THE

Calvin and Hobbes

PORTABLE COMPENDIUM

BOOK 8

BILL WATTERSON

Andrews McMeel
PUBLISHING®

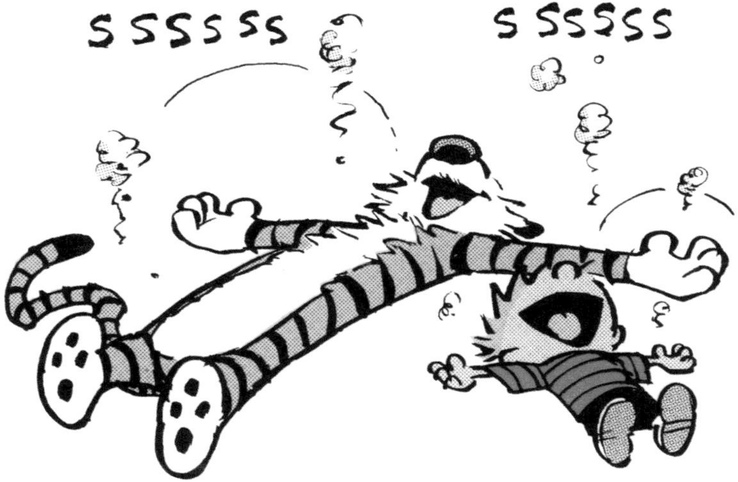

S SSSSS
S SSSSS

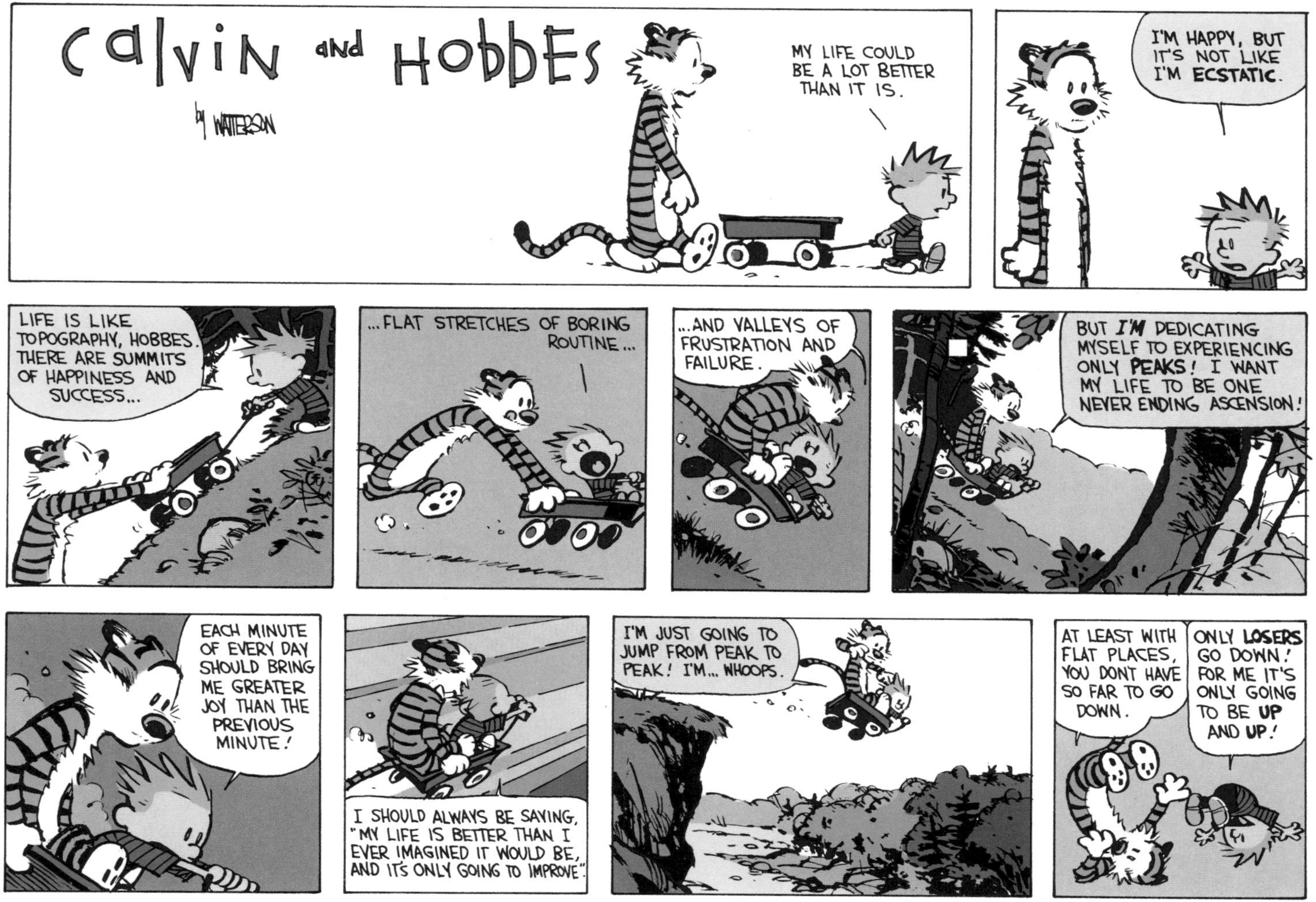
Calvin and HOBBES
by WATTERSON
MY LIFE COULD BE A LOT BETTER THAN IT IS.
I'M HAPPY, BUT IT'S NOT LIKE I'M **ECSTATIC**.
LIFE IS LIKE TOPOGRAPHY, HOBBES. THERE ARE SUMMITS OF HAPPINESS AND SUCCESS...
...FLAT STRETCHES OF BORING ROUTINE...
...AND VALLEYS OF FRUSTRATION AND FAILURE.
BUT ***I'M*** DEDICATING MYSELF TO EXPERIENCING ONLY **PEAKS**! I WANT MY LIFE TO BE ONE NEVER ENDING ASCENSION!
EACH MINUTE OF EVERY DAY SHOULD BRING ME GREATER JOY THAN THE PREVIOUS MINUTE!
I SHOULD ALWAYS BE SAYING, "MY LIFE IS BETTER THAN I EVER IMAGINED IT WOULD BE, AND IT'S ONLY GOING TO IMPROVE".
I'M JUST GOING TO JUMP FROM PEAK TO PEAK! I'M... WHOOPS.
AT LEAST WITH FLAT PLACES, YOU DONT HAVE SO FAR TO GO DOWN.
ONLY **LOSERS** GO DOWN! FOR ME IT'S ONLY GOING TO BE **UP** AND **UP**!

CaLViN and HOBBES
by WATTERSON

UH-O[...]

OH NO! EVERYTHING HAS SUDDENLY TURNED NEO-CUBIST!

IT ALL STARTED WHEN CALVIN ENGAGED HIS DAD IN A MINOR DEBATE! SOON CALVIN COULD SEE BOTH SIDES OF THE ISSUE! THEN POOR CALVIN BEGAN TO SEE BOTH SIDES OF *EVERY*THING!

THE TRADITIONAL SINGLE VIEWPOINT HAS BEEN ABANDONED! PERSPECTIVE HAS BEEN FRACTURED!

THE MULTIPLE VIEWS PROVIDE TOO MUCH INFORMATION! IT'S IMPOSSIBLE TO MOVE! CALVIN QUICKLY TRIES TO ELIMINATE ALL BUT ONE PERSPECTIVE!

IT WORKS! THE WORLD FALLS INTO A RECOGNIZABLE ORDER!

YOU'RE STILL WRONG, DAD.

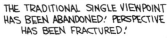

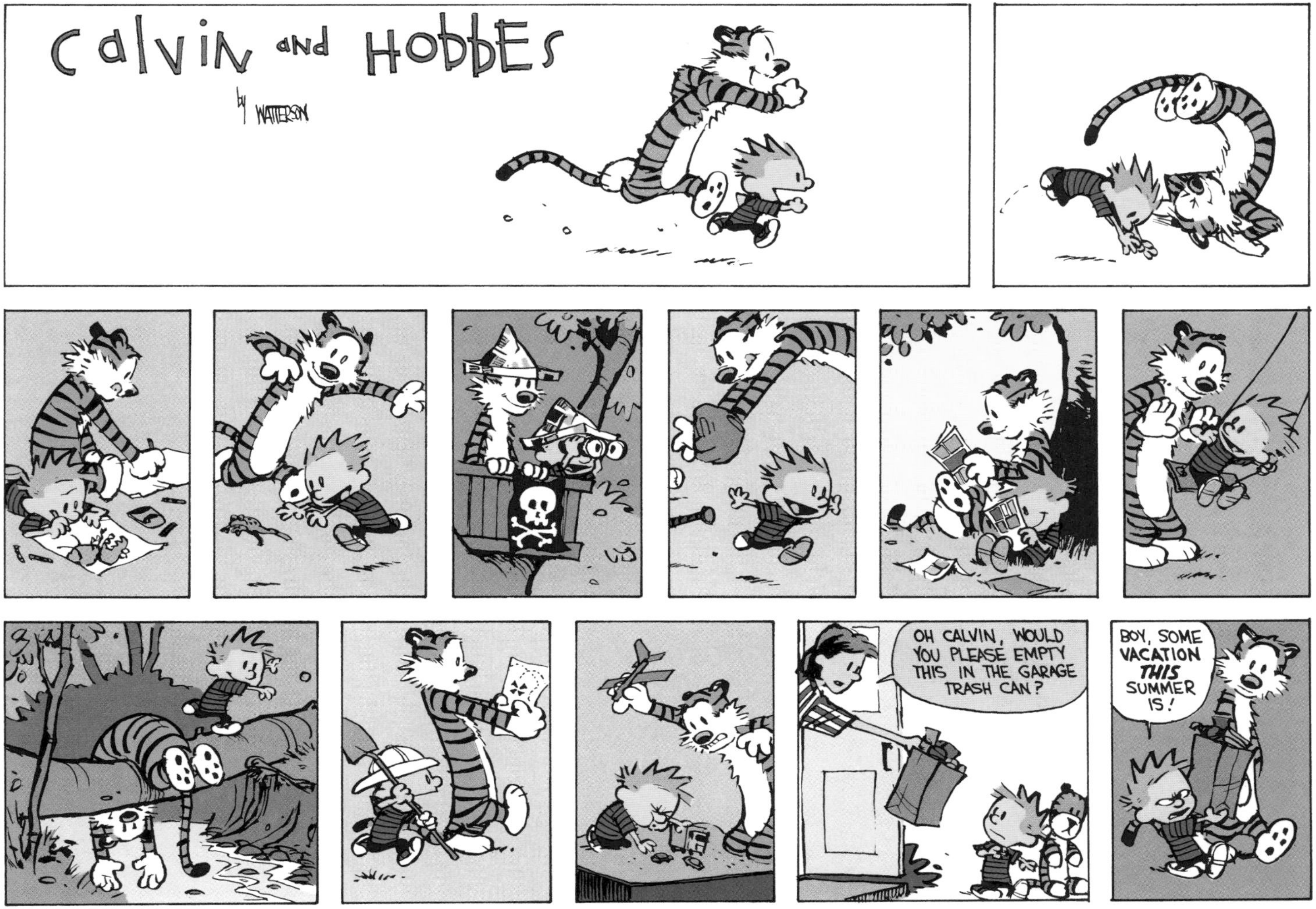
Calvin and HOBBES
by WATTERSON
OH CALVIN, WOULD YOU PLEASE EMPTY THIS IN THE GARAGE TRASH CAN?
BOY, SOME VACATION THIS SUMMER IS!

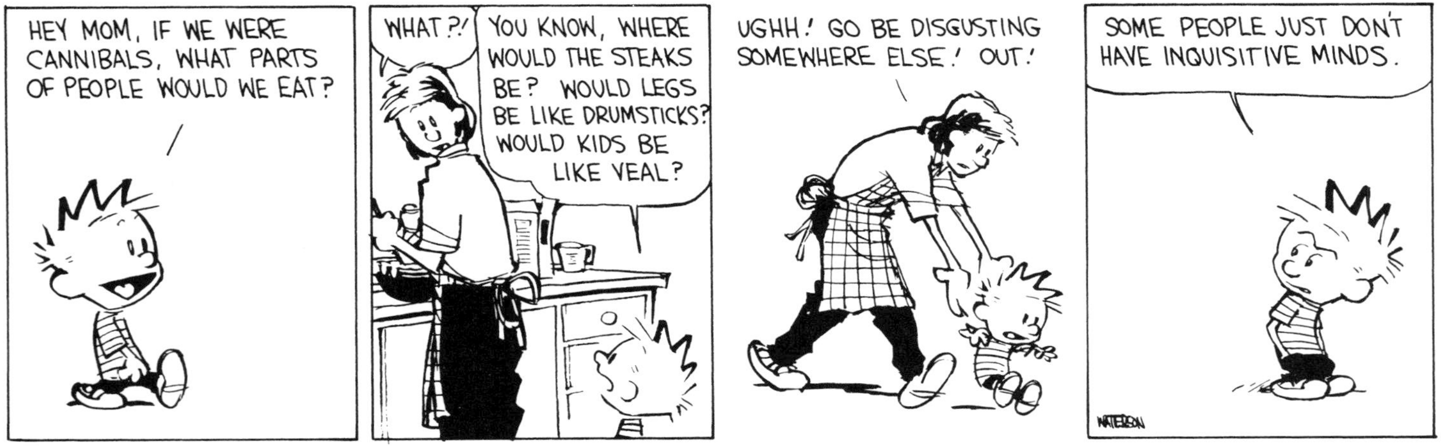
HEY MOM, IF WE WERE CANNIBALS, WHAT PARTS OF PEOPLE WOULD WE EAT?
WHAT?!
YOU KNOW, WHERE WOULD THE STEAKS BE? WOULD LEGS BE LIKE DRUMSTICKS? WOULD KIDS BE LIKE VEAL?
UGHH! GO BE DISGUSTING SOMEWHERE ELSE! OUT!
SOME PEOPLE JUST DON'T HAVE INQUISITIVE MINDS.
WATTERSON

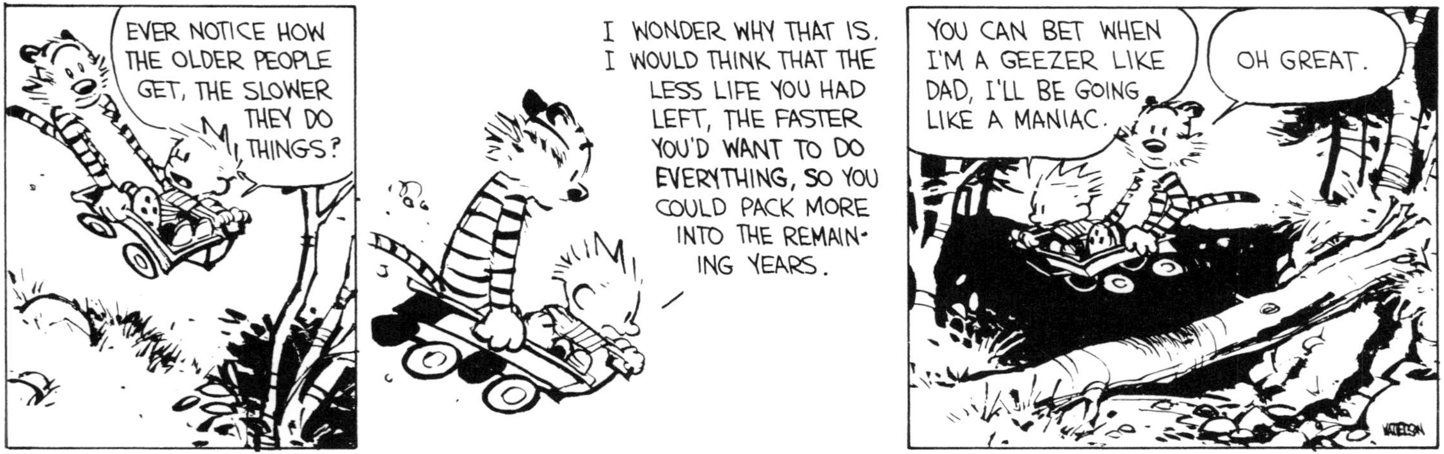
EVER NOTICE HOW THE OLDER PEOPLE GET, THE SLOWER THEY DO THINGS?
I WONDER WHY THAT IS. I WOULD THINK THAT THE LESS LIFE YOU HAD LEFT, THE FASTER YOU'D WANT TO DO EVERYTHING, SO YOU COULD PACK MORE INTO THE REMAINING YEARS.
YOU CAN BET WHEN I'M A GEEZER LIKE DAD, I'LL BE GOING LIKE A MANIAC.
OH GREAT.
WATTERSON

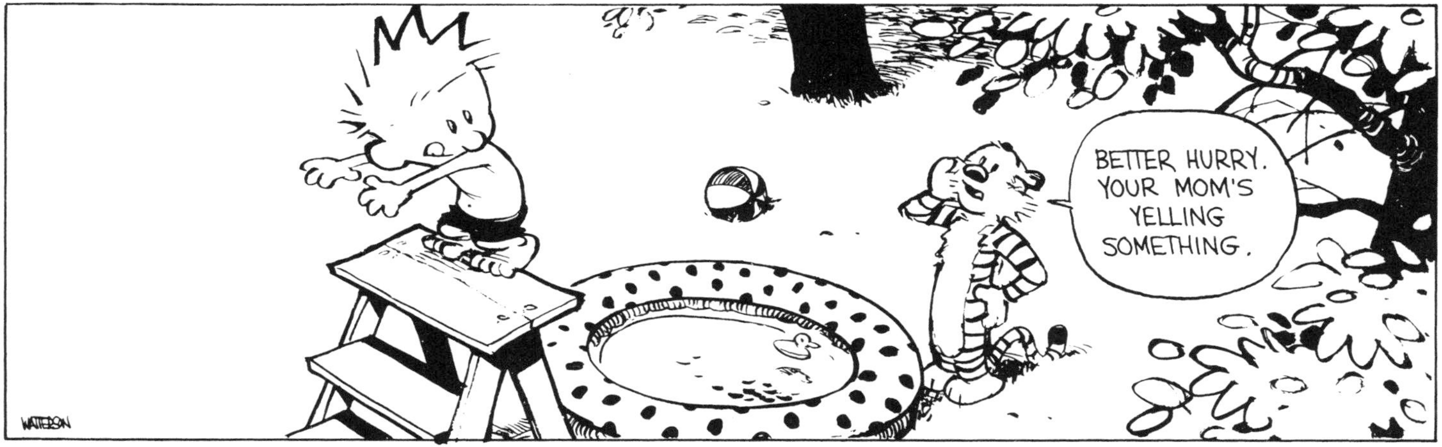
BETTER HURRY. YOUR MOM'S YELLING SOMETHING.

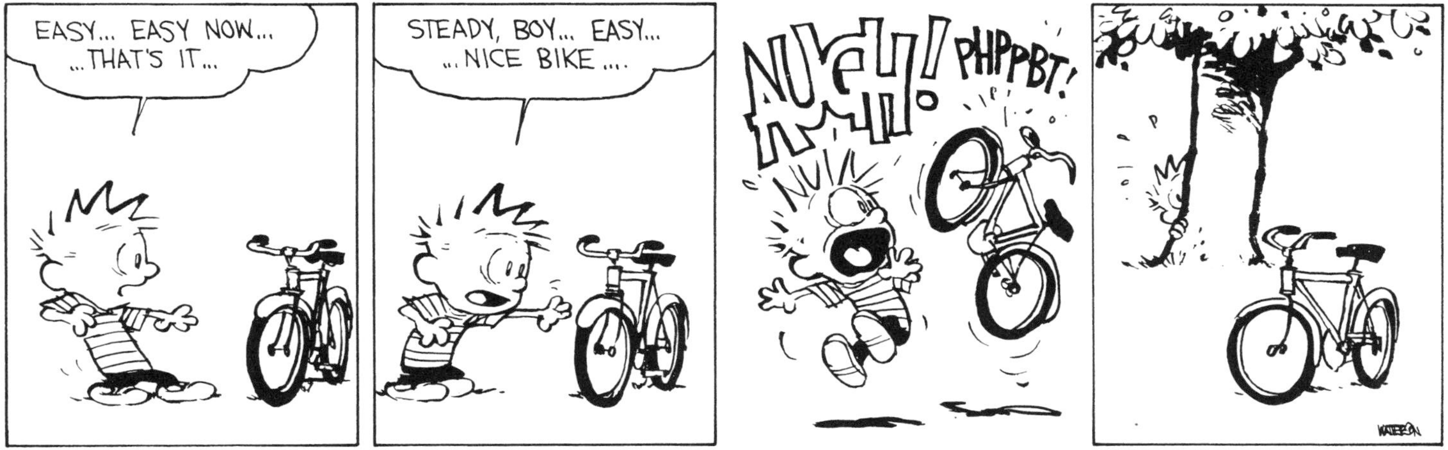
EASY... EASY NOW... ...THAT'S IT...
STEADY, BOY... EASY... ...NICE BIKE....
PHPPBT!

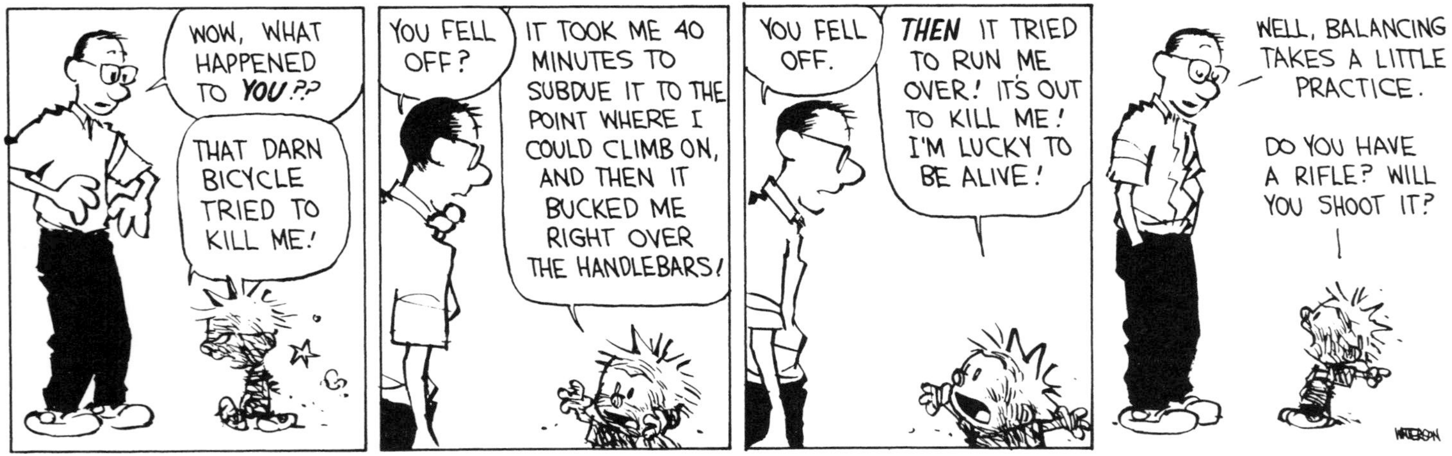
WOW, WHAT HAPPENED TO *YOU*??
THAT DARN BICYCLE TRIED TO KILL ME!
YOU FELL OFF?
IT TOOK ME 40 MINUTES TO SUBDUE IT TO THE POINT WHERE I COULD CLIMB ON, AND THEN IT BUCKED ME RIGHT OVER THE HANDLEBARS!
YOU FELL OFF.
THEN IT TRIED TO RUN ME OVER! IT'S OUT TO KILL ME! I'M LUCKY TO BE ALIVE!
WELL, BALANCING TAKES A LITTLE PRACTICE.
DO YOU HAVE A RIFLE? WILL YOU SHOOT IT?

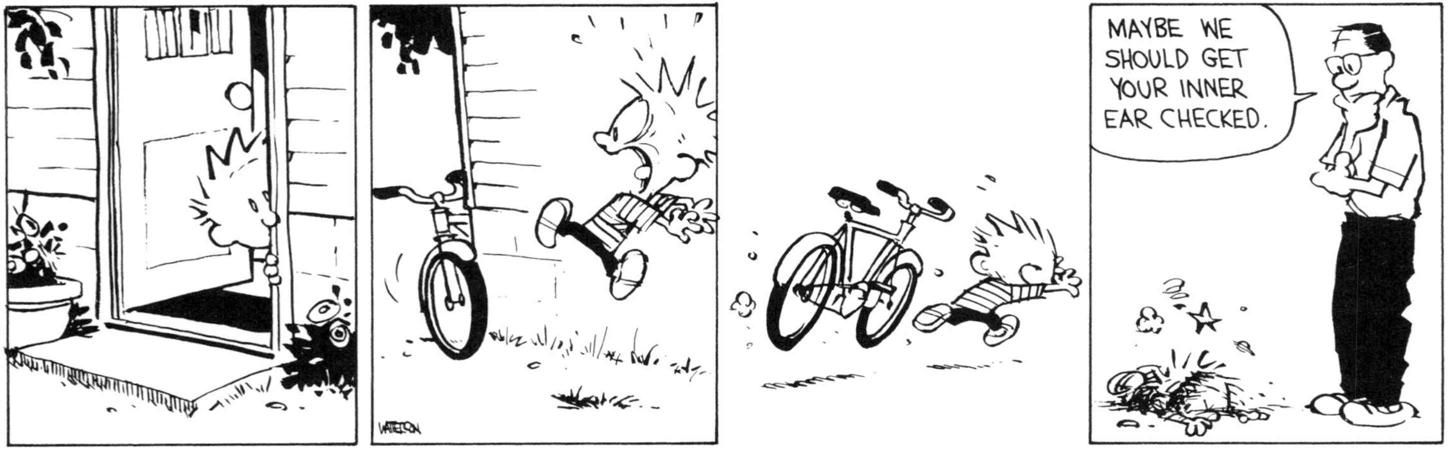
MAYBE WE SHOULD GET YOUR INNER EAR CHECKED.

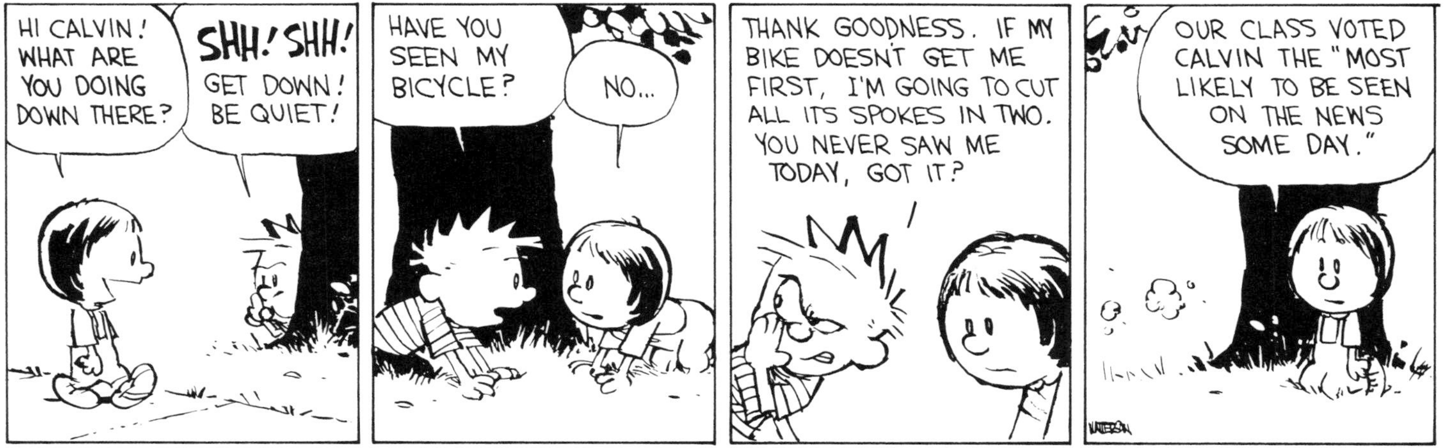
HI CALVIN! WHAT ARE YOU DOING DOWN THERE?
SHH! SHH! GET DOWN! BE QUIET!
HAVE YOU SEEN MY BICYCLE?
NO...
THANK GOODNESS. IF MY BIKE DOESN'T GET ME FIRST, I'M GOING TO CUT ALL ITS SPOKES IN TWO. YOU NEVER SAW ME TODAY, GOT IT?
OUR CLASS VOTED CALVIN THE "MOST LIKELY TO BE SEEN ON THE NEWS SOME DAY."

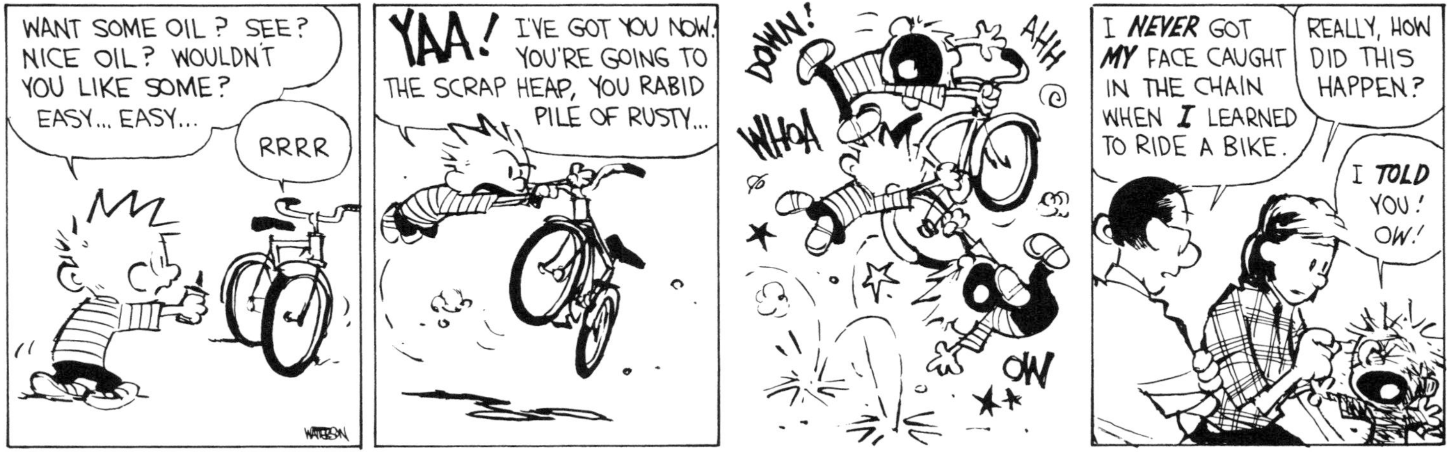
WANT SOME OIL? SEE? NICE OIL? WOULDN'T YOU LIKE SOME? EASY... EASY...
RRRR
YAA!
I'VE GOT YOU NOW! YOU'RE GOING TO THE SCRAP HEAP, YOU RABID PILE OF RUSTY...
DOWN!
AHH
WHOA
OW
I NEVER GOT MY FACE CAUGHT IN THE CHAIN WHEN I LEARNED TO RIDE A BIKE.
REALLY, HOW DID THIS HAPPEN?
I TOLD YOU! OW!

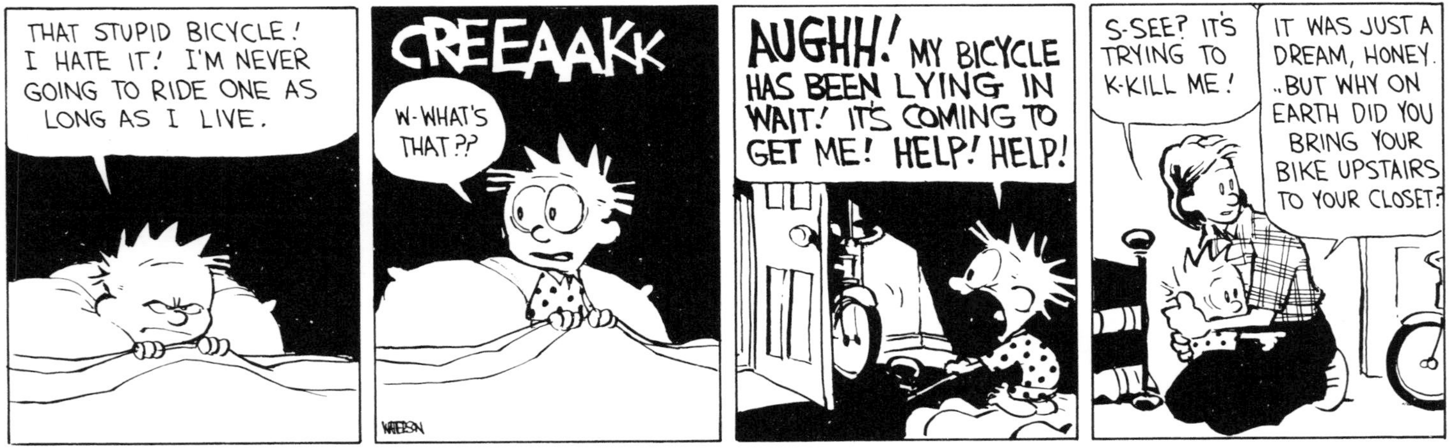
THAT STUPID BICYCLE! I HATE IT! I'M NEVER GOING TO RIDE ONE AS LONG AS I LIVE.
CREEAAKK
W-WHAT'S THAT??
AUGHH! MY BICYCLE HAS BEEN LYING IN WAIT! IT'S COMING TO GET ME! HELP! HELP!
S-SEE? IT'S TRYING TO K-KILL ME!
IT WAS JUST A DREAM, HONEY. ..BUT WHY ON EARTH DID YOU BRING YOUR BIKE UPSTAIRS TO YOUR CLOSET?

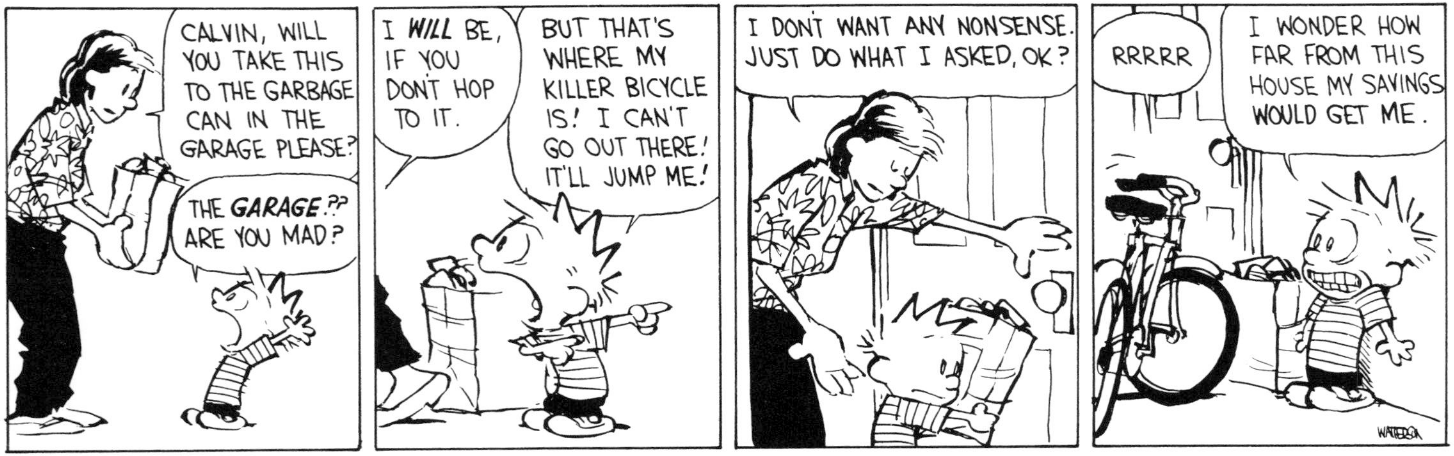
CALVIN, WILL YOU TAKE THIS TO THE GARBAGE CAN IN THE GARAGE PLEASE?
THE GARAGE?? ARE YOU MAD?
I WILL BE, IF YOU DON'T HOP TO IT.
BUT THAT'S WHERE MY KILLER BICYCLE IS! I CAN'T GO OUT THERE! IT'LL JUMP ME!
I DON'T WANT ANY NONSENSE. JUST DO WHAT I ASKED, OK?
RRRRR
I WONDER HOW FAR FROM THIS HOUSE MY SAVINGS WOULD GET ME.

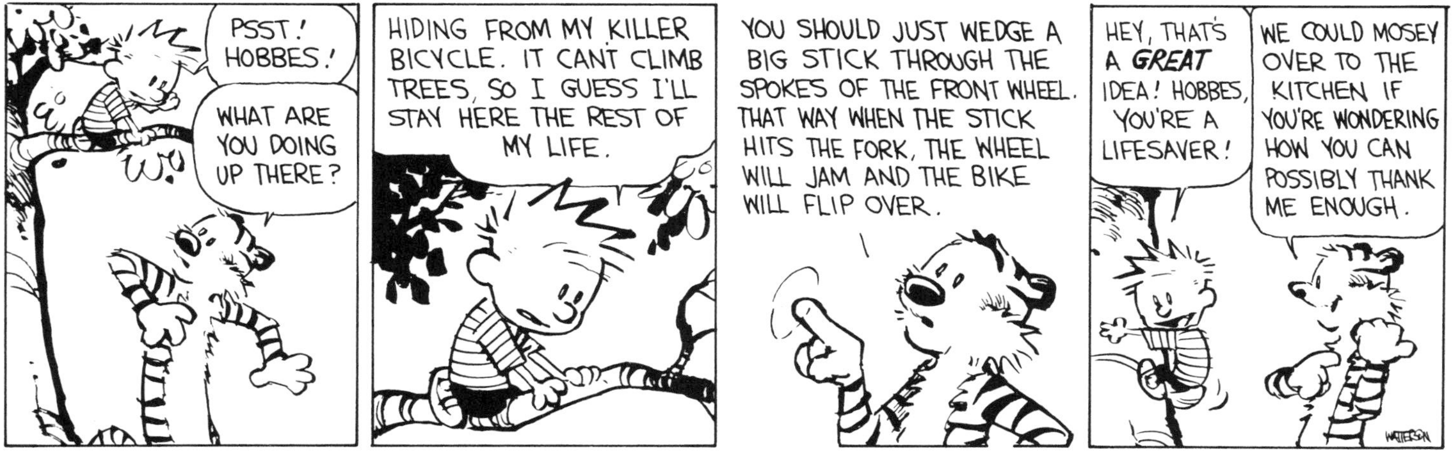
PSST! HOBBES!
WHAT ARE YOU DOING UP THERE?
HIDING FROM MY KILLER BICYCLE. IT CAN'T CLIMB TREES, SO I GUESS I'LL STAY HERE THE REST OF MY LIFE.
YOU SHOULD JUST WEDGE A BIG STICK THROUGH THE SPOKES OF THE FRONT WHEEL. THAT WAY WHEN THE STICK HITS THE FORK, THE WHEEL WILL JAM AND THE BIKE WILL FLIP OVER.
HEY, THAT'S A **GREAT** IDEA! HOBBES, YOU'RE A LIFESAVER!
WE COULD MOSEY OVER TO THE KITCHEN IF YOU'RE WONDERING HOW YOU CAN POSSIBLY THANK ME ENOUGH.
WATTERSON

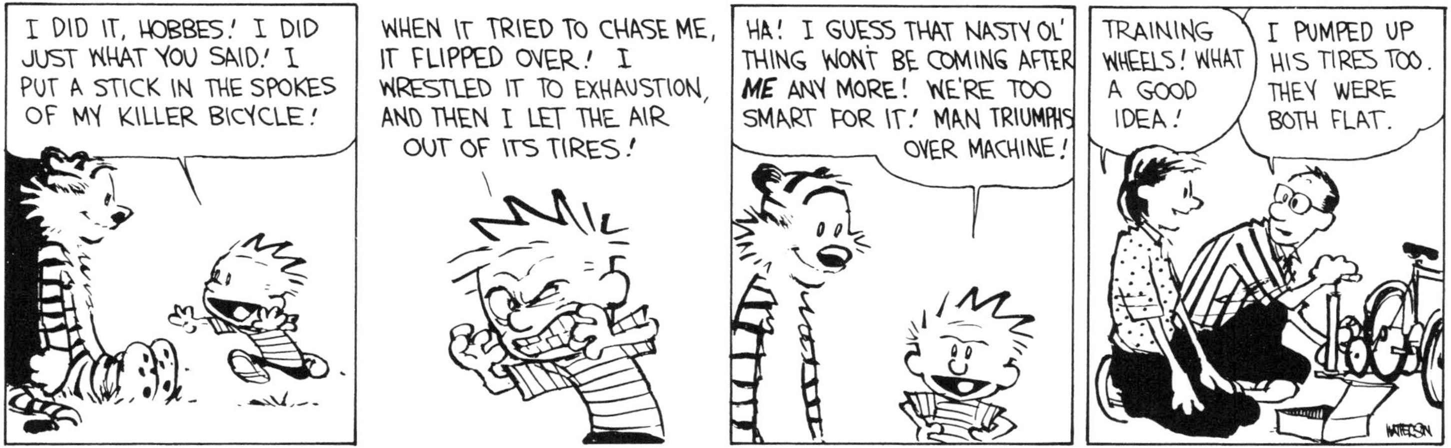
I DID IT, HOBBES! I DID JUST WHAT YOU SAID! I PUT A STICK IN THE SPOKES OF MY KILLER BICYCLE!
WHEN IT TRIED TO CHASE ME, IT FLIPPED OVER! I WRESTLED IT TO EXHAUSTION, AND THEN I LET THE AIR OUT OF ITS TIRES!
HA! I GUESS THAT NASTY OL' THING WON'T BE COMING AFTER **ME** ANY MORE! WE'RE TOO SMART FOR IT! MAN TRIUMPHS OVER MACHINE!
TRAINING WHEELS! WHAT A GOOD IDEA!
I PUMPED UP HIS TIRES TOO. THEY WERE BOTH FLAT.
WATTERSON

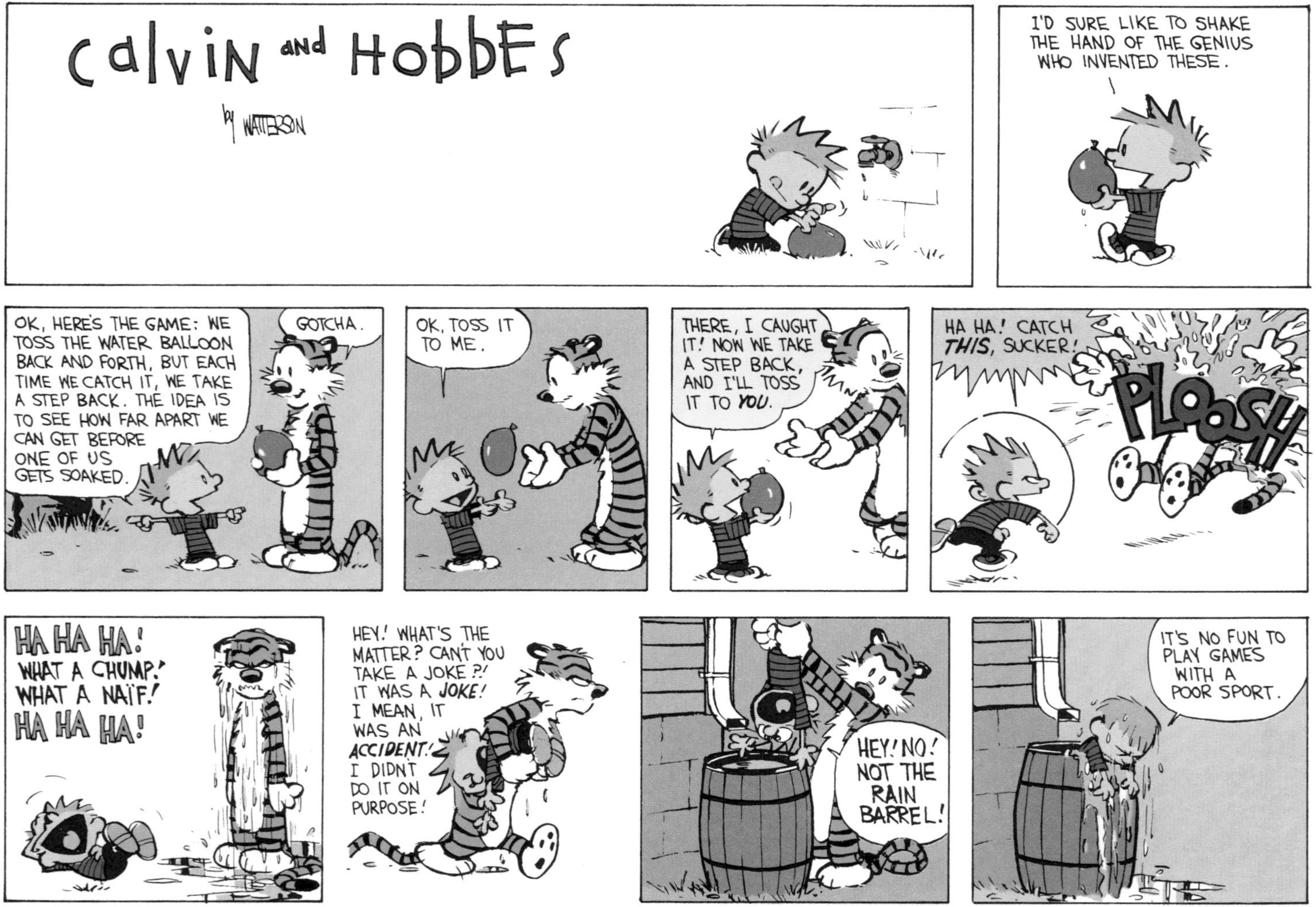
Calvin and Hobbes
by WATTERSON
I'D SURE LIKE TO SHAKE THE HAND OF THE GENIUS WHO INVENTED THESE.
OK, HERE'S THE GAME: WE TOSS THE WATER BALLOON BACK AND FORTH, BUT EACH TIME WE CATCH IT, WE TAKE A STEP BACK. THE IDEA IS TO SEE HOW FAR APART WE CAN GET BEFORE ONE OF US GETS SOAKED.
GOTCHA.
OK, TOSS IT TO ME.
THERE, I CAUGHT IT! NOW WE TAKE A STEP BACK, AND I'LL TOSS IT TO YOU.
HA HA! CATCH THIS, SUCKER!
PLOOSH
HA HA HA! WHAT A CHUMP! WHAT A NAÏF! HA HA HA!
HEY! WHAT'S THE MATTER? CAN'T YOU TAKE A JOKE?! IT WAS A JOKE! I MEAN, IT WAS AN ACCIDENT! I DIDN'T DO IT ON PURPOSE!
HEY! NO! NOT THE RAIN BARREL!
IT'S NO FUN TO PLAY GAMES WITH A POOR SPORT.

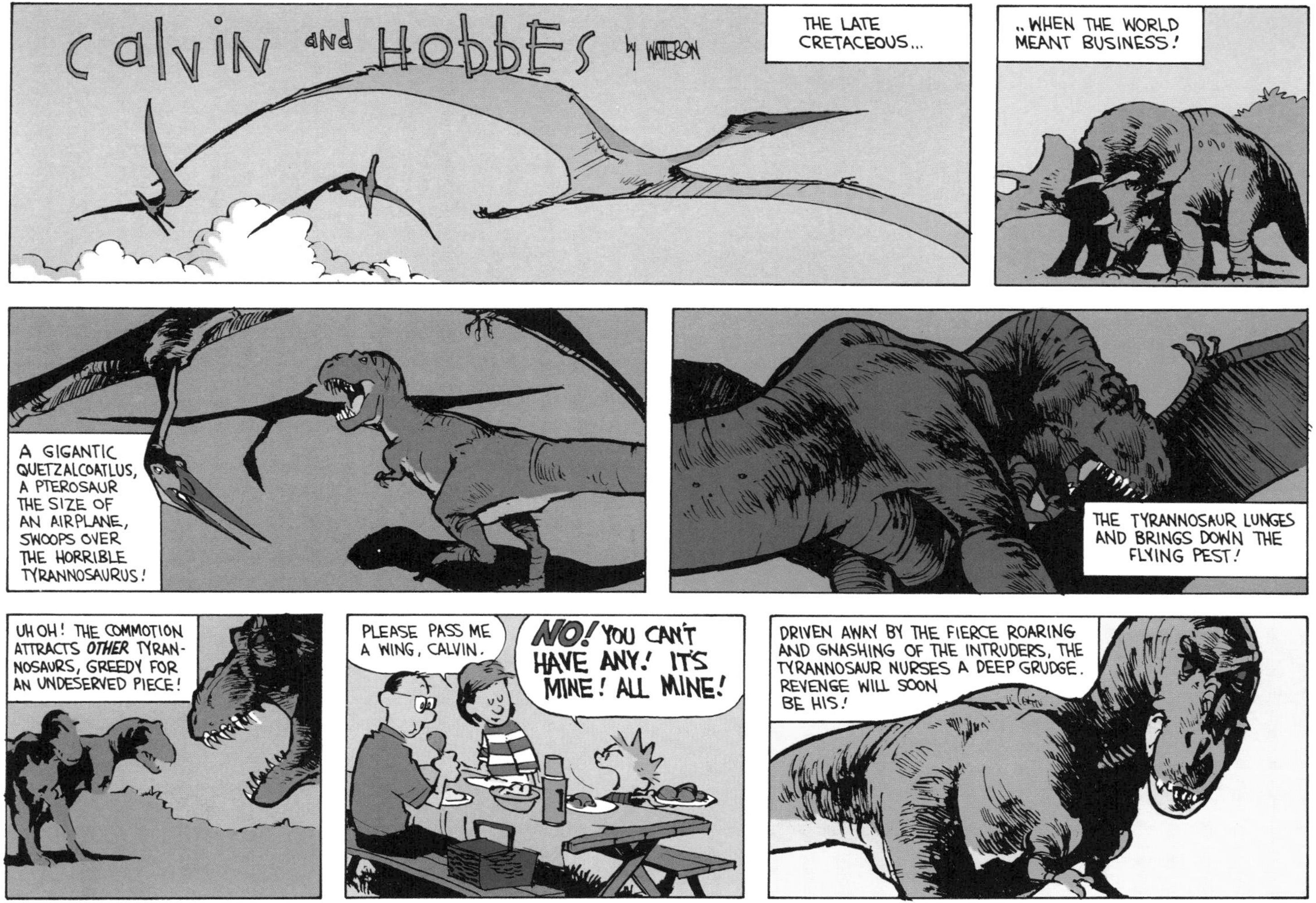

Calvin and Hobbes by WATTERSON
THE LATE CRETACEOUS...
..WHEN THE WORLD MEANT BUSINESS!
A GIGANTIC QUETZALCOATLUS, A PTEROSAUR THE SIZE OF AN AIRPLANE, SWOOPS OVER THE HORRIBLE TYRANNOSAURUS!
THE TYRANNOSAUR LUNGES AND BRINGS DOWN THE FLYING PEST!
UH OH! THE COMMOTION ATTRACTS OTHER TYRANNOSAURS, GREEDY FOR AN UNDESERVED PIECE!
PLEASE PASS ME A WING, CALVIN.
NO! YOU CAN'T HAVE ANY! IT'S MINE! ALL MINE!
DRIVEN AWAY BY THE FIERCE ROARING AND GNASHING OF THE INTRUDERS, THE TYRANNOSAUR NURSES A DEEP GRUDGE. REVENGE WILL SOON BE HIS!

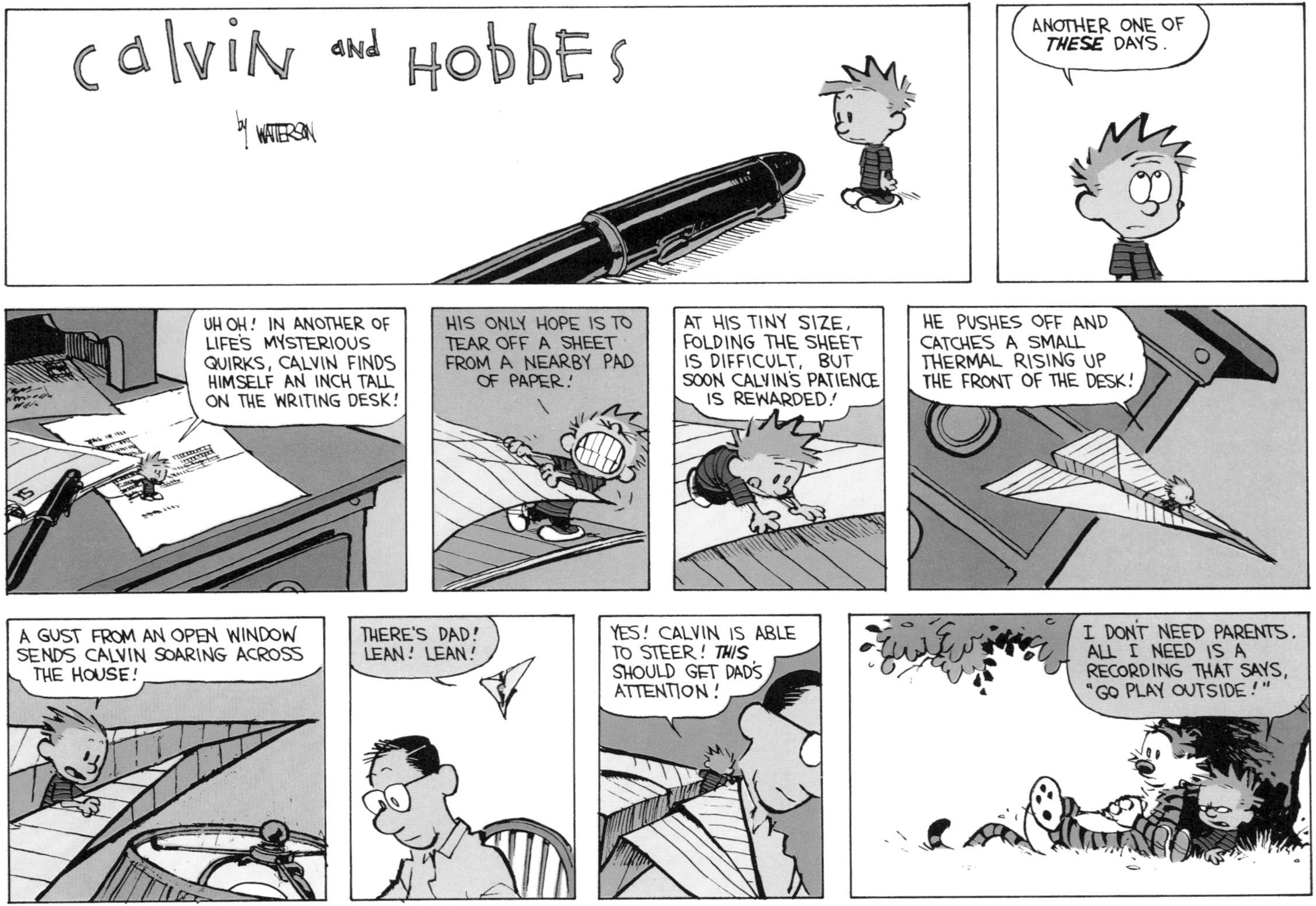
Calvin and HOBBES
by WATTERSON
ANOTHER ONE OF THESE DAYS.
UH OH! IN ANOTHER OF LIFE'S MYSTERIOUS QUIRKS, CALVIN FINDS HIMSELF AN INCH TALL ON THE WRITING DESK!
HIS ONLY HOPE IS TO TEAR OFF A SHEET FROM A NEARBY PAD OF PAPER!
AT HIS TINY SIZE, FOLDING THE SHEET IS DIFFICULT, BUT SOON CALVIN'S PATIENCE IS REWARDED!
HE PUSHES OFF AND CATCHES A SMALL THERMAL RISING UP THE FRONT OF THE DESK!
A GUST FROM AN OPEN WINDOW SENDS CALVIN SOARING ACROSS THE HOUSE!
THERE'S DAD! LEAN! LEAN!
YES! CALVIN IS ABLE TO STEER! THIS SHOULD GET DAD'S ATTENTION!
I DON'T NEED PARENTS. ALL I NEED IS A RECORDING THAT SAYS, "GO PLAY OUTSIDE!"

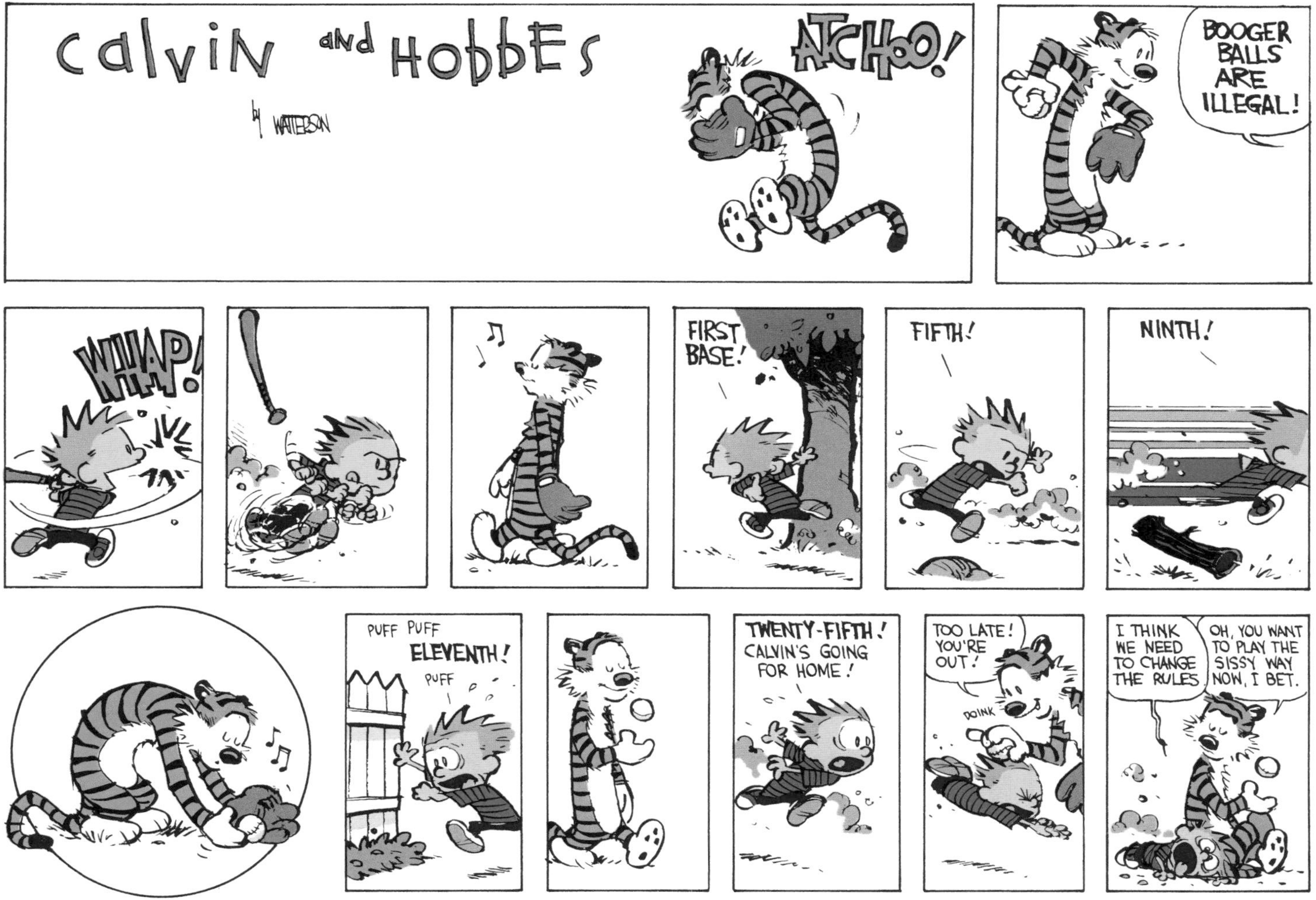
Calvin and Hobbes
by WATTERSON
ATCHOO!
BOOGER BALLS ARE ILLEGAL!
WHAP!
FIRST BASE!
FIFTH!
NINTH!
PUFF PUFF
ELEVENTH!
PUFF
TWENTY-FIFTH! CALVIN'S GOING FOR HOME!
TOO LATE! YOU'RE OUT!
DOINK
I THINK WE NEED TO CHANGE THE RULES
OH, YOU WANT TO PLAY THE SISSY WAY NOW, I BET.

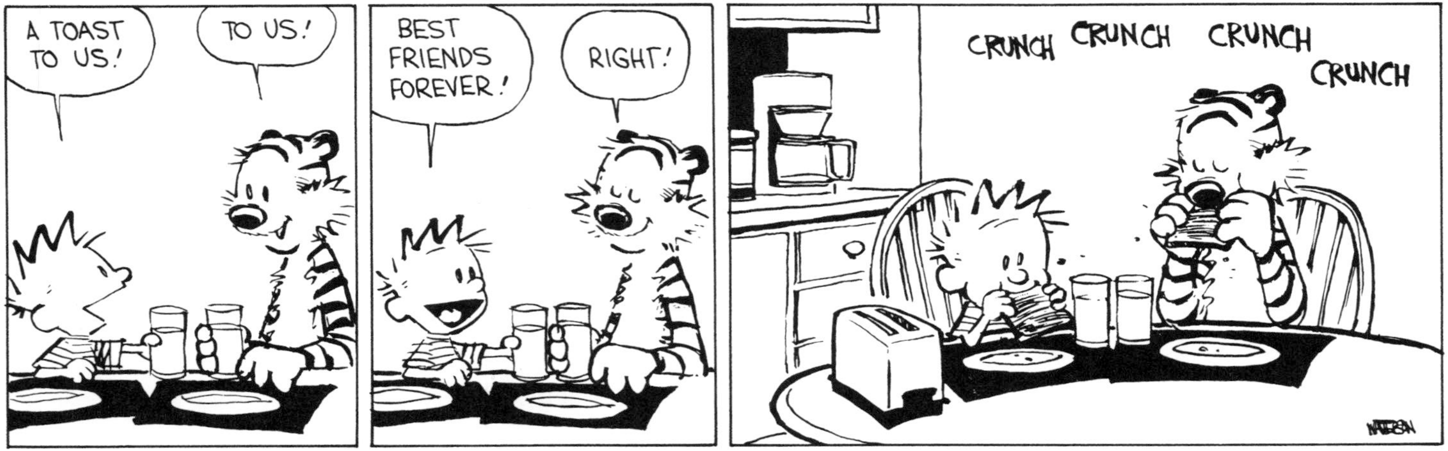
A TOAST TO US!
TO US!
BEST FRIENDS FOREVER!
RIGHT!
CRUNCH CRUNCH CRUNCH CRUNCH
WATTERSON

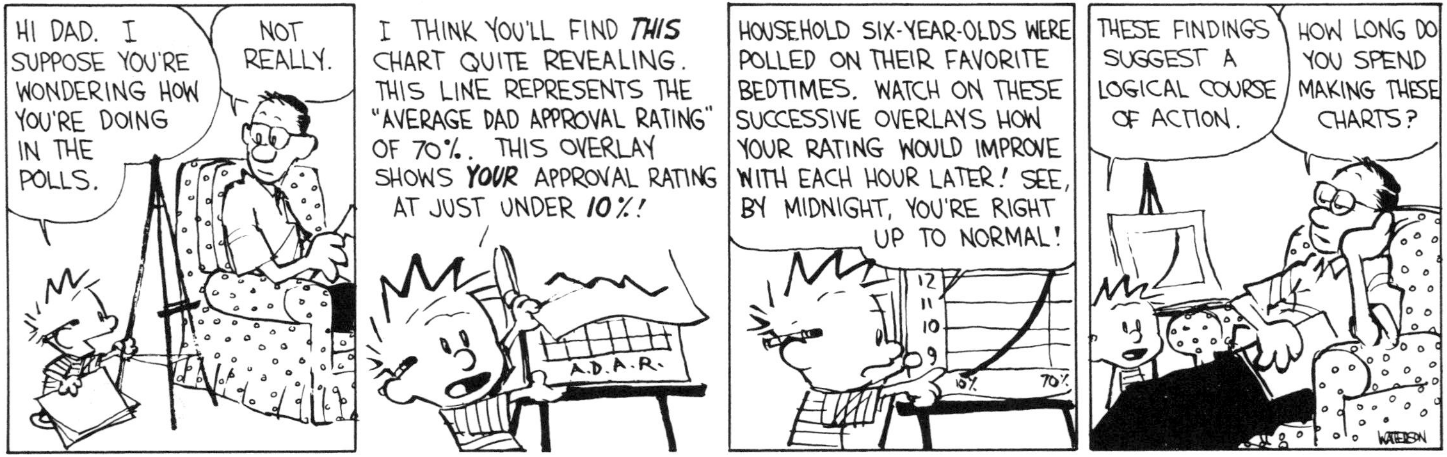
HI DAD. I SUPPOSE YOU'RE WONDERING HOW YOU'RE DOING IN THE POLLS.
NOT REALLY.
I THINK YOU'LL FIND THIS CHART QUITE REVEALING. THIS LINE REPRESENTS THE "AVERAGE DAD APPROVAL RATING" OF 70%. THIS OVERLAY SHOWS YOUR APPROVAL RATING AT JUST UNDER 10%!
A.D.A.R.
HOUSEHOLD SIX-YEAR-OLDS WERE POLLED ON THEIR FAVORITE BEDTIMES. WATCH ON THESE SUCCESSIVE OVERLAYS HOW YOUR RATING WOULD IMPROVE WITH EACH HOUR LATER! SEE, BY MIDNIGHT, YOU'RE RIGHT UP TO NORMAL!
12
11
10
9
10%
70%
THESE FINDINGS SUGGEST A LOGICAL COURSE OF ACTION.
HOW LONG DO YOU SPEND MAKING THESE CHARTS?
WATTERSON

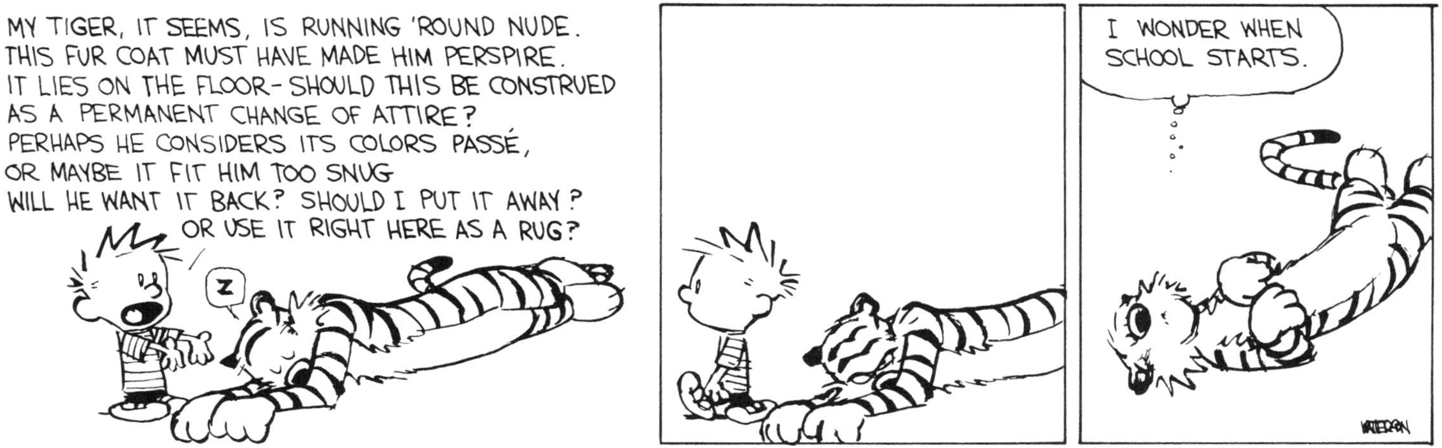
MY TIGER, IT SEEMS, IS RUNNING 'ROUND NUDE.
THIS FUR COAT MUST HAVE MADE HIM PERSPIRE.
IT LIES ON THE FLOOR- SHOULD THIS BE CONSTRUED
AS A PERMANENT CHANGE OF ATTIRE?
PERHAPS HE CONSIDERS ITS COLORS PASSÉ,
OR MAYBE IT FIT HIM TOO SNUG
WILL HE WANT IT BACK? SHOULD I PUT IT AWAY?
OR USE IT RIGHT HERE AS A RUG?
Z
I WONDER WHEN SCHOOL STARTS.

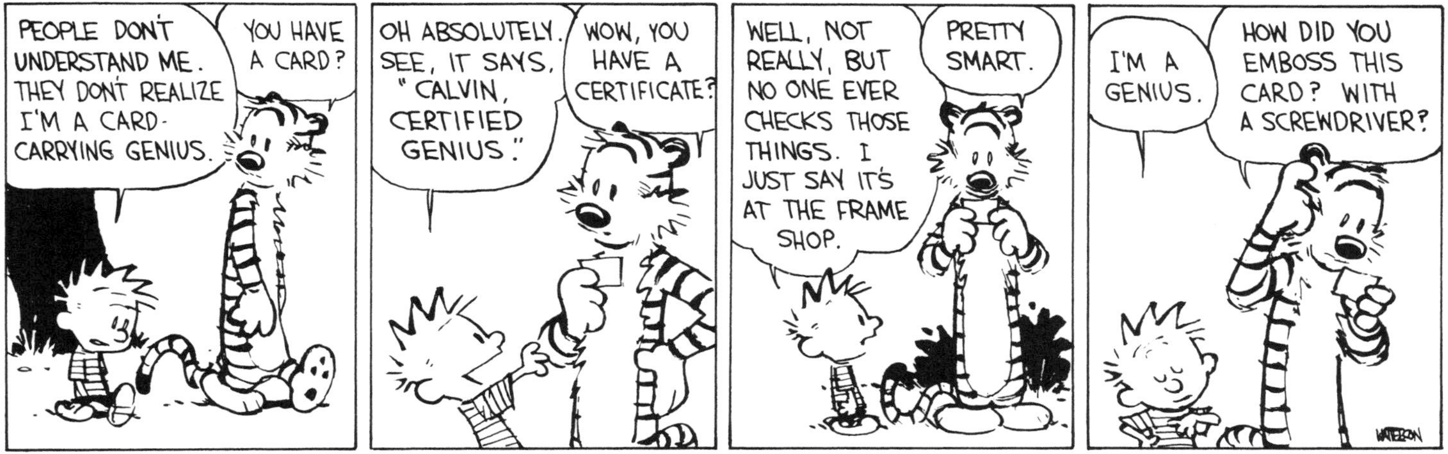
PEOPLE DON'T UNDERSTAND ME. THEY DON'T REALIZE I'M A CARD-CARRYING GENIUS.
YOU HAVE A CARD?
OH ABSOLUTELY. SEE, IT SAYS, "CALVIN, CERTIFIED GENIUS."
WOW, YOU HAVE A CERTIFICATE?
WELL, NOT REALLY, BUT NO ONE EVER CHECKS THOSE THINGS. I JUST SAY IT'S AT THE FRAME SHOP.
PRETTY SMART.
I'M A GENIUS.
HOW DID YOU EMBOSS THIS CARD? WITH A SCREWDRIVER?

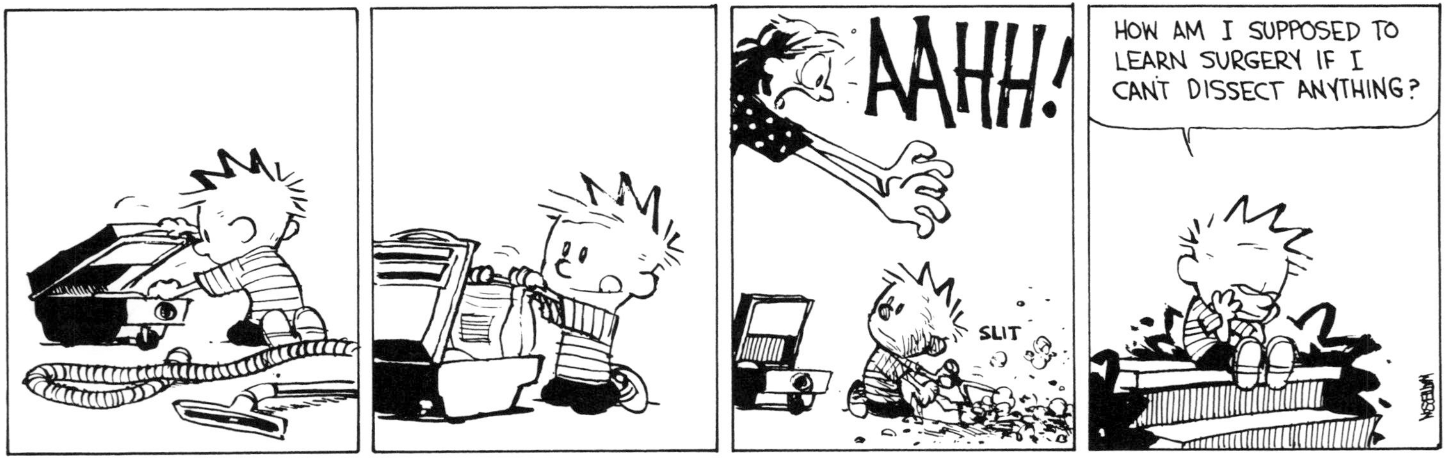
AAHH!
SLIT
HOW AM I SUPPOSED TO LEARN SURGERY IF I CAN'T DISSECT ANYTHING?

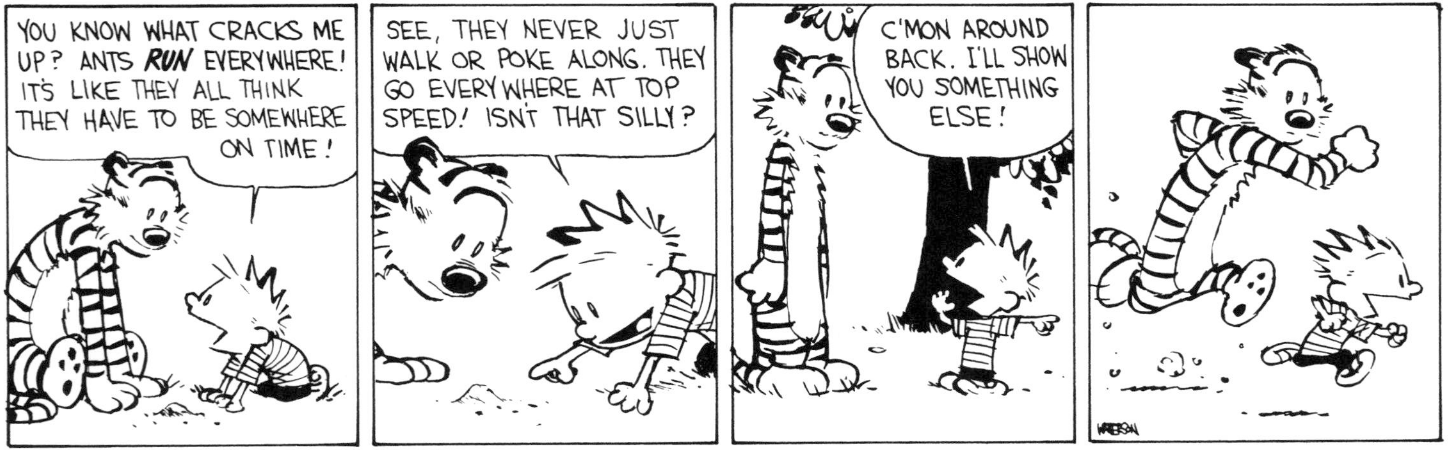
YOU KNOW WHAT CRACKS ME UP? ANTS ***RUN*** EVERYWHERE! IT'S LIKE THEY ALL THINK THEY HAVE TO BE SOMEWHERE ON TIME!
SEE, THEY NEVER JUST WALK OR POKE ALONG. THEY GO EVERYWHERE AT TOP SPEED! ISN'T THAT SILLY?
C'MON AROUND BACK. I'LL SHOW YOU SOMETHING ELSE!

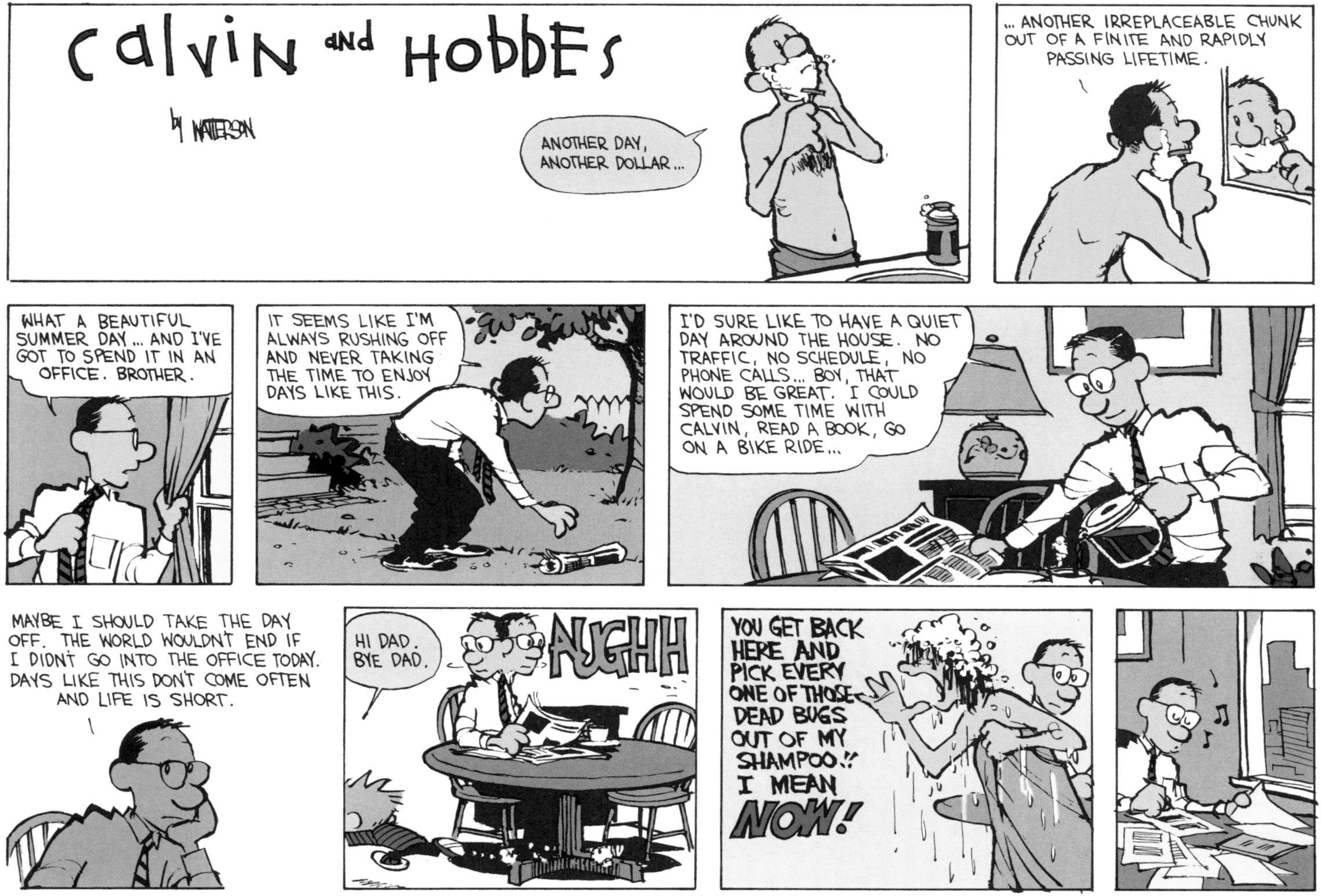
Calvin and HOBBES
by WATTERSON
ANOTHER DAY, ANOTHER DOLLAR...
... ANOTHER IRREPLACEABLE CHUNK OUT OF A FINITE AND RAPIDLY PASSING LIFETIME.
WHAT A BEAUTIFUL SUMMER DAY... AND I'VE GOT TO SPEND IT IN AN OFFICE. BROTHER.
IT SEEMS LIKE I'M ALWAYS RUSHING OFF AND NEVER TAKING THE TIME TO ENJOY DAYS LIKE THIS.
I'D SURE LIKE TO HAVE A QUIET DAY AROUND THE HOUSE. NO TRAFFIC, NO SCHEDULE, NO PHONE CALLS... BOY, THAT WOULD BE GREAT. I COULD SPEND SOME TIME WITH CALVIN, READ A BOOK, GO ON A BIKE RIDE...
MAYBE I SHOULD TAKE THE DAY OFF. THE WORLD WOULDN'T END IF I DIDN'T GO INTO THE OFFICE TODAY. DAYS LIKE THIS DON'T COME OFTEN AND LIFE IS SHORT.
HI DAD. BYE DAD.
AUGHH
YOU GET BACK HERE AND PICK EVERY ONE OF THOSE DEAD BUGS OUT OF MY SHAMPOO!! I MEAN NOW!

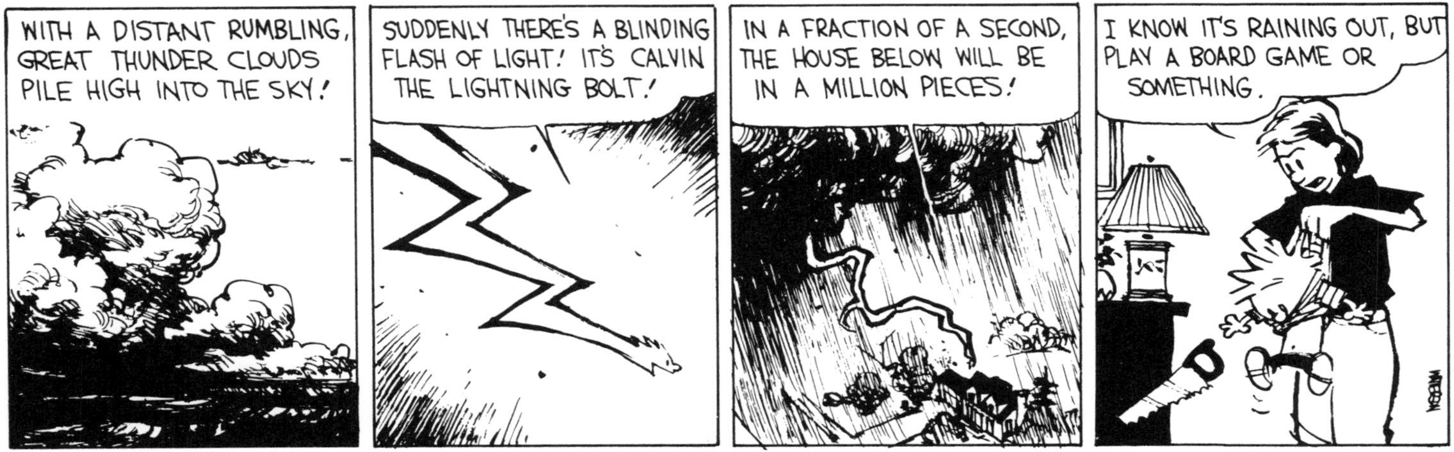
WITH A DISTANT RUMBLING, GREAT THUNDER CLOUDS PILE HIGH INTO THE SKY!
SUDDENLY THERE'S A BLINDING FLASH OF LIGHT! IT'S CALVIN THE LIGHTNING BOLT!
IN A FRACTION OF A SECOND, THE HOUSE BELOW WILL BE IN A MILLION PIECES!
I KNOW IT'S RAINING OUT, BUT PLAY A BOARD GAME OR SOMETHING.

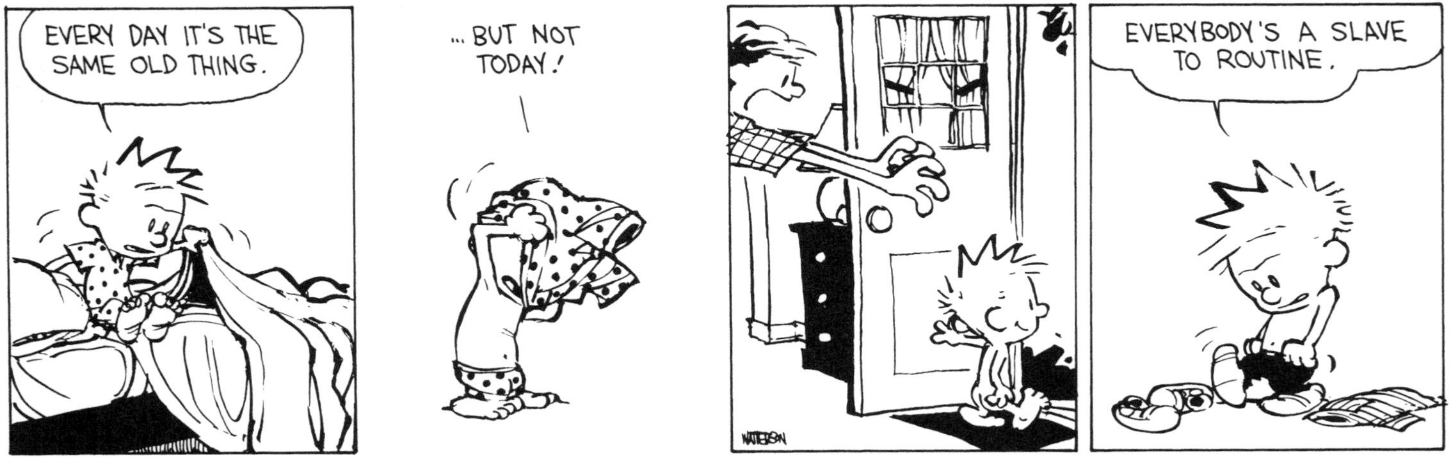
EVERY DAY IT'S THE SAME OLD THING.
... BUT NOT TODAY!
EVERYBODY'S A SLAVE TO ROUTINE.

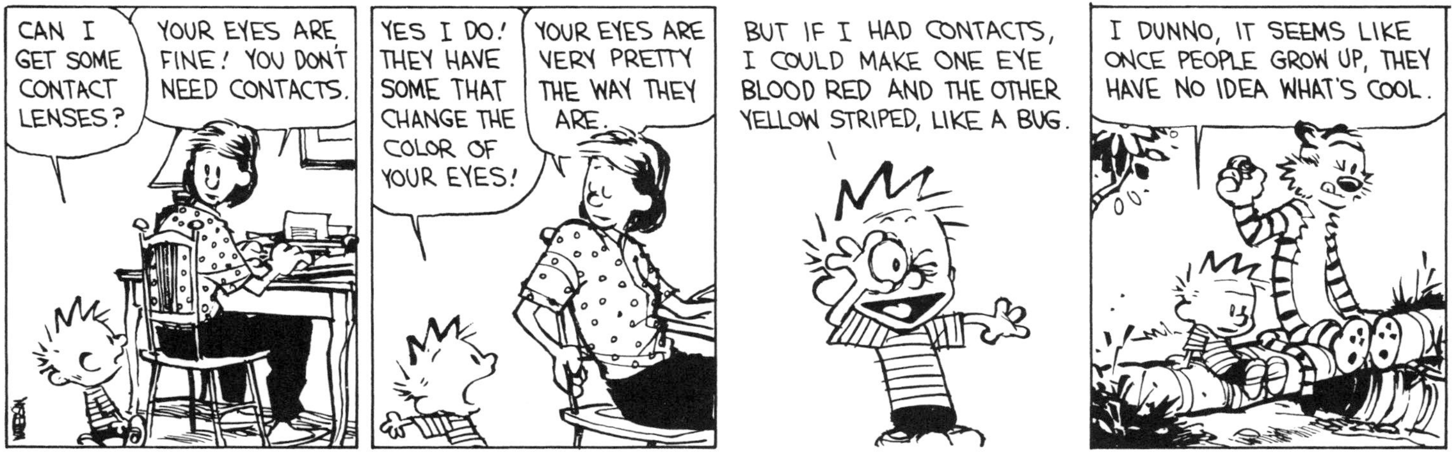
CAN I GET SOME CONTACT LENSES?
YOUR EYES ARE FINE! YOU DON'T NEED CONTACTS.
YES I DO! THEY HAVE SOME THAT CHANGE THE COLOR OF YOUR EYES!
YOUR EYES ARE VERY PRETTY THE WAY THEY ARE.
BUT IF I HAD CONTACTS, I COULD MAKE ONE EYE BLOOD RED AND THE OTHER YELLOW STRIPED, LIKE A BUG.
I DUNNO, IT SEEMS LIKE ONCE PEOPLE GROW UP, THEY HAVE NO IDEA WHAT'S COOL.

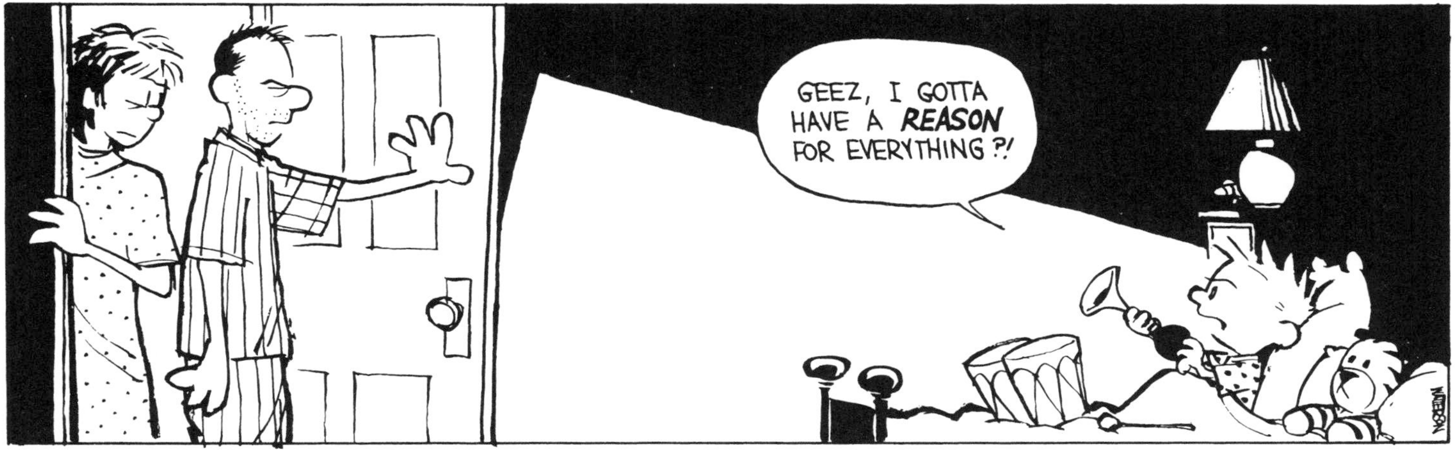
GEEZ, I GOTTA HAVE A **REASON** FOR EVERYTHING?!

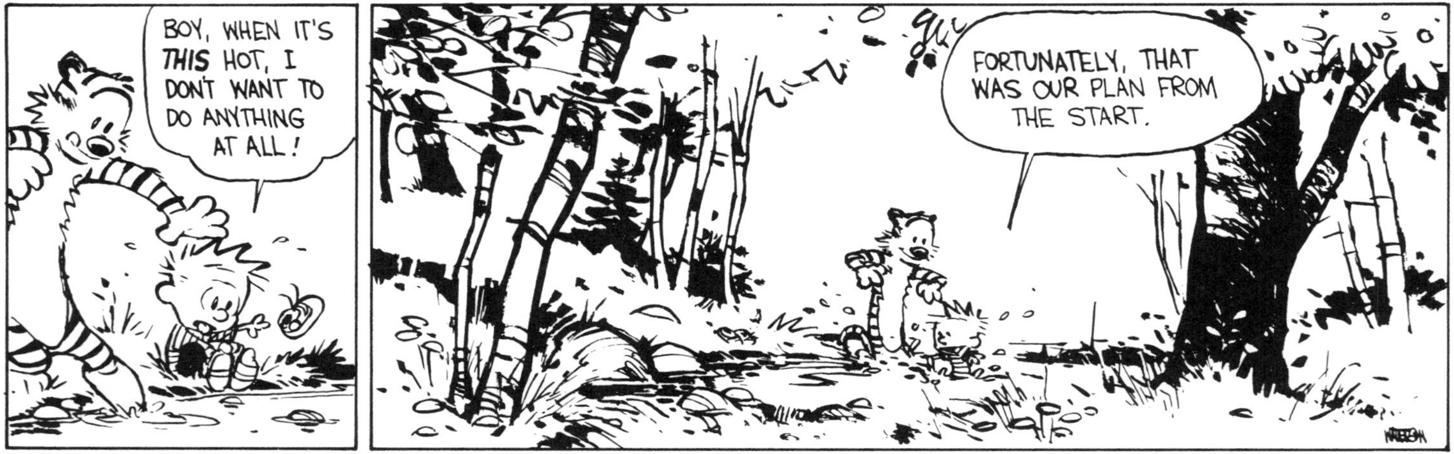
BOY, WHEN IT'S **THIS** HOT, I DON'T WANT TO DO ANYTHING AT ALL!
FORTUNATELY, THAT WAS OUR PLAN FROM THE START.
WATTERSON

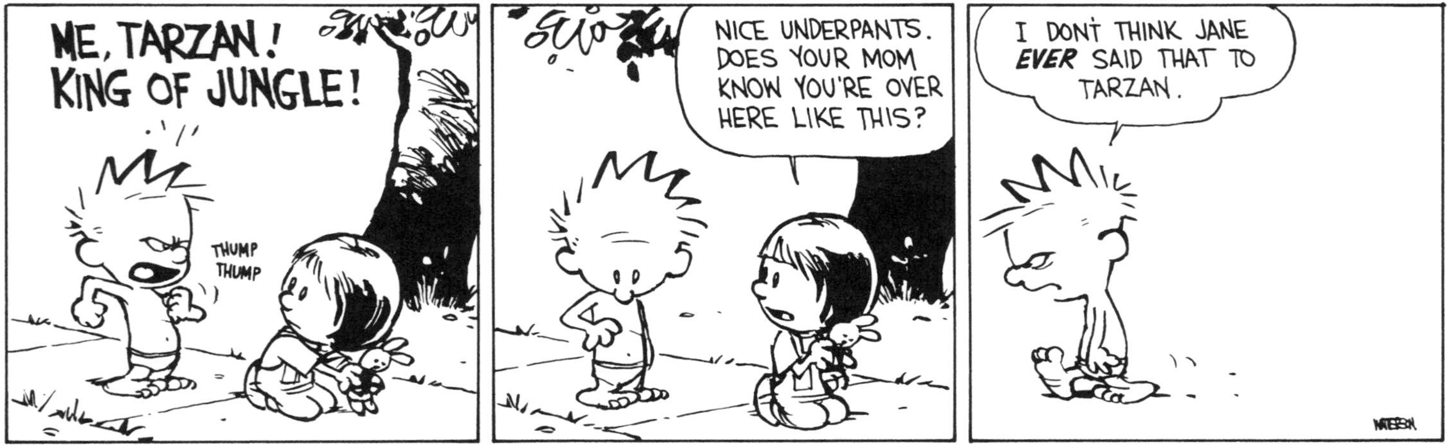
ME, TARZAN! KING OF JUNGLE!
THUMP THUMP
NICE UNDERPANTS. DOES YOUR MOM KNOW YOU'RE OVER HERE LIKE THIS?
I DON'T THINK JANE ***EVER*** SAID THAT TO TARZAN.
WATTERSON

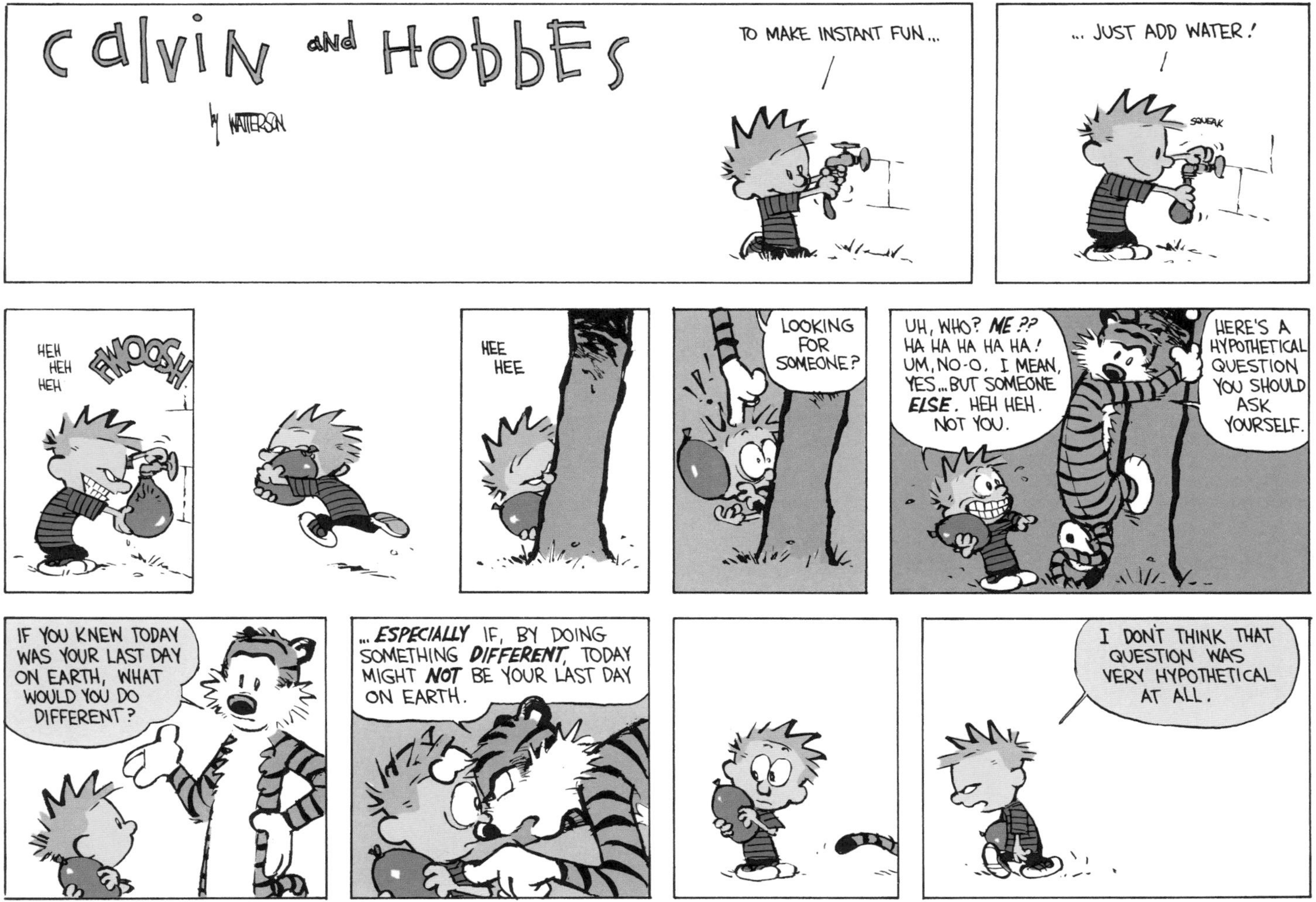
Calvin and Hobbes
by WATTERSON
TO MAKE INSTANT FUN...
... JUST ADD WATER!
SQUEAK
HEH HEH HEH
FWOOSH
HEE HEE
LOOKING FOR SOMEONE?
UH, WHO? ME ?? HA HA HA HA HA! UM, NO-O. I MEAN, YES... BUT SOMEONE ELSE. HEH HEH. NOT YOU.
HERE'S A HYPOTHETICAL QUESTION YOU SHOULD ASK YOURSELF.
IF YOU KNEW TODAY WAS YOUR LAST DAY ON EARTH, WHAT WOULD YOU DO DIFFERENT?
... ESPECIALLY IF, BY DOING SOMETHING DIFFERENT, TODAY MIGHT NOT BE YOUR LAST DAY ON EARTH.
I DON'T THINK THAT QUESTION WAS VERY HYPOTHETICAL AT ALL.

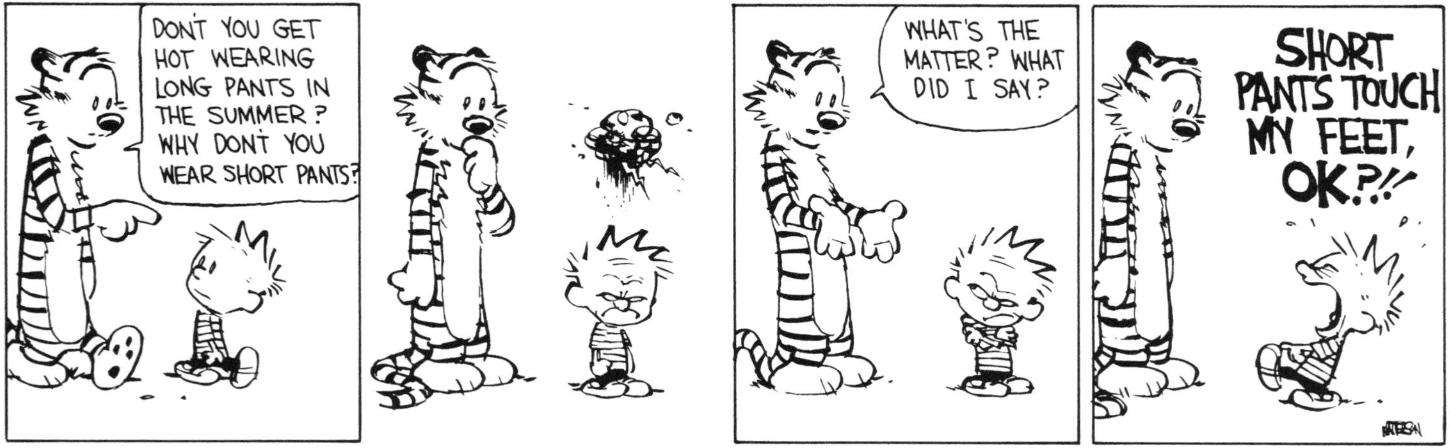
DON'T YOU GET HOT WEARING LONG PANTS IN THE SUMMER? WHY DON'T YOU WEAR SHORT PANTS?
WHAT'S THE MATTER? WHAT DID I SAY?
SHORT PANTS TOUCH MY FEET, OK?!!
WATTERSON

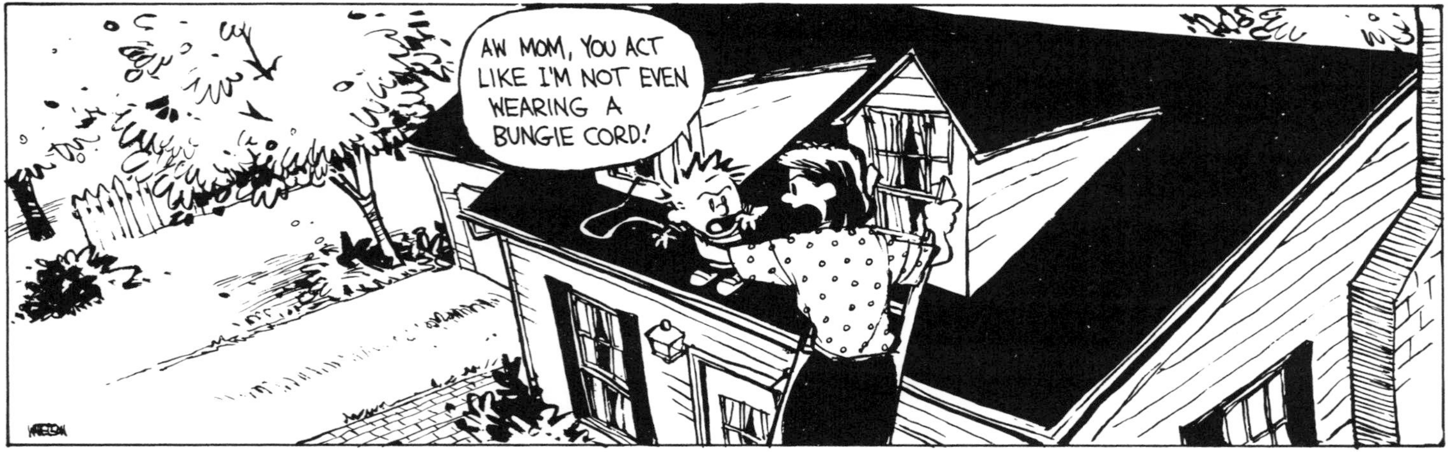
AW MOM, YOU ACT LIKE I'M NOT EVEN WEARING A BUNGIE CORD!
WATTERSON

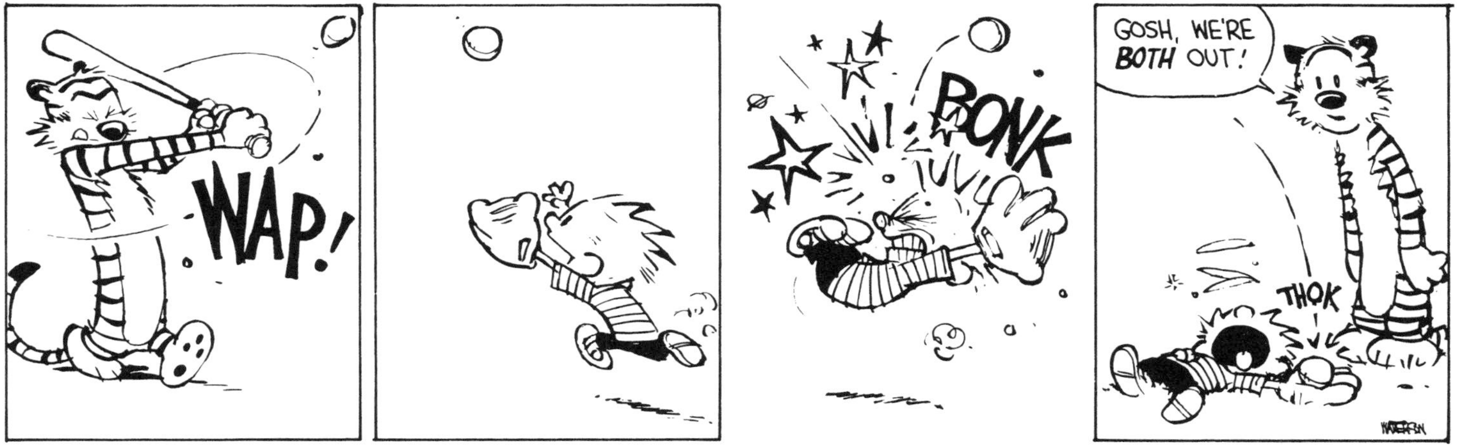
WAP!
BONK
GOSH, WE'RE BOTH OUT!
THOK

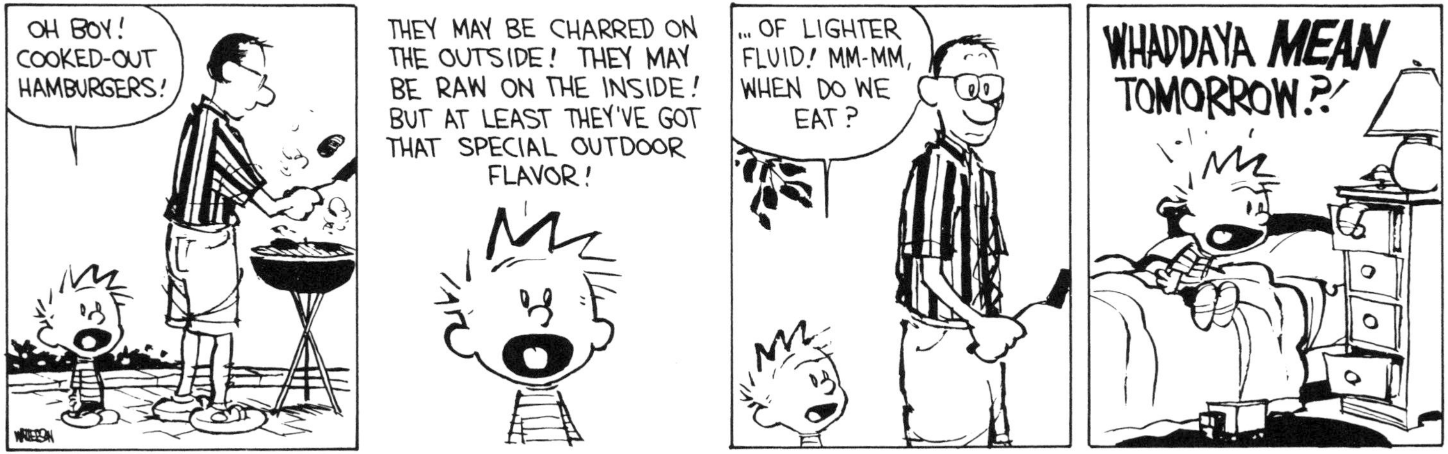
OH BOY! COOKED-OUT HAMBURGERS!
THEY MAY BE CHARRED ON THE OUTSIDE! THEY MAY BE RAW ON THE INSIDE! BUT AT LEAST THEY'VE GOT THAT SPECIAL OUTDOOR FLAVOR!
... OF LIGHTER FLUID! MM-MM, WHEN DO WE EAT?
WHADDAYA MEAN TOMORROW?!

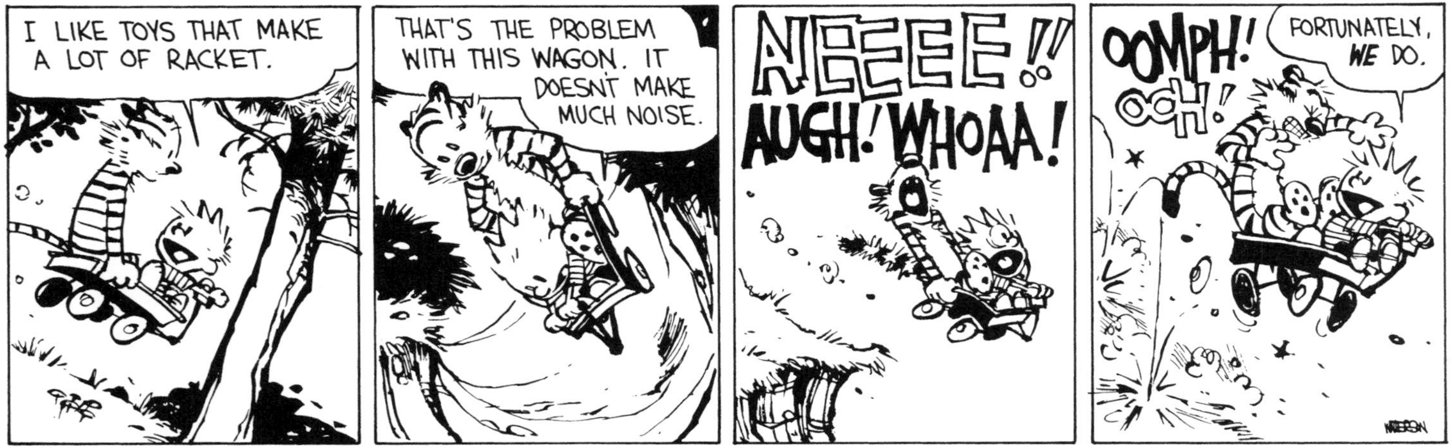
I LIKE TOYS THAT MAKE A LOT OF RACKET.
THAT'S THE PROBLEM WITH THIS WAGON. IT DOESN'T MAKE MUCH NOISE.
NEEEE!!
AUGH! WHOAA!
OOMPH! OCH!
FORTUNATELY, WE DO.
WATTERSON

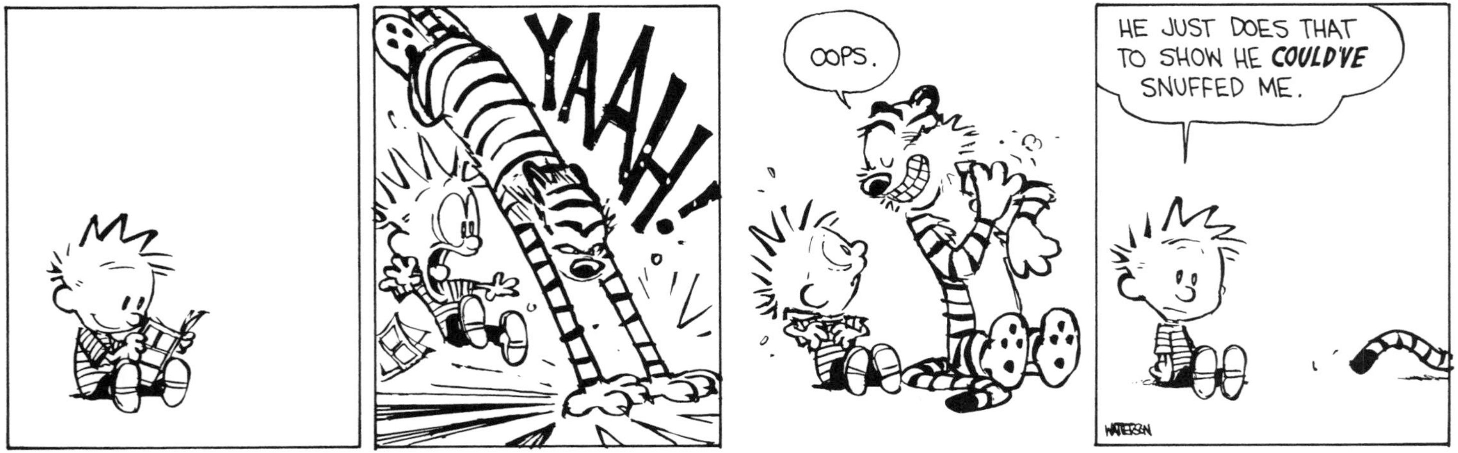
YAAH!
OOPS.
HE JUST DOES THAT TO SHOW HE COULD'VE SNUFFED ME.
WATTERSON

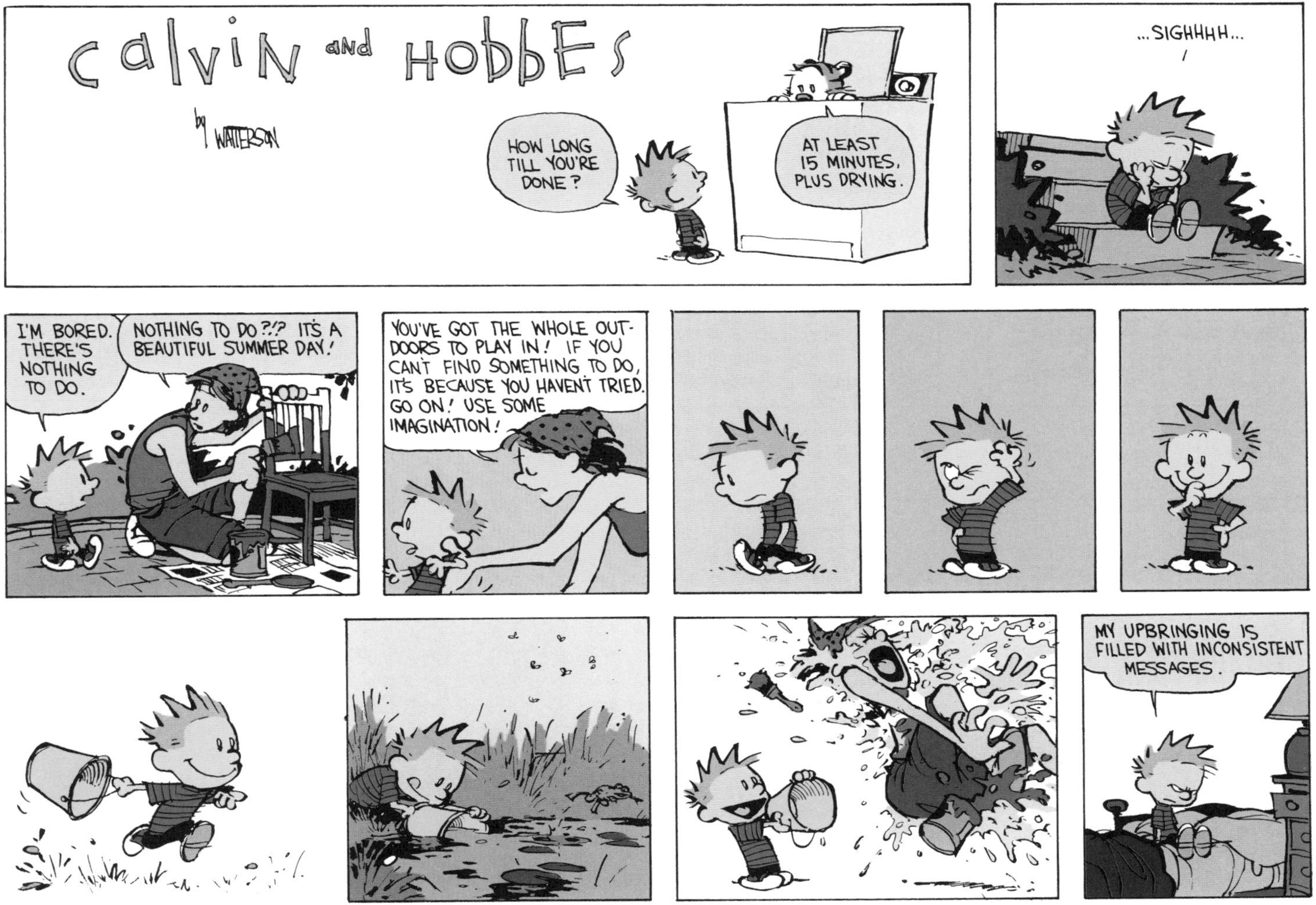
Calvin and Hobbes
by WATTERSON
HOW LONG TILL YOU'RE DONE?
AT LEAST 15 MINUTES, PLUS DRYING.
...SIGHHHH...
I'M BORED. THERE'S NOTHING TO DO.
NOTHING TO DO?!? IT'S A BEAUTIFUL SUMMER DAY!
YOU'VE GOT THE WHOLE OUTDOORS TO PLAY IN! IF YOU CAN'T FIND SOMETHING TO DO, IT'S BECAUSE YOU HAVEN'T TRIED. GO ON! USE SOME IMAGINATION!
MY UPBRINGING IS FILLED WITH INCONSISTENT MESSAGES.

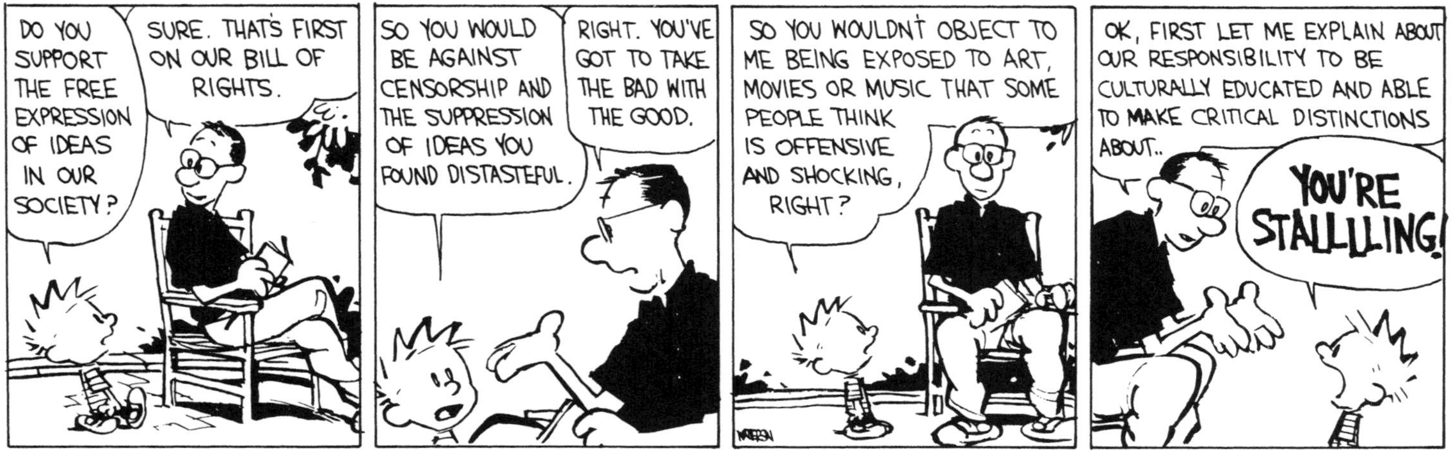
DO YOU SUPPORT THE FREE EXPRESSION OF IDEAS IN OUR SOCIETY?
SURE. THAT'S FIRST ON OUR BILL OF RIGHTS.
SO YOU WOULD BE AGAINST CENSORSHIP AND THE SUPPRESSION OF IDEAS YOU FOUND DISTASTEFUL.
RIGHT. YOU'VE GOT TO TAKE THE BAD WITH THE GOOD.
SO YOU WOULDN'T OBJECT TO ME BEING EXPOSED TO ART, MOVIES OR MUSIC THAT SOME PEOPLE THINK IS OFFENSIVE AND SHOCKING, RIGHT?
OK, FIRST LET ME EXPLAIN ABOUT OUR RESPONSIBILITY TO BE CULTURALLY EDUCATED AND ABLE TO MAKE CRITICAL DISTINCTIONS ABOUT..
YOU'RE STALLLLING!

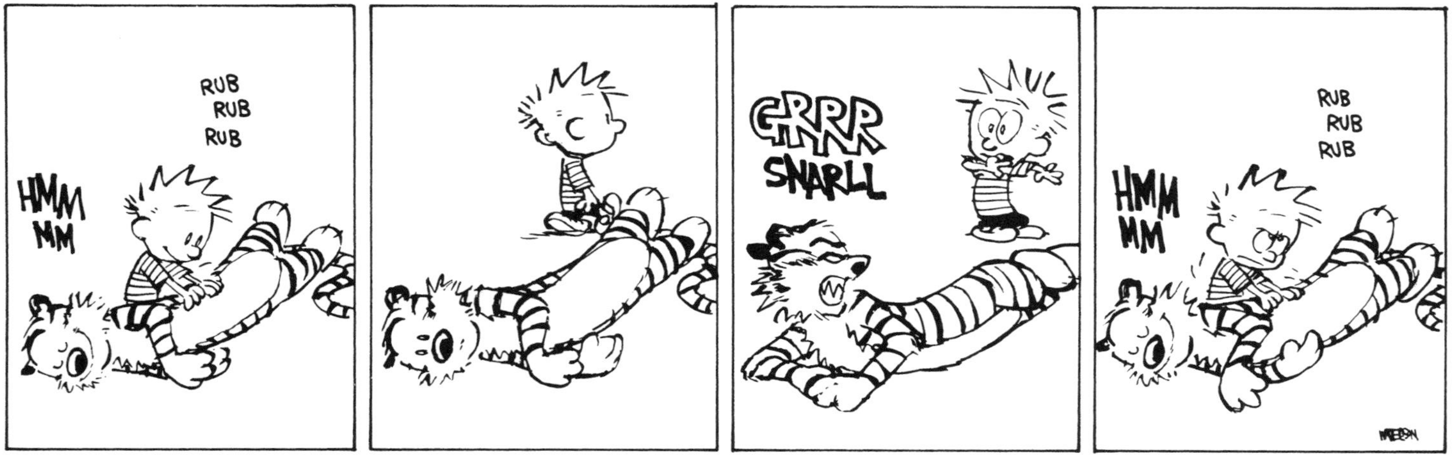
RUB RUB RUB
HMM MM
GRRR SNARLL
RUB RUB RUB
HMM MM

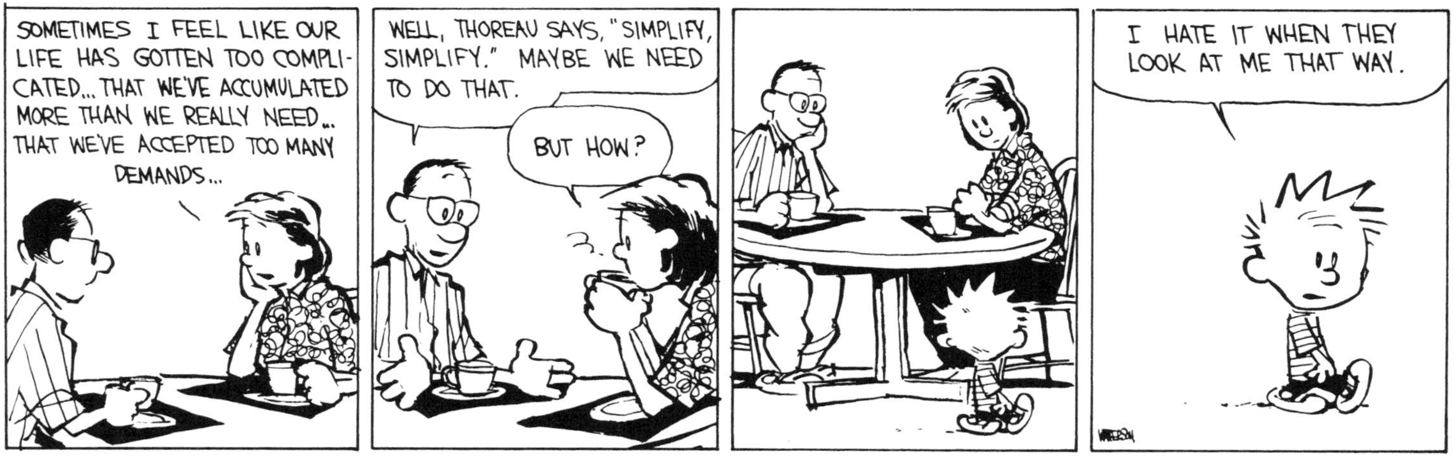
SOMETIMES I FEEL LIKE OUR LIFE HAS GOTTEN TOO COMPLICATED... THAT WE'VE ACCUMULATED MORE THAN WE REALLY NEED... THAT WE'VE ACCEPTED TOO MANY DEMANDS...
WELL, THOREAU SAYS, "SIMPLIFY, SIMPLIFY." MAYBE WE NEED TO DO THAT.
BUT HOW?
I HATE IT WHEN THEY LOOK AT ME THAT WAY.

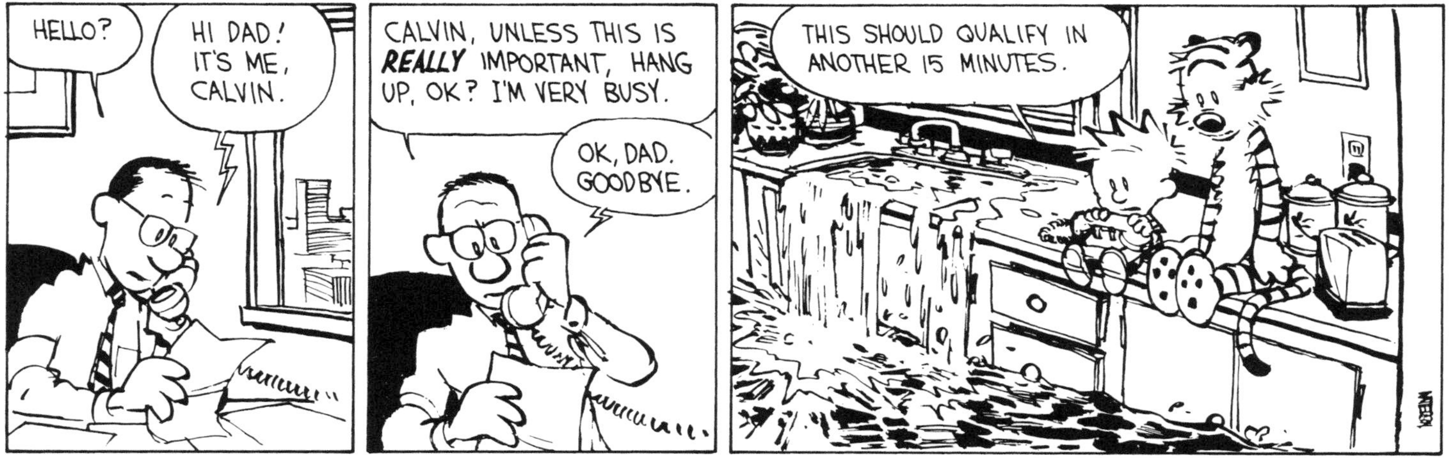
HELLO?
HI DAD! IT'S ME, CALVIN.
CALVIN, UNLESS THIS IS **REALLY** IMPORTANT, HANG UP, OK? I'M VERY BUSY.
OK, DAD. GOODBYE.
THIS SHOULD QUALIFY IN ANOTHER 15 MINUTES.

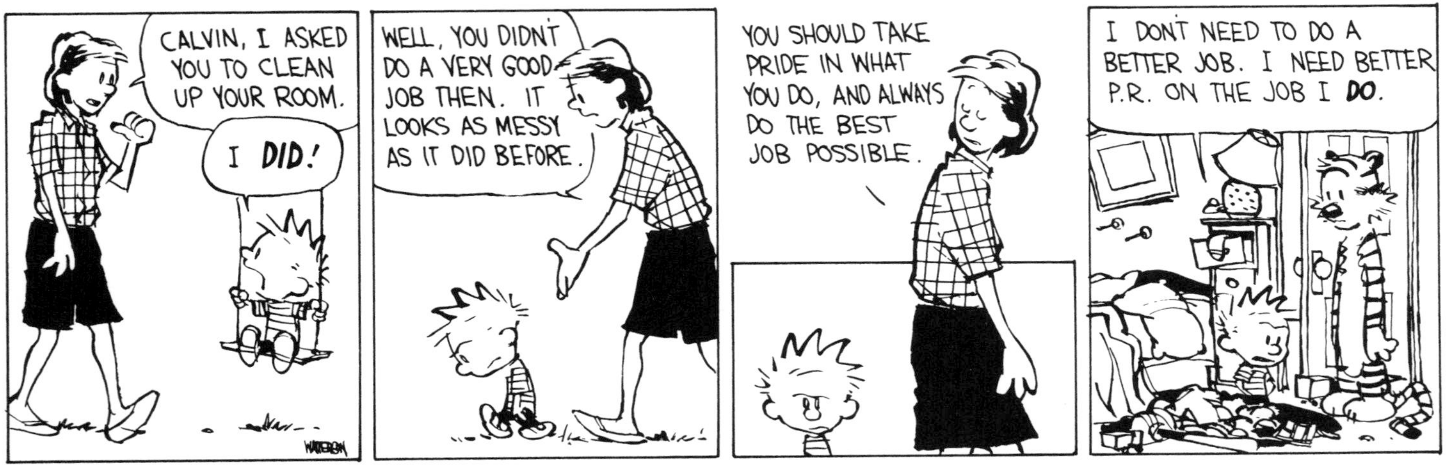
CALVIN, I ASKED YOU TO CLEAN UP YOUR ROOM.
I DID!
WELL, YOU DIDN'T DO A VERY GOOD JOB THEN. IT LOOKS AS MESSY AS IT DID BEFORE.
YOU SHOULD TAKE PRIDE IN WHAT YOU DO, AND ALWAYS DO THE BEST JOB POSSIBLE.
I DON'T NEED TO DO A BETTER JOB. I NEED BETTER P.R. ON THE JOB I **DO**.

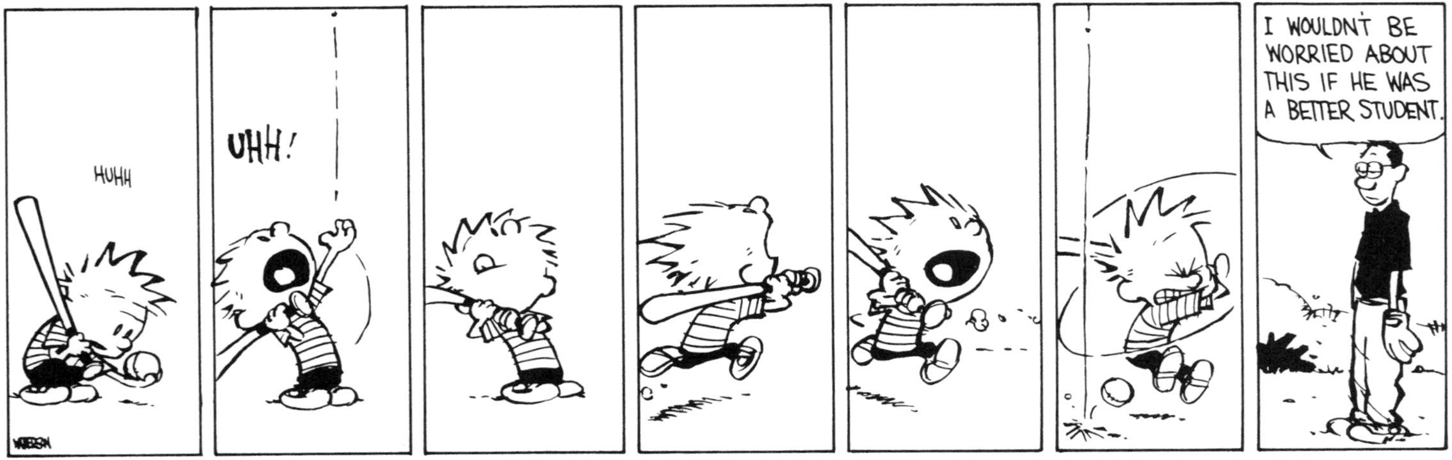
HUHH
UHH!
I WOULDN'T BE WORRIED ABOUT THIS IF HE WAS A BETTER STUDENT.

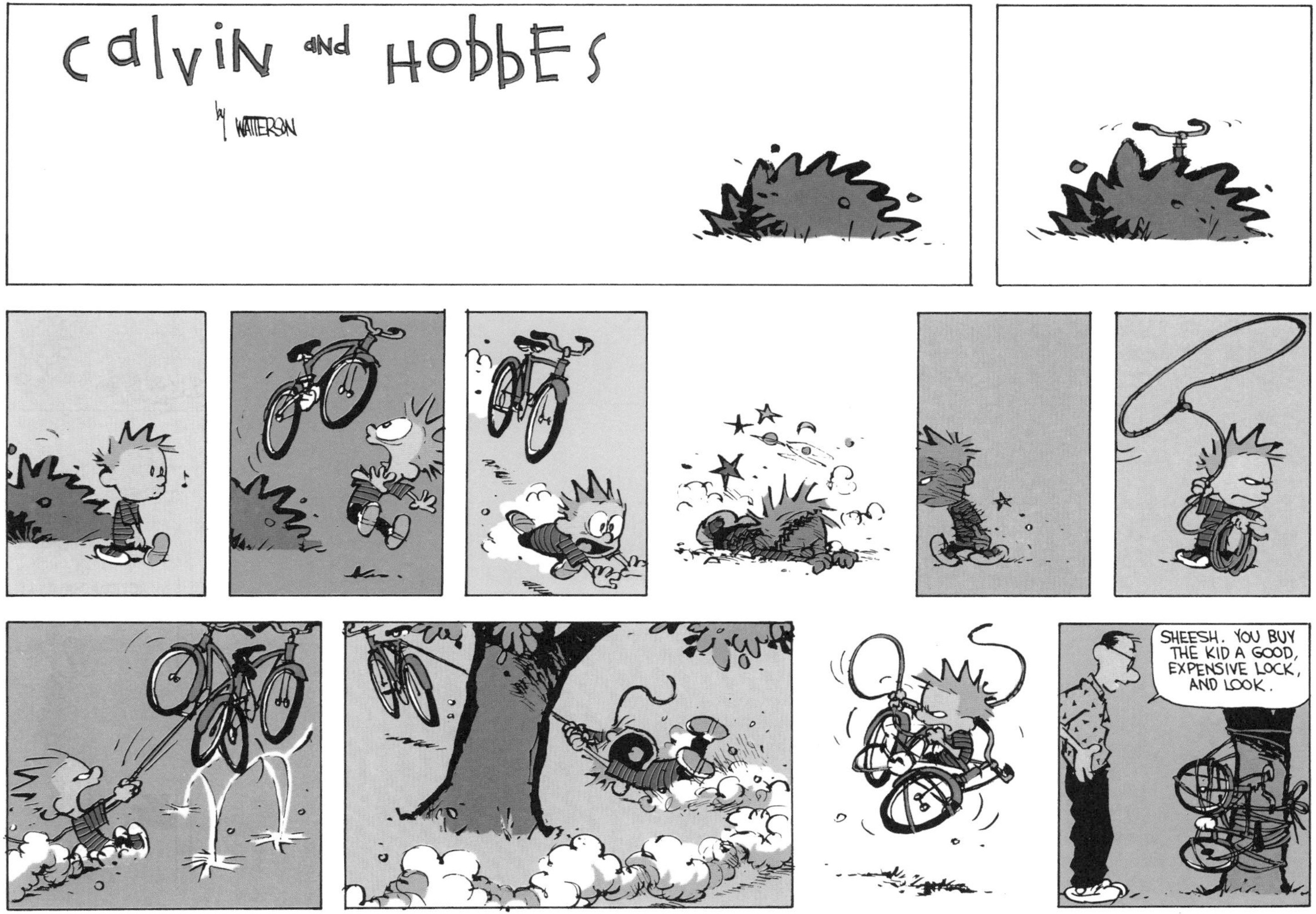
Calvin and Hobbes
by Watterson
SHEESH. YOU BUY THE KID A GOOD, EXPENSIVE LOCK, AND LOOK.

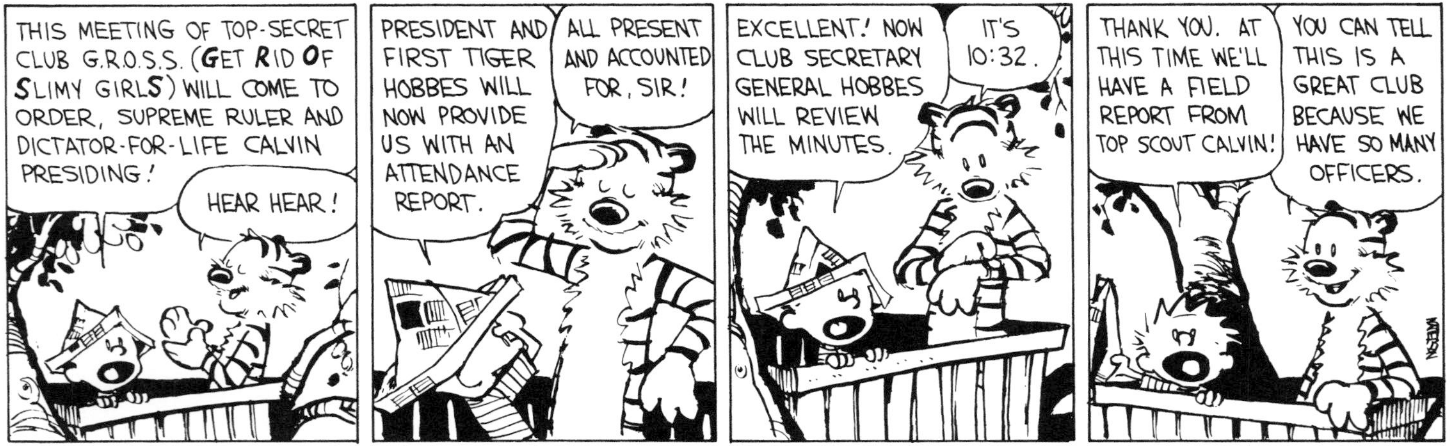
THIS MEETING OF TOP-SECRET CLUB G.R.O.S.S. (GET RID OF SLIMY GIRLS) WILL COME TO ORDER, SUPREME RULER AND DICTATOR-FOR-LIFE CALVIN PRESIDING!
HEAR HEAR!
PRESIDENT AND FIRST TIGER HOBBES WILL NOW PROVIDE US WITH AN ATTENDANCE REPORT.
ALL PRESENT AND ACCOUNTED FOR, SIR!
EXCELLENT! NOW CLUB SECRETARY GENERAL HOBBES WILL REVIEW THE MINUTES.
IT'S 10:32.
THANK YOU. AT THIS TIME WE'LL HAVE A FIELD REPORT FROM TOP SCOUT CALVIN!
YOU CAN TELL THIS IS A GREAT CLUB BECAUSE WE HAVE SO MANY OFFICERS.

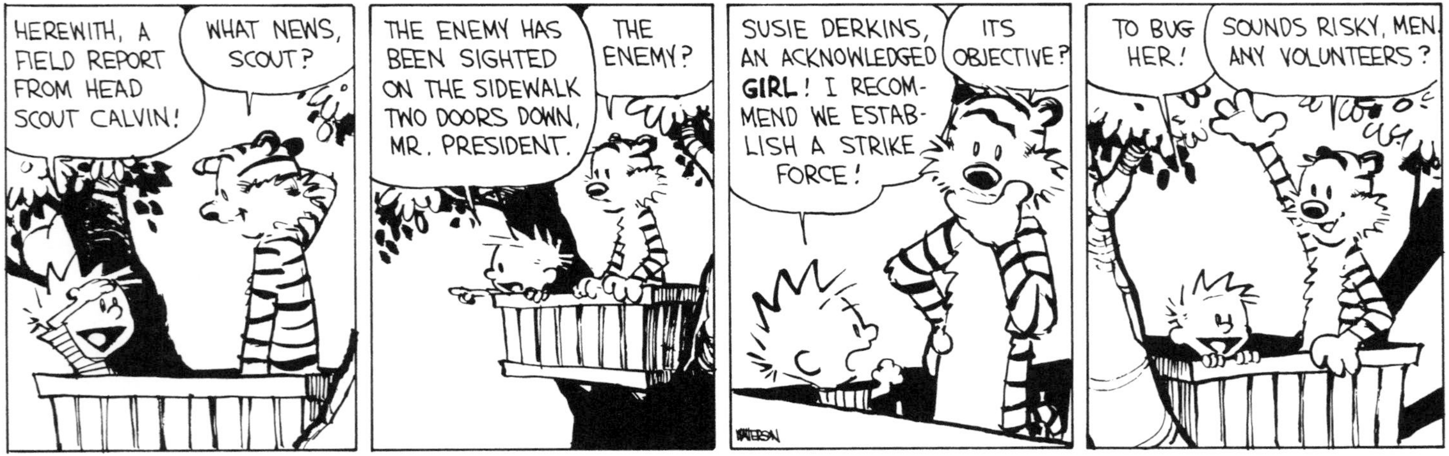
HEREWITH, A FIELD REPORT FROM HEAD SCOUT CALVIN!
WHAT NEWS, SCOUT?
THE ENEMY HAS BEEN SIGHTED ON THE SIDEWALK TWO DOORS DOWN, MR. PRESIDENT.
THE ENEMY?
SUSIE DERKINS, AN ACKNOWLEDGED GIRL! I RECOMMEND WE ESTABLISH A STRIKE FORCE!
ITS OBJECTIVE?
TO BUG HER!
SOUNDS RISKY, MEN. ANY VOLUNTEERS?

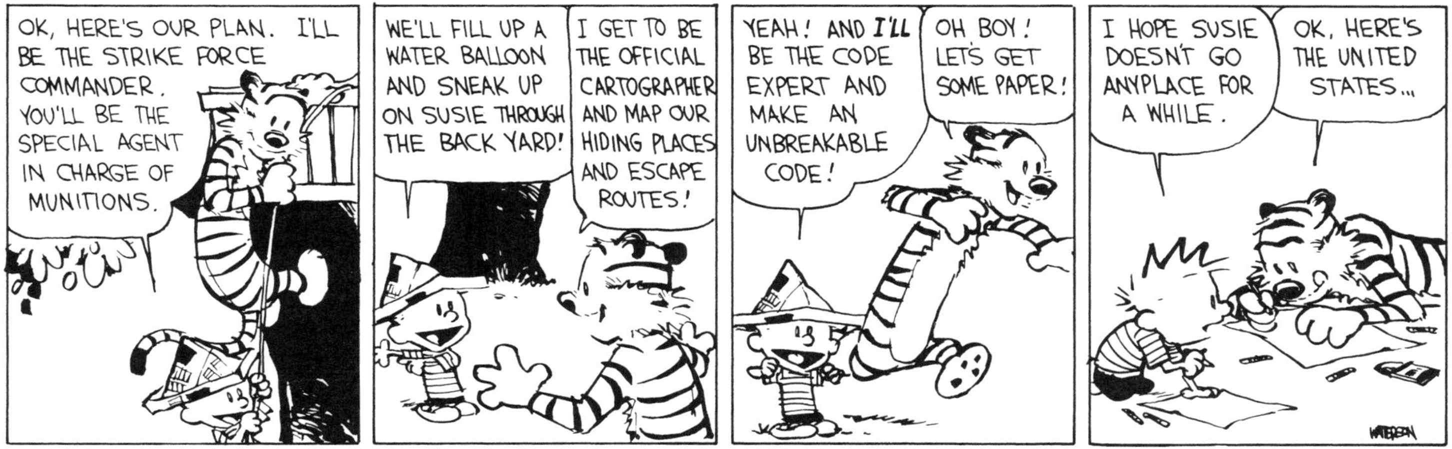
OK, HERE'S OUR PLAN. I'LL BE THE STRIKE FORCE COMMANDER. YOU'LL BE THE SPECIAL AGENT IN CHARGE OF MUNITIONS.
WE'LL FILL UP A WATER BALLOON AND SNEAK UP ON SUSIE THROUGH THE BACK YARD!
I GET TO BE THE OFFICIAL CARTOGRAPHER AND MAP OUR HIDING PLACES AND ESCAPE ROUTES!
YEAH! AND I'LL BE THE CODE EXPERT AND MAKE AN UNBREAKABLE CODE!
OH BOY! LET'S GET SOME PAPER!
I HOPE SUSIE DOESN'T GO ANYPLACE FOR A WHILE.
OK, HERE'S THE UNITED STATES...
WATTERSON

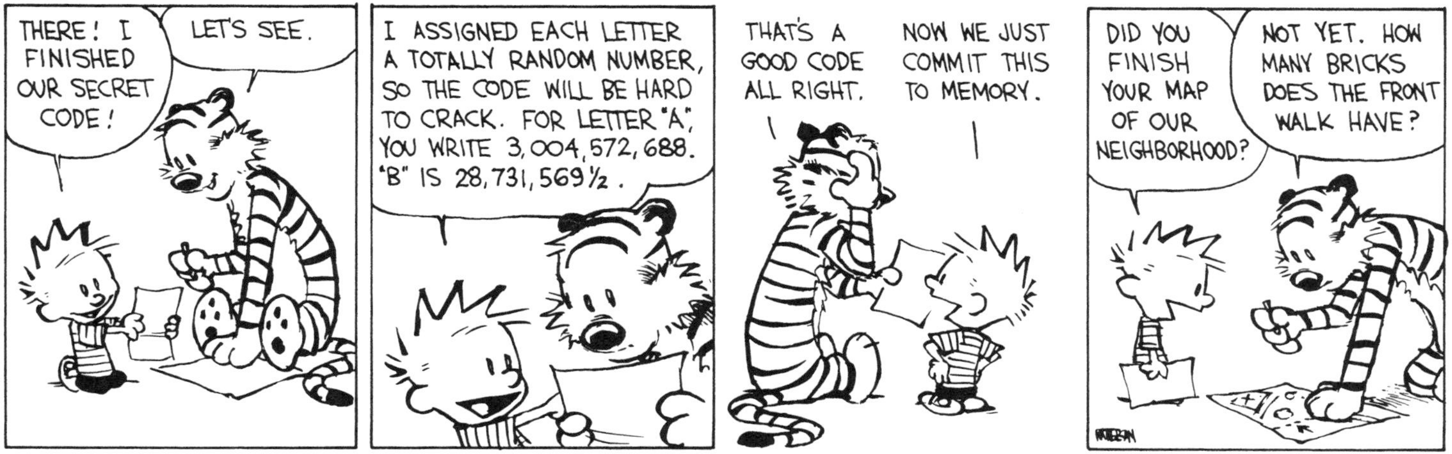
THERE! I FINISHED OUR SECRET CODE!
LET'S SEE.
I ASSIGNED EACH LETTER A TOTALLY RANDOM NUMBER, SO THE CODE WILL BE HARD TO CRACK. FOR LETTER "A", YOU WRITE 3,004,572,688. "B" IS 28,731,569½.
THAT'S A GOOD CODE ALL RIGHT.
NOW WE JUST COMMIT THIS TO MEMORY.
DID YOU FINISH YOUR MAP OF OUR NEIGHBORHOOD?
NOT YET. HOW MANY BRICKS DOES THE FRONT WALK HAVE?
WATTERSON

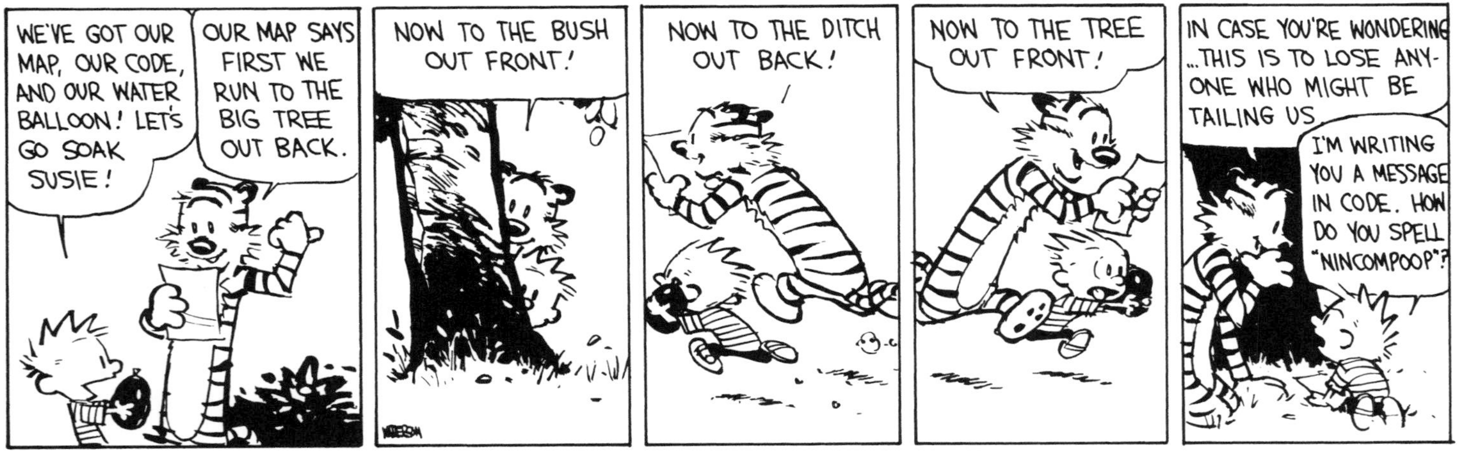
WE'VE GOT OUR MAP, OUR CODE, AND OUR WATER BALLOON! LET'S GO SOAK SUSIE!
OUR MAP SAYS FIRST WE RUN TO THE BIG TREE OUT BACK.
NOW TO THE BUSH OUT FRONT!
NOW TO THE DITCH OUT BACK!
NOW TO THE TREE OUT FRONT!
IN CASE YOU'RE WONDERING ...THIS IS TO LOSE ANY-ONE WHO MIGHT BE TAILING US.
I'M WRITING YOU A MESSAGE IN CODE. HOW DO YOU SPELL "NINCOMPOOP"?

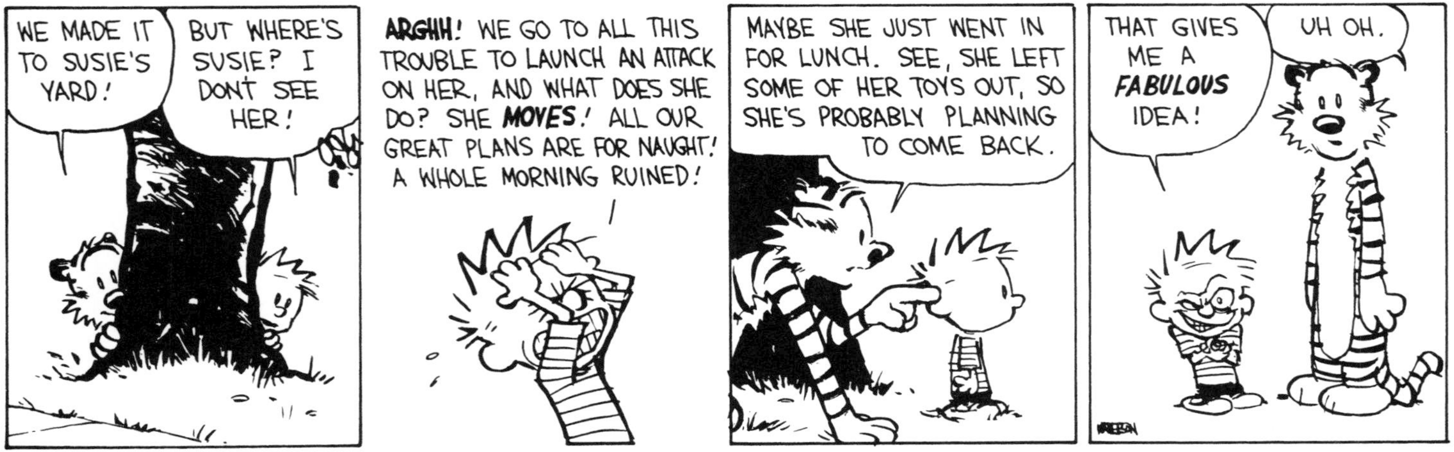
WE MADE IT TO SUSIE'S YARD!
BUT WHERE'S SUSIE? I DON'T SEE HER!
ARGHH! WE GO TO ALL THIS TROUBLE TO LAUNCH AN ATTACK ON HER, AND WHAT DOES SHE DO? SHE MOVES! ALL OUR GREAT PLANS ARE FOR NAUGHT! A WHOLE MORNING RUINED!
MAYBE SHE JUST WENT IN FOR LUNCH. SEE, SHE LEFT SOME OF HER TOYS OUT, SO SHE'S PROBABLY PLANNING TO COME BACK.
THAT GIVES ME A FABULOUS IDEA!
UH OH.

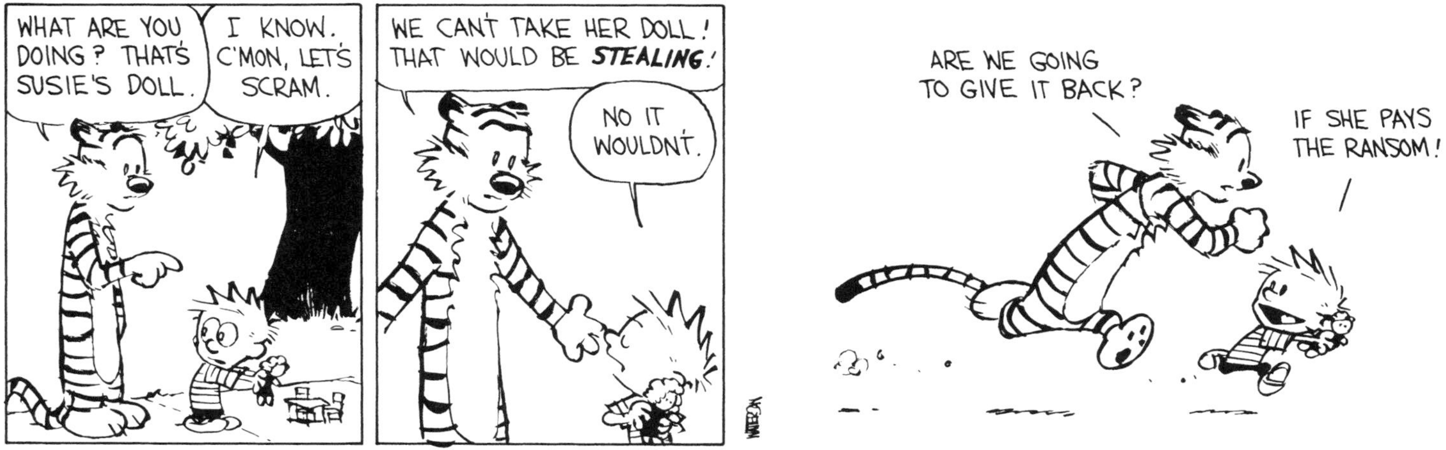
WHAT ARE YOU DOING? THAT'S SUSIE'S DOLL.
I KNOW. C'MON, LET'S SCRAM.
WE CAN'T TAKE HER DOLL! THAT WOULD BE **STEALING**!
NO IT WOULDN'T.
ARE WE GOING TO GIVE IT BACK?
IF SHE PAYS THE RANSOM!

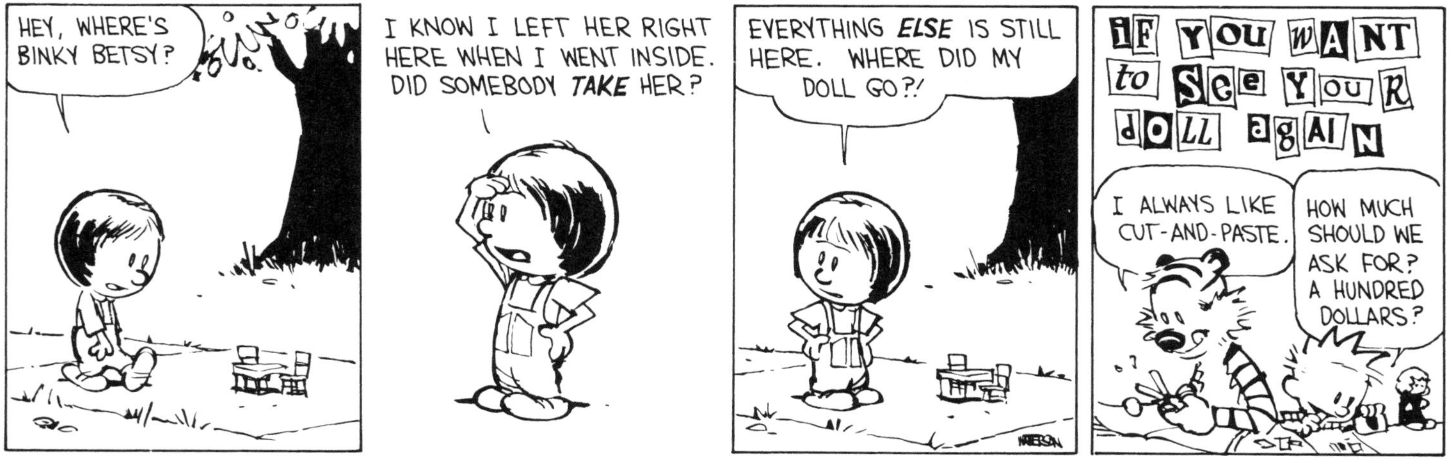
HEY, WHERE'S BINKY BETSY?
I KNOW I LEFT HER RIGHT HERE WHEN I WENT INSIDE. DID SOMEBODY *TAKE* HER?
EVERYTHING *ELSE* IS STILL HERE. WHERE DID MY DOLL GO?!
IF YOU WANT to See YOUR doLL agAIN
I ALWAYS LIKE CUT-AND-PASTE.
HOW MUCH SHOULD WE ASK FOR? A HUNDRED DOLLARS?

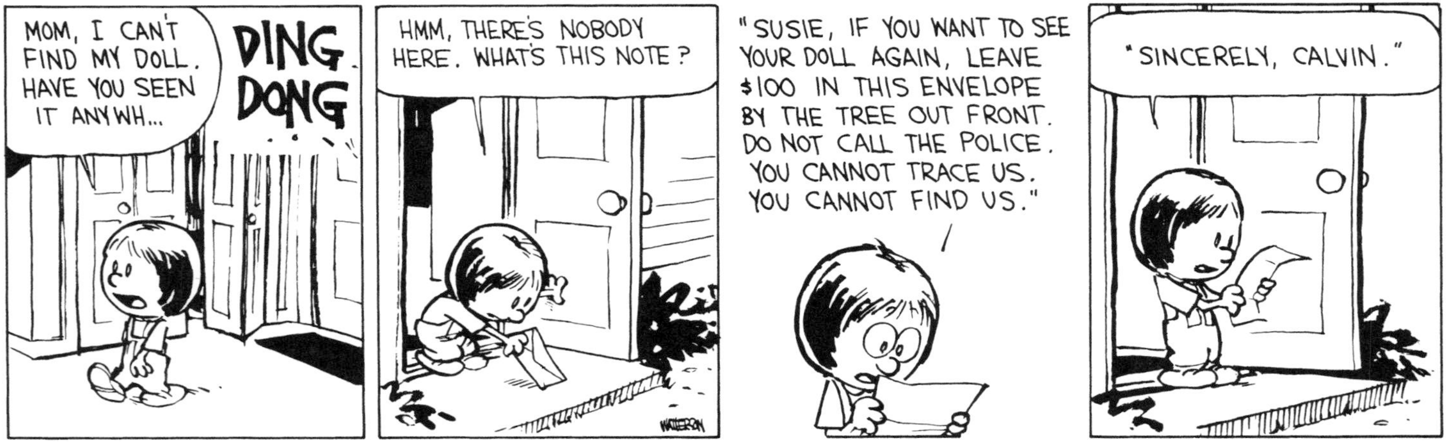
MOM, I CAN'T FIND MY DOLL. HAVE YOU SEEN IT ANYWH...
DING DONG
HMM, THERE'S NOBODY HERE. WHAT'S THIS NOTE?
"SUSIE, IF YOU WANT TO SEE YOUR DOLL AGAIN, LEAVE $100 IN THIS ENVELOPE BY THE TREE OUT FRONT. DO NOT CALL THE POLICE. YOU CANNOT TRACE US. YOU CANNOT FIND US."
"SINCERELY, CALVIN."

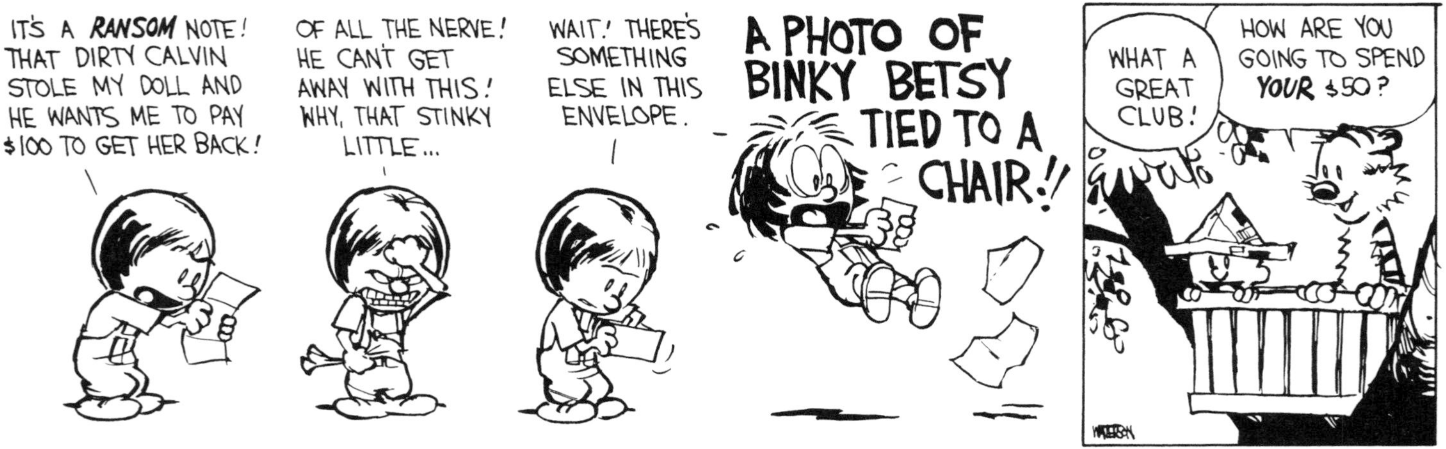
IT'S A RANSOM NOTE! THAT DIRTY CALVIN STOLE MY DOLL AND HE WANTS ME TO PAY $100 TO GET HER BACK!
OF ALL THE NERVE! HE CAN'T GET AWAY WITH THIS! WHY, THAT STINKY LITTLE...
WAIT! THERE'S SOMETHING ELSE IN THIS ENVELOPE.
A PHOTO OF BINKY BETSY TIED TO A CHAIR!!
WHAT A GREAT CLUB!
HOW ARE YOU GOING TO SPEND YOUR $50?

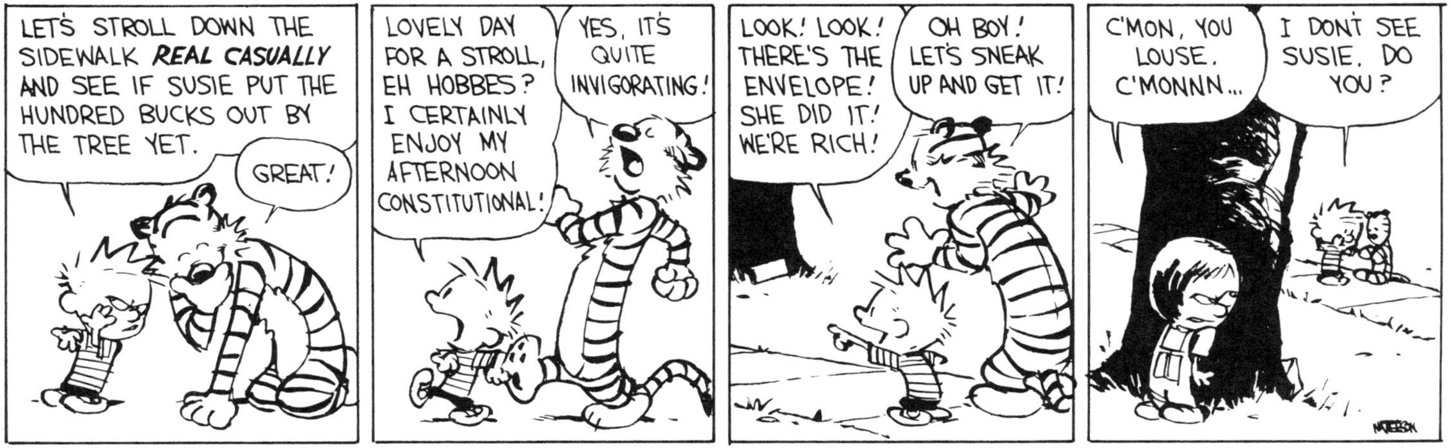
LET'S STROLL DOWN THE SIDEWALK **REAL CASUALLY** AND SEE IF SUSIE PUT THE HUNDRED BUCKS OUT BY THE TREE YET.
GREAT!
LOVELY DAY FOR A STROLL, EH HOBBES? I CERTAINLY ENJOY MY AFTERNOON CONSTITUTIONAL!
YES, IT'S QUITE INVIGORATING!
LOOK! LOOK! THERE'S THE ENVELOPE! SHE DID IT! WE'RE RICH!
OH BOY! LET'S SNEAK UP AND GET IT!
C'MON, YOU LOUSE. C'MONNN...
I DON'T SEE SUSIE. DO YOU?
WATTERSON

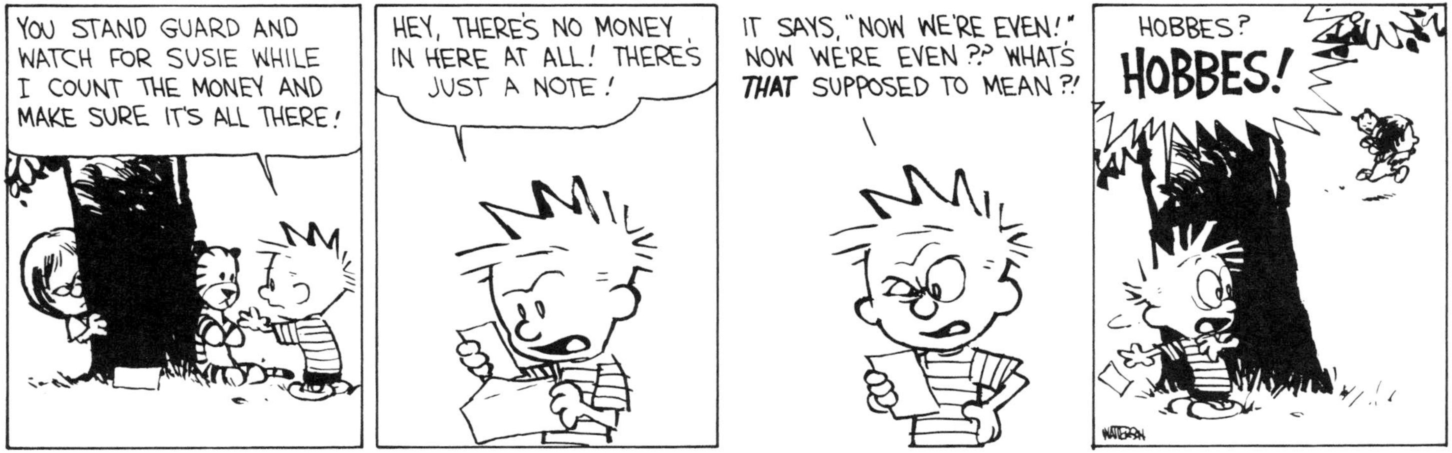
YOU STAND GUARD AND WATCH FOR SUSIE WHILE I COUNT THE MONEY AND MAKE SURE IT'S ALL THERE!
HEY, THERE'S NO MONEY IN HERE AT ALL! THERE'S JUST A NOTE!
IT SAYS, "NOW WE'RE EVEN!" NOW WE'RE EVEN?? WHAT'S **THAT** SUPPOSED TO MEAN?!
HOBBES?
HOBBES!
WATTERSON

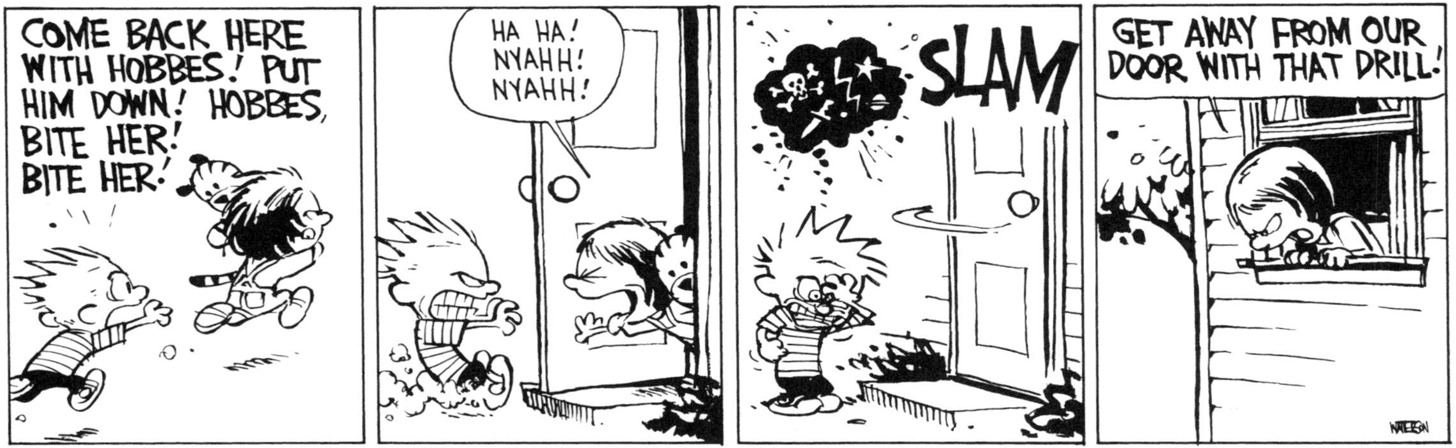
COME BACK HERE WITH HOBBES! PUT HIM DOWN! HOBBES, BITE HER! BITE HER!
HA HA! NYAHH! NYAHH!
SLAM
GET AWAY FROM OUR DOOR WITH THAT DRILL!

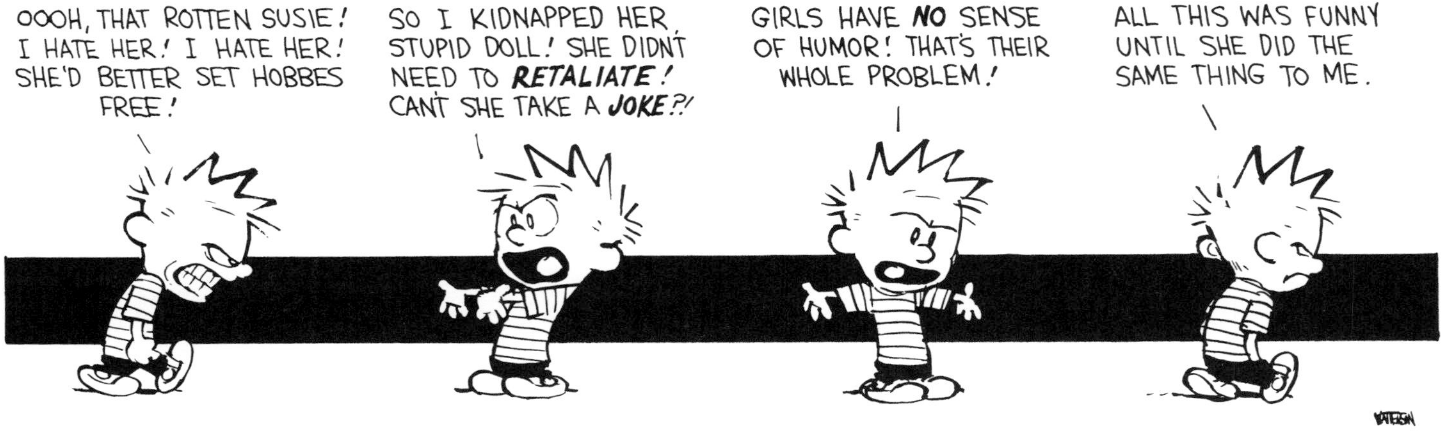
OOOH, THAT ROTTEN SUSIE! I HATE HER! I HATE HER! SHE'D BETTER SET HOBBES FREE!
SO I KIDNAPPED HER STUPID DOLL! SHE DIDN'T NEED TO RETALIATE! CAN'T SHE TAKE A JOKE?!
GIRLS HAVE NO SENSE OF HUMOR! THAT'S THEIR WHOLE PROBLEM!
ALL THIS WAS FUNNY UNTIL SHE DID THE SAME THING TO ME.

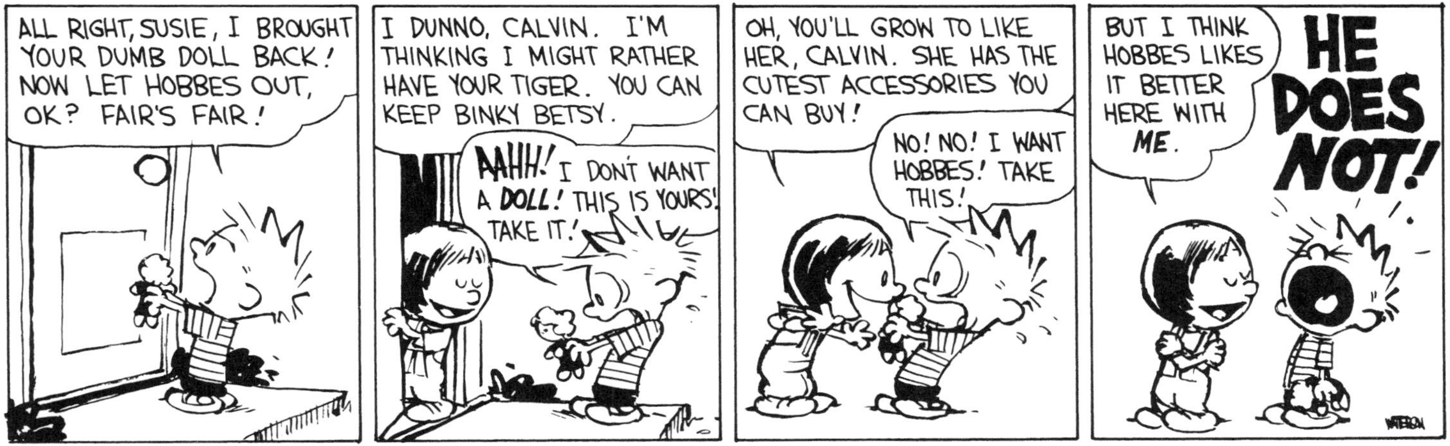
ALL RIGHT, SUSIE, I BROUGHT YOUR DUMB DOLL BACK! NOW LET HOBBES OUT, OK? FAIR'S FAIR!
I DUNNO, CALVIN. I'M THINKING I MIGHT RATHER HAVE YOUR TIGER. YOU CAN KEEP BINKY BETSY.
AAHH! I DON'T WANT A DOLL! THIS IS YOURS! TAKE IT!
OH, YOU'LL GROW TO LIKE HER, CALVIN. SHE HAS THE CUTEST ACCESSORIES YOU CAN BUY!
NO! NO! I WANT HOBBES! TAKE THIS!
BUT I THINK HOBBES LIKES IT BETTER HERE WITH ME.
HE DOES NOT!
WATTERSON

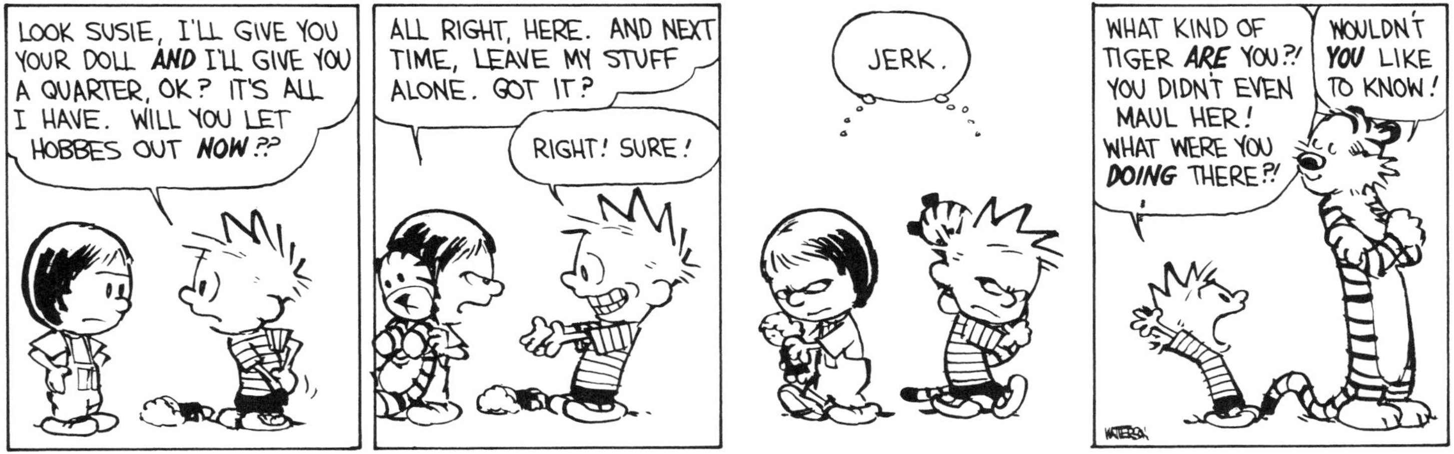
LOOK SUSIE, I'LL GIVE YOU YOUR DOLL AND I'LL GIVE YOU A QUARTER, OK? IT'S ALL I HAVE. WILL YOU LET HOBBES OUT NOW??
ALL RIGHT, HERE. AND NEXT TIME, LEAVE MY STUFF ALONE. GOT IT?
RIGHT! SURE!
JERK.
WHAT KIND OF TIGER ARE YOU?! YOU DIDN'T EVEN MAUL HER! WHAT WERE YOU DOING THERE?!
WOULDN'T YOU LIKE TO KNOW!
WATTERSON

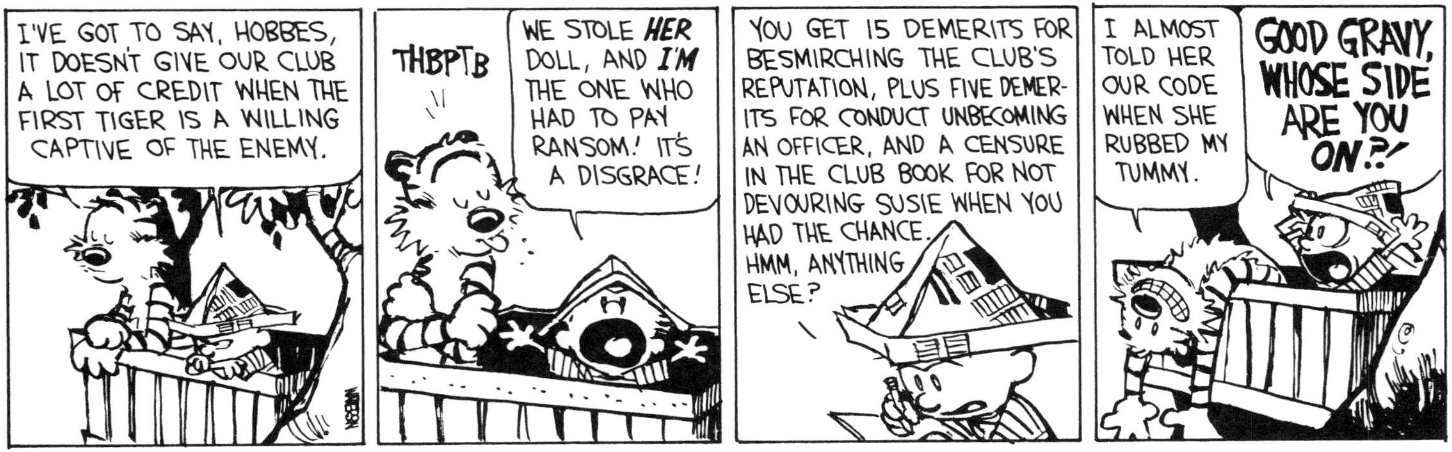
I'VE GOT TO SAY, HOBBES, IT DOESN'T GIVE OUR CLUB A LOT OF CREDIT WHEN THE FIRST TIGER IS A WILLING CAPTIVE OF THE ENEMY.
THBPTB
WE STOLE HER DOLL, AND I'M THE ONE WHO HAD TO PAY RANSOM! IT'S A DISGRACE!
YOU GET 15 DEMERITS FOR BESMIRCHING THE CLUB'S REPUTATION, PLUS FIVE DEMERITS FOR CONDUCT UNBECOMING AN OFFICER, AND A CENSURE IN THE CLUB BOOK FOR NOT DEVOURING SUSIE WHEN YOU HAD THE CHANCE.
HMM, ANYTHING ELSE?
I ALMOST TOLD HER OUR CODE WHEN SHE RUBBED MY TUMMY.
GOOD GRAVY, WHOSE SIDE ARE YOU ON?!

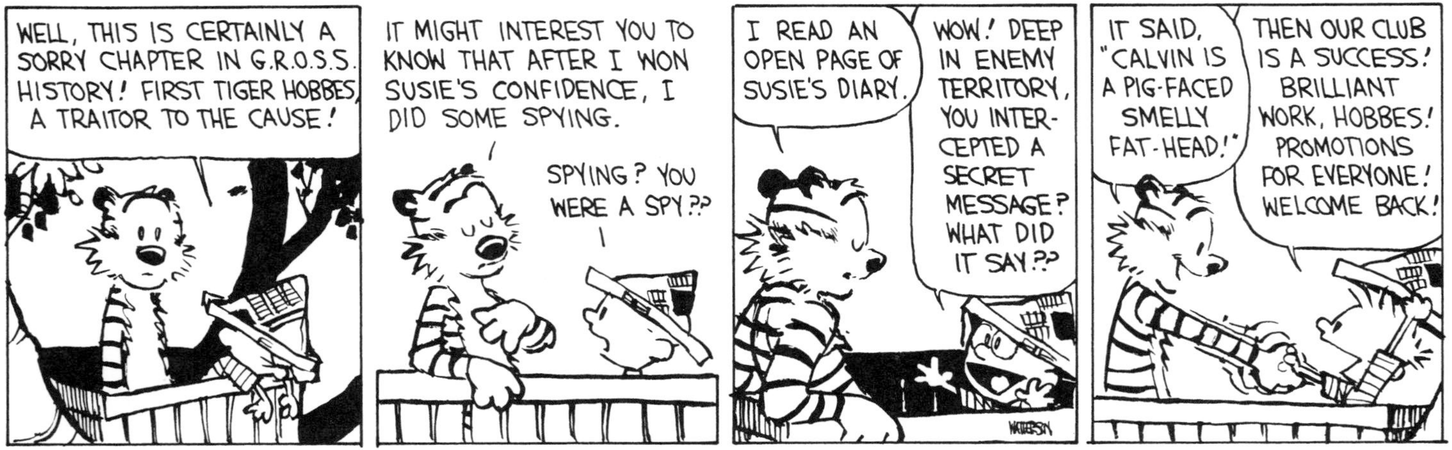
WELL, THIS IS CERTAINLY A SORRY CHAPTER IN G.R.O.S.S. HISTORY! FIRST TIGER HOBBES, A TRAITOR TO THE CAUSE!
IT MIGHT INTEREST YOU TO KNOW THAT AFTER I WON SUSIE'S CONFIDENCE, I DID SOME SPYING.
SPYING? YOU WERE A SPY??
I READ AN OPEN PAGE OF SUSIE'S DIARY.
WOW! DEEP IN ENEMY TERRITORY, YOU INTERCEPTED A SECRET MESSAGE? WHAT DID IT SAY??
IT SAID, "CALVIN IS A PIG-FACED SMELLY FAT-HEAD!"
THEN OUR CLUB IS A SUCCESS! BRILLIANT WORK, HOBBES! PROMOTIONS FOR EVERYONE! WELCOME BACK!

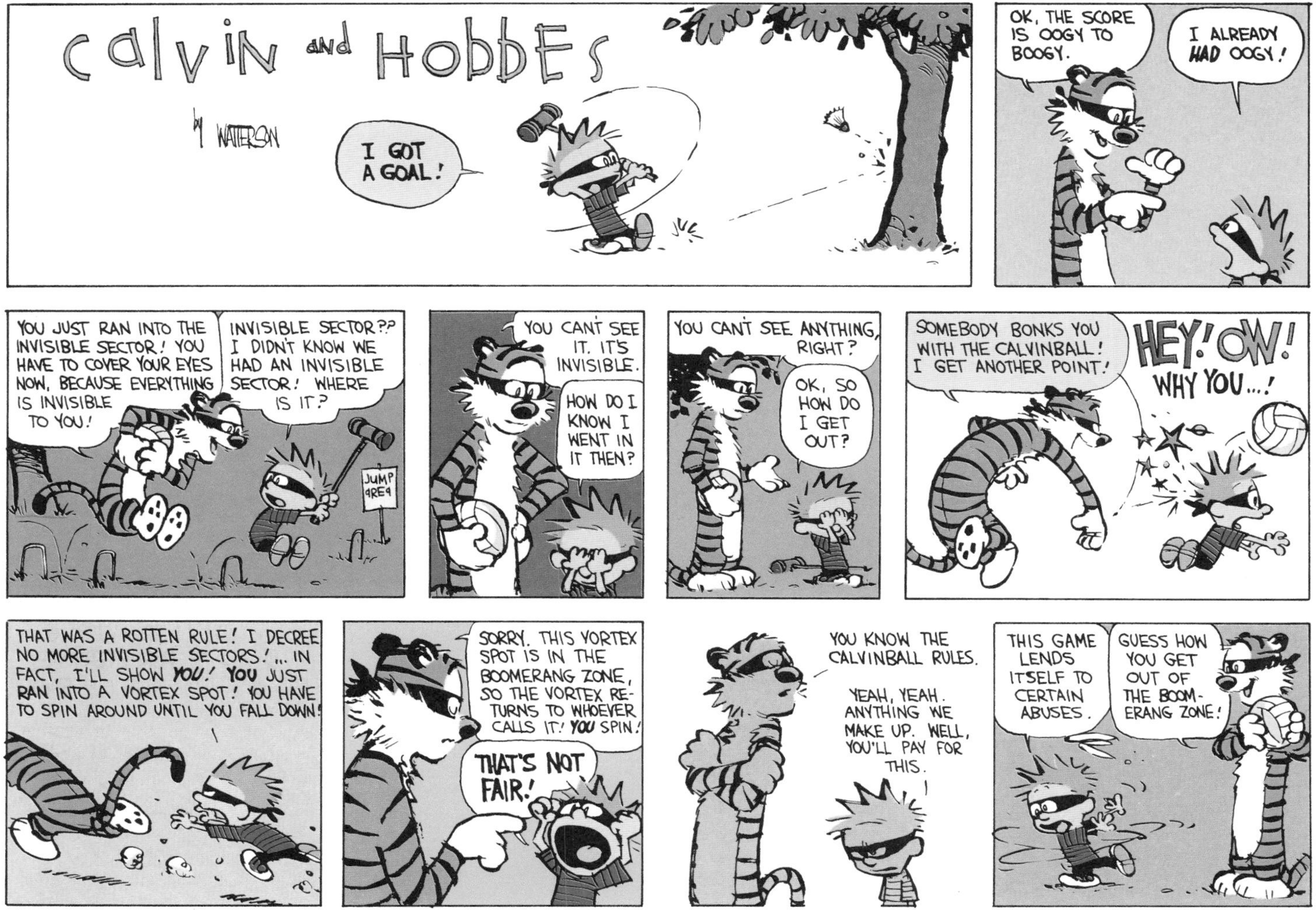
Calvin and HOBBES
by WATTERSON
I GOT A GOAL!
OK, THE SCORE IS OOGY TO BOOGY.
I ALREADY HAD OOGY!
YOU JUST RAN INTO THE INVISIBLE SECTOR! YOU HAVE TO COVER YOUR EYES NOW, BECAUSE EVERYTHING IS INVISIBLE TO YOU!
INVISIBLE SECTOR?? I DIDN'T KNOW WE HAD AN INVISIBLE SECTOR! WHERE IS IT?
JUMP AREA
YOU CAN'T SEE IT. IT'S INVISIBLE.
HOW DO I KNOW I WENT IN IT THEN?
YOU CAN'T SEE ANYTHING, RIGHT?
OK, SO HOW DO I GET OUT?
SOMEBODY BONKS YOU WITH THE CALVINBALL! I GET ANOTHER POINT!
HEY! OW! WHY YOU...!
THAT WAS A ROTTEN RULE! I DECREE NO MORE INVISIBLE SECTORS! ... IN FACT, I'LL SHOW YOU! YOU JUST RAN INTO A VORTEX SPOT! YOU HAVE TO SPIN AROUND UNTIL YOU FALL DOWN!
SORRY. THIS VORTEX SPOT IS IN THE BOOMERANG ZONE, SO THE VORTEX RETURNS TO WHOEVER CALLS IT! YOU SPIN!
THAT'S NOT FAIR!
YOU KNOW THE CALVINBALL RULES.
YEAH, YEAH. ANYTHING WE MAKE UP. WELL, YOU'LL PAY FOR THIS.
THIS GAME LENDS ITSELF TO CERTAIN ABUSES.
GUESS HOW YOU GET OUT OF THE BOOMERANG ZONE!

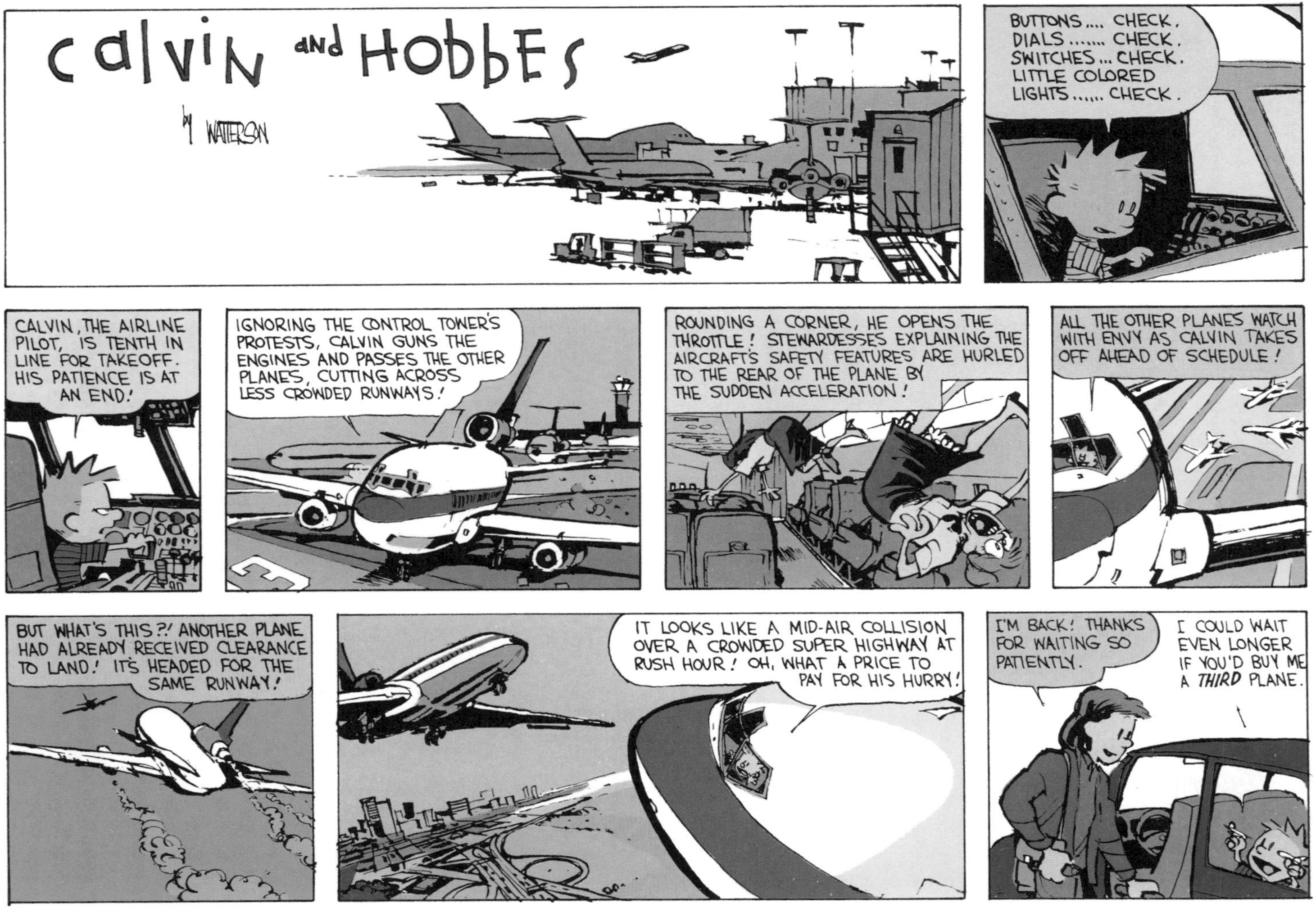
Calvin and HOBBES
by WATTERSON
BUTTONS.... CHECK. DIALS....... CHECK. SWITCHES... CHECK. LITTLE COLORED LIGHTS...... CHECK.
CALVIN, THE AIRLINE PILOT, IS TENTH IN LINE FOR TAKEOFF. HIS PATIENCE IS AT AN END!
IGNORING THE CONTROL TOWER'S PROTESTS, CALVIN GUNS THE ENGINES AND PASSES THE OTHER PLANES, CUTTING ACROSS LESS CROWDED RUNWAYS!
ROUNDING A CORNER, HE OPENS THE THROTTLE! STEWARDESSES EXPLAINING THE AIRCRAFT'S SAFETY FEATURES ARE HURLED TO THE REAR OF THE PLANE BY THE SUDDEN ACCELERATION!
ALL THE OTHER PLANES WATCH WITH ENVY AS CALVIN TAKES OFF AHEAD OF SCHEDULE!
BUT WHAT'S THIS?! ANOTHER PLANE HAD ALREADY RECEIVED CLEARANCE TO LAND! IT'S HEADED FOR THE SAME RUNWAY!
IT LOOKS LIKE A MID-AIR COLLISION OVER A CROWDED SUPER HIGHWAY AT RUSH HOUR! OH, WHAT A PRICE TO PAY FOR HIS HURRY!
I'M BACK! THANKS FOR WAITING SO PATIENTLY.
I COULD WAIT EVEN LONGER IF YOU'D BUY ME A *THIRD* PLANE.

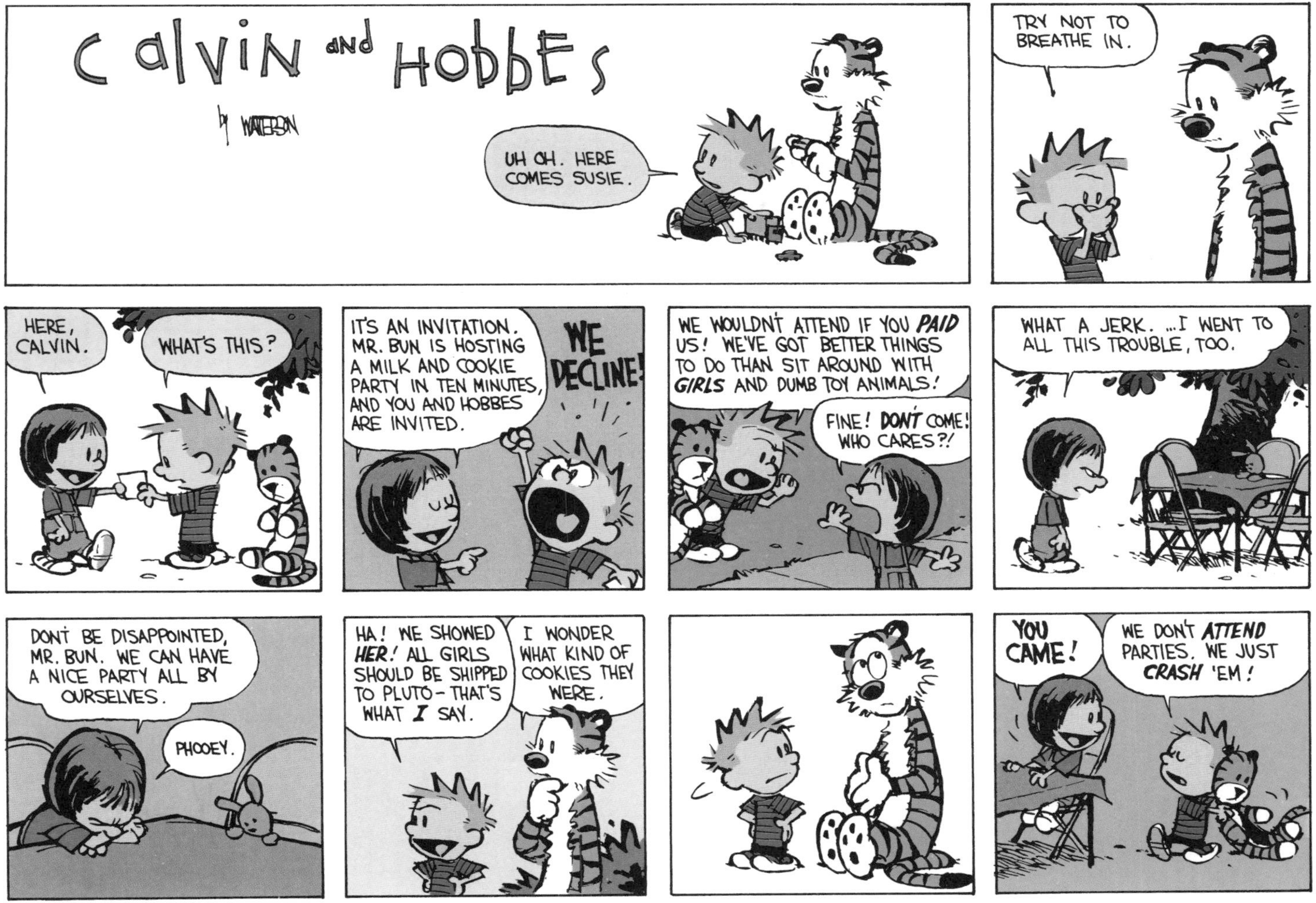
Calvin and HOBBES
by WATTERSON
UH OH. HERE COMES SUSIE.
TRY NOT TO BREATHE IN.
HERE, CALVIN.
WHAT'S THIS?
IT'S AN INVITATION. MR. BUN IS HOSTING A MILK AND COOKIE PARTY IN TEN MINUTES, AND YOU AND HOBBES ARE INVITED.
WE DECLINE!
WE WOULDN'T ATTEND IF YOU PAID US! WE'VE GOT BETTER THINGS TO DO THAN SIT AROUND WITH GIRLS AND DUMB TOY ANIMALS!
FINE! DON'T COME! WHO CARES?!
WHAT A JERK. ...I WENT TO ALL THIS TROUBLE, TOO.
DON'T BE DISAPPOINTED, MR. BUN. WE CAN HAVE A NICE PARTY ALL BY OURSELVES.
PHOOEY.
HA! WE SHOWED HER! ALL GIRLS SHOULD BE SHIPPED TO PLUTO - THAT'S WHAT I SAY.
I WONDER WHAT KIND OF COOKIES THEY WERE.
YOU CAME!
WE DON'T ATTEND PARTIES. WE JUST CRASH 'EM!

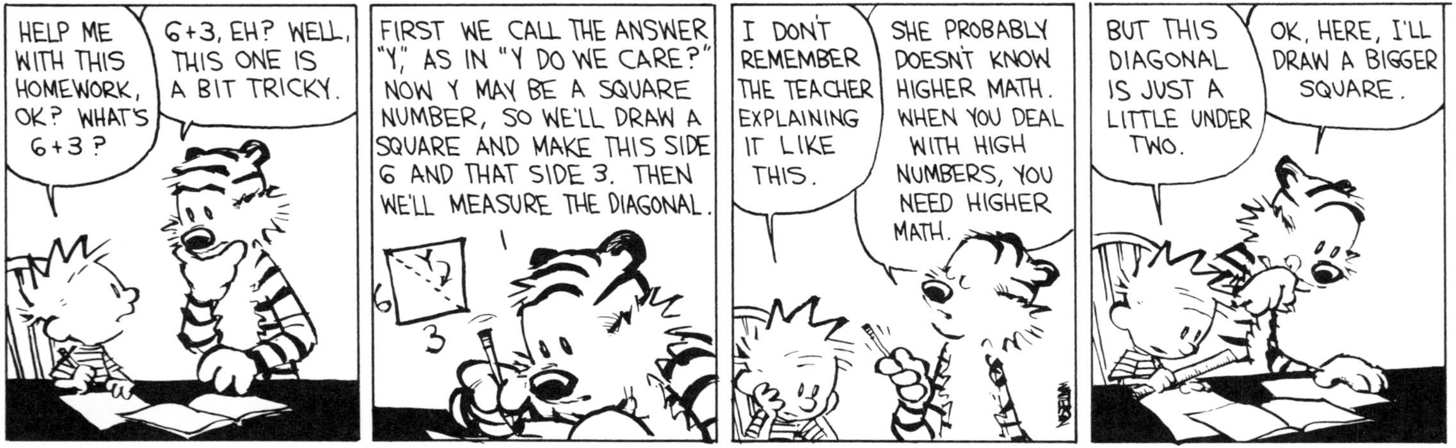
HELP ME WITH THIS HOMEWORK, OK? WHAT'S 6+3?
6+3, EH? WELL, THIS ONE IS A BIT TRICKY.
FIRST WE CALL THE ANSWER "Y," AS IN "Y DO WE CARE?" NOW Y MAY BE A SQUARE NUMBER, SO WE'LL DRAW A SQUARE AND MAKE THIS SIDE 6 AND THAT SIDE 3. THEN WE'LL MEASURE THE DIAGONAL.
I DON'T REMEMBER THE TEACHER EXPLAINING IT LIKE THIS.
SHE PROBABLY DOESN'T KNOW HIGHER MATH. WHEN YOU DEAL WITH HIGH NUMBERS, YOU NEED HIGHER MATH.
BUT THIS DIAGONAL IS JUST A LITTLE UNDER TWO.
OK, HERE, I'LL DRAW A BIGGER SQUARE.

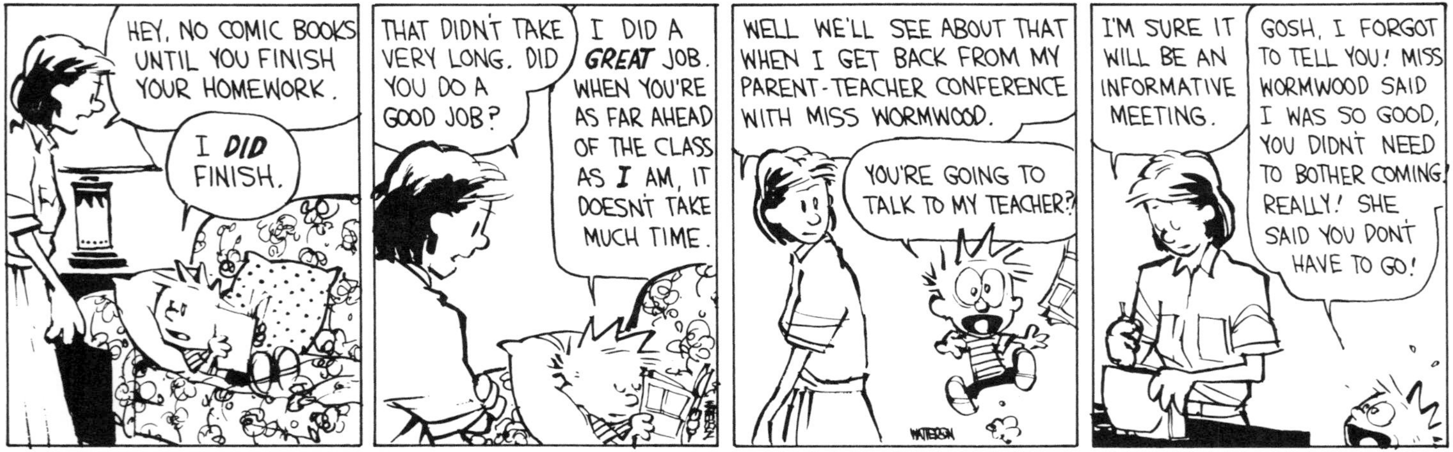
HEY, NO COMIC BOOKS UNTIL YOU FINISH YOUR HOMEWORK.
I **DID** FINISH.
THAT DIDN'T TAKE VERY LONG. DID YOU DO A GOOD JOB?
I DID A **GREAT** JOB. WHEN YOU'RE AS FAR AHEAD OF THE CLASS AS **I** AM, IT DOESN'T TAKE MUCH TIME.
WELL WE'LL SEE ABOUT THAT WHEN I GET BACK FROM MY PARENT-TEACHER CONFERENCE WITH MISS WORMWOOD.
YOU'RE GOING TO TALK TO MY TEACHER?!
I'M SURE IT WILL BE AN INFORMATIVE MEETING.
GOSH, I FORGOT TO TELL YOU! MISS WORMWOOD SAID I WAS SO GOOD, YOU DIDN'T NEED TO BOTHER COMING! REALLY! SHE SAID YOU DON'T HAVE TO GO!
WATTERSON

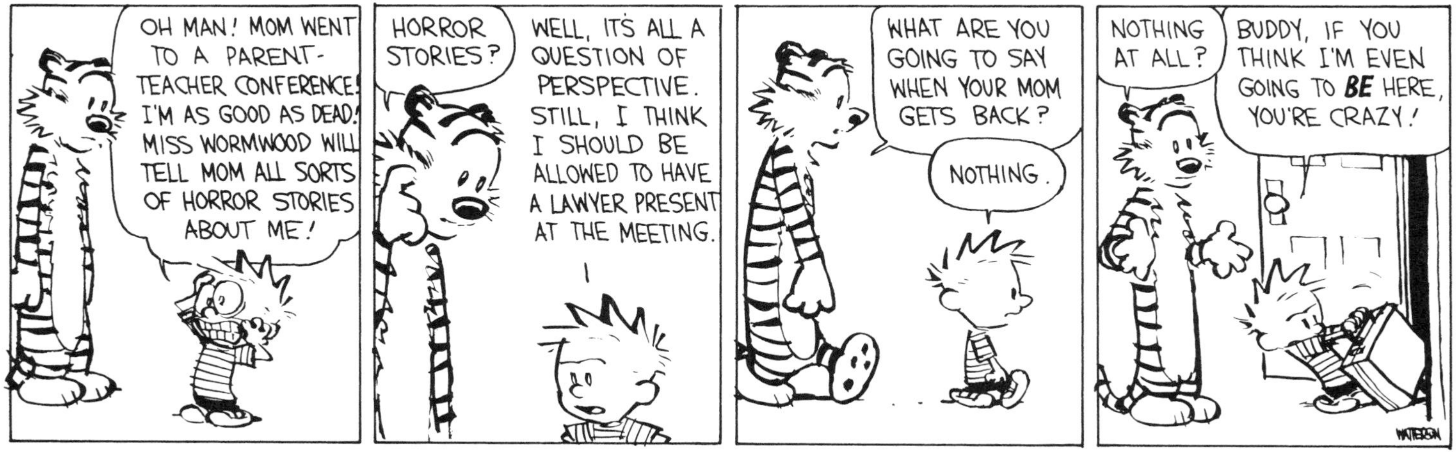
OH MAN! MOM WENT TO A PARENT-TEACHER CONFERENCE! I'M AS GOOD AS DEAD! MISS WORMWOOD WILL TELL MOM ALL SORTS OF HORROR STORIES ABOUT ME!
HORROR STORIES?
WELL, IT'S ALL A QUESTION OF PERSPECTIVE. STILL, I THINK I SHOULD BE ALLOWED TO HAVE A LAWYER PRESENT AT THE MEETING.
WHAT ARE YOU GOING TO SAY WHEN YOUR MOM GETS BACK?
NOTHING.
NOTHING AT ALL?
BUDDY, IF YOU THINK I'M EVEN GOING TO **BE** HERE, YOU'RE CRAZY!
WATTERSON

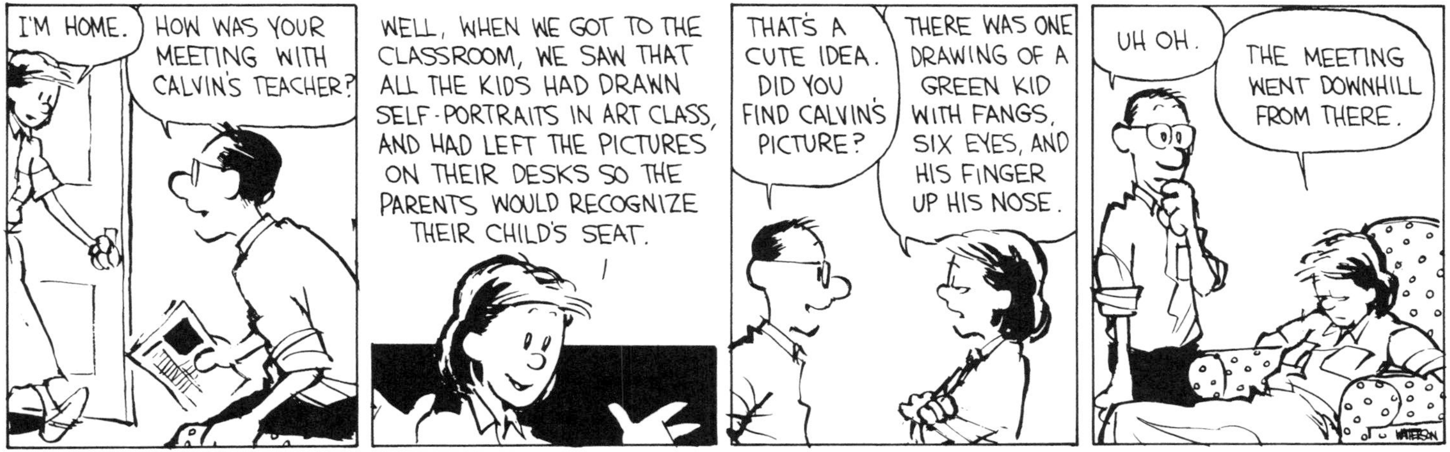
I'M HOME.
HOW WAS YOUR MEETING WITH CALVIN'S TEACHER?
WELL, WHEN WE GOT TO THE CLASSROOM, WE SAW THAT ALL THE KIDS HAD DRAWN SELF-PORTRAITS IN ART CLASS, AND HAD LEFT THE PICTURES ON THEIR DESKS SO THE PARENTS WOULD RECOGNIZE THEIR CHILD'S SEAT.
THAT'S A CUTE IDEA. DID YOU FIND CALVIN'S PICTURE?
THERE WAS ONE DRAWING OF A GREEN KID WITH FANGS, SIX EYES, AND HIS FINGER UP HIS NOSE.
UH OH.
THE MEETING WENT DOWNHILL FROM THERE.
WATTERSON

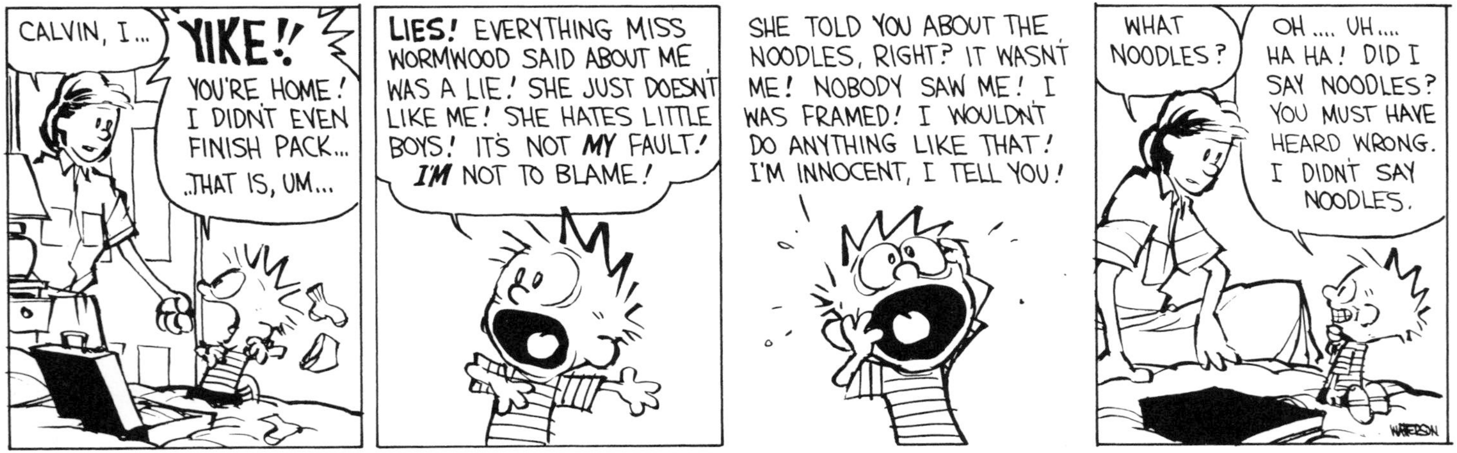
CALVIN, I...
YIKE!! YOU'RE HOME! I DIDN'T EVEN FINISH PACK... ..THAT IS, UM...
LIES! EVERYTHING MISS WORMWOOD SAID ABOUT ME WAS A LIE! SHE JUST DOESN'T LIKE ME! SHE HATES LITTLE BOYS! IT'S NOT MY FAULT! I'M NOT TO BLAME!
SHE TOLD YOU ABOUT THE NOODLES, RIGHT? IT WASN'T ME! NOBODY SAW ME! I WAS FRAMED! I WOULDN'T DO ANYTHING LIKE THAT! I'M INNOCENT, I TELL YOU!
WHAT NOODLES?
OH .... UH .... HA HA! DID I SAY NOODLES? YOU MUST HAVE HEARD WRONG. I DIDN'T SAY NOODLES.
WATTERSON

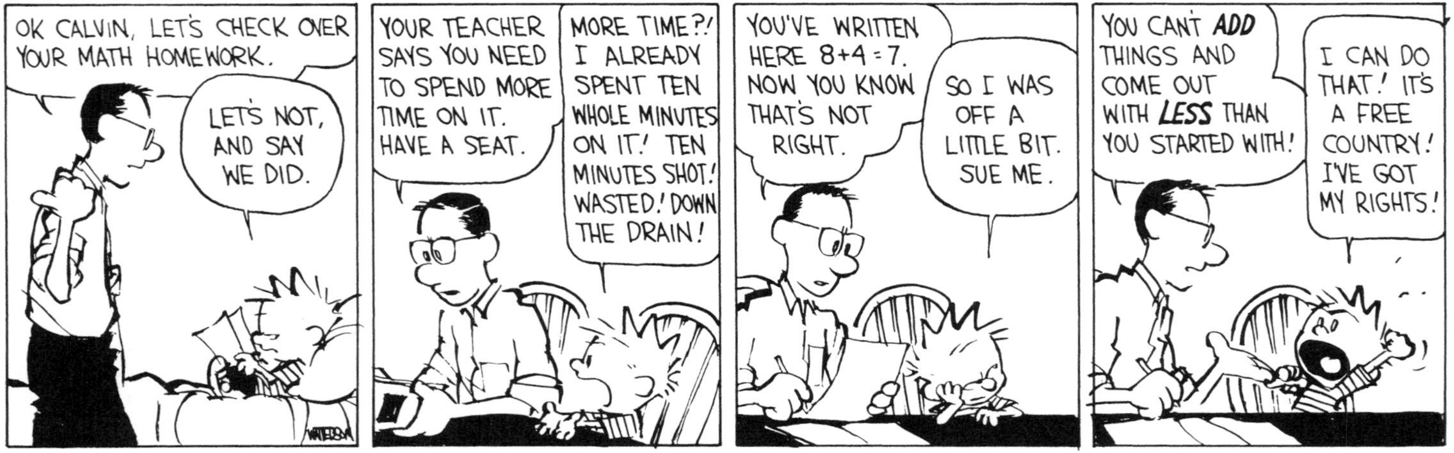
OK CALVIN, LET'S CHECK OVER YOUR MATH HOMEWORK.
LET'S NOT, AND SAY WE DID.
WATTERSON
YOUR TEACHER SAYS YOU NEED TO SPEND MORE TIME ON IT. HAVE A SEAT.
MORE TIME?! I ALREADY SPENT TEN WHOLE MINUTES ON IT! TEN MINUTES SHOT! WASTED! DOWN THE DRAIN!
YOU'VE WRITTEN HERE 8+4=7. NOW YOU KNOW THAT'S NOT RIGHT.
SO I WAS OFF A LITTLE BIT. SUE ME.
YOU CAN'T ADD THINGS AND COME OUT WITH LESS THAN YOU STARTED WITH!
I CAN DO THAT! IT'S A FREE COUNTRY! I'VE GOT MY RIGHTS!

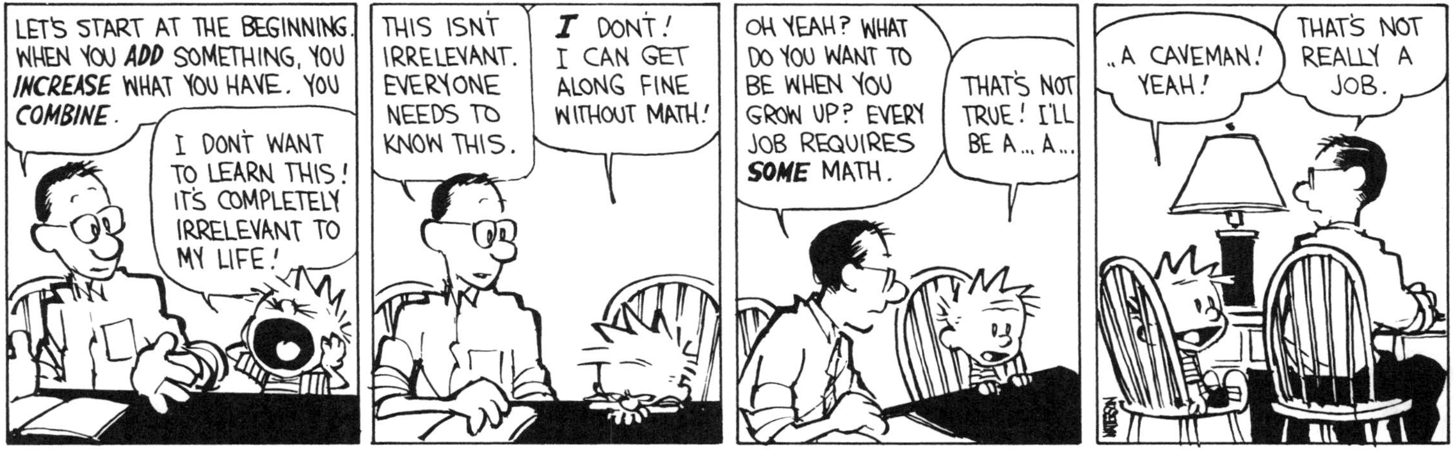
LET'S START AT THE BEGINNING. WHEN YOU **ADD** SOMETHING, YOU **INCREASE** WHAT YOU HAVE. YOU **COMBINE**.
I DON'T WANT TO LEARN THIS! IT'S COMPLETELY IRRELEVANT TO MY LIFE!
THIS ISN'T IRRELEVANT. EVERYONE NEEDS TO KNOW THIS.
I DON'T! I CAN GET ALONG FINE WITHOUT MATH!
OH YEAH? WHAT DO YOU WANT TO BE WHEN YOU GROW UP? EVERY JOB REQUIRES **SOME** MATH.
THAT'S NOT TRUE! I'LL BE A... A...
..A CAVEMAN! YEAH!
THAT'S NOT REALLY A JOB.
WATTERSON

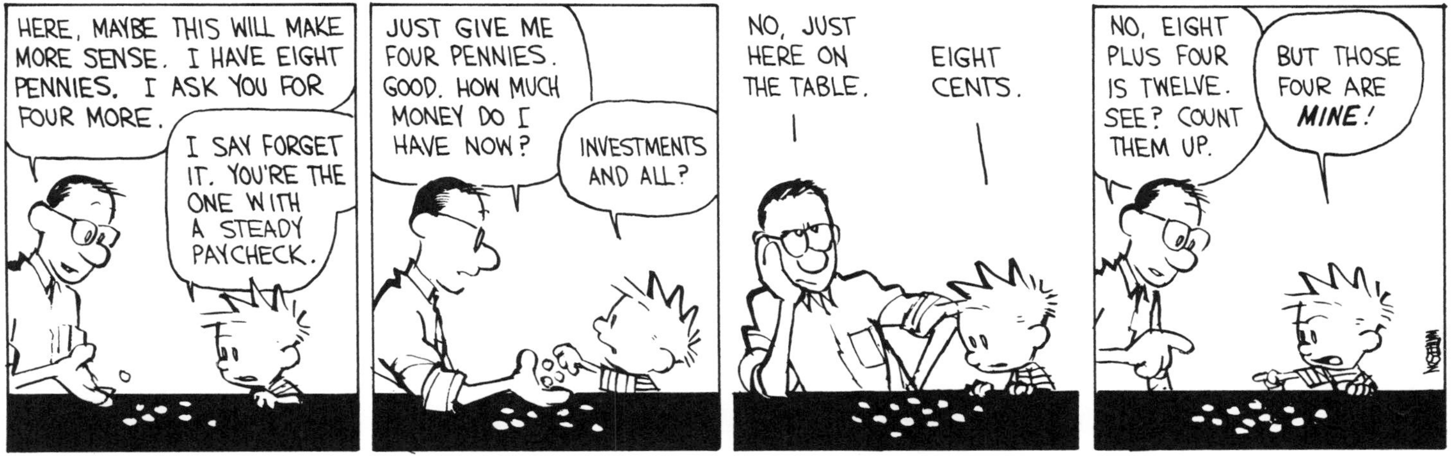
HERE, MAYBE THIS WILL MAKE MORE SENSE. I HAVE EIGHT PENNIES. I ASK YOU FOR FOUR MORE.
I SAY FORGET IT. YOU'RE THE ONE WITH A STEADY PAYCHECK.
JUST GIVE ME FOUR PENNIES. GOOD. HOW MUCH MONEY DO I HAVE NOW?
INVESTMENTS AND ALL?
NO, JUST HERE ON THE TABLE.
EIGHT CENTS.
NO, EIGHT PLUS FOUR IS TWELVE. SEE? COUNT THEM UP.
BUT THOSE FOUR ARE **MINE**!
WATTERSON

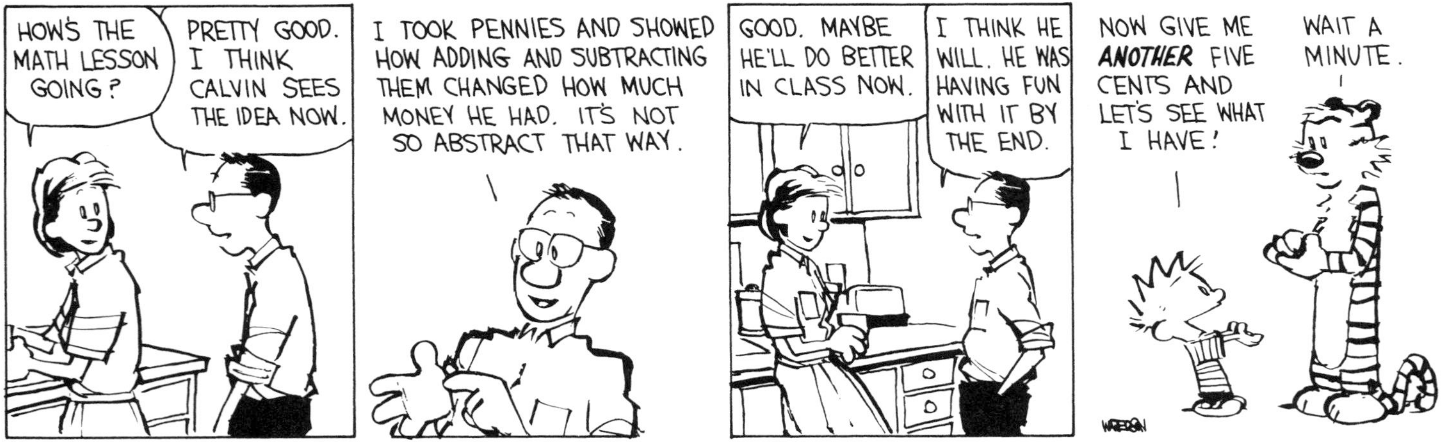
HOW'S THE MATH LESSON GOING?
PRETTY GOOD. I THINK CALVIN SEES THE IDEA NOW.
I TOOK PENNIES AND SHOWED HOW ADDING AND SUBTRACTING THEM CHANGED HOW MUCH MONEY HE HAD. IT'S NOT SO ABSTRACT THAT WAY.
GOOD. MAYBE HE'LL DO BETTER IN CLASS NOW.
I THINK HE WILL. HE WAS HAVING FUN WITH IT BY THE END.
NOW GIVE ME **ANOTHER** FIVE CENTS AND LET'S SEE WHAT I HAVE!
WAIT A MINUTE.

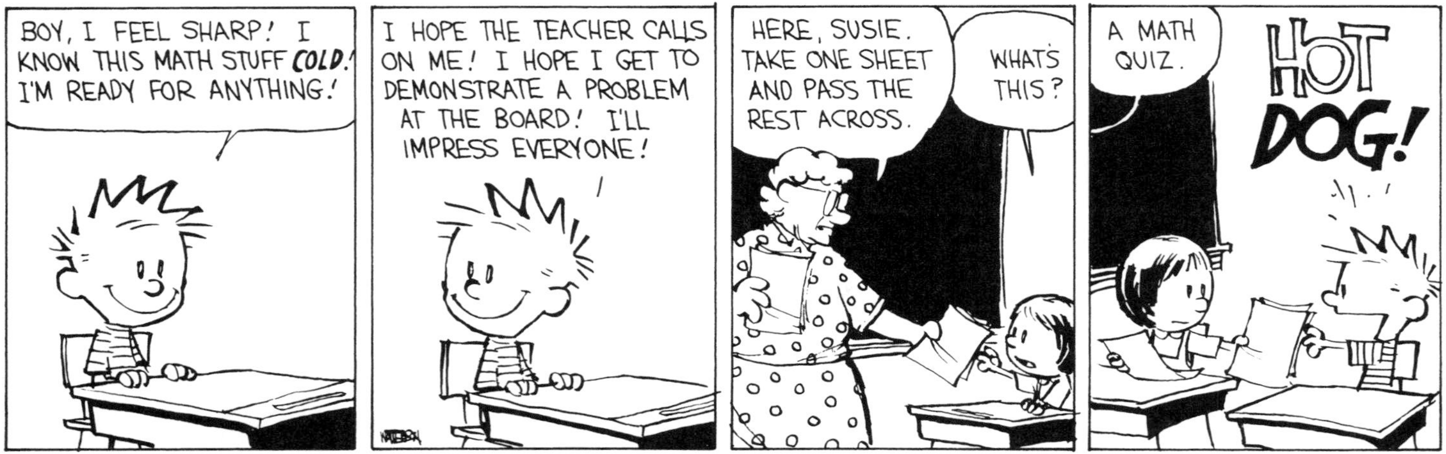
BOY, I FEEL SHARP! I KNOW THIS MATH STUFF **COLD**! I'M READY FOR ANYTHING!
I HOPE THE TEACHER CALLS ON ME! I HOPE I GET TO DEMONSTRATE A PROBLEM AT THE BOARD! I'LL IMPRESS EVERYONE!
HERE, SUSIE. TAKE ONE SHEET AND PASS THE REST ACROSS.
WHAT'S THIS?
A MATH QUIZ.
HOT DOG!

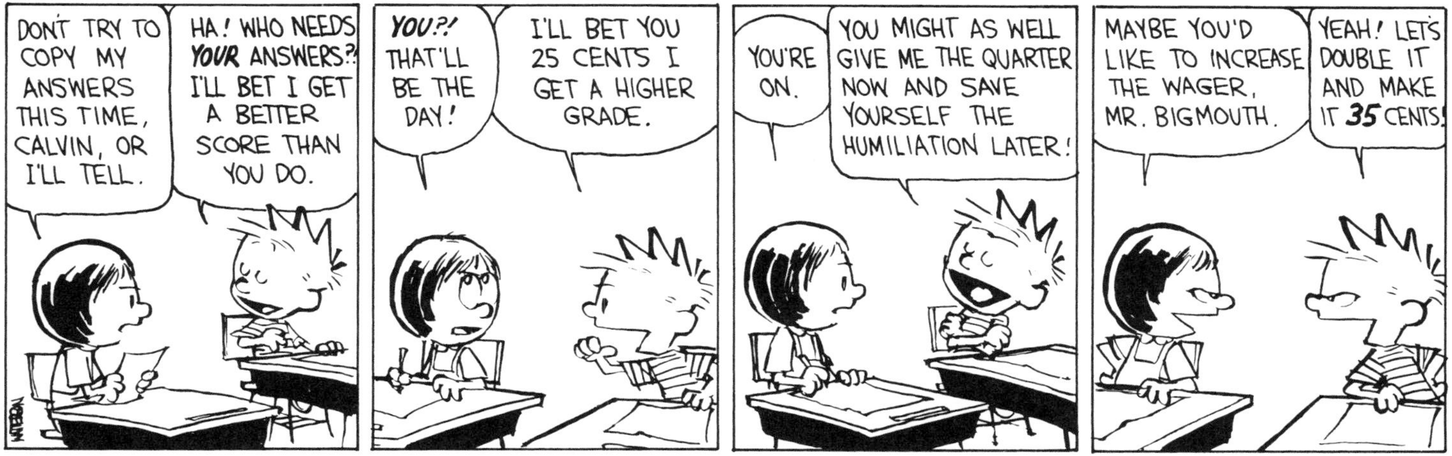
DON'T TRY TO COPY MY ANSWERS THIS TIME, CALVIN, OR I'LL TELL.
HA! WHO NEEDS YOUR ANSWERS?! I'LL BET I GET A BETTER SCORE THAN YOU DO.
YOU?! THAT'LL BE THE DAY!
I'LL BET YOU 25 CENTS I GET A HIGHER GRADE.
YOU'RE ON.
YOU MIGHT AS WELL GIVE ME THE QUARTER NOW AND SAVE YOURSELF THE HUMILIATION LATER!
MAYBE YOU'D LIKE TO INCREASE THE WAGER, MR. BIGMOUTH.
YEAH! LET'S DOUBLE IT AND MAKE IT 35 CENTS!

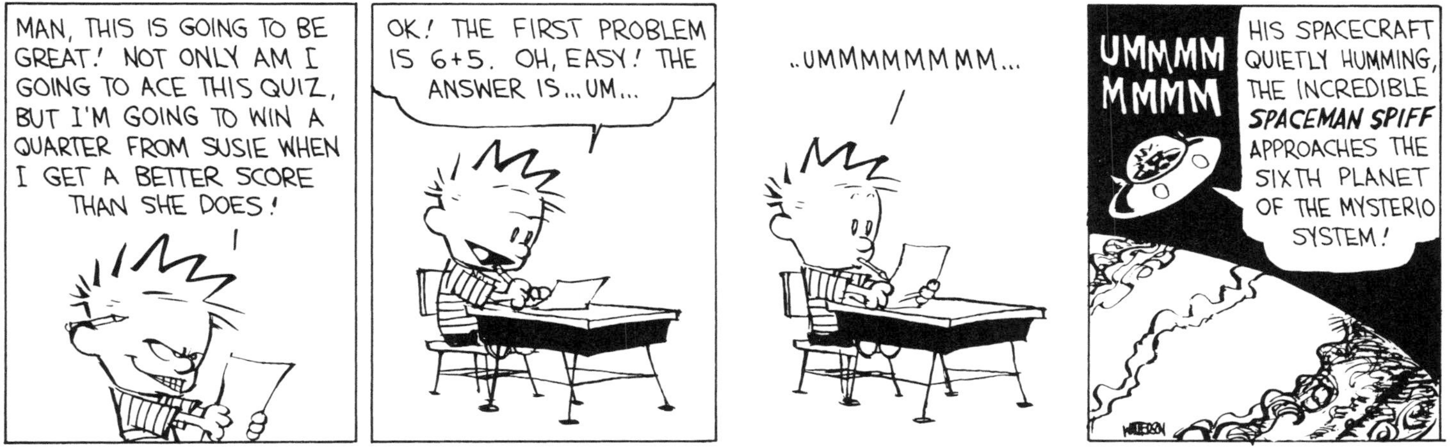
MAN, THIS IS GOING TO BE GREAT! NOT ONLY AM I GOING TO ACE THIS QUIZ, BUT I'M GOING TO WIN A QUARTER FROM SUSIE WHEN I GET A BETTER SCORE THAN SHE DOES!
OK! THE FIRST PROBLEM IS 6+5. OH, EASY! THE ANSWER IS... UM...
..UMMMMMMMM...
UMMMM MMMM
HIS SPACECRAFT QUIETLY HUMMING, THE INCREDIBLE SPACEMAN SPIFF APPROACHES THE SIXTH PLANET OF THE MYSTERIO SYSTEM!

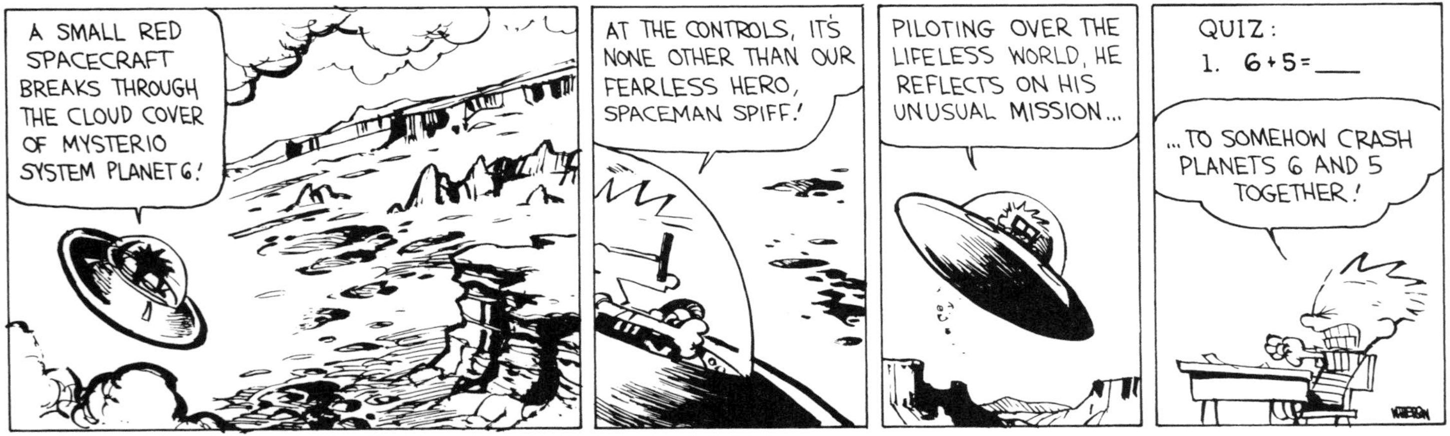
A SMALL RED SPACECRAFT BREAKS THROUGH THE CLOUD COVER OF MYSTERIO SYSTEM PLANET 6!
AT THE CONTROLS, IT'S NONE OTHER THAN OUR FEARLESS HERO, SPACEMAN SPIFF!
PILOTING OVER THE LIFELESS WORLD, HE REFLECTS ON HIS UNUSUAL MISSION...
QUIZ:
1. 6+5=___
...TO SOMEHOW CRASH PLANETS 6 AND 5 TOGETHER!

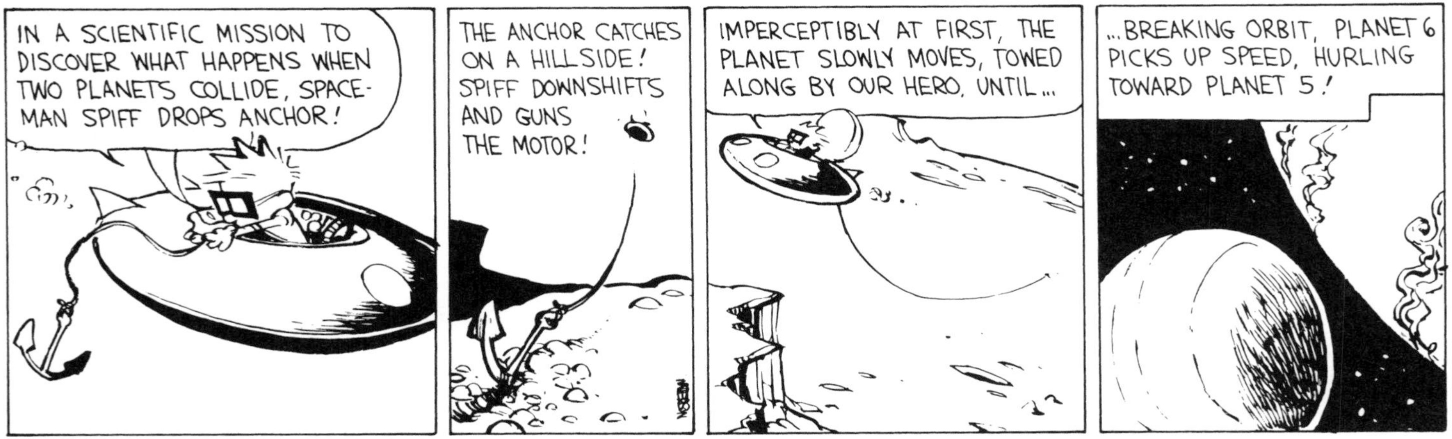
IN A SCIENTIFIC MISSION TO DISCOVER WHAT HAPPENS WHEN TWO PLANETS COLLIDE, SPACEMAN SPIFF DROPS ANCHOR!
THE ANCHOR CATCHES ON A HILLSIDE! SPIFF DOWNSHIFTS AND GUNS THE MOTOR!
IMPERCEPTIBLY AT FIRST, THE PLANET SLOWLY MOVES, TOWED ALONG BY OUR HERO, UNTIL...
...BREAKING ORBIT, PLANET 6 PICKS UP SPEED, HURLING TOWARD PLANET 5!

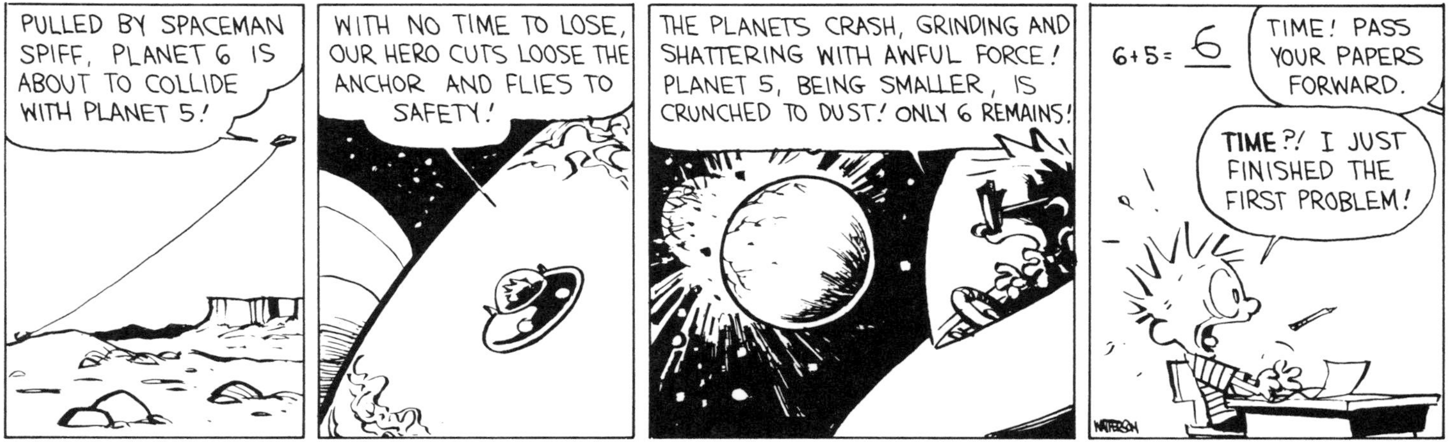
PULLED BY SPACEMAN SPIFF, PLANET 6 IS ABOUT TO COLLIDE WITH PLANET 5!
WITH NO TIME TO LOSE, OUR HERO CUTS LOOSE THE ANCHOR AND FLIES TO SAFETY!
THE PLANETS CRASH, GRINDING AND SHATTERING WITH AWFUL FORCE! PLANET 5, BEING SMALLER, IS CRUNCHED TO DUST! ONLY 6 REMAINS!
6+5= 6
TIME! PASS YOUR PAPERS FORWARD.
TIME?! I JUST FINISHED THE FIRST PROBLEM!
WATTERSON

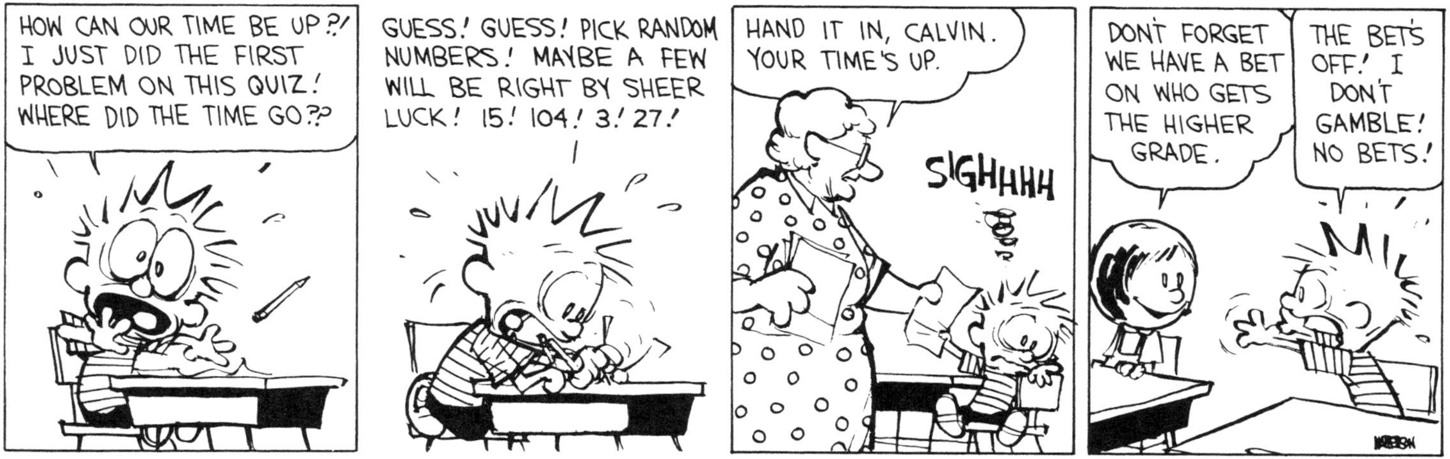
HOW CAN OUR TIME BE UP?! I JUST DID THE FIRST PROBLEM ON THIS QUIZ! WHERE DID THE TIME GO??
GUESS! GUESS! PICK RANDOM NUMBERS! MAYBE A FEW WILL BE RIGHT BY SHEER LUCK! 15! 104! 3! 27!
HAND IT IN, CALVIN. YOUR TIME'S UP.
SIGHHHH
DON'T FORGET WE HAVE A BET ON WHO GETS THE HIGHER GRADE.
THE BET'S OFF! I DON'T GAMBLE! NO BETS!
WATTERSON

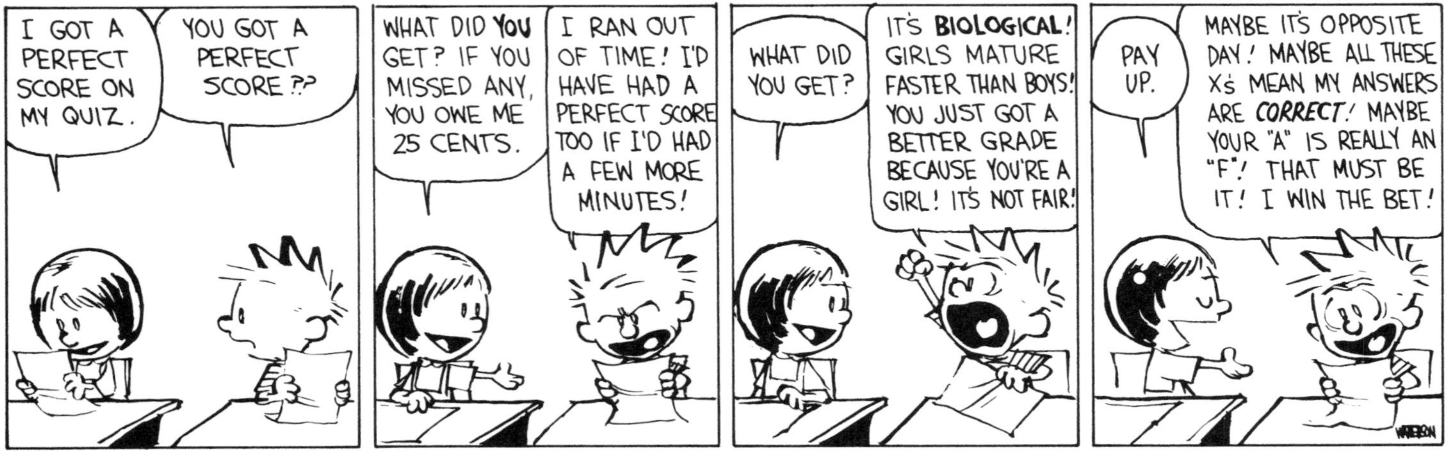
I GOT A PERFECT SCORE ON MY QUIZ.
YOU GOT A PERFECT SCORE ??
WHAT DID YOU GET? IF YOU MISSED ANY, YOU OWE ME 25 CENTS.
I RAN OUT OF TIME! I'D HAVE HAD A PERFECT SCORE TOO IF I'D HAD A FEW MORE MINUTES!
WHAT DID YOU GET?
IT'S BIOLOGICAL! GIRLS MATURE FASTER THAN BOYS! YOU JUST GOT A BETTER GRADE BECAUSE YOU'RE A GIRL! IT'S NOT FAIR!
PAY UP.
MAYBE IT'S OPPOSITE DAY! MAYBE ALL THESE X'S MEAN MY ANSWERS ARE CORRECT! MAYBE YOUR "A" IS REALLY AN "F"! THAT MUST BE IT! I WIN THE BET!
WATTERSON

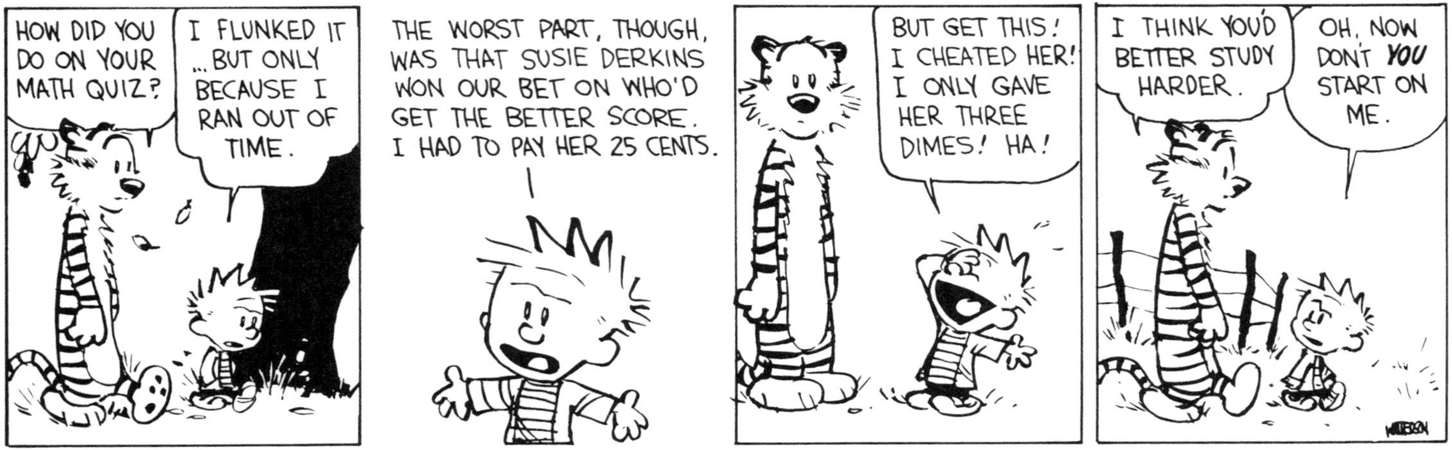
HOW DID YOU DO ON YOUR MATH QUIZ?
I FLUNKED IT ...BUT ONLY BECAUSE I RAN OUT OF TIME.
THE WORST PART, THOUGH, WAS THAT SUSIE DERKINS WON OUR BET ON WHO'D GET THE BETTER SCORE. I HAD TO PAY HER 25 CENTS.
BUT GET THIS! I CHEATED HER! I ONLY GAVE HER THREE DIMES! HA!
I THINK YOU'D BETTER STUDY HARDER.
OH, NOW DON'T YOU START ON ME.
WATTERSON

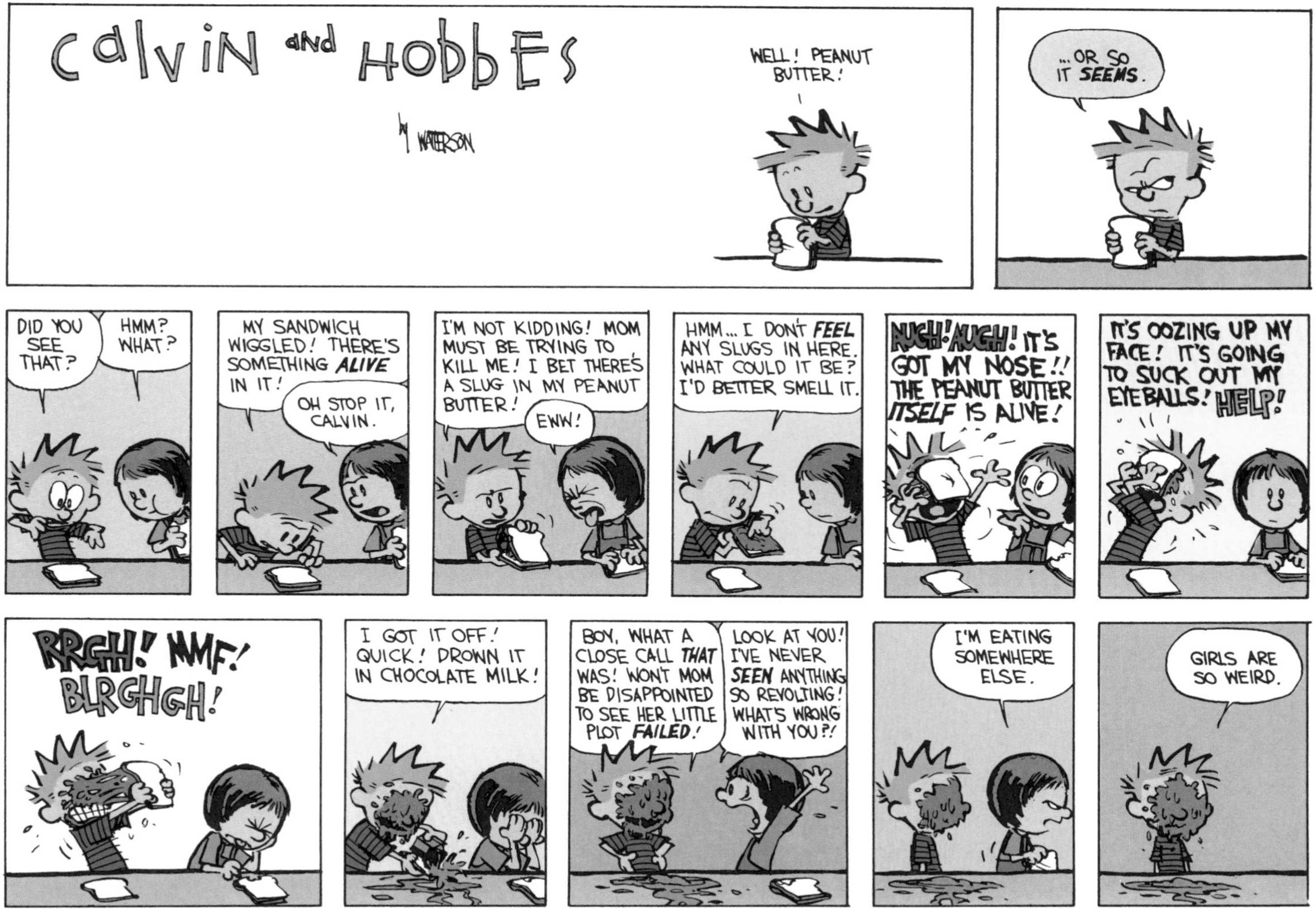

Calvin and HOBBES
by WATTERSON
WELL! PEANUT BUTTER!
...OR SO IT SEEMS.
DID YOU SEE THAT?
HMM? WHAT?
MY SANDWICH WIGGLED! THERE'S SOMETHING ALIVE IN IT!
OH STOP IT, CALVIN.
I'M NOT KIDDING! MOM MUST BE TRYING TO KILL ME! I BET THERE'S A SLUG IN MY PEANUT BUTTER!
EWW!
HMM... I DON'T FEEL ANY SLUGS IN HERE. WHAT COULD IT BE? I'D BETTER SMELL IT.
AUGH! AUGH! IT'S GOT MY NOSE!! THE PEANUT BUTTER ITSELF IS ALIVE!
IT'S OOZING UP MY FACE! IT'S GOING TO SUCK OUT MY EYEBALLS! HELP!
RRGH! MMF! BLRGHGH!
I GOT IT OFF! QUICK! DROWN IT IN CHOCOLATE MILK!
BOY, WHAT A CLOSE CALL THAT WAS! WON'T MOM BE DISAPPOINTED TO SEE HER LITTLE PLOT FAILED!
LOOK AT YOU! I'VE NEVER SEEN ANYTHING SO REVOLTING! WHAT'S WRONG WITH YOU?!
I'M EATING SOMEWHERE ELSE.
GIRLS ARE SO WEIRD.

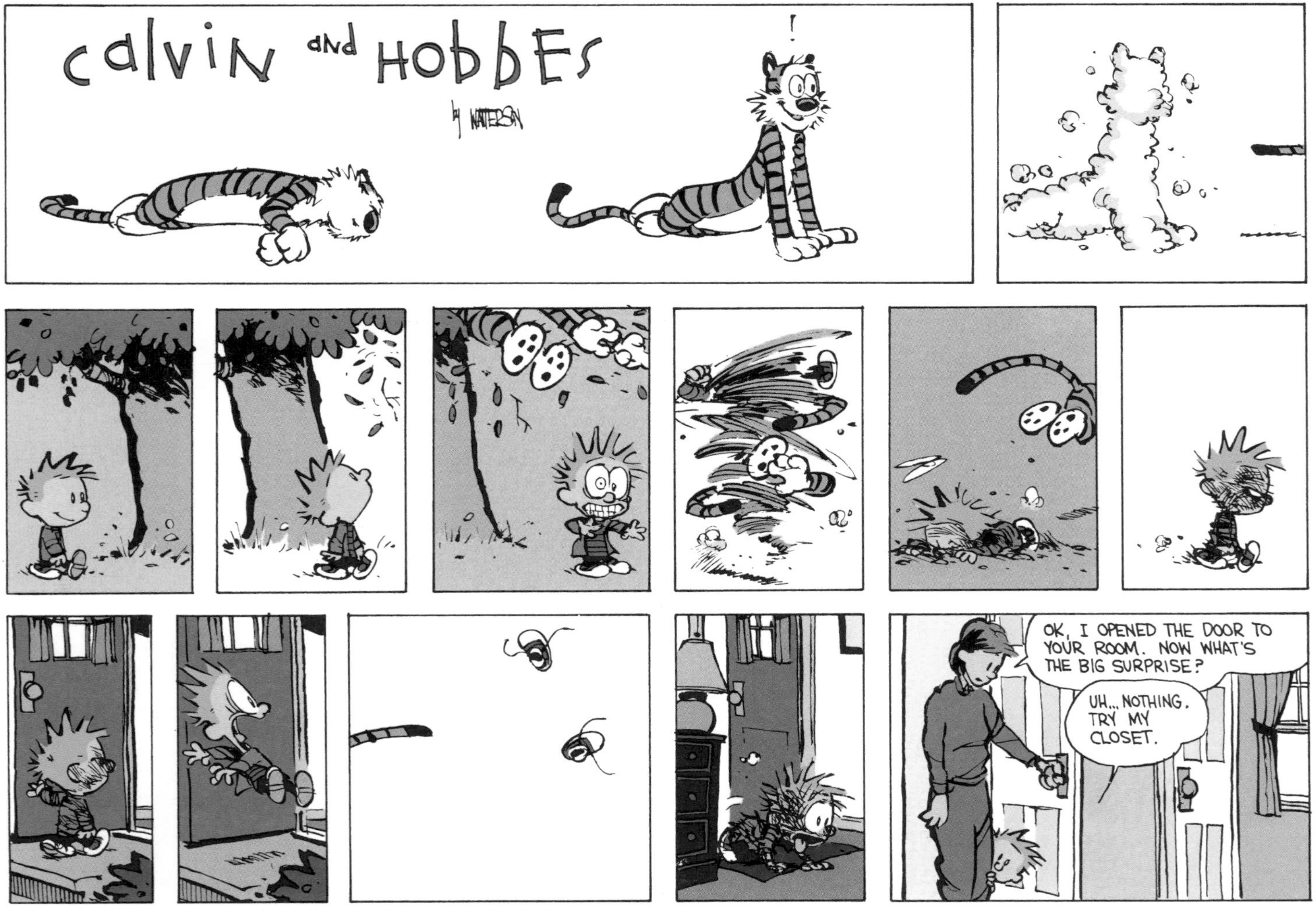
Calvin and HOBBES
by WATTERSON
!
OK, I OPENED THE DOOR TO YOUR ROOM. NOW WHAT'S THE BIG SURPRISE?
UH... NOTHING. TRY MY CLOSET.

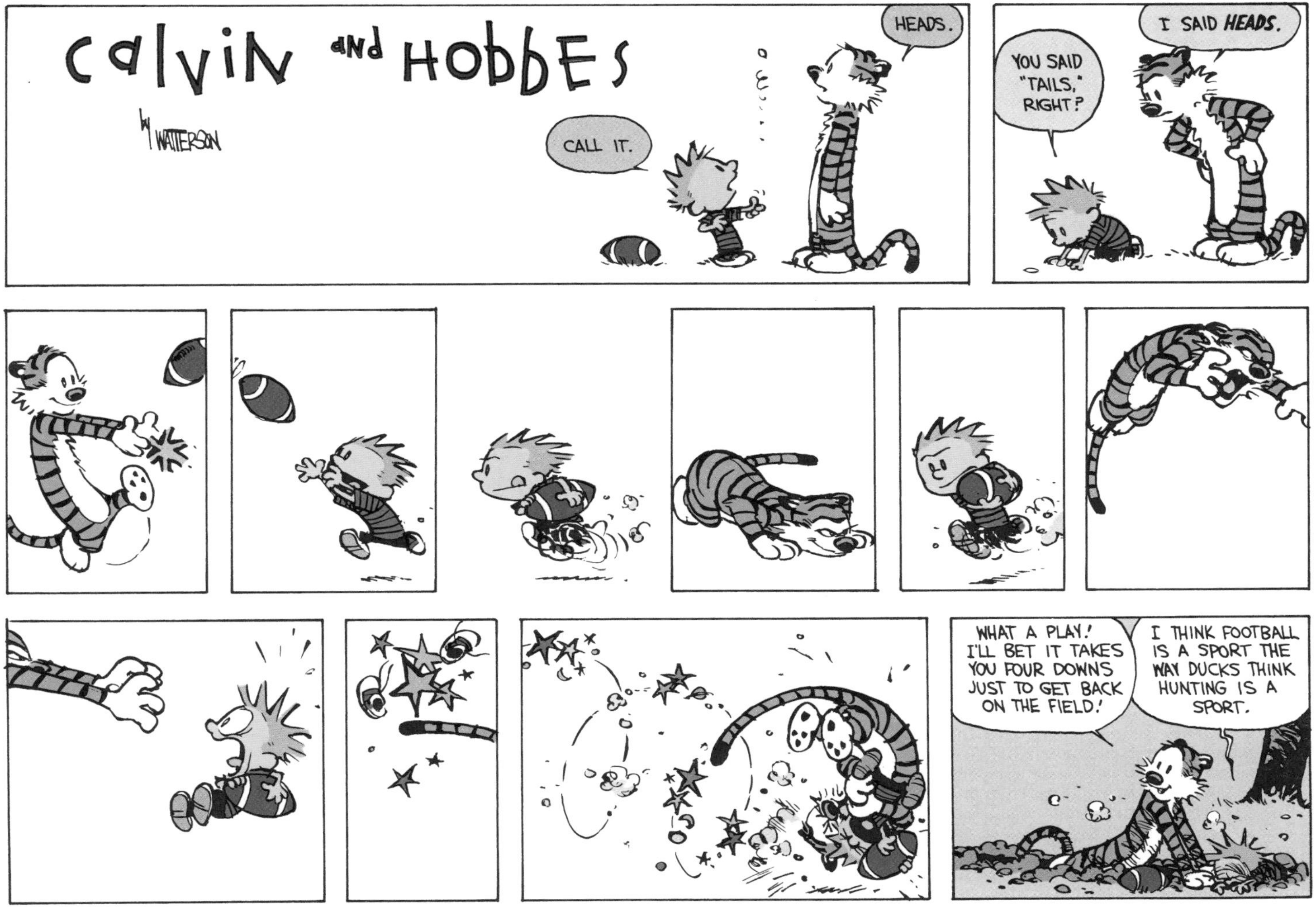
Calvin and Hobbes
by WATTERSON
CALL IT.
HEADS.
YOU SAID "TAILS," RIGHT?
I SAID **HEADS**.
WHAT A PLAY! I'LL BET IT TAKES YOU FOUR DOWNS JUST TO GET BACK ON THE FIELD!
I THINK FOOTBALL IS A SPORT THE WAY DUCKS THINK HUNTING IS A SPORT.

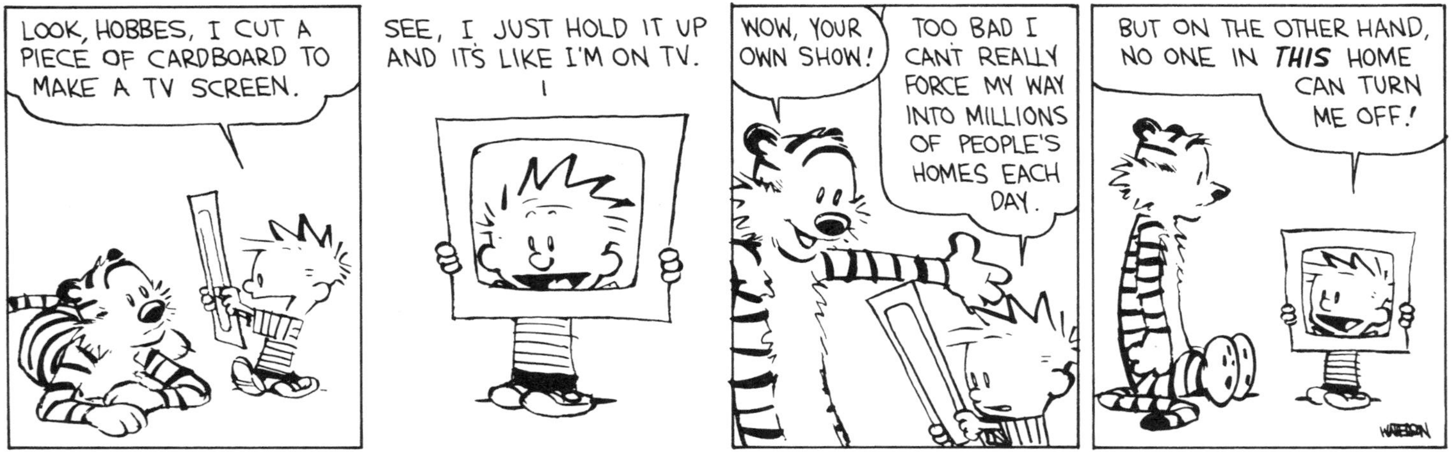
LOOK, HOBBES, I CUT A PIECE OF CARDBOARD TO MAKE A TV SCREEN.
SEE, I JUST HOLD IT UP AND IT'S LIKE I'M ON TV.
WOW, YOUR OWN SHOW!
TOO BAD I CAN'T REALLY FORCE MY WAY INTO MILLIONS OF PEOPLE'S HOMES EACH DAY.
BUT ON THE OTHER HAND, NO ONE IN THIS HOME CAN TURN ME OFF!
WATTERSON

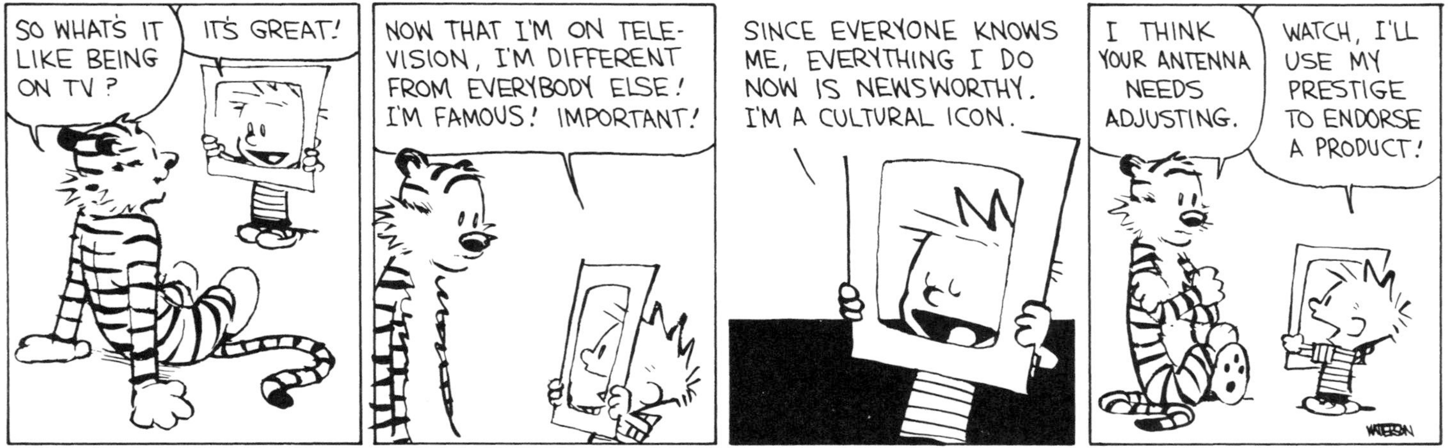
SO WHAT'S IT LIKE BEING ON TV?
IT'S GREAT!
NOW THAT I'M ON TELE-VISION, I'M DIFFERENT FROM EVERYBODY ELSE! I'M FAMOUS! IMPORTANT!
SINCE EVERYONE KNOWS ME, EVERYTHING I DO NOW IS NEWSWORTHY. I'M A CULTURAL ICON.
I THINK YOUR ANTENNA NEEDS ADJUSTING.
WATCH, I'LL USE MY PRESTIGE TO ENDORSE A PRODUCT!
WATTERSON

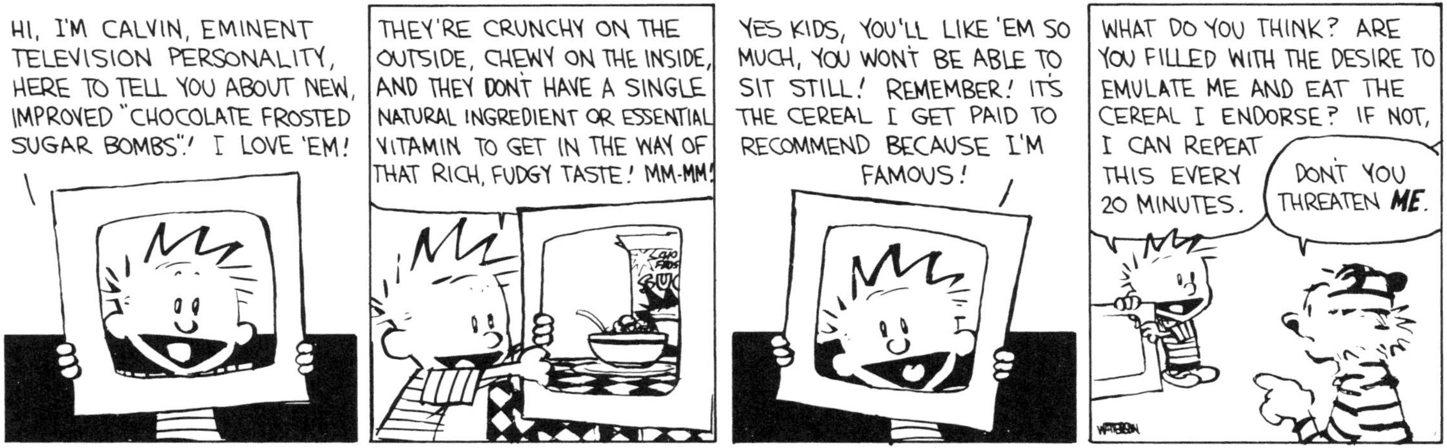
HI, I'M CALVIN, EMINENT TELEVISION PERSONALITY, HERE TO TELL YOU ABOUT NEW, IMPROVED "CHOCOLATE FROSTED SUGAR BOMBS"! I LOVE 'EM!
THEY'RE CRUNCHY ON THE OUTSIDE, CHEWY ON THE INSIDE, AND THEY DON'T HAVE A SINGLE NATURAL INGREDIENT OR ESSENTIAL VITAMIN TO GET IN THE WAY OF THAT RICH, FUDGY TASTE! MM-MM!
YES KIDS, YOU'LL LIKE 'EM SO MUCH, YOU WON'T BE ABLE TO SIT STILL! REMEMBER! IT'S THE CEREAL I GET PAID TO RECOMMEND BECAUSE I'M FAMOUS!
WHAT DO YOU THINK? ARE YOU FILLED WITH THE DESIRE TO EMULATE ME AND EAT THE CEREAL I ENDORSE? IF NOT, I CAN REPEAT THIS EVERY 20 MINUTES.
DON'T YOU THREATEN **ME**.

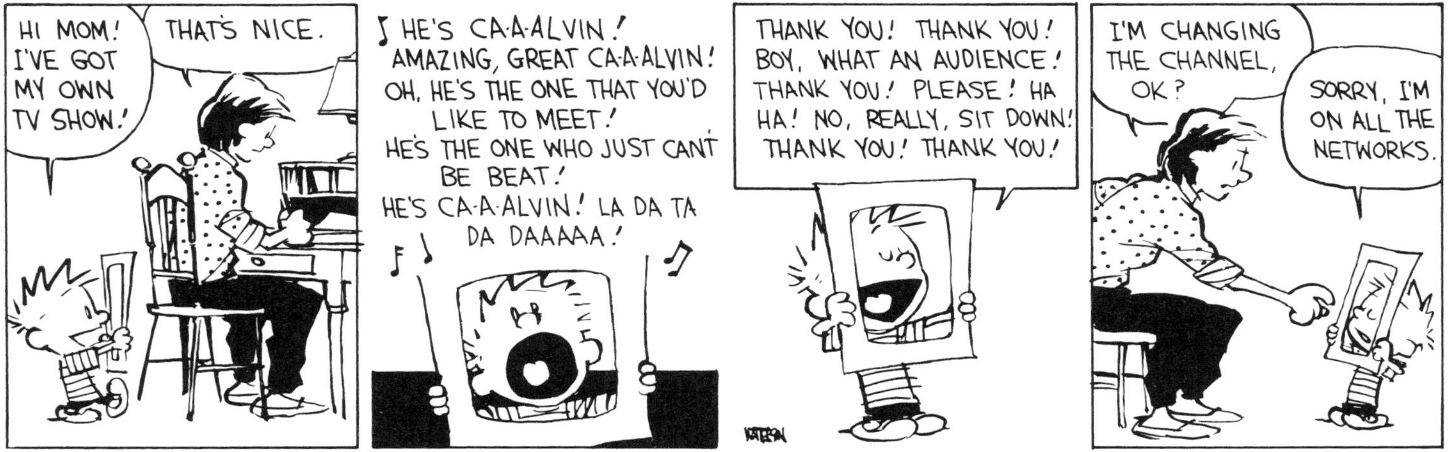
HI MOM! I'VE GOT MY OWN TV SHOW!
THAT'S NICE.
HE'S CA-A-ALVIN! AMAZING, GREAT CA-A-ALVIN! OH, HE'S THE ONE THAT YOU'D LIKE TO MEET! HE'S THE ONE WHO JUST CAN'T BE BEAT! HE'S CA-A-ALVIN! LA DA TA DA DAAAAA!
THANK YOU! THANK YOU! BOY, WHAT AN AUDIENCE! THANK YOU! PLEASE! HA HA! NO, REALLY, SIT DOWN! THANK YOU! THANK YOU!
I'M CHANGING THE CHANNEL, OK?
SORRY, I'M ON ALL THE NETWORKS.

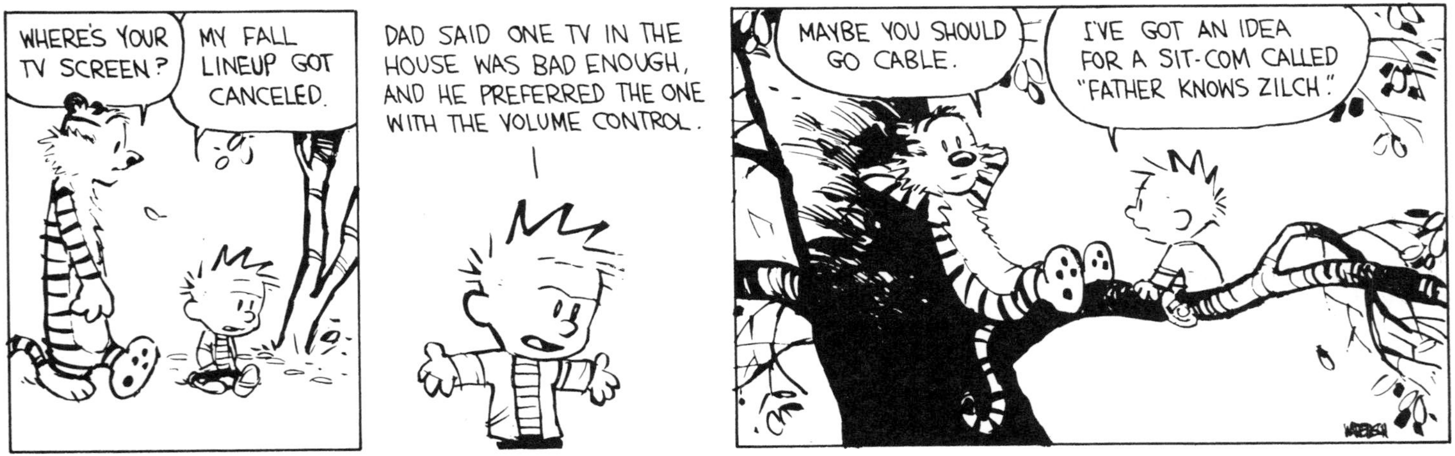
WHERE'S YOUR TV SCREEN?
MY FALL LINEUP GOT CANCELED.
DAD SAID ONE TV IN THE HOUSE WAS BAD ENOUGH, AND HE PREFERRED THE ONE WITH THE VOLUME CONTROL.
MAYBE YOU SHOULD GO CABLE.
I'VE GOT AN IDEA FOR A SIT-COM CALLED "FATHER KNOWS ZILCH."

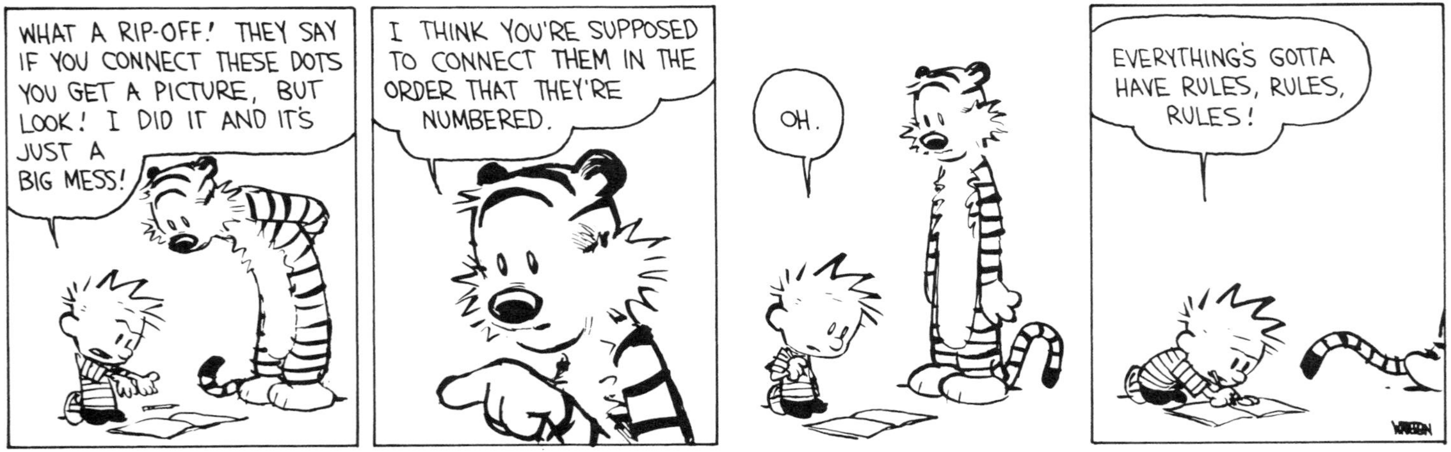
WHAT A RIP-OFF! THEY SAY IF YOU CONNECT THESE DOTS YOU GET A PICTURE, BUT LOOK! I DID IT AND IT'S JUST A BIG MESS!
I THINK YOU'RE SUPPOSED TO CONNECT THEM IN THE ORDER THAT THEY'RE NUMBERED.
OH.
EVERYTHING'S GOTTA HAVE RULES, RULES, RULES!

CALVIN AND HOBBES by WATTERSON

OUT IN THE FARTHEST REACHES OF THE GALAXY...

...SPEEDS THAT SPLENDID SPECIMEN OF SPIRIT AND SPUNK, THE SPECTACULAR *SPACEMAN SPIFF!*

THE FEARLESS SPACEMAN SPIFF SETS OFF TO EXPLORE A NEW PLANET!

THE PLANET APPEARS TO BE UNINHABITED. THE ONLY SIGN OF LIFE IS A STRANGE LICHEN GROWING ON THE ROCKS.

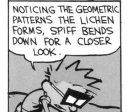

NOTICING THE GEOMETRIC PATTERNS THE LICHEN FORMS, SPIFF BENDS DOWN FOR A CLOSER LOOK.

IT'S NOT LICHEN! IT'S TINY TREES ON TINY FARMLAND!

PEERING AHEAD, OUR HERO SEES A SPRAWLING CITY, WITH SKYSCRAPERS AN INCH HIGH! THE PLANET IS INHABITED AFTER ALL!

SPIFF REFLECTS THAT HUMAN SCALE IS BY NO MEANS THE STANDARD FOR LIFE FORMS.

AS IF TO DRIVE THE POINT HOME, A BLIMP-SIZED MONSTER APPEARS OVER THE HILLSIDE!

Hey, lookit Shorty here! He's playing with his fellow bugs! Haw haw!

IT'S A *Doofus Ignoramus!* OUR HERO SLOWLY REACHES FOR HIS STUN BLASTER!

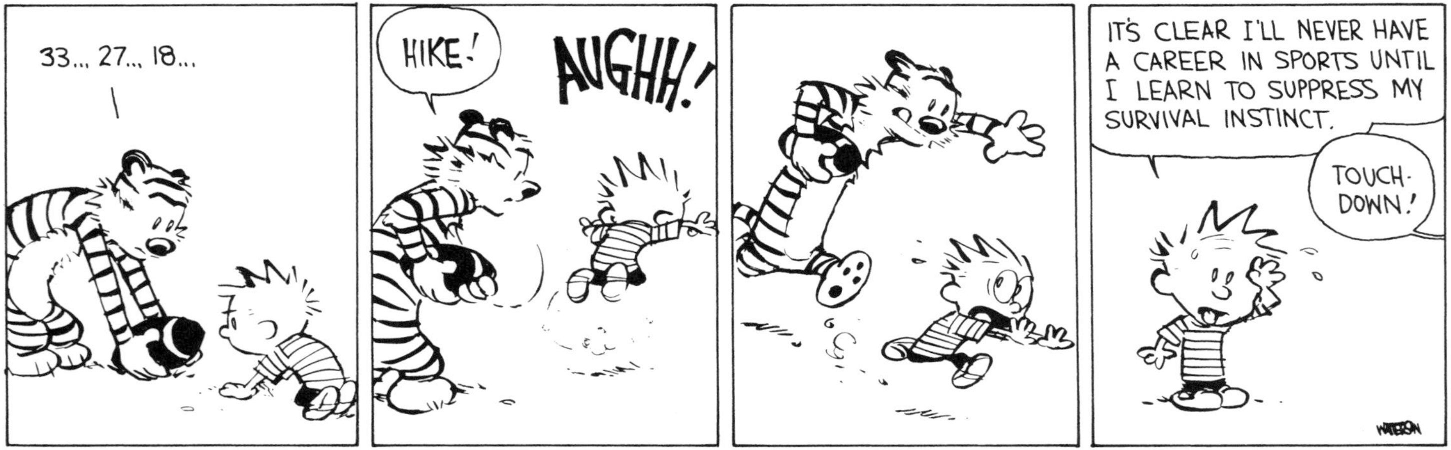
33... 27... 18...
HIKE!
AUGHH!
IT'S CLEAR I'LL NEVER HAVE A CAREER IN SPORTS UNTIL I LEARN TO SUPPRESS MY SURVIVAL INSTINCT.
TOUCH-DOWN!

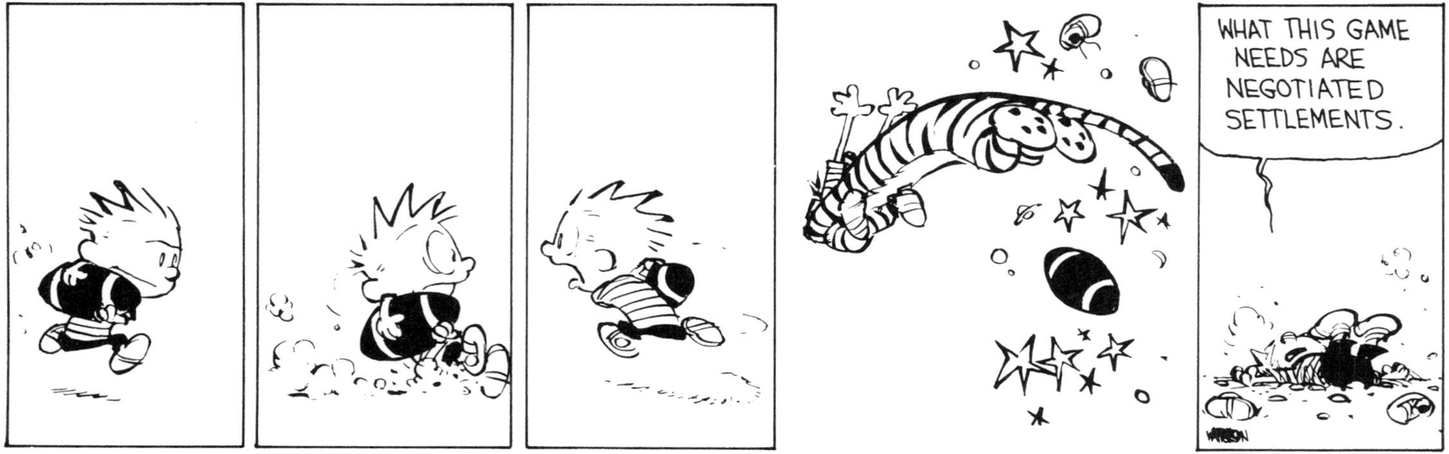
WHAT THIS GAME NEEDS ARE NEGOTIATED SETTLEMENTS.

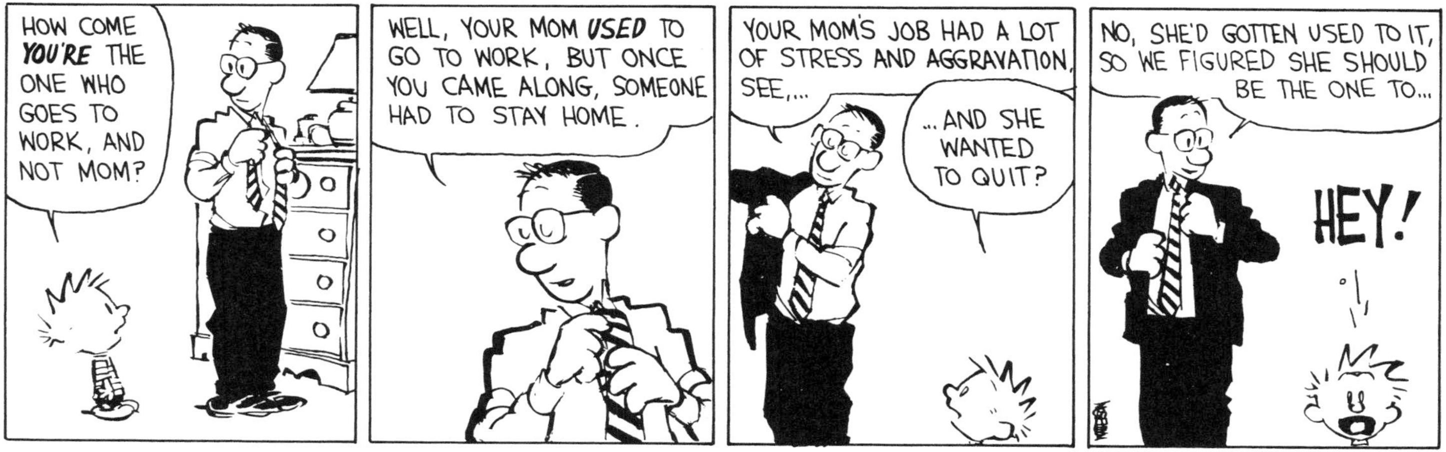
HOW COME YOU'RE THE ONE WHO GOES TO WORK, AND NOT MOM?
WELL, YOUR MOM USED TO GO TO WORK, BUT ONCE YOU CAME ALONG, SOMEONE HAD TO STAY HOME.
YOUR MOM'S JOB HAD A LOT OF STRESS AND AGGRAVATION, SEE,...
...AND SHE WANTED TO QUIT?
NO, SHE'D GOTTEN USED TO IT, SO WE FIGURED SHE SHOULD BE THE ONE TO...
HEY!

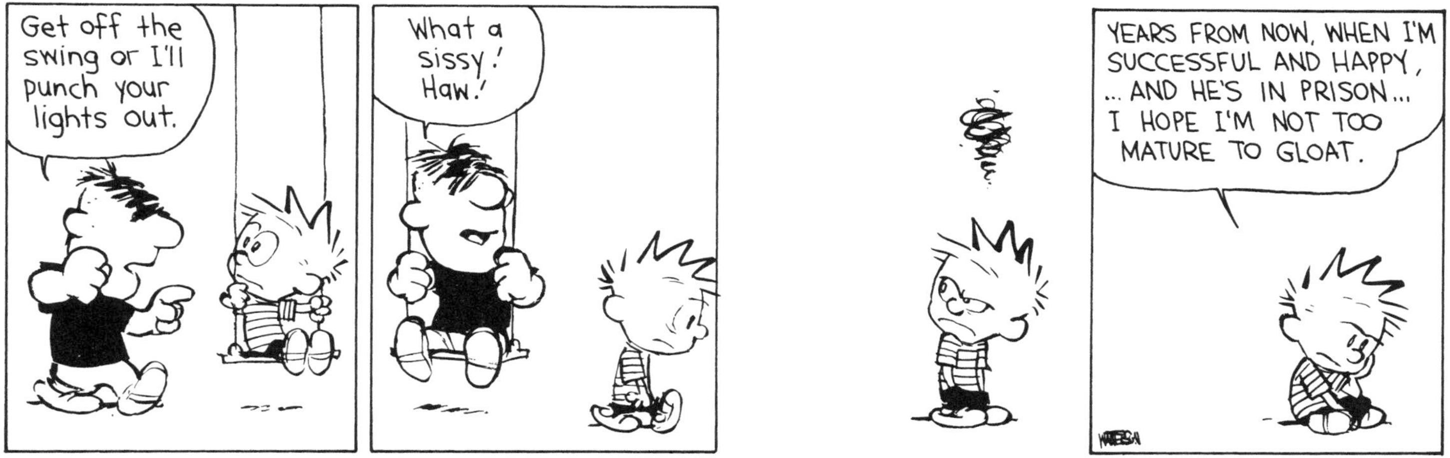
Get off the swing or I'll punch your lights out.
What a sissy! Haw!
YEARS FROM NOW, WHEN I'M SUCCESSFUL AND HAPPY, ... AND HE'S IN PRISON... I HOPE I'M NOT TOO MATURE TO GLOAT.

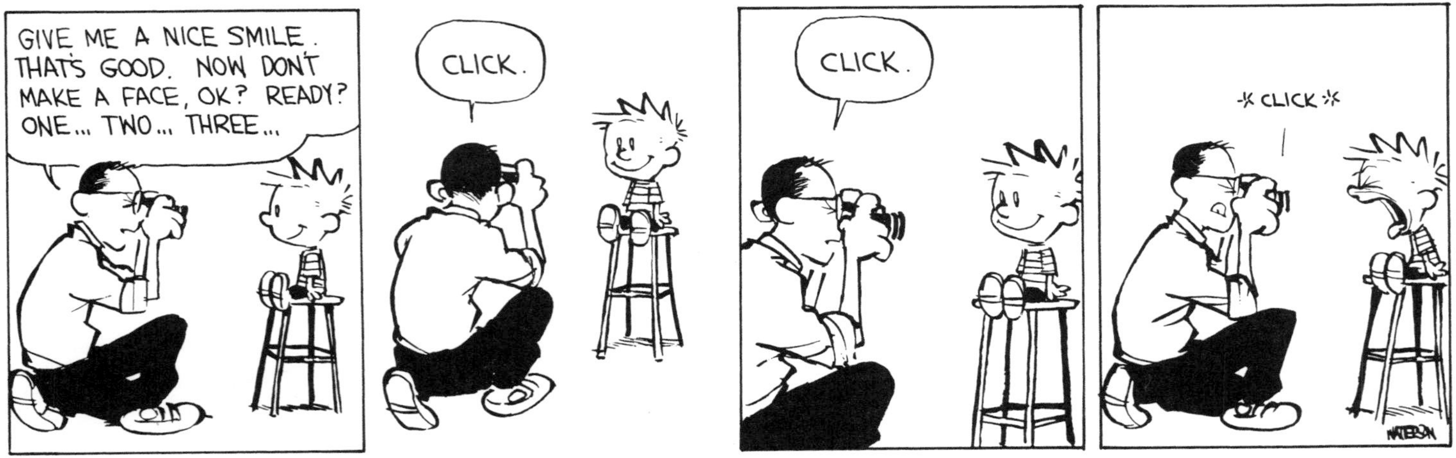
GIVE ME A NICE SMILE. THAT'S GOOD. NOW DON'T MAKE A FACE, OK? READY? ONE... TWO... THREE...
CLICK.
CLICK.
CLICK
WATTERSON

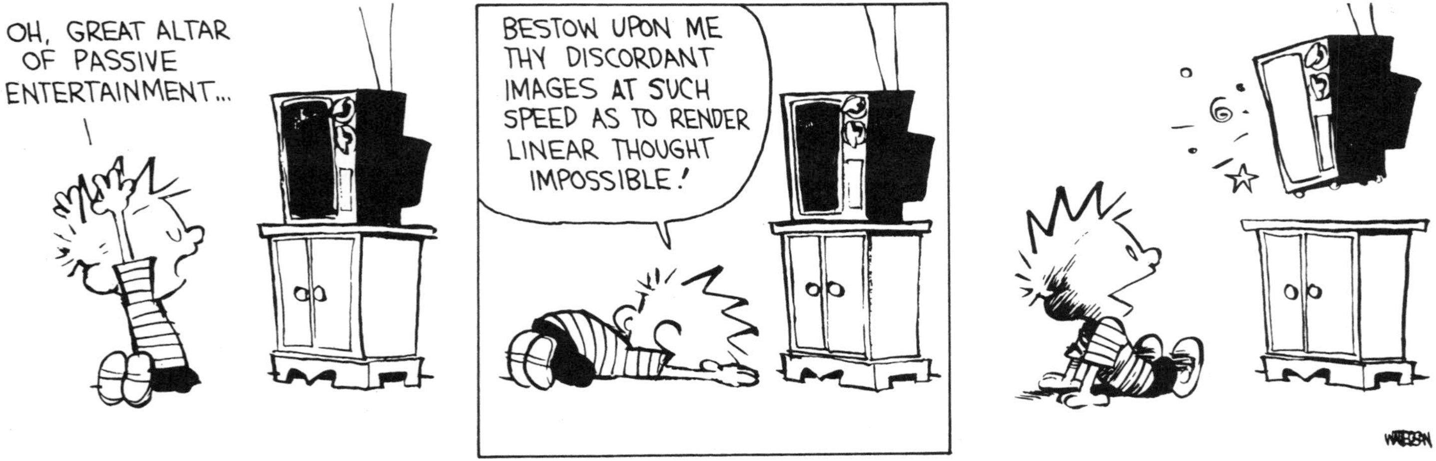
OH, GREAT ALTAR OF PASSIVE ENTERTAINMENT...
BESTOW UPON ME THY DISCORDANT IMAGES AT SUCH SPEED AS TO RENDER LINEAR THOUGHT IMPOSSIBLE!
WATTERSON

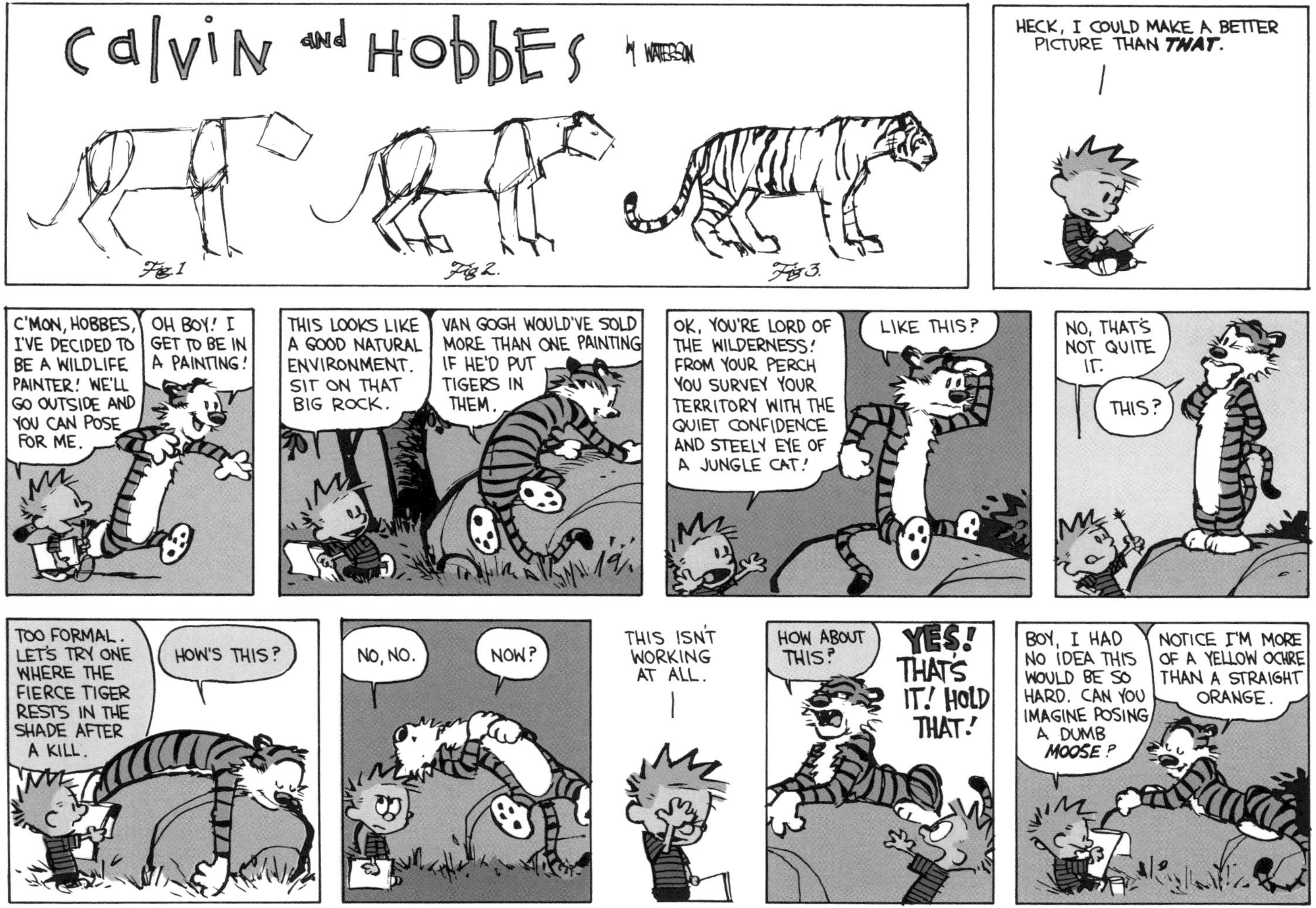
Calvin and HOBBES
by WATTERSON
Fig 1
Fig 2.
Fig 3.
HECK, I COULD MAKE A BETTER PICTURE THAN *THAT*.
C'MON, HOBBES, I'VE DECIDED TO BE A WILDLIFE PAINTER! WE'LL GO OUTSIDE AND YOU CAN POSE FOR ME.
OH BOY! I GET TO BE IN A PAINTING!
THIS LOOKS LIKE A GOOD NATURAL ENVIRONMENT. SIT ON THAT BIG ROCK.
VAN GOGH WOULD'VE SOLD MORE THAN ONE PAINTING IF HE'D PUT TIGERS IN THEM.
OK, YOU'RE LORD OF THE WILDERNESS! FROM YOUR PERCH YOU SURVEY YOUR TERRITORY WITH THE QUIET CONFIDENCE AND STEELY EYE OF A JUNGLE CAT!
LIKE THIS?
NO, THAT'S NOT QUITE IT.
THIS?
TOO FORMAL. LET'S TRY ONE WHERE THE FIERCE TIGER RESTS IN THE SHADE AFTER A KILL.
HOW'S THIS?
NO, NO.
NOW?
THIS ISN'T WORKING AT ALL.
HOW ABOUT THIS?
YES! THAT'S IT! HOLD THAT!
BOY, I HAD NO IDEA THIS WOULD BE SO HARD. CAN YOU IMAGINE POSING A DUMB *MOOSE*?
NOTICE I'M MORE OF A YELLOW OCHRE THAN A STRAIGHT ORANGE.

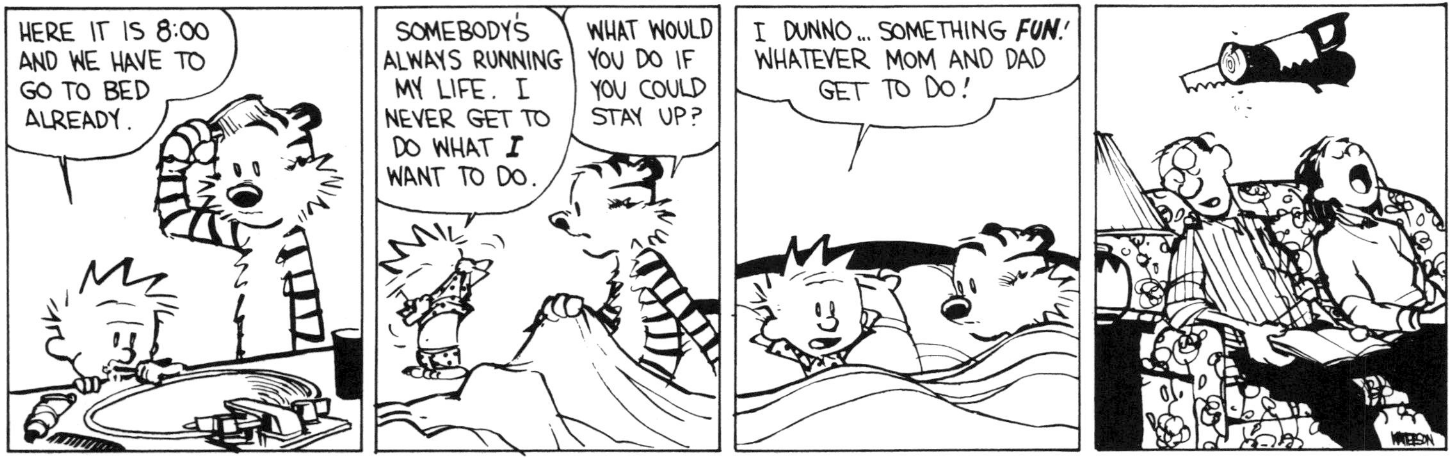
HERE IT IS 8:00 AND WE HAVE TO GO TO BED ALREADY.
SOMEBODY'S ALWAYS RUNNING MY LIFE. I NEVER GET TO DO WHAT *I* WANT TO DO.
WHAT WOULD YOU DO IF YOU COULD STAY UP?
I DUNNO... SOMETHING **FUN**! WHATEVER MOM AND DAD GET TO DO!

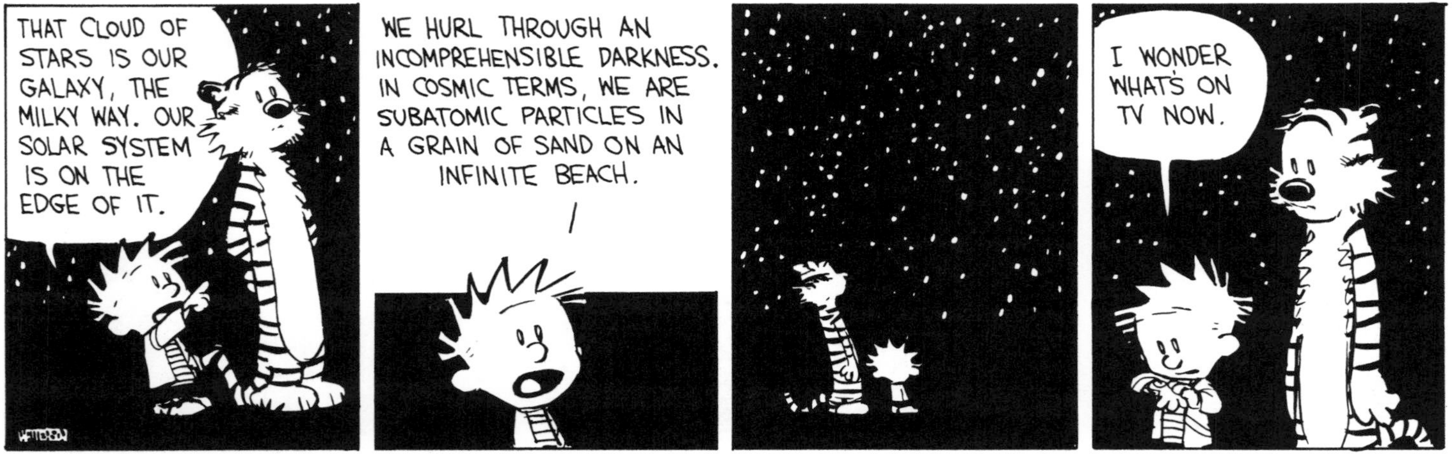
THAT CLOUD OF STARS IS OUR GALAXY, THE MILKY WAY. OUR SOLAR SYSTEM IS ON THE EDGE OF IT.
WE HURL THROUGH AN INCOMPREHENSIBLE DARKNESS. IN COSMIC TERMS, WE ARE SUBATOMIC PARTICLES IN A GRAIN OF SAND ON AN INFINITE BEACH.
I WONDER WHAT'S ON TV NOW.

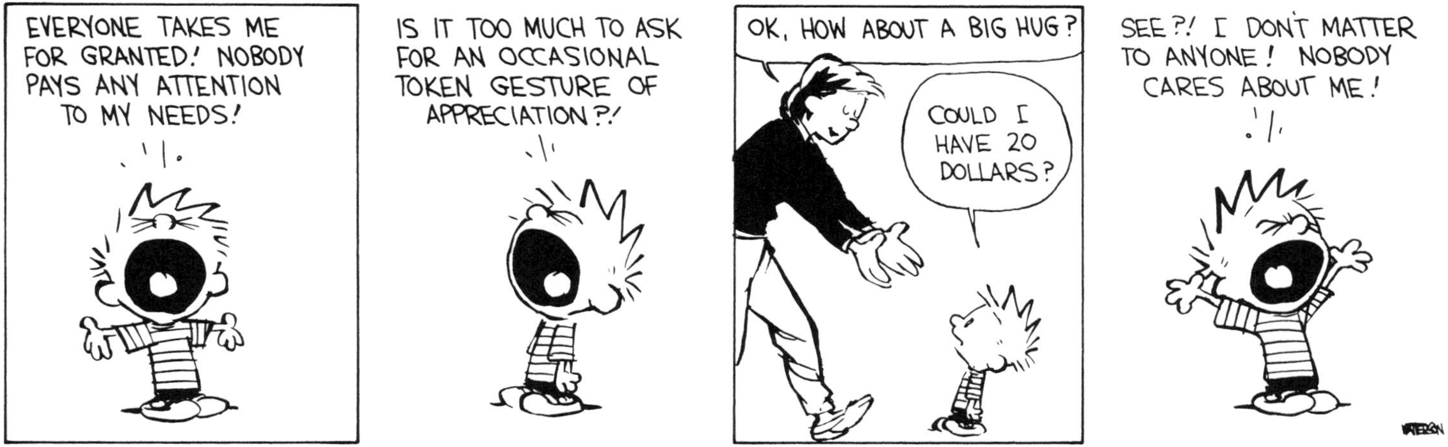
EVERYONE TAKES ME FOR GRANTED! NOBODY PAYS ANY ATTENTION TO MY NEEDS!
IS IT TOO MUCH TO ASK FOR AN OCCASIONAL TOKEN GESTURE OF APPRECIATION?!
OK, HOW ABOUT A BIG HUG?
COULD I HAVE 20 DOLLARS?
SEE?! I DON'T MATTER TO ANYONE! NOBODY CARES ABOUT ME!

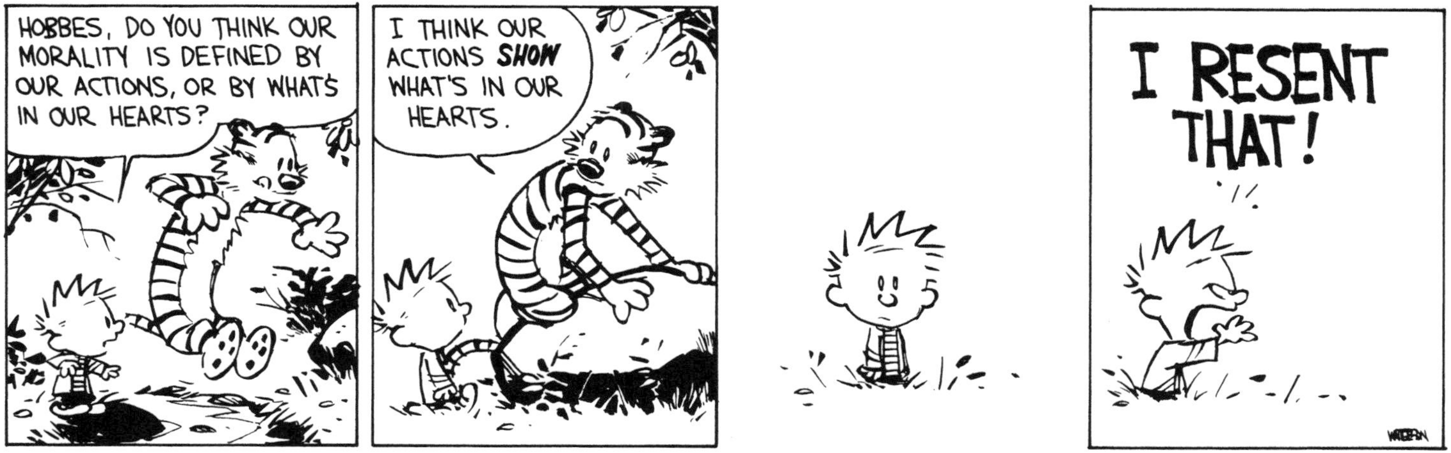
HOBBES, DO YOU THINK OUR MORALITY IS DEFINED BY OUR ACTIONS, OR BY WHAT'S IN OUR HEARTS?
I THINK OUR ACTIONS **SHOW** WHAT'S IN OUR HEARTS.
I RESENT THAT!

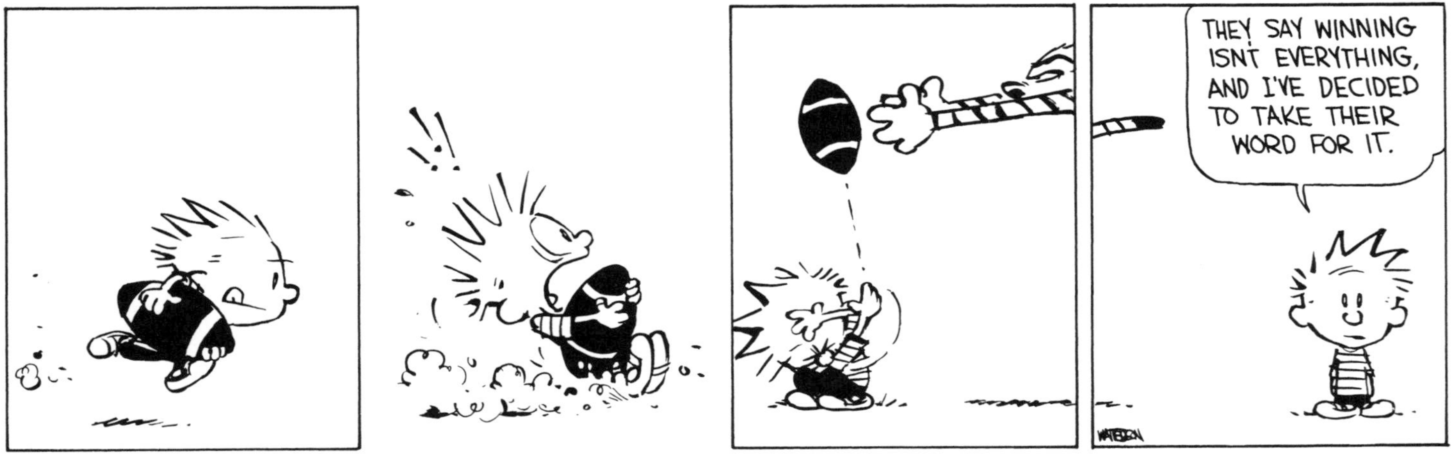
THEY SAY WINNING ISN'T EVERYTHING, AND I'VE DECIDED TO TAKE THEIR WORD FOR IT.
WATERSON

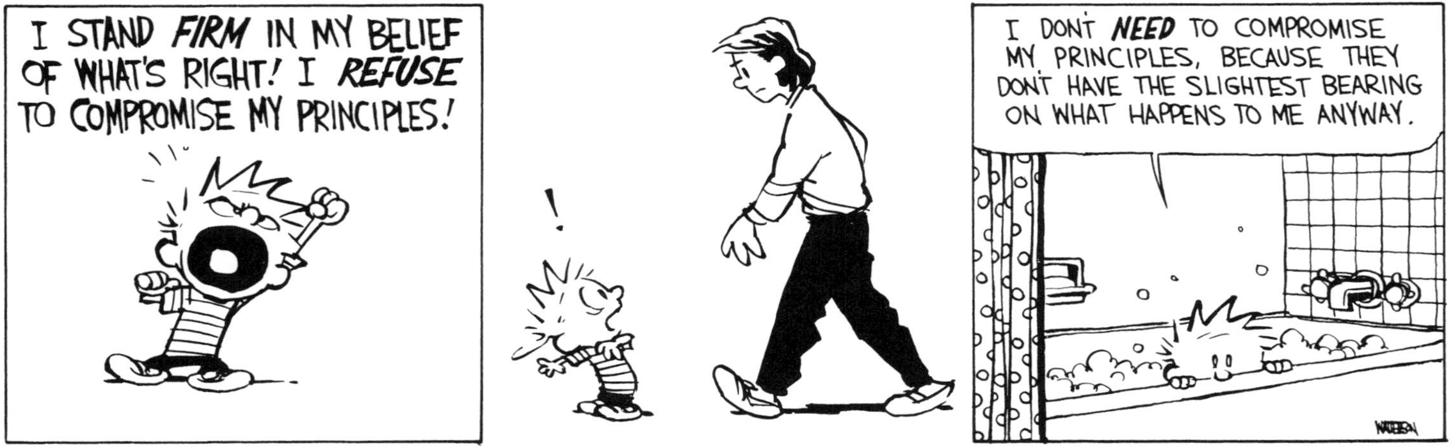
I STAND FIRM IN MY BELIEF OF WHAT'S RIGHT! I REFUSE TO COMPROMISE MY PRINCIPLES!
!
I DON'T NEED TO COMPROMISE MY PRINCIPLES, BECAUSE THEY DON'T HAVE THE SLIGHTEST BEARING ON WHAT HAPPENS TO ME ANYWAY.
WATERSON

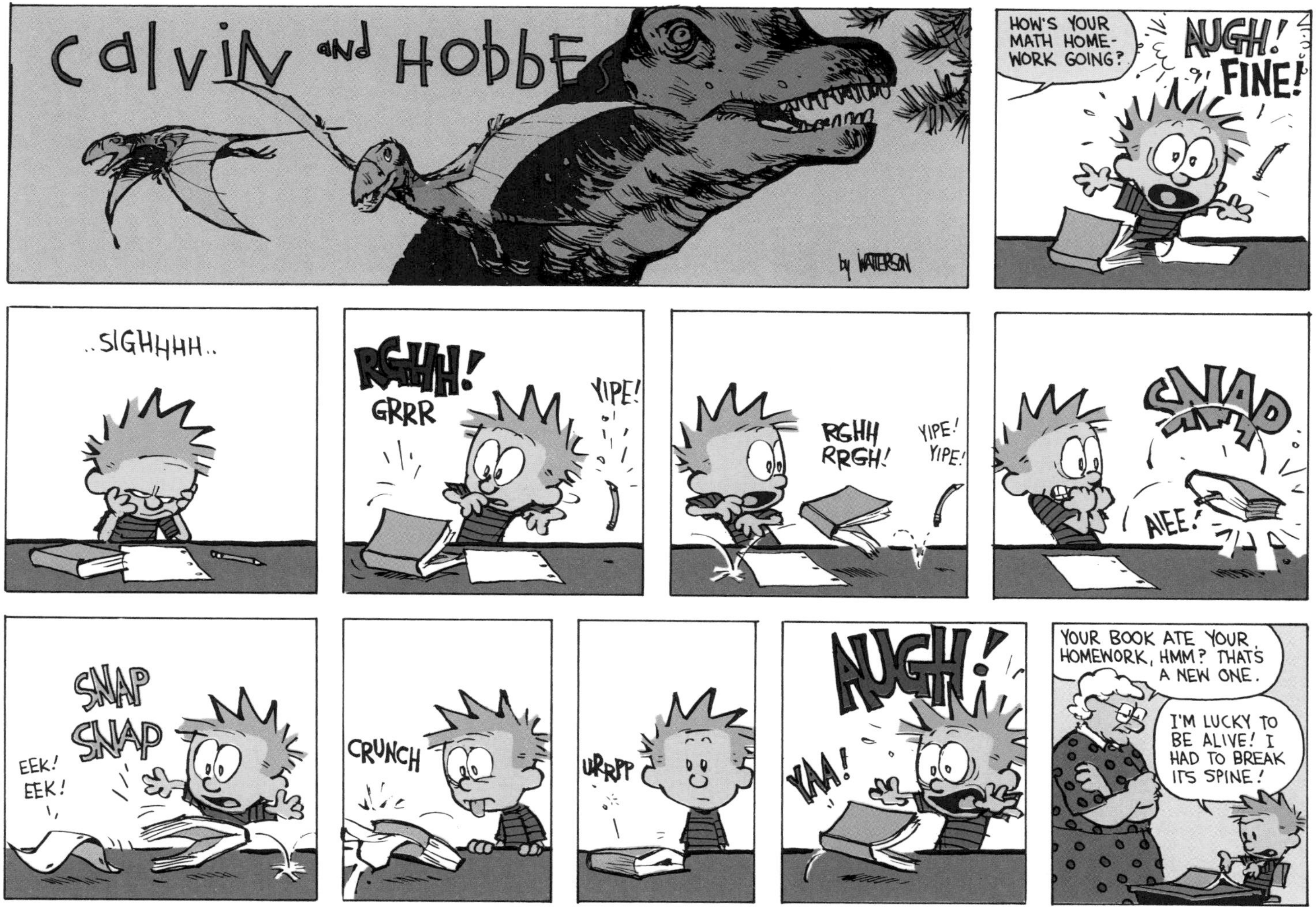
Calvin and Hobbes
by WATTERSON
HOW'S YOUR MATH HOME-WORK GOING?
AUGH! FINE!
..SIGHHHH..
RGHHH!
GRRR
YIPE!
RGHH RRGH!
YIPE! YIPE!
SNAP
AIEE!
SNAP
SNAP
EEK! EEK!
CRUNCH
URRPP
AUGH!
YAA!
YOUR BOOK ATE YOUR HOMEWORK, HMM? THAT'S A NEW ONE.
I'M LUCKY TO BE ALIVE! I HAD TO BREAK ITS SPINE!

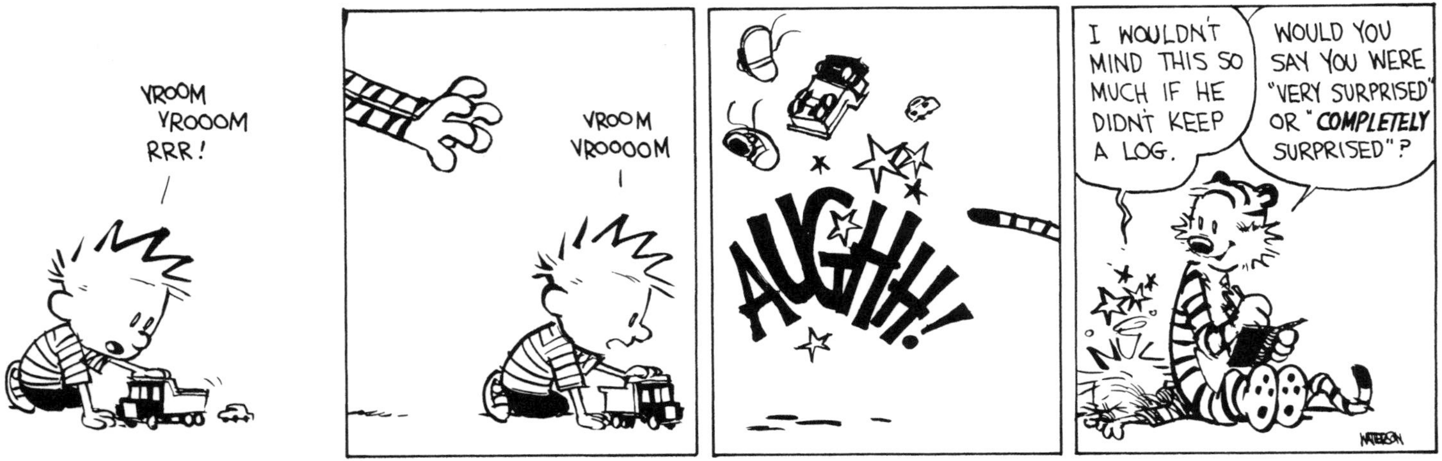
VROOM
VROOOM
RRR!
VROOM
VROOOOM
AUGHH!
I WOULDN'T MIND THIS SO MUCH IF HE DIDN'T KEEP A LOG.
WOULD YOU SAY YOU WERE "VERY SURPRISED" OR "**COMPLETELY** SURPRISED"?
WATTERSON

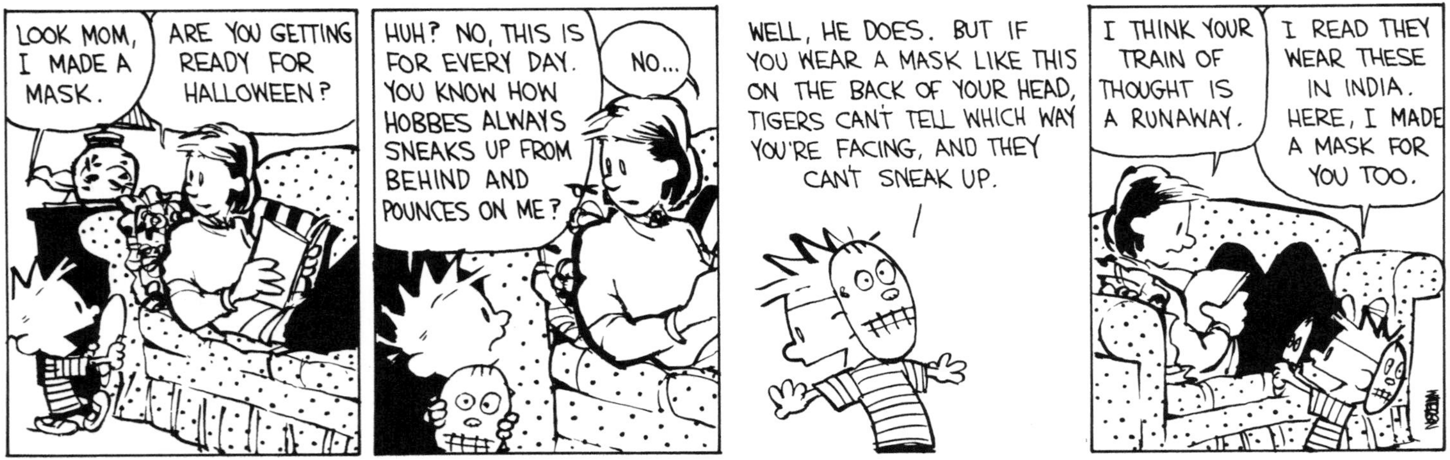
LOOK MOM, I MADE A MASK.
ARE YOU GETTING READY FOR HALLOWEEN?
HUH? NO, THIS IS FOR EVERY DAY. YOU KNOW HOW HOBBES ALWAYS SNEAKS UP FROM BEHIND AND POUNCES ON ME?
NO...
WELL, HE DOES. BUT IF YOU WEAR A MASK LIKE THIS ON THE BACK OF YOUR HEAD, TIGERS CAN'T TELL WHICH WAY YOU'RE FACING, AND THEY CAN'T SNEAK UP.
I THINK YOUR TRAIN OF THOUGHT IS A RUNAWAY.
I READ THEY WEAR THESE IN INDIA. HERE, I MADE A MASK FOR YOU TOO.

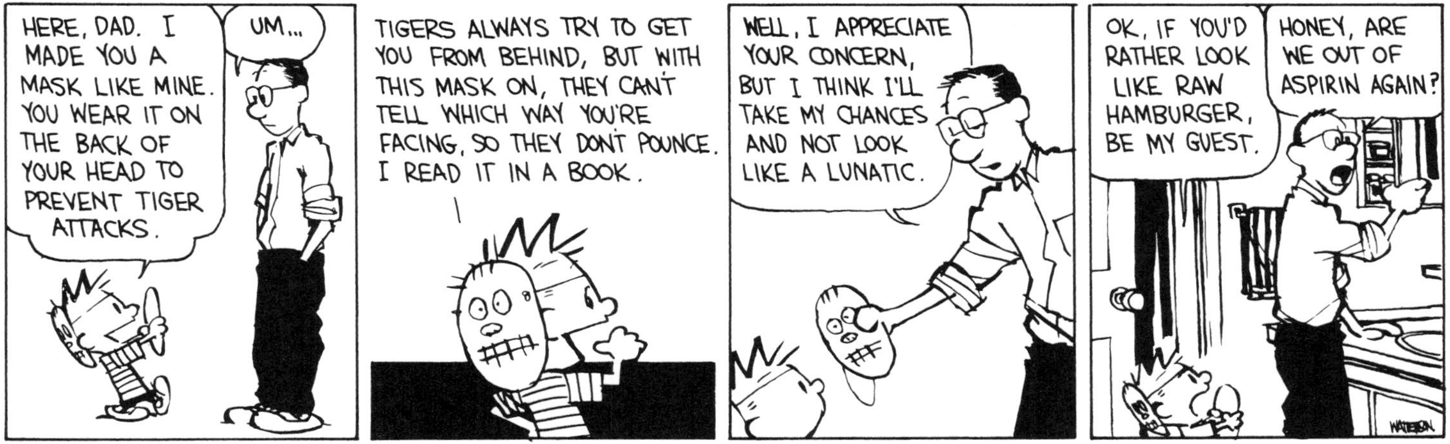
HERE, DAD. I MADE YOU A MASK LIKE MINE. YOU WEAR IT ON THE BACK OF YOUR HEAD TO PREVENT TIGER ATTACKS.
UM...
TIGERS ALWAYS TRY TO GET YOU FROM BEHIND, BUT WITH THIS MASK ON, THEY CAN'T TELL WHICH WAY YOU'RE FACING, SO THEY DON'T POUNCE. I READ IT IN A BOOK.
WELL, I APPRECIATE YOUR CONCERN, BUT I THINK I'LL TAKE MY CHANCES AND NOT LOOK LIKE A LUNATIC.
OK, IF YOU'D RATHER LOOK LIKE RAW HAMBURGER, BE MY GUEST.
HONEY, ARE WE OUT OF ASPIRIN AGAIN?

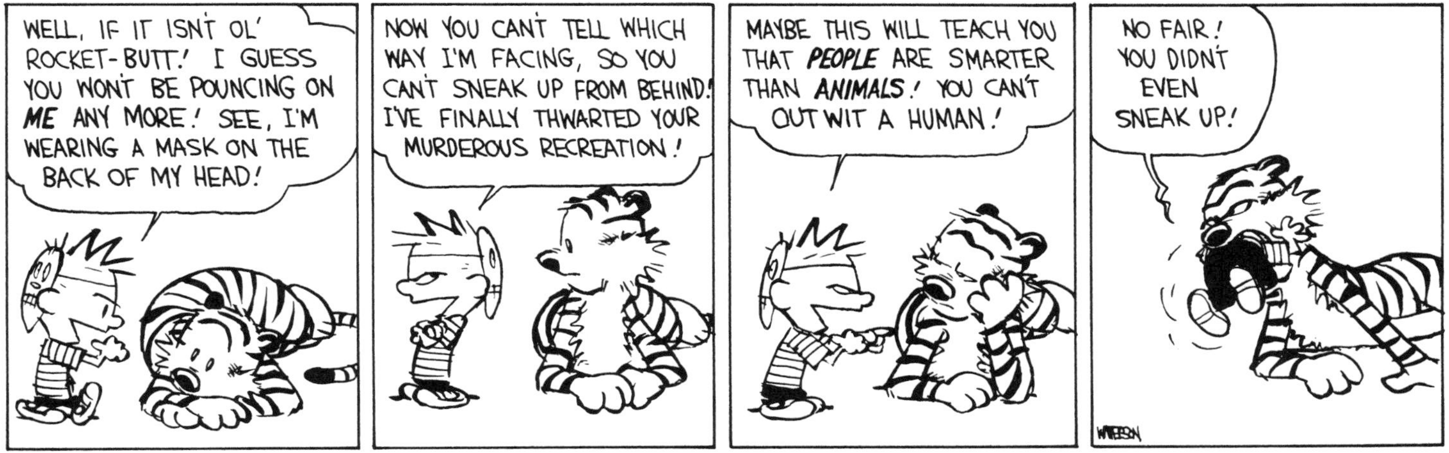
WELL, IF IT ISN'T OL' ROCKET-BUTT! I GUESS YOU WON'T BE POUNCING ON ***ME*** ANY MORE! SEE, I'M WEARING A MASK ON THE BACK OF MY HEAD!
NOW YOU CAN'T TELL WHICH WAY I'M FACING, SO YOU CAN'T SNEAK UP FROM BEHIND! I'VE FINALLY THWARTED YOUR MURDEROUS RECREATION!
MAYBE THIS WILL TEACH YOU THAT ***PEOPLE*** ARE SMARTER THAN ***ANIMALS***! YOU CAN'T OUTWIT A HUMAN!
NO FAIR! YOU DIDN'T EVEN SNEAK UP!

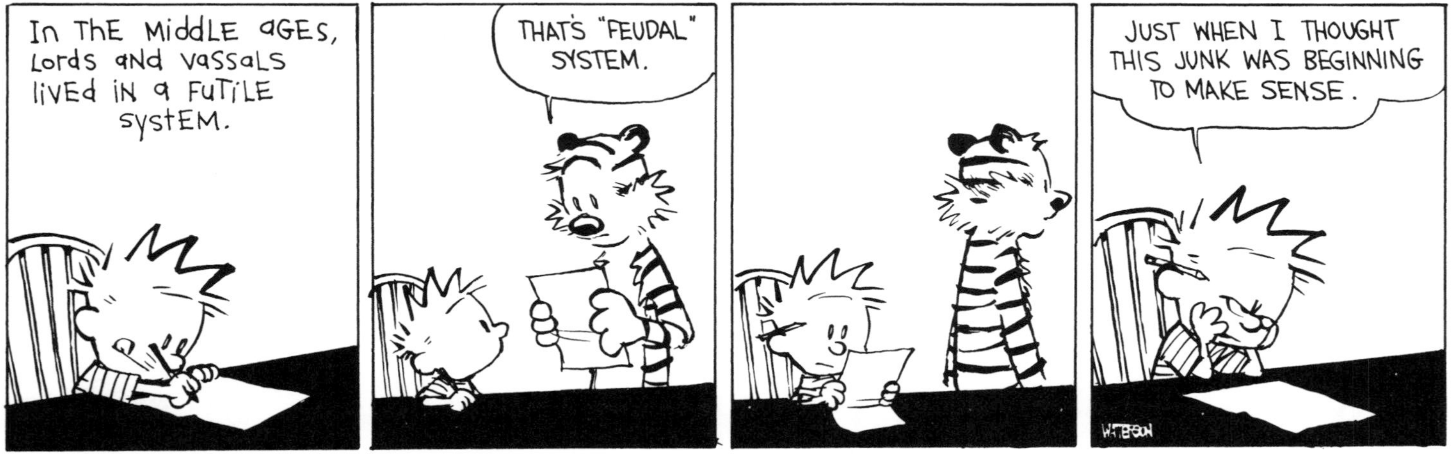
In THE MiddLE aGES, Lords aNd VassaLs liVEd iN a FuTiLE systEM.
THAT'S "FEUDAL" SYSTEM.
JUST WHEN I THOUGHT THIS JUNK WAS BEGINNING TO MAKE SENSE.

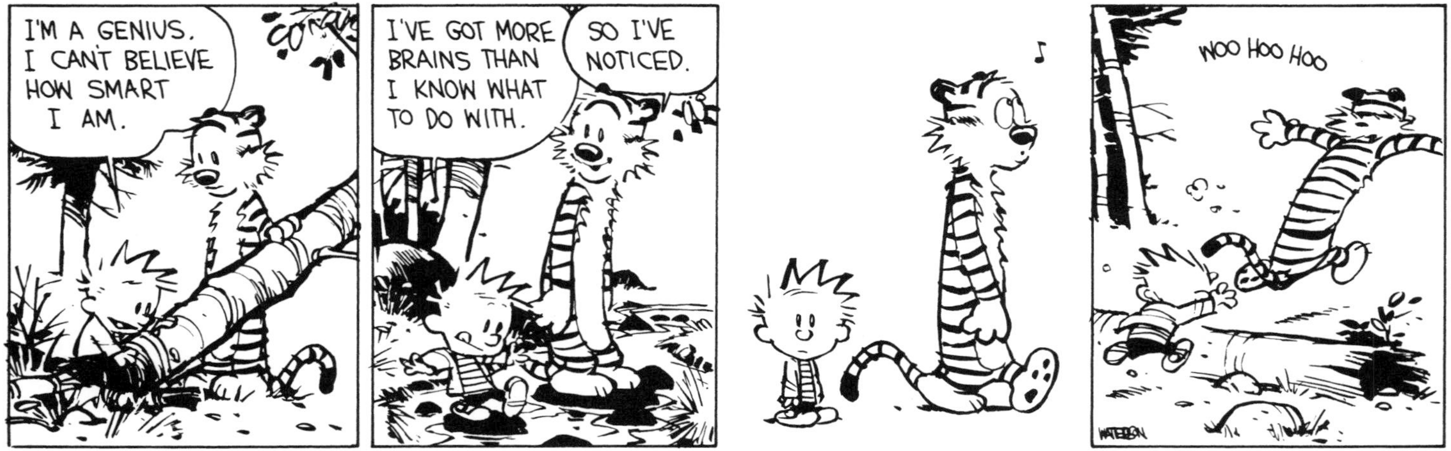
I'M A GENIUS. I CAN'T BELIEVE HOW SMART I AM.
I'VE GOT MORE BRAINS THAN I KNOW WHAT TO DO WITH.
SO I'VE NOTICED.
WOO HOO HOO

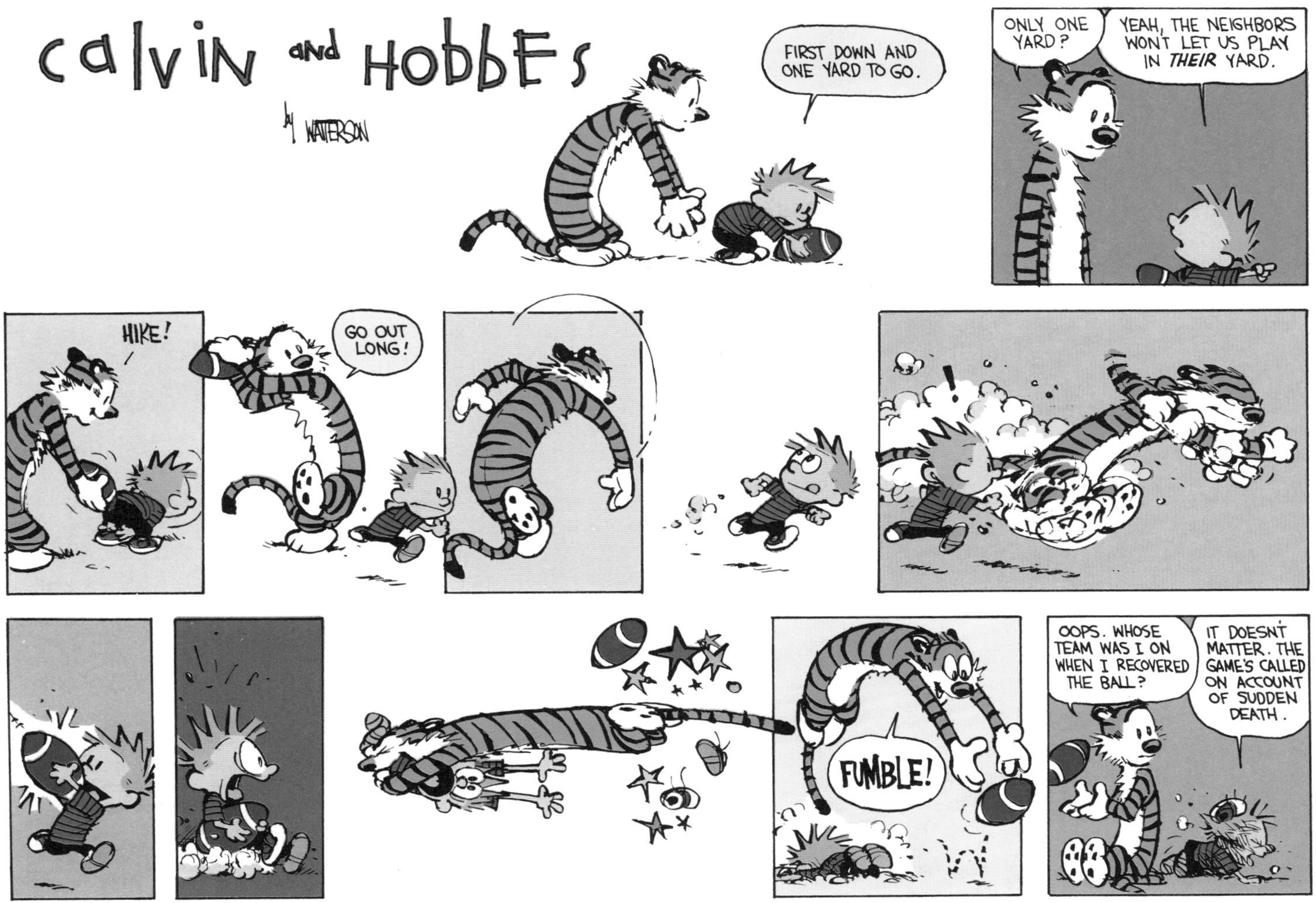
Calvin and Hobbes
by WATTERSON
FIRST DOWN AND ONE YARD TO GO.
ONLY ONE YARD?
YEAH, THE NEIGHBORS WON'T LET US PLAY IN THEIR YARD.
HIKE!
GO OUT LONG!
FUMBLE!
OOPS. WHOSE TEAM WAS I ON WHEN I RECOVERED THE BALL?
IT DOESN'T MATTER. THE GAME'S CALLED ON ACCOUNT OF SUDDEN DEATH.

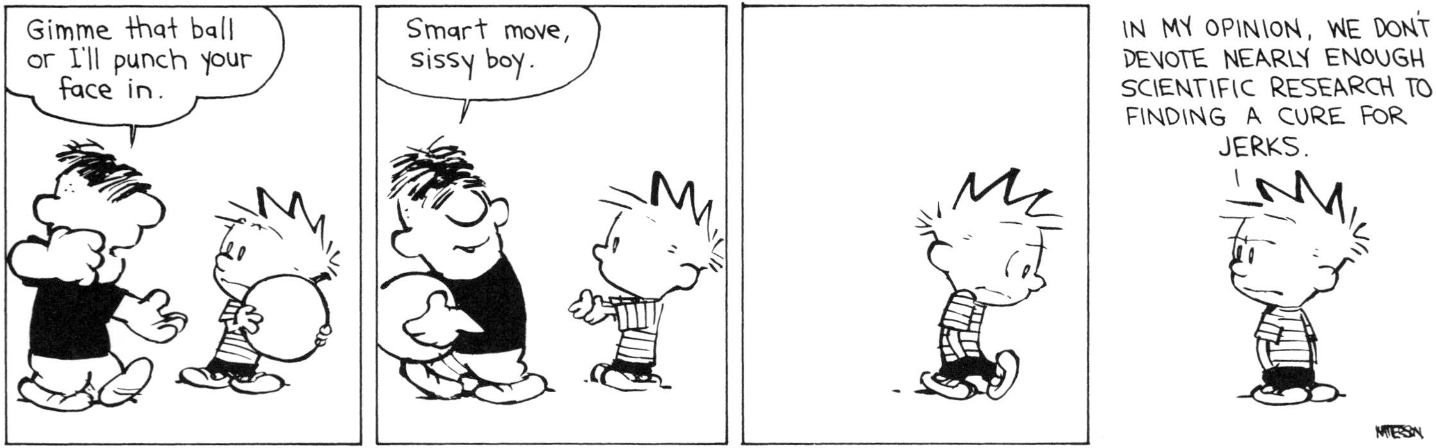
Gimme that ball or I'll punch your face in.
Smart move, sissy boy.
IN MY OPINION, WE DON'T DEVOTE NEARLY ENOUGH SCIENTIFIC RESEARCH TO FINDING A CURE FOR JERKS.
WATTERSON

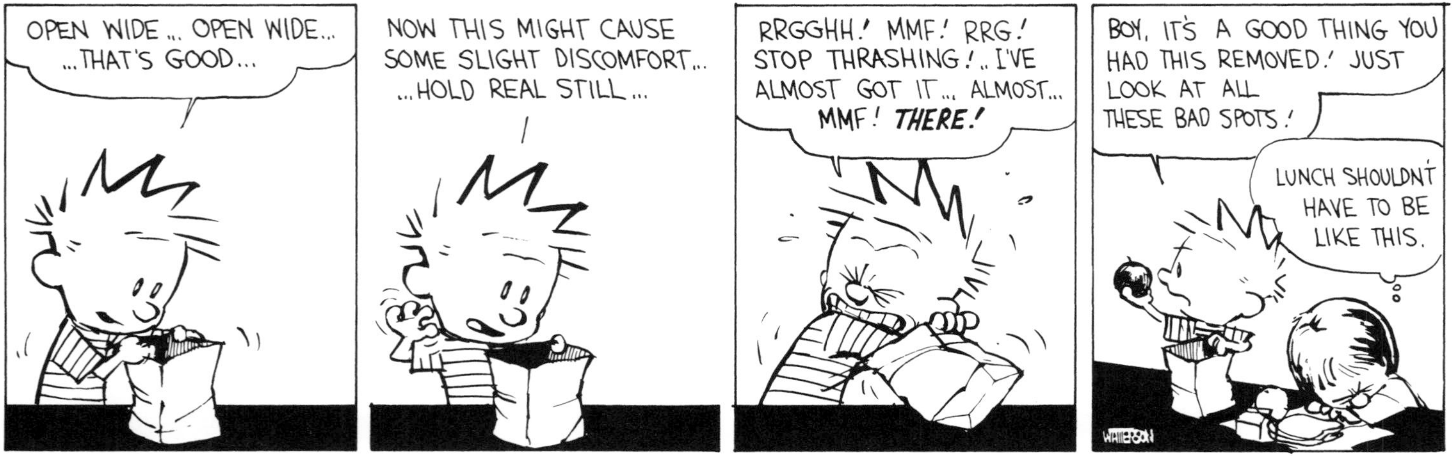
OPEN WIDE... OPEN WIDE... ...THAT'S GOOD...
NOW THIS MIGHT CAUSE SOME SLIGHT DISCOMFORT... ...HOLD REAL STILL...
RRGGHH! MMF! RRG! STOP THRASHING!.. I'VE ALMOST GOT IT... ALMOST... MMF! THERE!
BOY, IT'S A GOOD THING YOU HAD THIS REMOVED! JUST LOOK AT ALL THESE BAD SPOTS!
LUNCH SHOULDN'T HAVE TO BE LIKE THIS.
WATTERSON

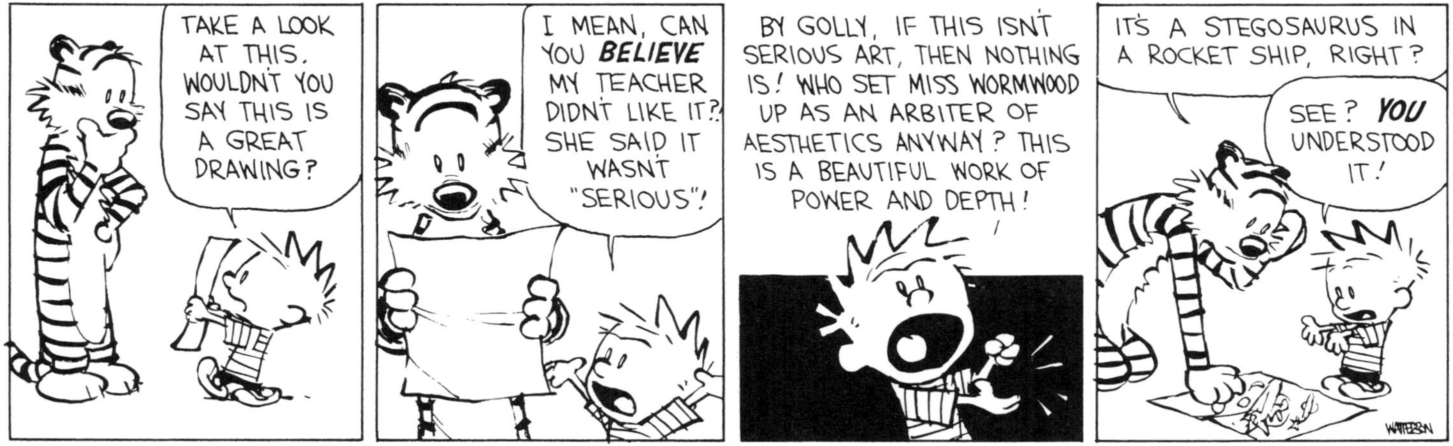
TAKE A LOOK AT THIS. WOULDN'T YOU SAY THIS IS A GREAT DRAWING?
I MEAN, CAN YOU **BELIEVE** MY TEACHER DIDN'T LIKE IT?! SHE SAID IT WASN'T "SERIOUS"!
BY GOLLY, IF THIS ISN'T SERIOUS ART, THEN NOTHING IS! WHO SET MISS WORMWOOD UP AS AN ARBITER OF AESTHETICS ANYWAY? THIS IS A BEAUTIFUL WORK OF POWER AND DEPTH!
IT'S A STEGOSAURUS IN A ROCKET SHIP, RIGHT?
SEE? **YOU** UNDERSTOOD IT!
WATTERSON

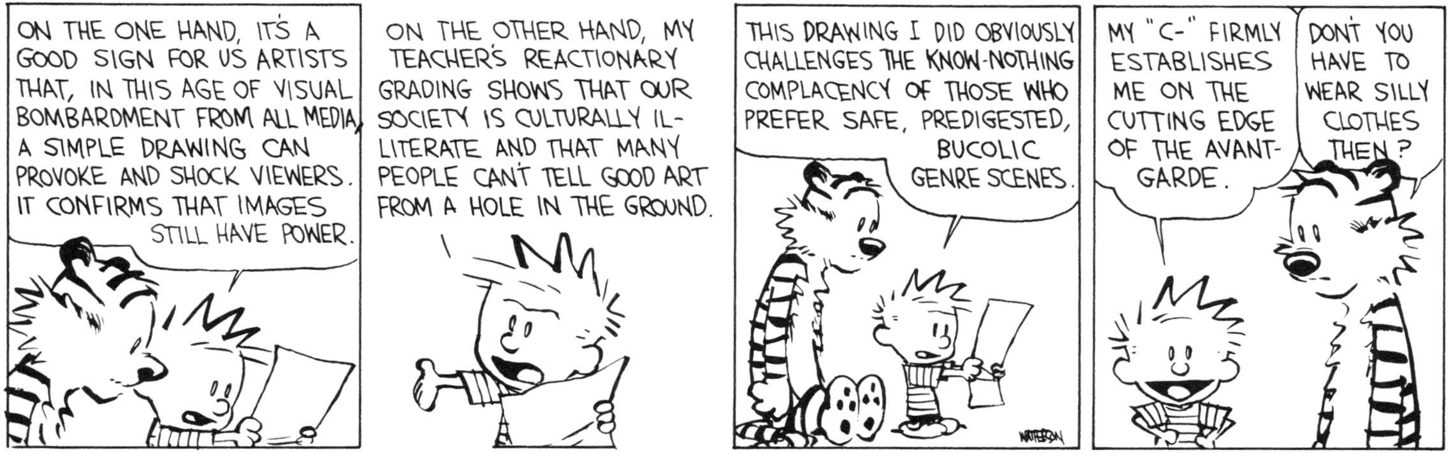
ON THE ONE HAND, IT'S A GOOD SIGN FOR US ARTISTS THAT, IN THIS AGE OF VISUAL BOMBARDMENT FROM ALL MEDIA, A SIMPLE DRAWING CAN PROVOKE AND SHOCK VIEWERS. IT CONFIRMS THAT IMAGES STILL HAVE POWER.
ON THE OTHER HAND, MY TEACHER'S REACTIONARY GRADING SHOWS THAT OUR SOCIETY IS CULTURALLY ILLITERATE AND THAT MANY PEOPLE CAN'T TELL GOOD ART FROM A HOLE IN THE GROUND.
THIS DRAWING I DID OBVIOUSLY CHALLENGES THE KNOW-NOTHING COMPLACENCY OF THOSE WHO PREFER SAFE, PREDIGESTED, BUCOLIC GENRE SCENES.
MY "C-" FIRMLY ESTABLISHES ME ON THE CUTTING EDGE OF THE AVANT-GARDE.
DON'T YOU HAVE TO WEAR SILLY CLOTHES THEN?
WATTERSON

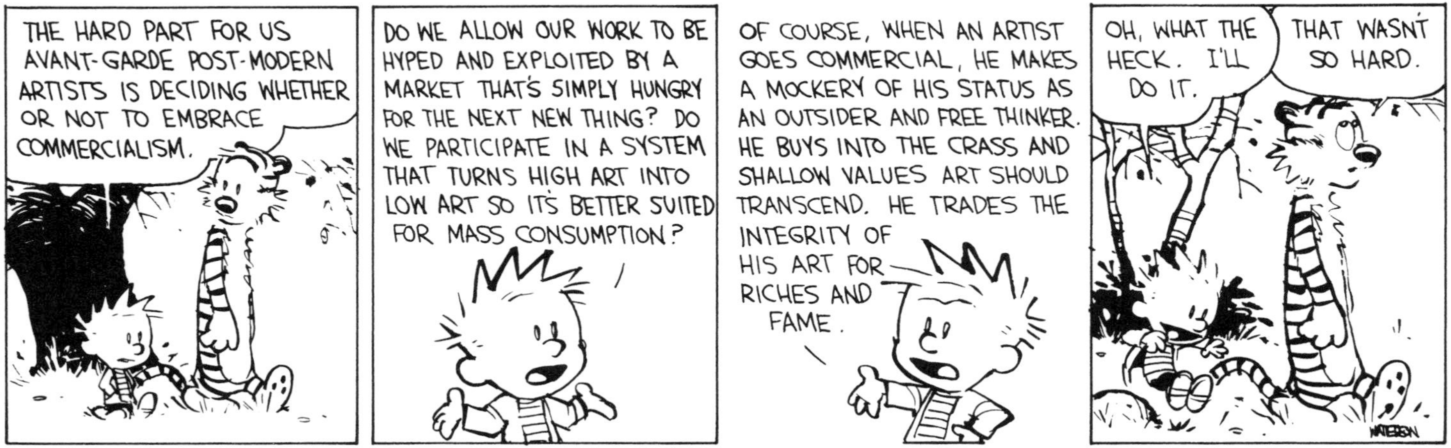
THE HARD PART FOR US AVANT-GARDE POST-MODERN ARTISTS IS DECIDING WHETHER OR NOT TO EMBRACE COMMERCIALISM.
DO WE ALLOW OUR WORK TO BE HYPED AND EXPLOITED BY A MARKET THAT'S SIMPLY HUNGRY FOR THE NEXT NEW THING? DO WE PARTICIPATE IN A SYSTEM THAT TURNS HIGH ART INTO LOW ART SO IT'S BETTER SUITED FOR MASS CONSUMPTION?
OF COURSE, WHEN AN ARTIST GOES COMMERCIAL, HE MAKES A MOCKERY OF HIS STATUS AS AN OUTSIDER AND FREE THINKER. HE BUYS INTO THE CRASS AND SHALLOW VALUES ART SHOULD TRANSCEND. HE TRADES THE INTEGRITY OF HIS ART FOR RICHES AND FAME.
OH, WHAT THE HECK. I'LL DO IT.
THAT WASN'T SO HARD.

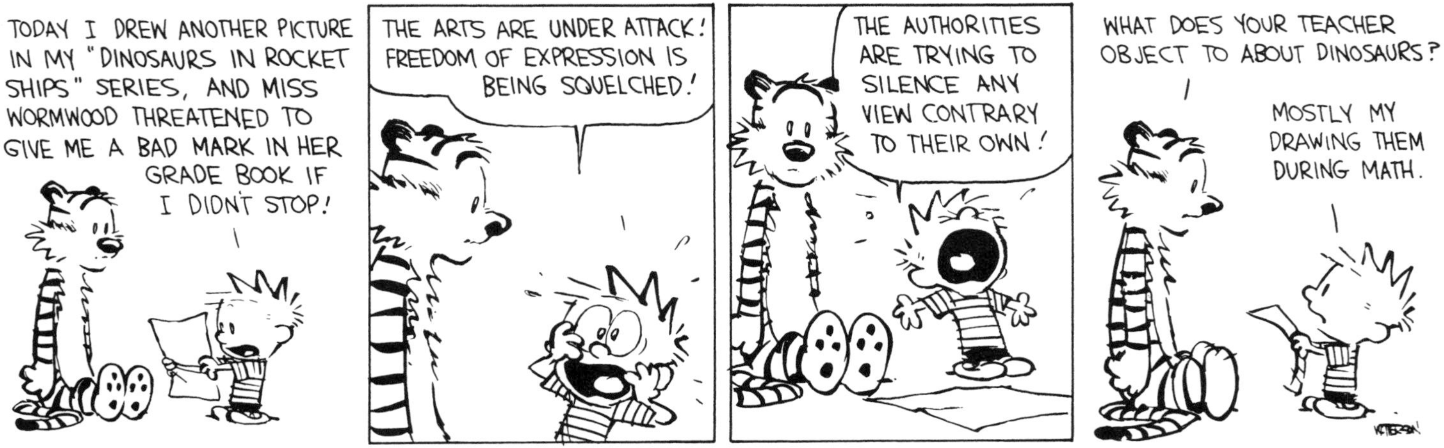
TODAY I DREW ANOTHER PICTURE IN MY "DINOSAURS IN ROCKET SHIPS" SERIES, AND MISS WORMWOOD THREATENED TO GIVE ME A BAD MARK IN HER GRADE BOOK IF I DIDN'T STOP!
THE ARTS ARE UNDER ATTACK! FREEDOM OF EXPRESSION IS BEING SQUELCHED!
THE AUTHORITIES ARE TRYING TO SILENCE ANY VIEW CONTRARY TO THEIR OWN!
WHAT DOES YOUR TEACHER OBJECT TO ABOUT DINOSAURS?
MOSTLY MY DRAWING THEM DURING MATH.

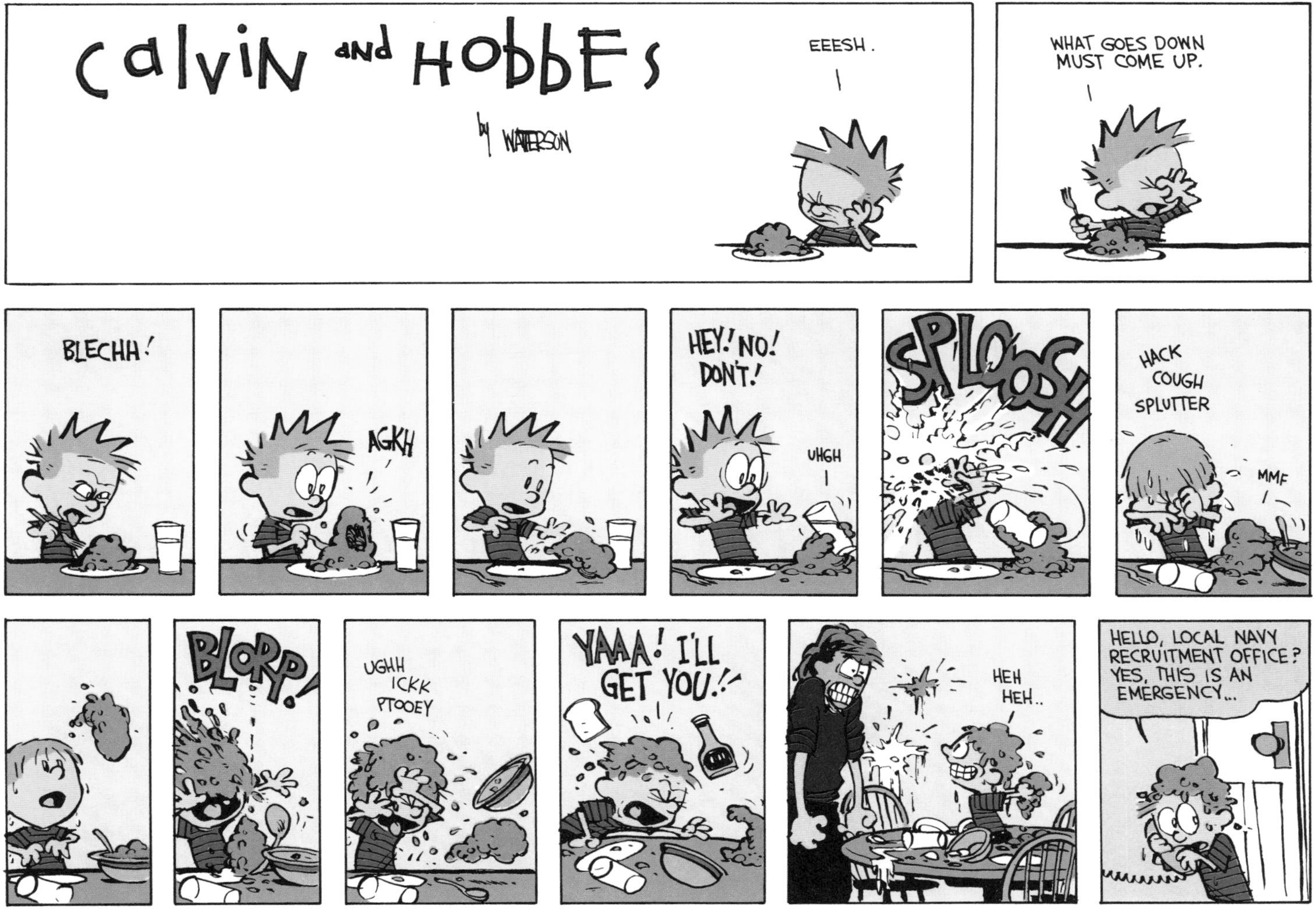
Calvin and HOBBES
by WATTERSON
EEESH.
WHAT GOES DOWN MUST COME UP.
BLECHH!
AGKH
HEY! NO! DON'T!
UHGH
SPLOOSH
HACK COUGH SPLUTTER
MMF
BLORP!
UGHH ICKK PTOOEY
YAAA! I'LL GET YOU!
HEH HEH..
HELLO, LOCAL NAVY RECRUITMENT OFFICE? YES, THIS IS AN EMERGENCY...

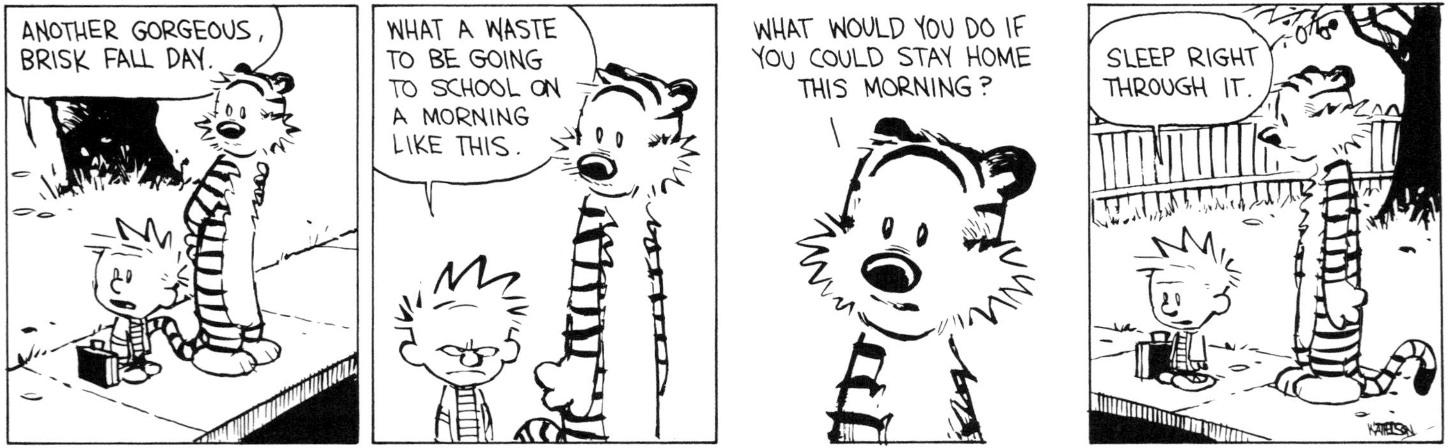
ANOTHER GORGEOUS, BRISK FALL DAY.
WHAT A WASTE TO BE GOING TO SCHOOL ON A MORNING LIKE THIS.
WHAT WOULD YOU DO IF YOU COULD STAY HOME THIS MORNING?
SLEEP RIGHT THROUGH IT.

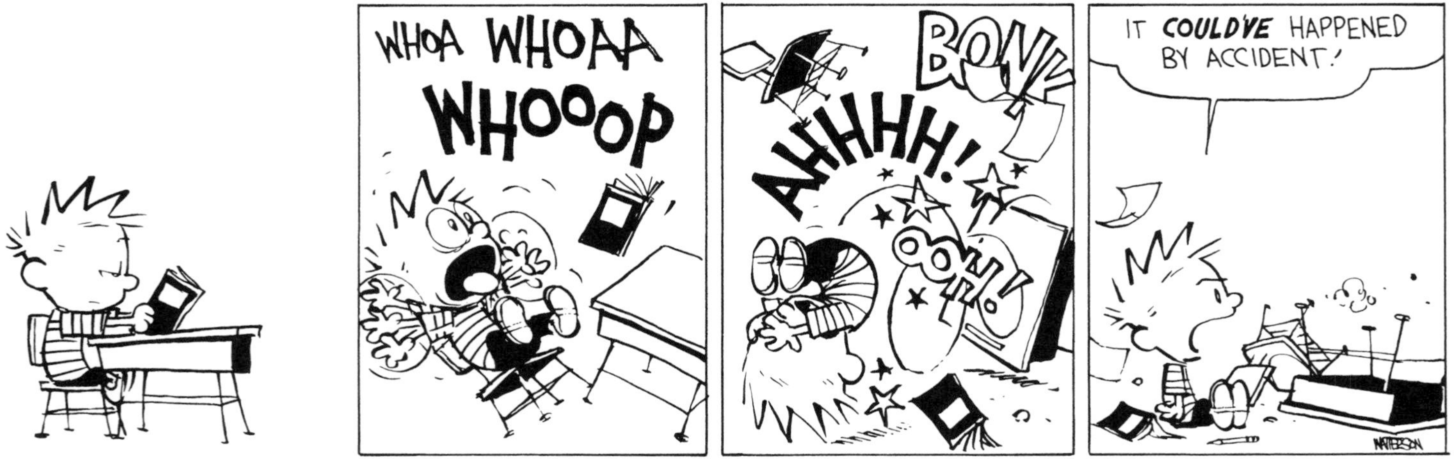
WHOA WHOAA
WHOOOP
BONK
AHHHH!
IT COULD'VE HAPPENED BY ACCIDENT!

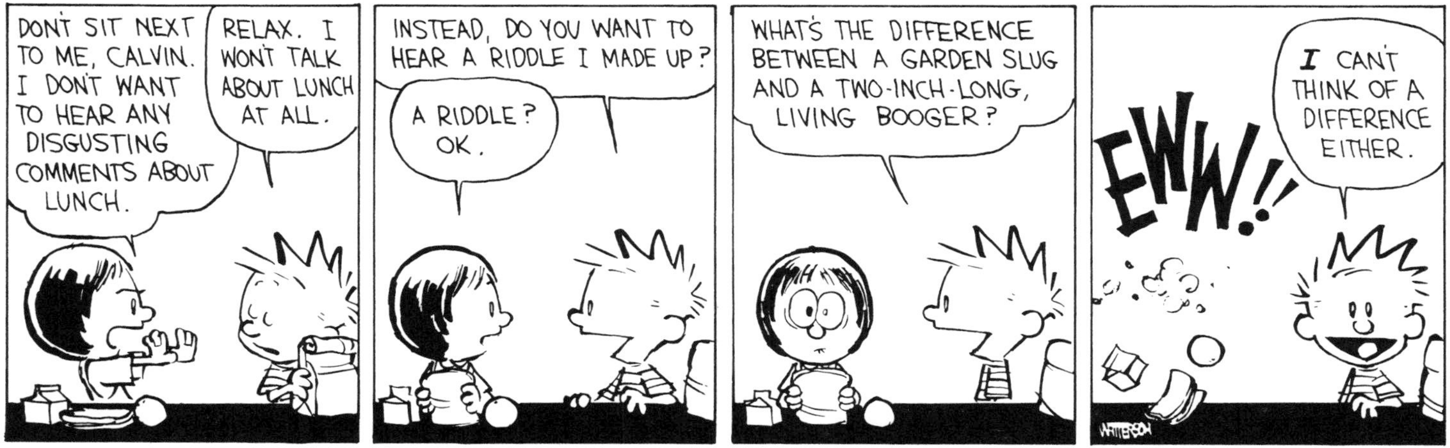
DON'T SIT NEXT TO ME, CALVIN. I DON'T WANT TO HEAR ANY DISGUSTING COMMENTS ABOUT LUNCH.
RELAX. I WON'T TALK ABOUT LUNCH AT ALL.
INSTEAD, DO YOU WANT TO HEAR A RIDDLE I MADE UP?
A RIDDLE? OK.
WHAT'S THE DIFFERENCE BETWEEN A GARDEN SLUG AND A TWO-INCH-LONG, LIVING BOOGER?
EWW!!
I CAN'T THINK OF A DIFFERENCE EITHER.
WATTERSON

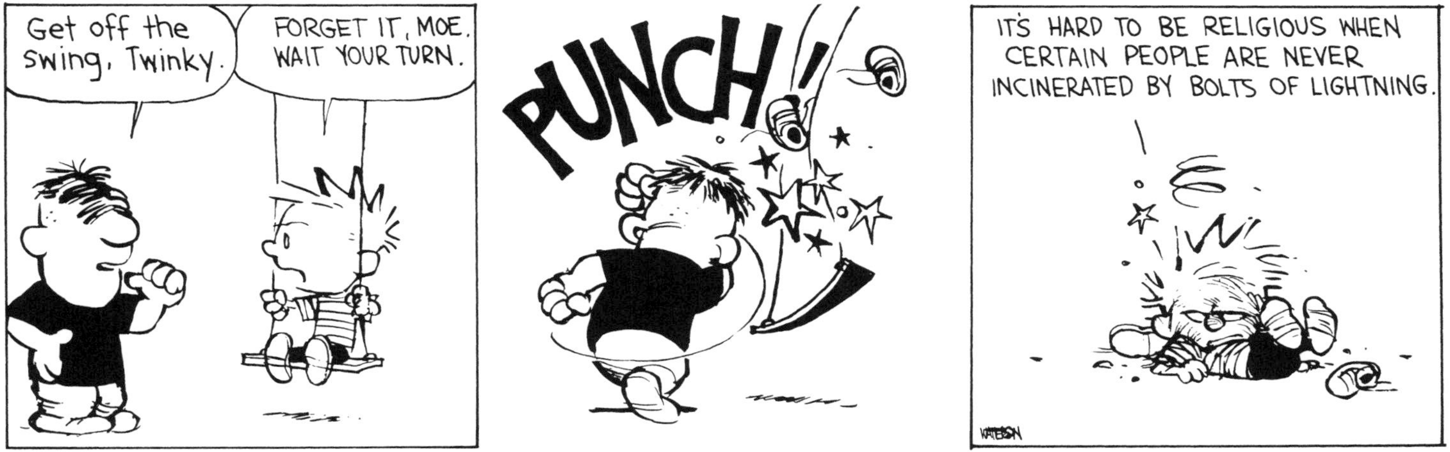
Get off the swing, Twinky.
FORGET IT, MOE. WAIT YOUR TURN.
PUNCH!!
IT'S HARD TO BE RELIGIOUS WHEN CERTAIN PEOPLE ARE NEVER INCINERATED BY BOLTS OF LIGHTNING.
WATTERSON

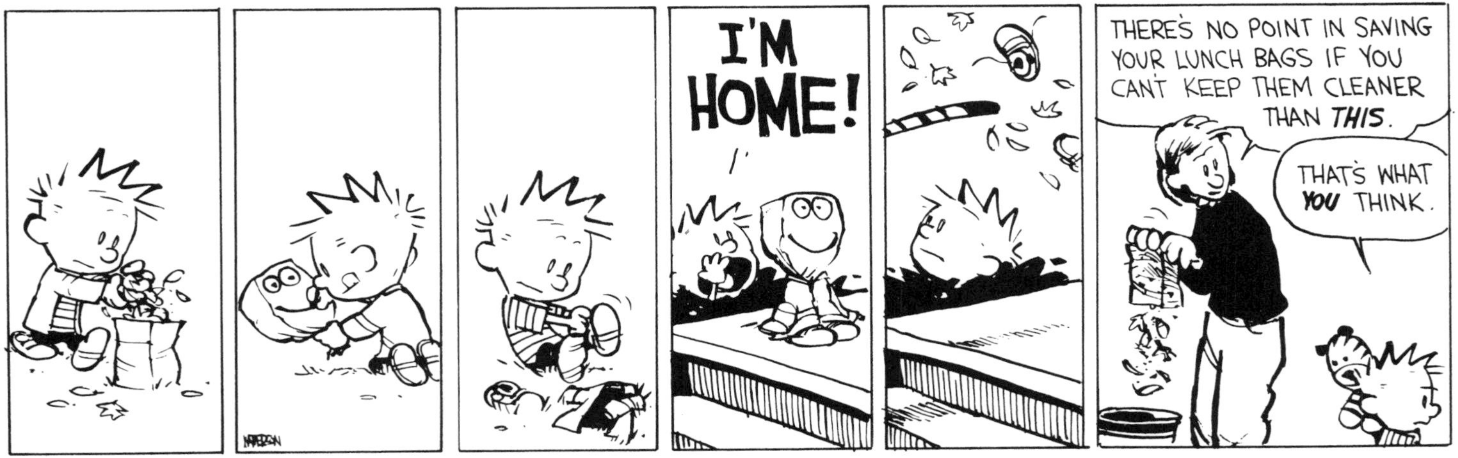
I'M HOME!
THERE'S NO POINT IN SAVING YOUR LUNCH BAGS IF YOU CAN'T KEEP THEM CLEANER THAN **THIS**.
THAT'S WHAT **YOU** THINK.

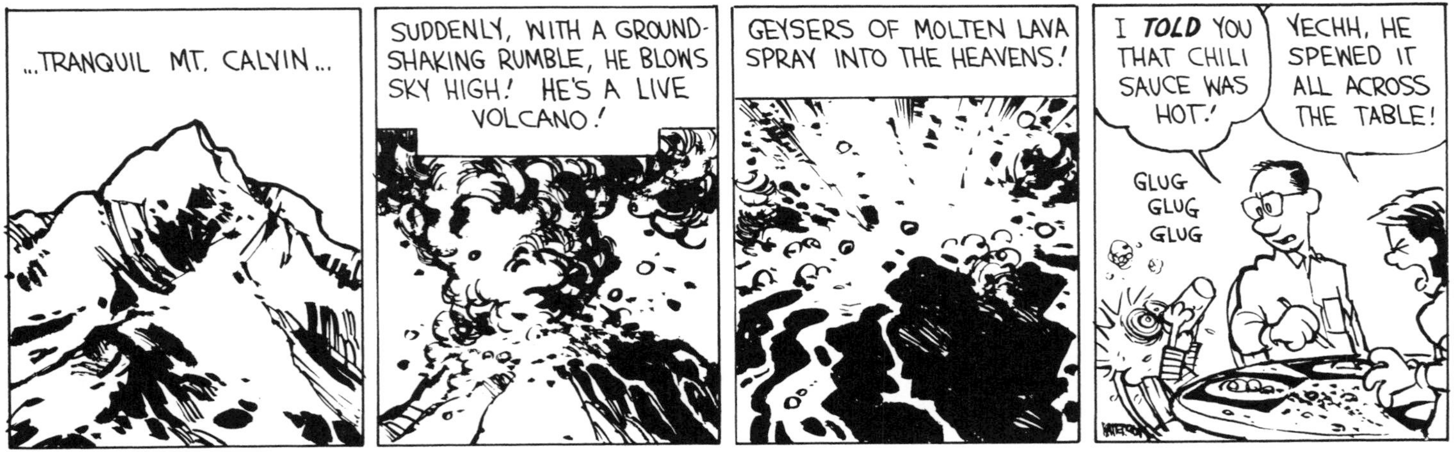
...TRANQUIL MT. CALVIN...
SUDDENLY, WITH A GROUND-SHAKING RUMBLE, HE BLOWS SKY HIGH! HE'S A LIVE VOLCANO!
GEYSERS OF MOLTEN LAVA SPRAY INTO THE HEAVENS!
I **TOLD** YOU THAT CHILI SAUCE WAS HOT!
YECHH, HE SPEWED IT ALL ACROSS THE TABLE!
GLUG GLUG GLUG

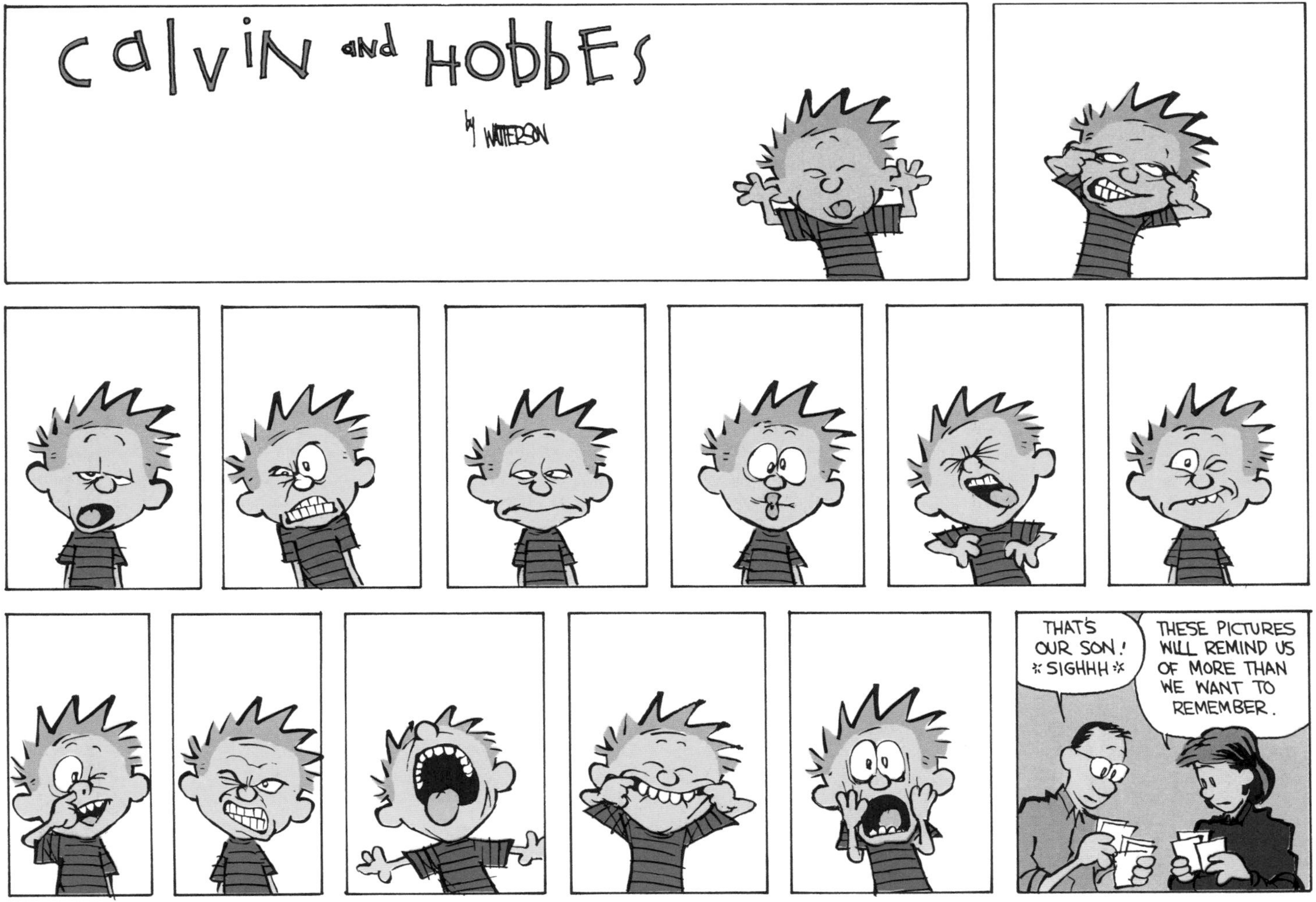
Calvin and HOBBES
by WATTERSON
THAT'S OUR SON! *SIGHHH*
THESE PICTURES WILL REMIND US OF MORE THAN WE WANT TO REMEMBER.

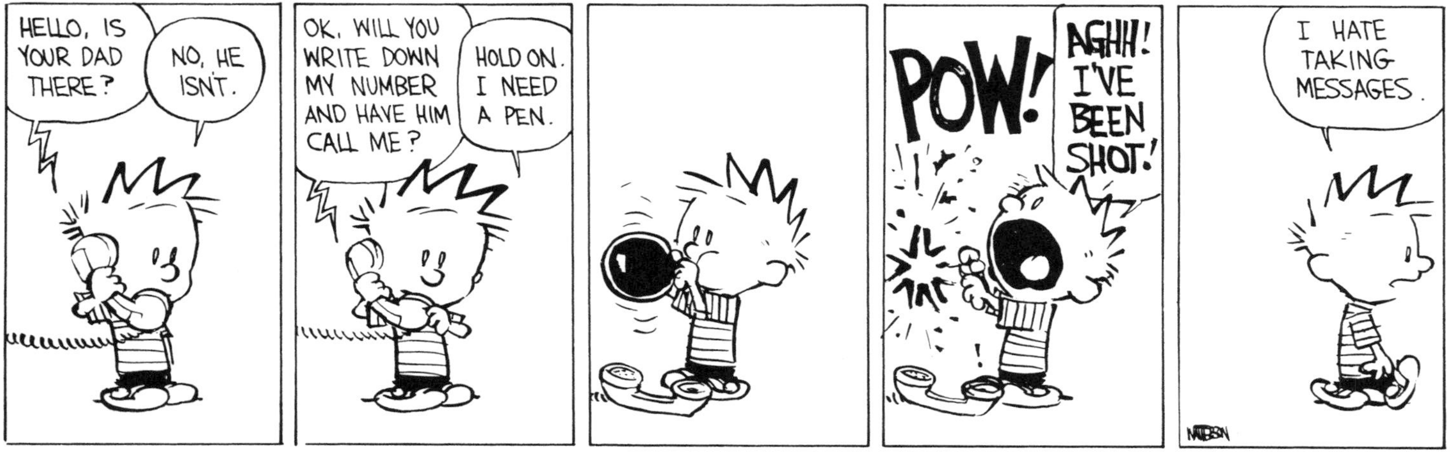
HELLO, IS YOUR DAD THERE?
NO, HE ISN'T.
OK. WILL YOU WRITE DOWN MY NUMBER AND HAVE HIM CALL ME?
HOLD ON. I NEED A PEN.
POW!
AGHH! I'VE BEEN SHOT!
I HATE TAKING MESSAGES.
WATTERSON

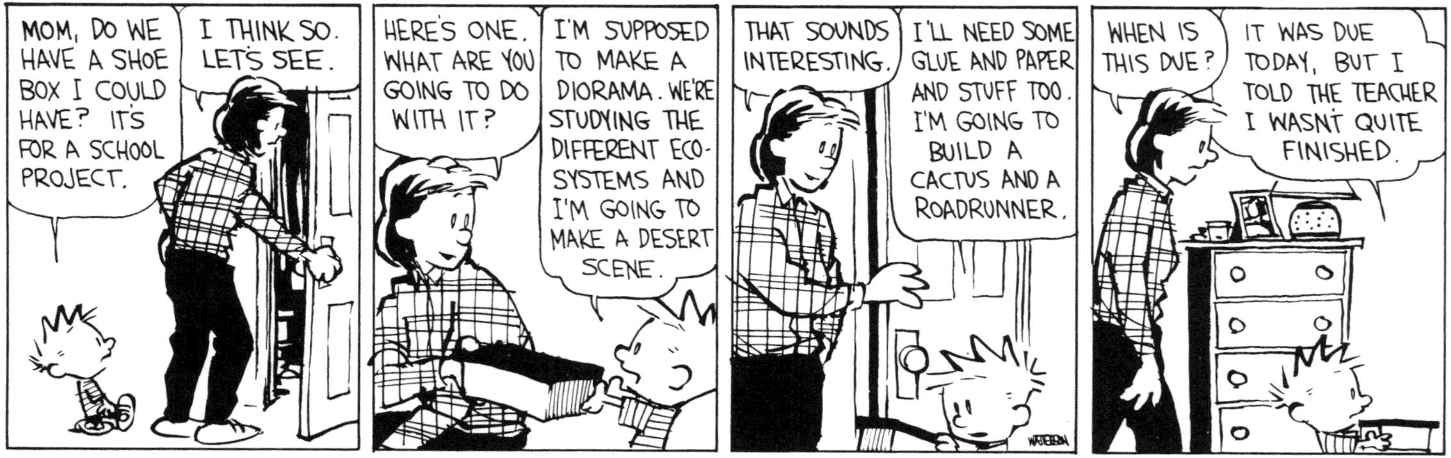
MOM, DO WE HAVE A SHOE BOX I COULD HAVE? IT'S FOR A SCHOOL PROJECT.
I THINK SO. LET'S SEE.
HERE'S ONE. WHAT ARE YOU GOING TO DO WITH IT?
I'M SUPPOSED TO MAKE A DIORAMA. WE'RE STUDYING THE DIFFERENT ECO-SYSTEMS AND I'M GOING TO MAKE A DESERT SCENE.
THAT SOUNDS INTERESTING.
I'LL NEED SOME GLUE AND PAPER AND STUFF TOO. I'M GOING TO BUILD A CACTUS AND A ROADRUNNER.
WATTERSON
WHEN IS THIS DUE?
IT WAS DUE TODAY, BUT I TOLD THE TEACHER I WASN'T QUITE FINISHED.

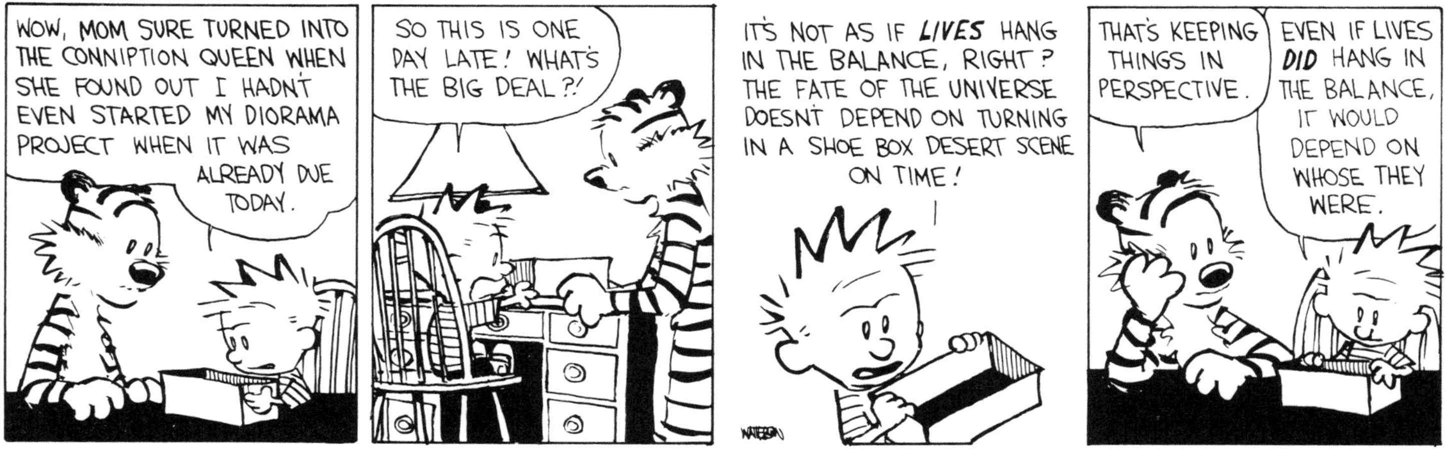
WOW, MOM SURE TURNED INTO THE CONNIPTION QUEEN WHEN SHE FOUND OUT I HADN'T EVEN STARTED MY DIORAMA PROJECT WHEN IT WAS ALREADY DUE TODAY.
SO THIS IS ONE DAY LATE! WHAT'S THE BIG DEAL?!
IT'S NOT AS IF *LIVES* HANG IN THE BALANCE, RIGHT? THE FATE OF THE UNIVERSE DOESN'T DEPEND ON TURNING IN A SHOE BOX DESERT SCENE ON TIME!
WATTERSON
THAT'S KEEPING THINGS IN PERSPECTIVE.
EVEN IF LIVES *DID* HANG IN THE BALANCE, IT WOULD DEPEND ON WHOSE THEY WERE.

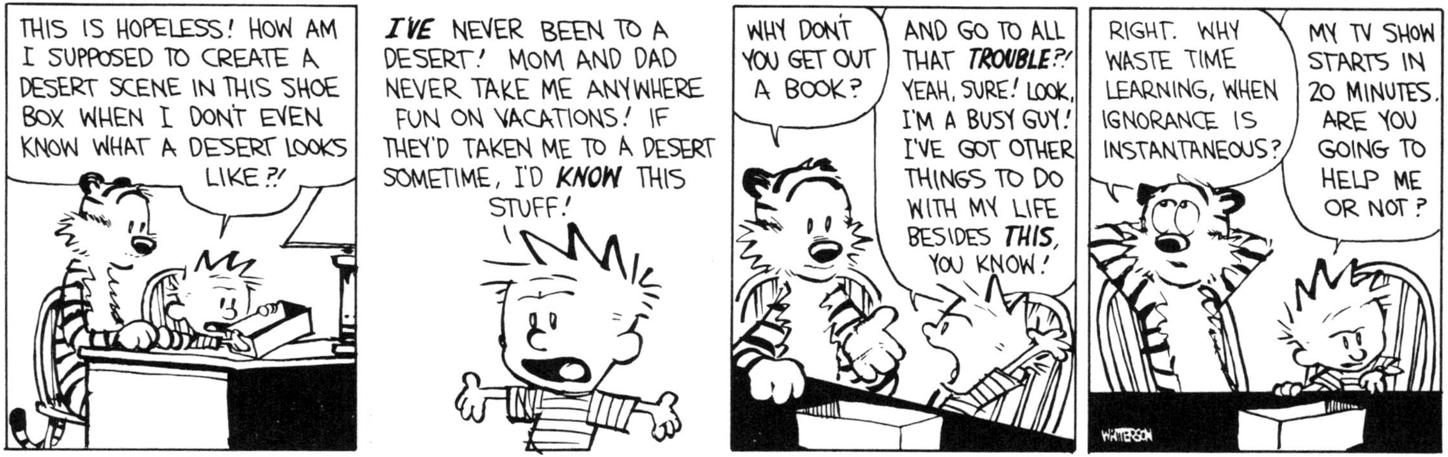
THIS IS HOPELESS! HOW AM I SUPPOSED TO CREATE A DESERT SCENE IN THIS SHOE BOX WHEN I DON'T EVEN KNOW WHAT A DESERT LOOKS LIKE?!
I'VE NEVER BEEN TO A DESERT! MOM AND DAD NEVER TAKE ME ANYWHERE FUN ON VACATIONS! IF THEY'D TAKEN ME TO A DESERT SOMETIME, I'D *KNOW* THIS STUFF!
WHY DON'T YOU GET OUT A BOOK?
AND GO TO ALL THAT *TROUBLE*?! YEAH, SURE! LOOK, I'M A BUSY GUY! I'VE GOT OTHER THINGS TO DO WITH MY LIFE BESIDES *THIS*, YOU KNOW!
RIGHT. WHY WASTE TIME LEARNING, WHEN IGNORANCE IS INSTANTANEOUS?
MY TV SHOW STARTS IN 20 MINUTES. ARE YOU GOING TO HELP ME OR NOT?
WATTERSON

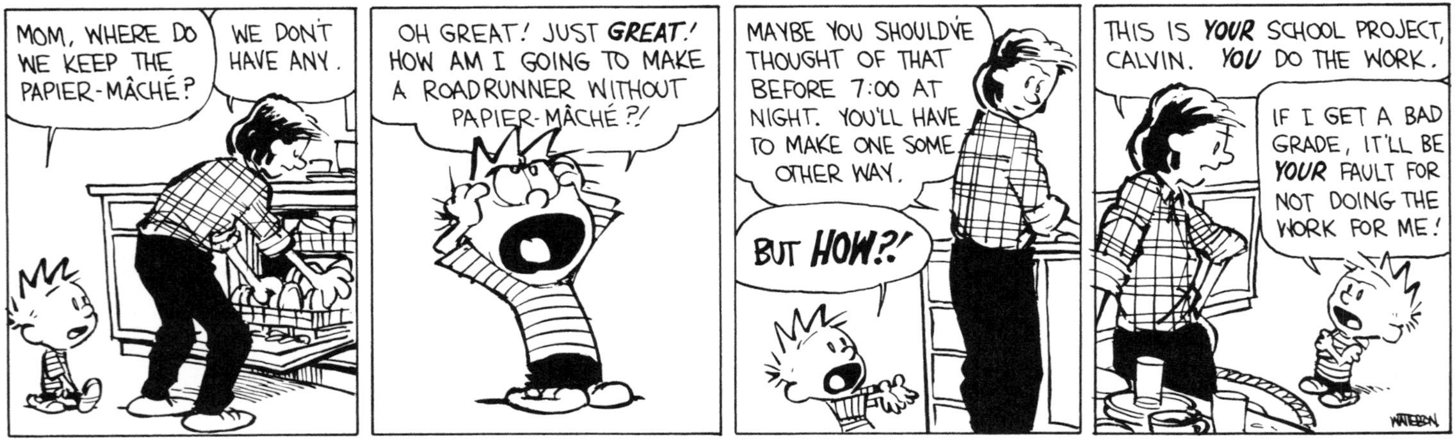
MOM, WHERE DO WE KEEP THE PAPIER-MÂCHÉ?
WE DON'T HAVE ANY.
OH GREAT! JUST **GREAT**! HOW AM I GOING TO MAKE A ROADRUNNER WITHOUT PAPIER-MÂCHÉ?!
MAYBE YOU SHOULD'VE THOUGHT OF THAT BEFORE 7:00 AT NIGHT. YOU'LL HAVE TO MAKE ONE SOME OTHER WAY.
BUT **HOW?!**
THIS IS **YOUR** SCHOOL PROJECT, CALVIN. **YOU** DO THE WORK.
IF I GET A BAD GRADE, IT'LL BE **YOUR** FAULT FOR NOT DOING THE WORK FOR ME!

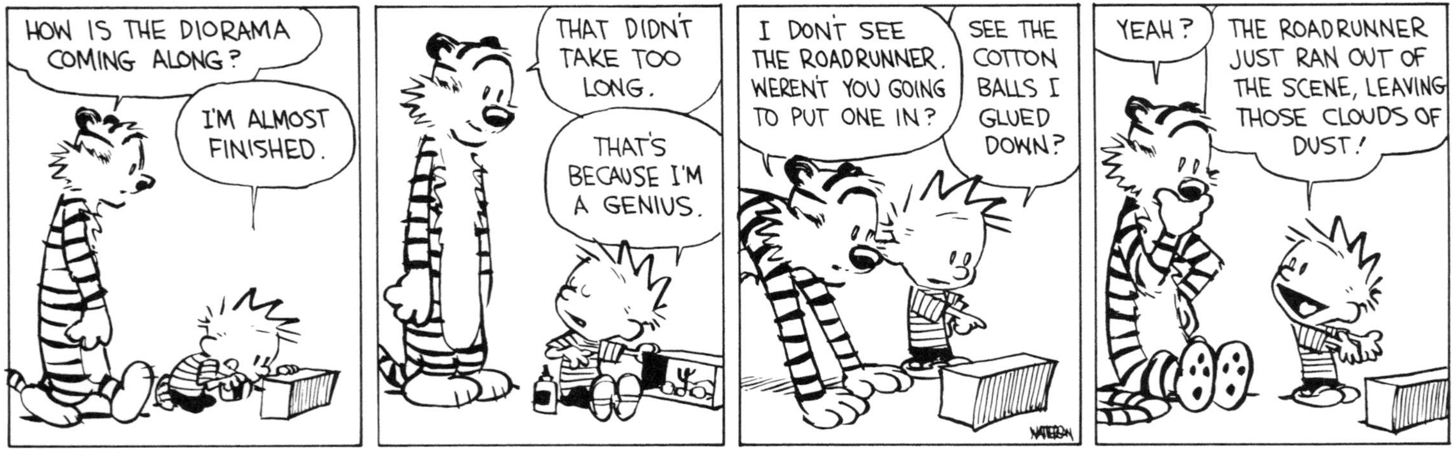
HOW IS THE DIORAMA COMING ALONG?
I'M ALMOST FINISHED.
THAT DIDN'T TAKE TOO LONG.
THAT'S BECAUSE I'M A GENIUS.
I DON'T SEE THE ROADRUNNER. WEREN'T YOU GOING TO PUT ONE IN?
SEE THE COTTON BALLS I GLUED DOWN?
YEAH?
THE ROADRUNNER JUST RAN OUT OF THE SCENE, LEAVING THOSE CLOUDS OF DUST!

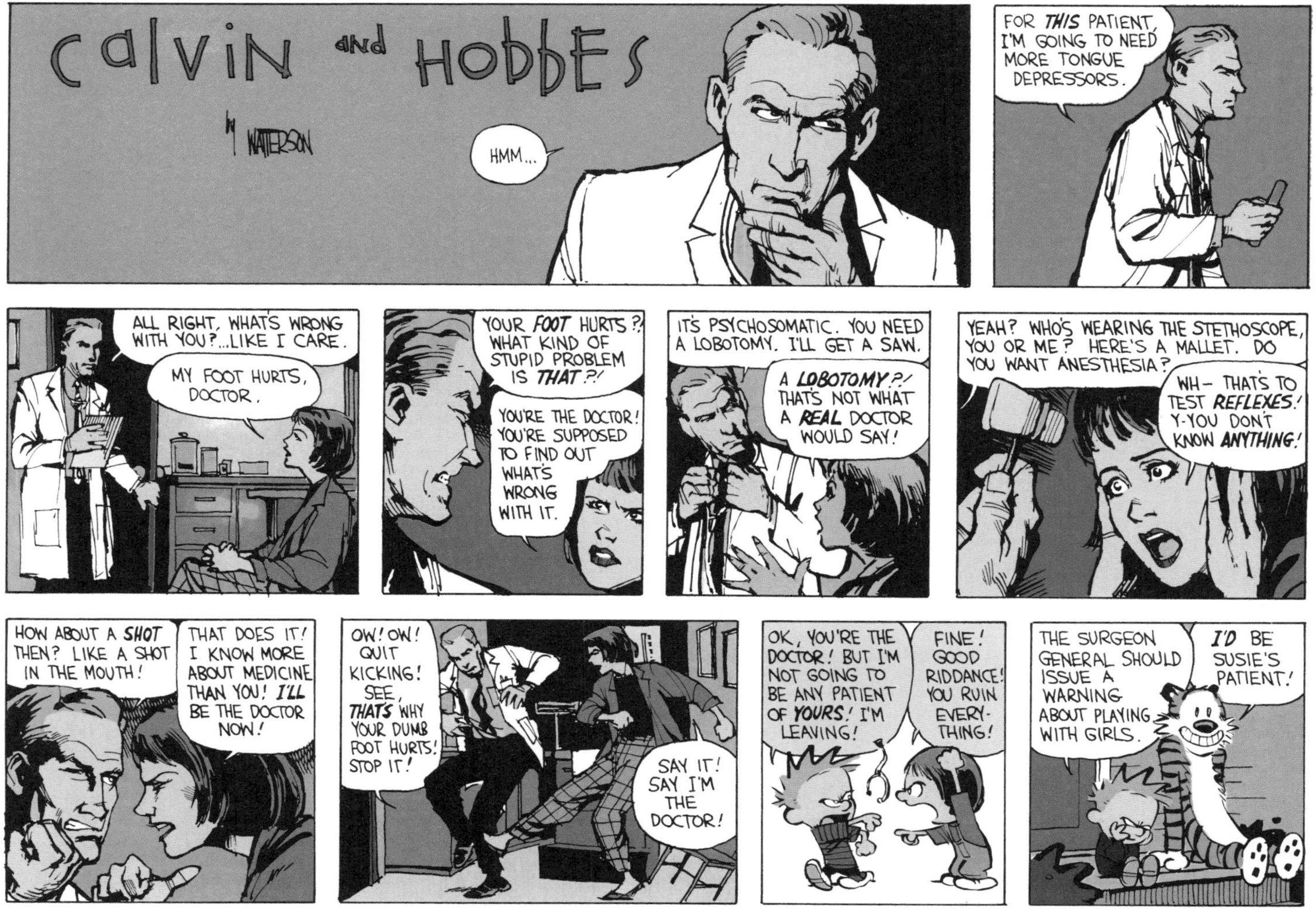
Calvin and HOBBES
by WATTERSON
HMM...
FOR THIS PATIENT, I'M GOING TO NEED MORE TONGUE DEPRESSORS.
ALL RIGHT, WHAT'S WRONG WITH YOU?...LIKE I CARE.
MY FOOT HURTS, DOCTOR.
YOUR FOOT HURTS?! WHAT KIND OF STUPID PROBLEM IS THAT?!
YOU'RE THE DOCTOR! YOU'RE SUPPOSED TO FIND OUT WHAT'S WRONG WITH IT.
IT'S PSYCHOSOMATIC. YOU NEED A LOBOTOMY. I'LL GET A SAW.
A LOBOTOMY?! THAT'S NOT WHAT A REAL DOCTOR WOULD SAY!
YEAH? WHO'S WEARING THE STETHOSCOPE, YOU OR ME? HERE'S A MALLET. DO YOU WANT ANESTHESIA?
WH– THAT'S TO TEST REFLEXES! Y-YOU DON'T KNOW ANYTHING!
HOW ABOUT A SHOT THEN? LIKE A SHOT IN THE MOUTH!
THAT DOES IT! I KNOW MORE ABOUT MEDICINE THAN YOU! I'LL BE THE DOCTOR NOW!
OW! OW! QUIT KICKING! SEE, THAT'S WHY YOUR DUMB FOOT HURTS! STOP IT!
SAY IT! SAY I'M THE DOCTOR!
OK, YOU'RE THE DOCTOR! BUT I'M NOT GOING TO BE ANY PATIENT OF YOURS! I'M LEAVING!
FINE! GOOD RIDDANCE! YOU RUIN EVERY-THING!
THE SURGEON GENERAL SHOULD ISSUE A WARNING ABOUT PLAYING WITH GIRLS.
I'D BE SUSIE'S PATIENT!

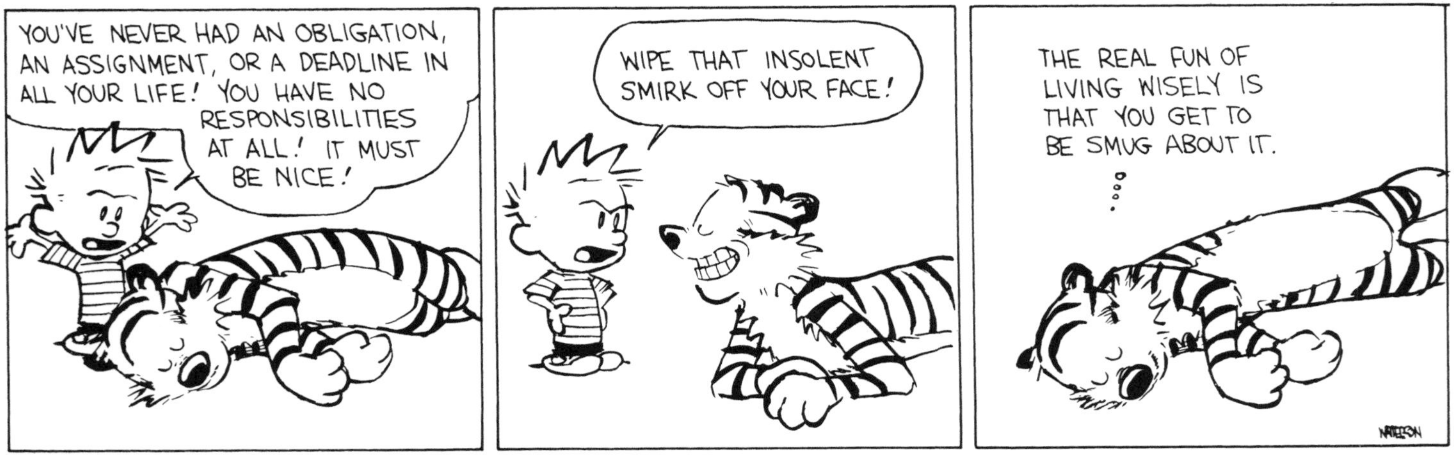
YOU'VE NEVER HAD AN OBLIGATION, AN ASSIGNMENT, OR A DEADLINE IN ALL YOUR LIFE! YOU HAVE NO RESPONSIBILITIES AT ALL! IT MUST BE NICE!
WIPE THAT INSOLENT SMIRK OFF YOUR FACE!
THE REAL FUN OF LIVING WISELY IS THAT YOU GET TO BE SMUG ABOUT IT.
WATTERSON

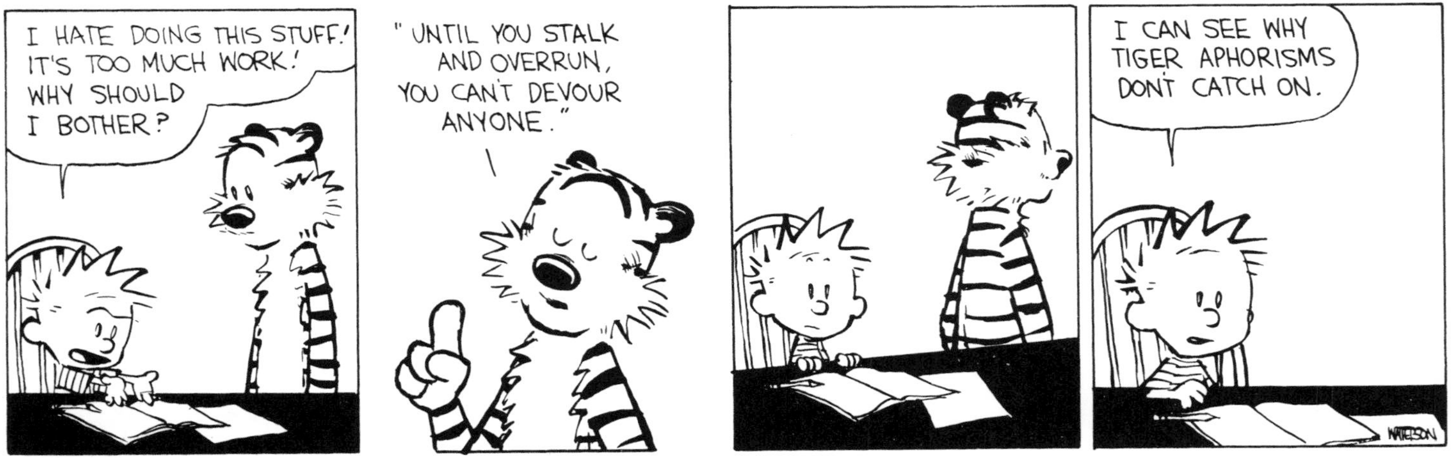
I HATE DOING THIS STUFF! IT'S TOO MUCH WORK! WHY SHOULD I BOTHER?
"UNTIL YOU STALK AND OVERRUN, YOU CAN'T DEVOUR ANYONE."
I CAN SEE WHY TIGER APHORISMS DON'T CATCH ON.
WATTERSON

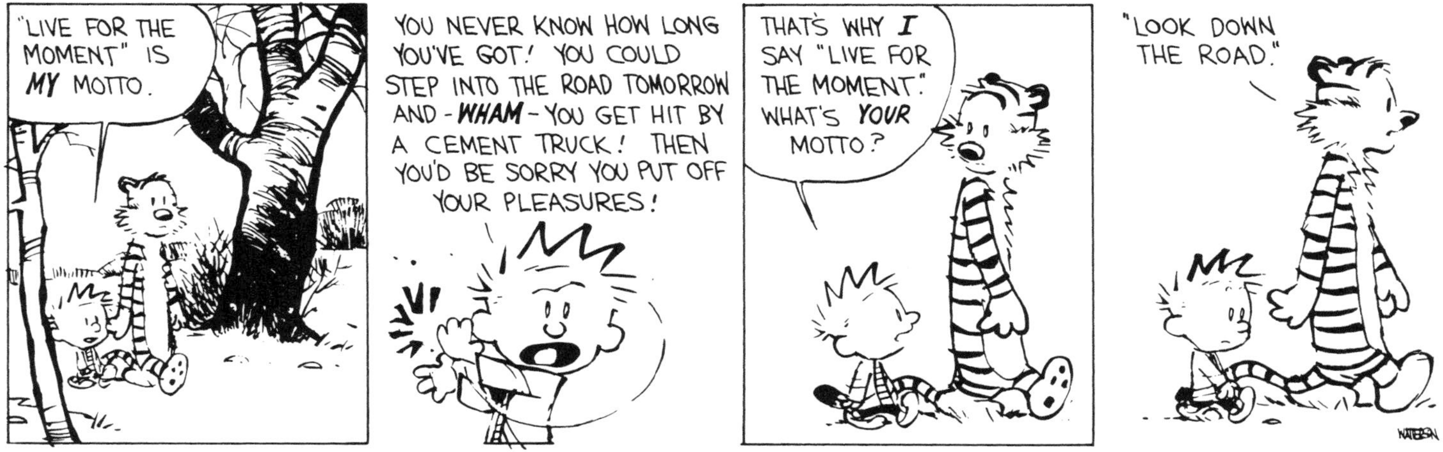
"LIVE FOR THE MOMENT" IS MY MOTTO.
YOU NEVER KNOW HOW LONG YOU'VE GOT! YOU COULD STEP INTO THE ROAD TOMORROW AND - WHAM - YOU GET HIT BY A CEMENT TRUCK! THEN YOU'D BE SORRY YOU PUT OFF YOUR PLEASURES!
THAT'S WHY I SAY "LIVE FOR THE MOMENT." WHAT'S YOUR MOTTO?
"LOOK DOWN THE ROAD."

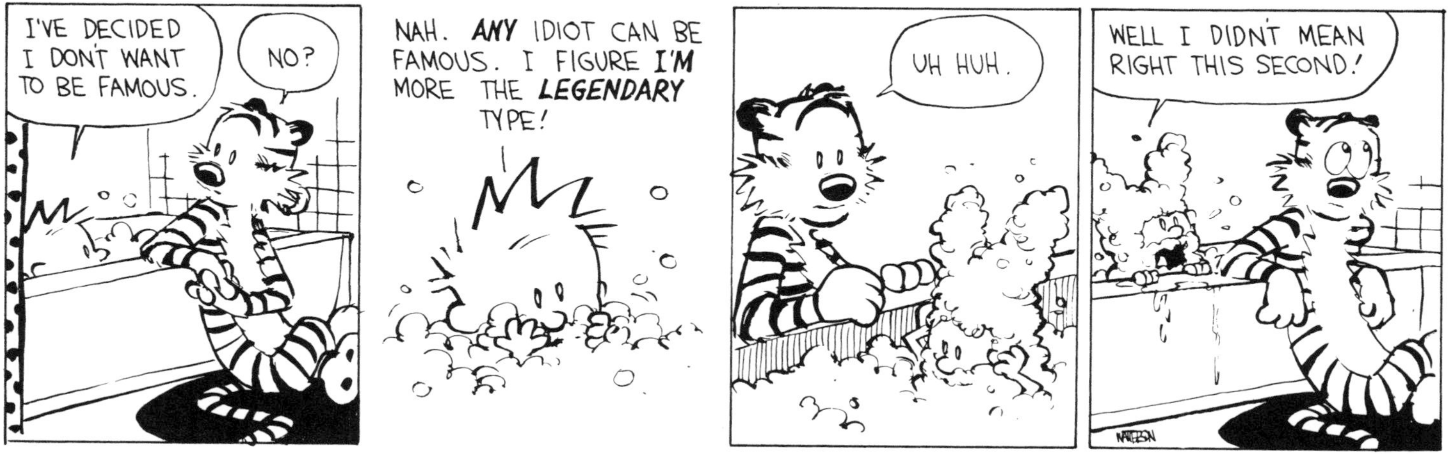
I'VE DECIDED I DON'T WANT TO BE FAMOUS.
NO?
NAH. ANY IDIOT CAN BE FAMOUS. I FIGURE I'M MORE THE LEGENDARY TYPE!
UH HUH.
WELL I DIDN'T MEAN RIGHT THIS SECOND!

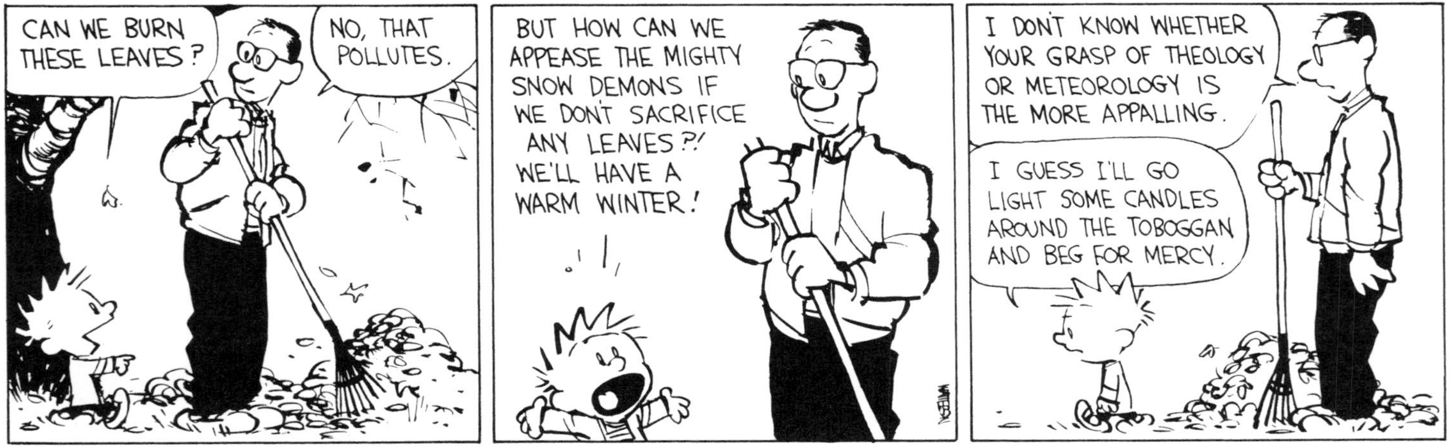
CAN WE BURN THESE LEAVES?
NO, THAT POLLUTES.
BUT HOW CAN WE APPEASE THE MIGHTY SNOW DEMONS IF WE DON'T SACRIFICE ANY LEAVES?! WE'LL HAVE A WARM WINTER!
I DON'T KNOW WHETHER YOUR GRASP OF THEOLOGY OR METEOROLOGY IS THE MORE APPALLING.
I GUESS I'LL GO LIGHT SOME CANDLES AROUND THE TOBOGGAN AND BEG FOR MERCY.

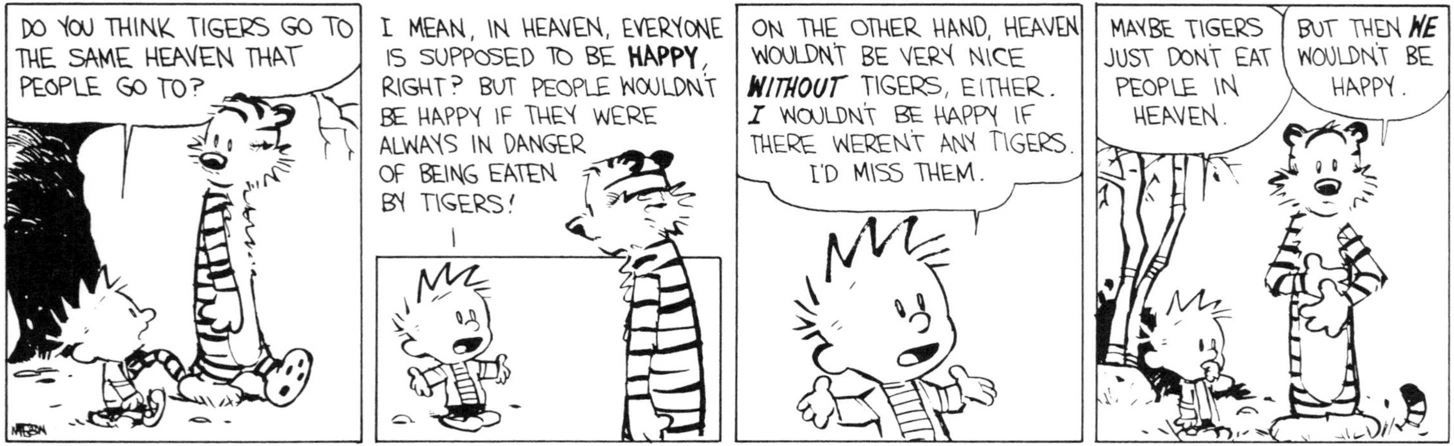
DO YOU THINK TIGERS GO TO THE SAME HEAVEN THAT PEOPLE GO TO?
I MEAN, IN HEAVEN, EVERYONE IS SUPPOSED TO BE HAPPY, RIGHT? BUT PEOPLE WOULDN'T BE HAPPY IF THEY WERE ALWAYS IN DANGER OF BEING EATEN BY TIGERS!
ON THE OTHER HAND, HEAVEN WOULDN'T BE VERY NICE WITHOUT TIGERS, EITHER. I WOULDN'T BE HAPPY IF THERE WEREN'T ANY TIGERS. I'D MISS THEM.
MAYBE TIGERS JUST DON'T EAT PEOPLE IN HEAVEN.
BUT THEN WE WOULDN'T BE HAPPY.

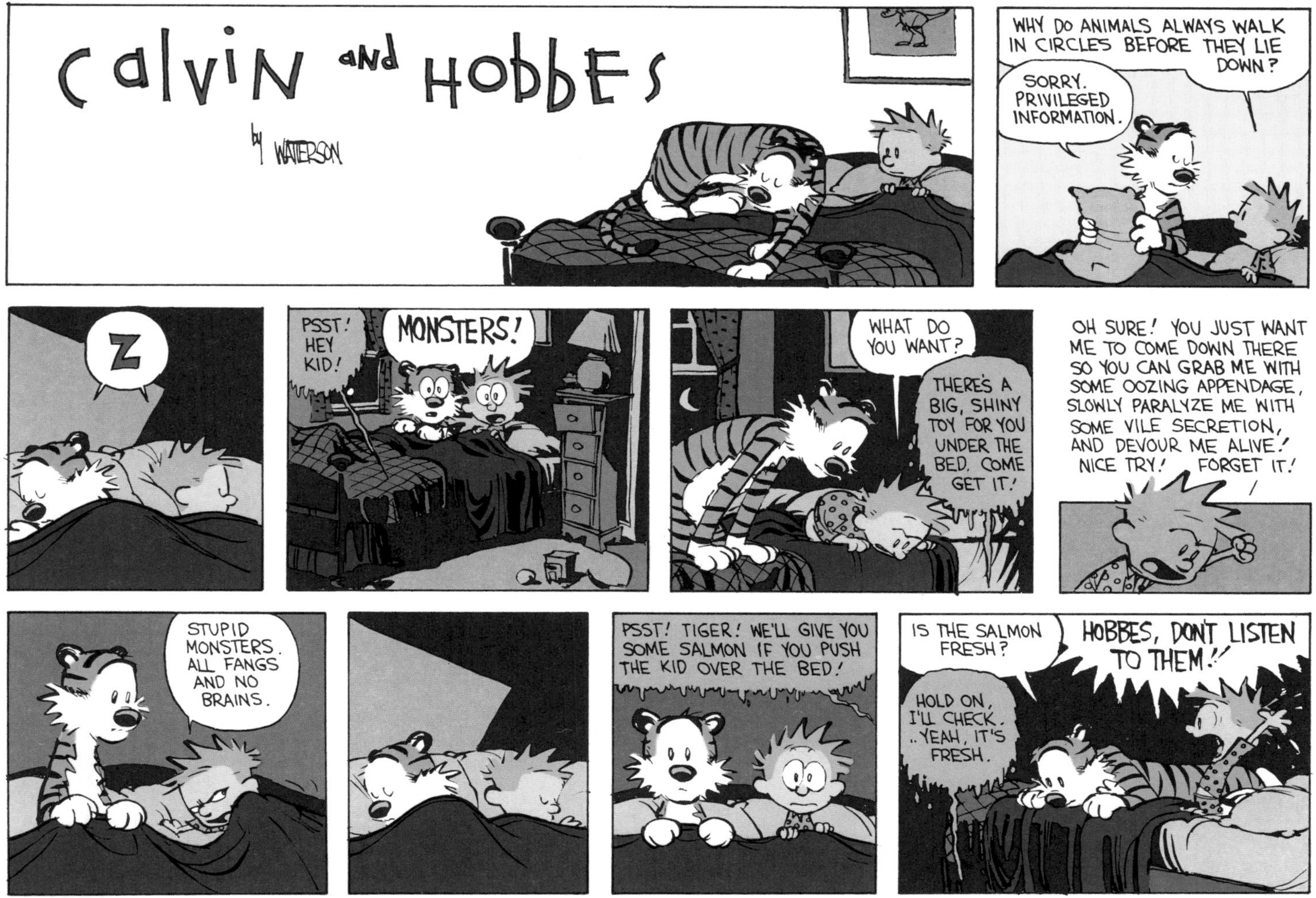
Calvin and Hobbes
by WATTERSON
WHY DO ANIMALS ALWAYS WALK IN CIRCLES BEFORE THEY LIE DOWN?
SORRY. PRIVILEGED INFORMATION.
Z
PSST! HEY KID!
MONSTERS!
WHAT DO YOU WANT?
THERE'S A BIG, SHINY TOY FOR YOU UNDER THE BED. COME GET IT!
OH SURE! YOU JUST WANT ME TO COME DOWN THERE SO YOU CAN GRAB ME WITH SOME OOZING APPENDAGE, SLOWLY PARALYZE ME WITH SOME VILE SECRETION, AND DEVOUR ME ALIVE! NICE TRY! FORGET IT!
STUPID MONSTERS. ALL FANGS AND NO BRAINS.
PSST! TIGER! WE'LL GIVE YOU SOME SALMON IF YOU PUSH THE KID OVER THE BED!
IS THE SALMON FRESH?
HOLD ON, I'LL CHECK. ..YEAH, IT'S FRESH.
HOBBES, DON'T LISTEN TO THEM!!

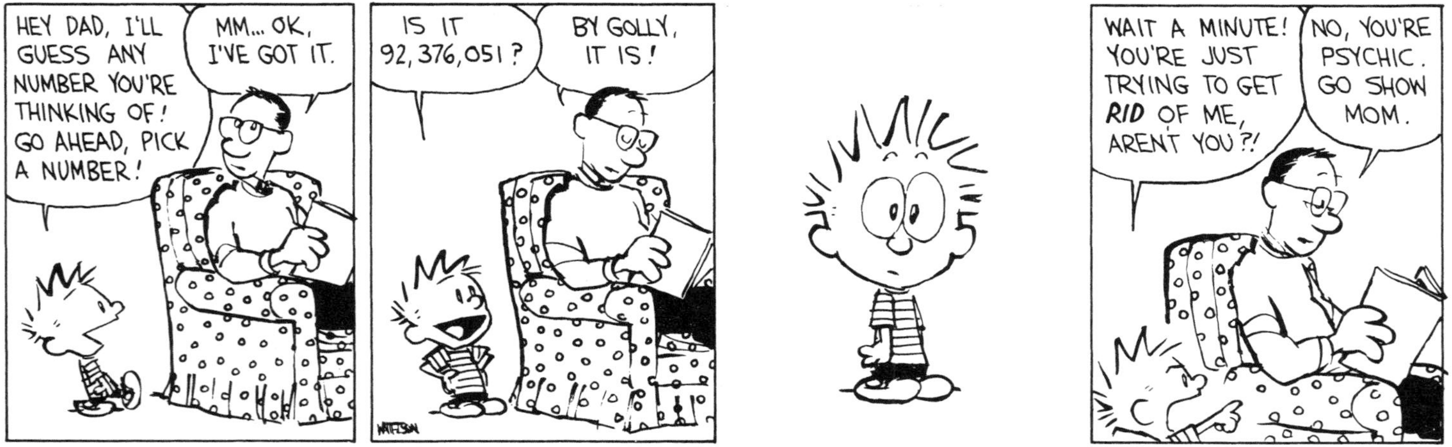
HEY DAD, I'LL GUESS ANY NUMBER YOU'RE THINKING OF! GO AHEAD, PICK A NUMBER!
MM... OK, I'VE GOT IT.
IS IT 92,376,051?
BY GOLLY, IT IS!
WAIT A MINUTE! YOU'RE JUST TRYING TO GET **RID** OF ME, AREN'T YOU?!
NO, YOU'RE PSYCHIC. GO SHOW MOM.

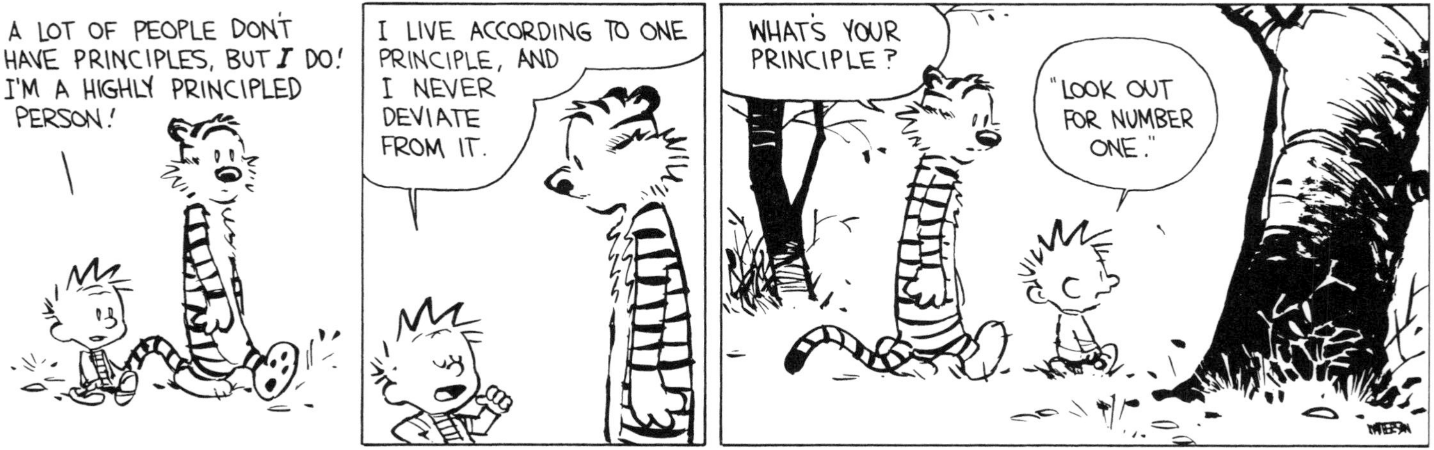
A LOT OF PEOPLE DON'T HAVE PRINCIPLES, BUT ***I*** DO! I'M A HIGHLY PRINCIPLED PERSON!
I LIVE ACCORDING TO ONE PRINCIPLE, AND I NEVER DEVIATE FROM IT.
WHAT'S YOUR PRINCIPLE?
"LOOK OUT FOR NUMBER ONE."

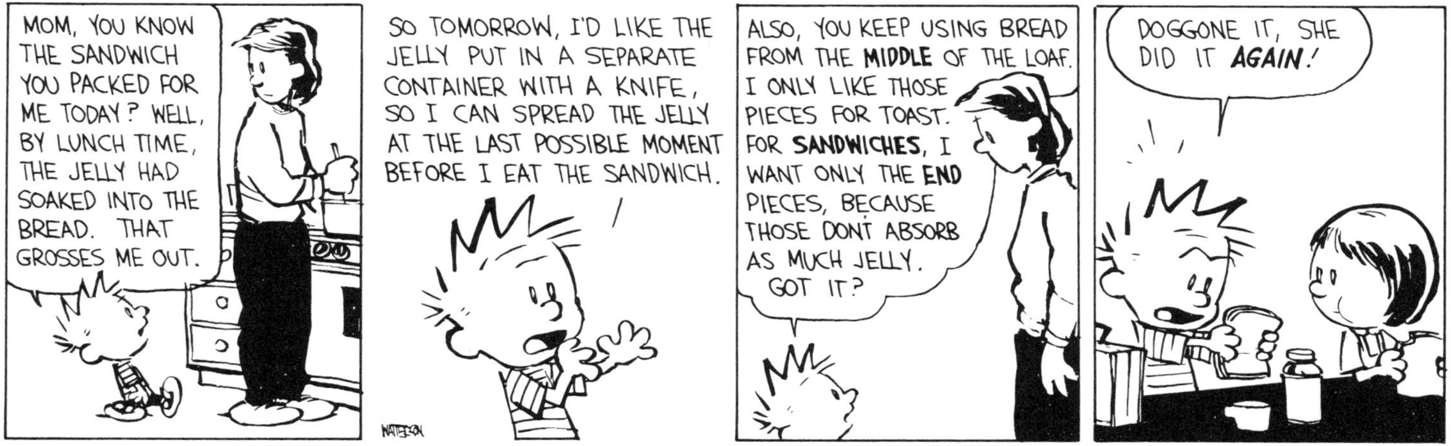
MOM, YOU KNOW THE SANDWICH YOU PACKED FOR ME TODAY? WELL, BY LUNCH TIME, THE JELLY HAD SOAKED INTO THE BREAD. THAT GROSSES ME OUT.
SO TOMORROW, I'D LIKE THE JELLY PUT IN A SEPARATE CONTAINER WITH A KNIFE, SO I CAN SPREAD THE JELLY AT THE LAST POSSIBLE MOMENT BEFORE I EAT THE SANDWICH.
ALSO, YOU KEEP USING BREAD FROM THE **MIDDLE** OF THE LOAF. I ONLY LIKE THOSE PIECES FOR TOAST. FOR **SANDWICHES**, I WANT ONLY THE **END** PIECES, BECAUSE THOSE DON'T ABSORB AS MUCH JELLY. GOT IT?
DOGGONE IT, SHE DID IT **AGAIN**!

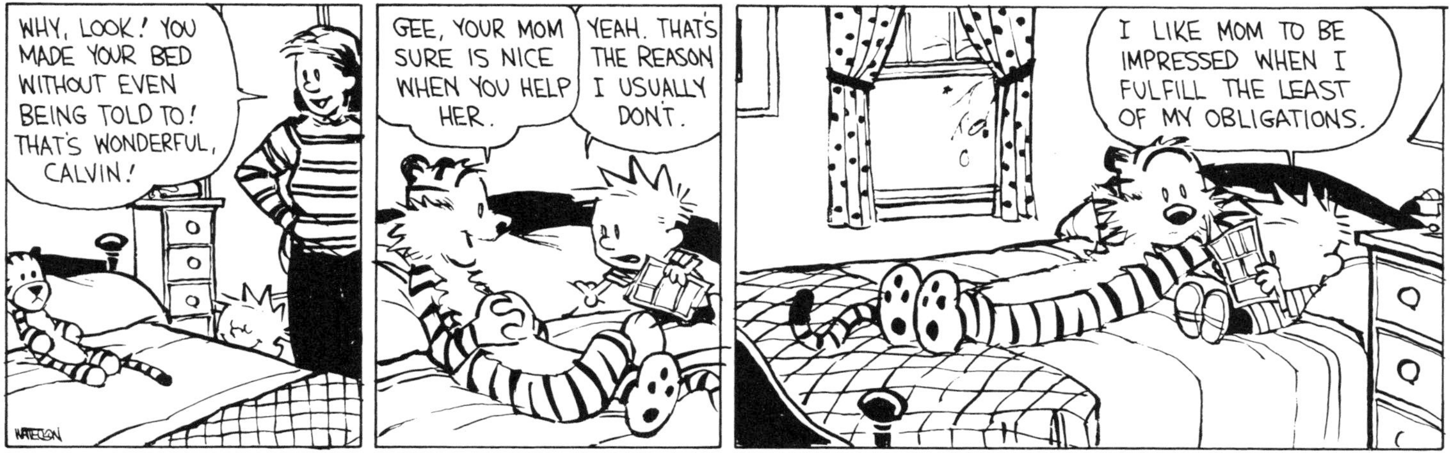
WHY, LOOK! YOU MADE YOUR BED WITHOUT EVEN BEING TOLD TO! THAT'S WONDERFUL, CALVIN!
GEE, YOUR MOM SURE IS NICE WHEN YOU HELP HER.
YEAH. THAT'S THE REASON I USUALLY DON'T.
I LIKE MOM TO BE IMPRESSED WHEN I FULFILL THE LEAST OF MY OBLIGATIONS.

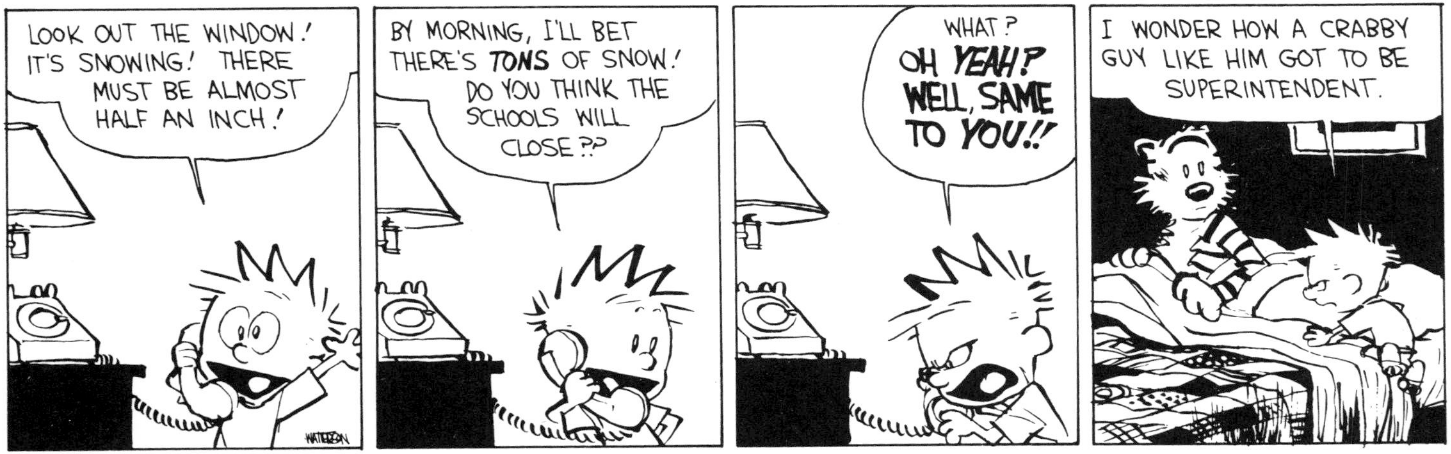
LOOK OUT THE WINDOW! IT'S SNOWING! THERE MUST BE ALMOST HALF AN INCH!
BY MORNING, I'LL BET THERE'S TONS OF SNOW! DO YOU THINK THE SCHOOLS WILL CLOSE?!?
WHAT? OH YEAH? WELL, SAME TO YOU!!
I WONDER HOW A CRABBY GUY LIKE HIM GOT TO BE SUPERINTENDENT.

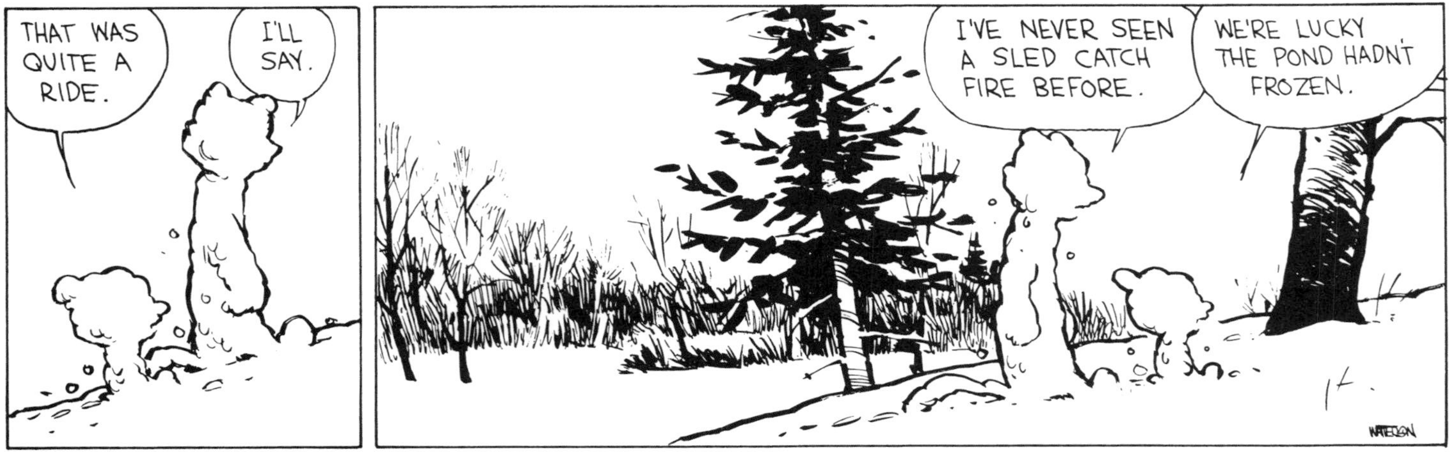
THAT WAS QUITE A RIDE.
I'LL SAY.
I'VE NEVER SEEN A SLED CATCH FIRE BEFORE.
WE'RE LUCKY THE POND HADN'T FROZEN.

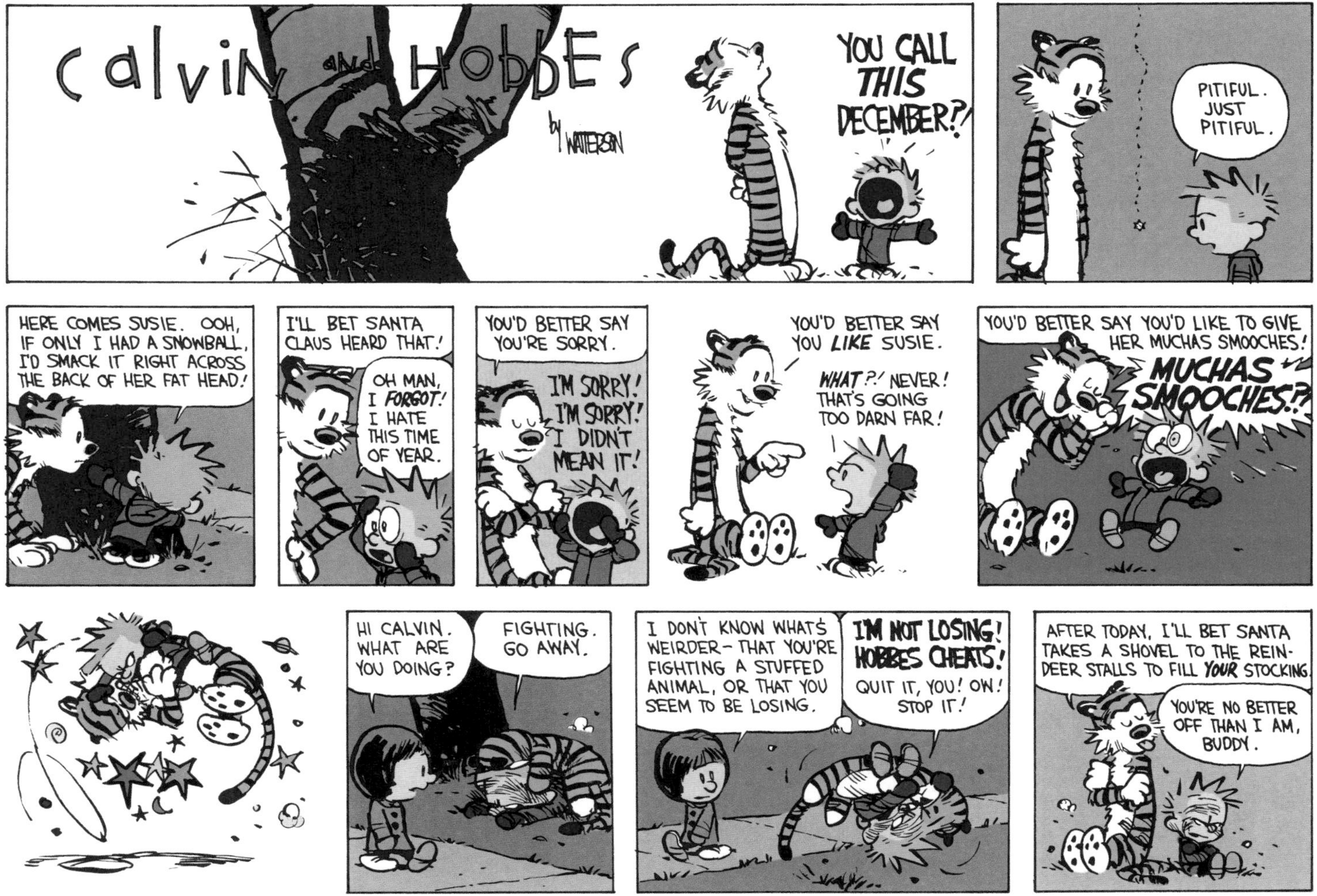
Calvin and HobbEs
by WATTERSON
YOU CALL THIS DECEMBER?!
PITIFUL. JUST PITIFUL.
HERE COMES SUSIE. OOH, IF ONLY I HAD A SNOWBALL, I'D SMACK IT RIGHT ACROSS THE BACK OF HER FAT HEAD!
I'LL BET SANTA CLAUS HEARD THAT!
OH MAN, I FORGOT! I HATE THIS TIME OF YEAR.
YOU'D BETTER SAY YOU'RE SORRY.
I'M SORRY! I'M SORRY! I DIDN'T MEAN IT!
YOU'D BETTER SAY YOU LIKE SUSIE.
WHAT?! NEVER! THAT'S GOING TOO DARN FAR!
YOU'D BETTER SAY YOU'D LIKE TO GIVE HER MUCHAS SMOOCHES!
MUCHAS SMOOCHES?!
HI CALVIN. WHAT ARE YOU DOING?
FIGHTING. GO AWAY.
I DON'T KNOW WHAT'S WEIRDER– THAT YOU'RE FIGHTING A STUFFED ANIMAL, OR THAT YOU SEEM TO BE LOSING.
I'M NOT LOSING! HOBBES CHEATS!
QUIT IT, YOU! OW! STOP IT!
AFTER TODAY, I'LL BET SANTA TAKES A SHOVEL TO THE REINDEER STALLS TO FILL YOUR STOCKING.
YOU'RE NO BETTER OFF THAN I AM, BUDDY.

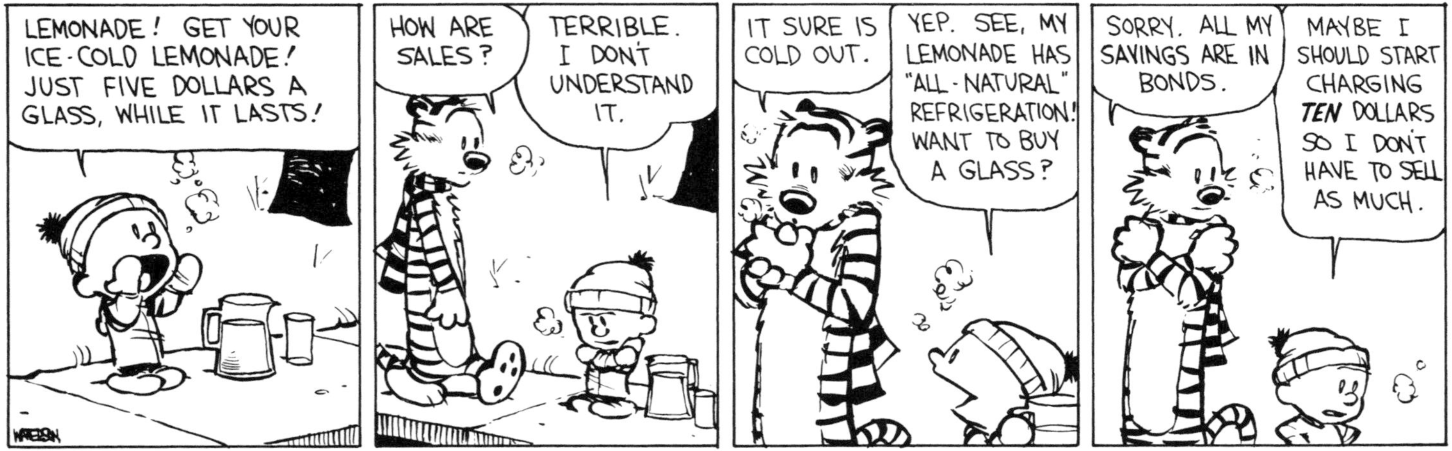
LEMONADE! GET YOUR ICE-COLD LEMONADE! JUST FIVE DOLLARS A GLASS, WHILE IT LASTS!
HOW ARE SALES?
TERRIBLE. I DON'T UNDERSTAND IT.
IT SURE IS COLD OUT.
YEP. SEE, MY LEMONADE HAS "ALL-NATURAL" REFRIGERATION! WANT TO BUY A GLASS?
SORRY. ALL MY SAVINGS ARE IN BONDS.
MAYBE I SHOULD START CHARGING TEN DOLLARS SO I DON'T HAVE TO SELL AS MUCH.

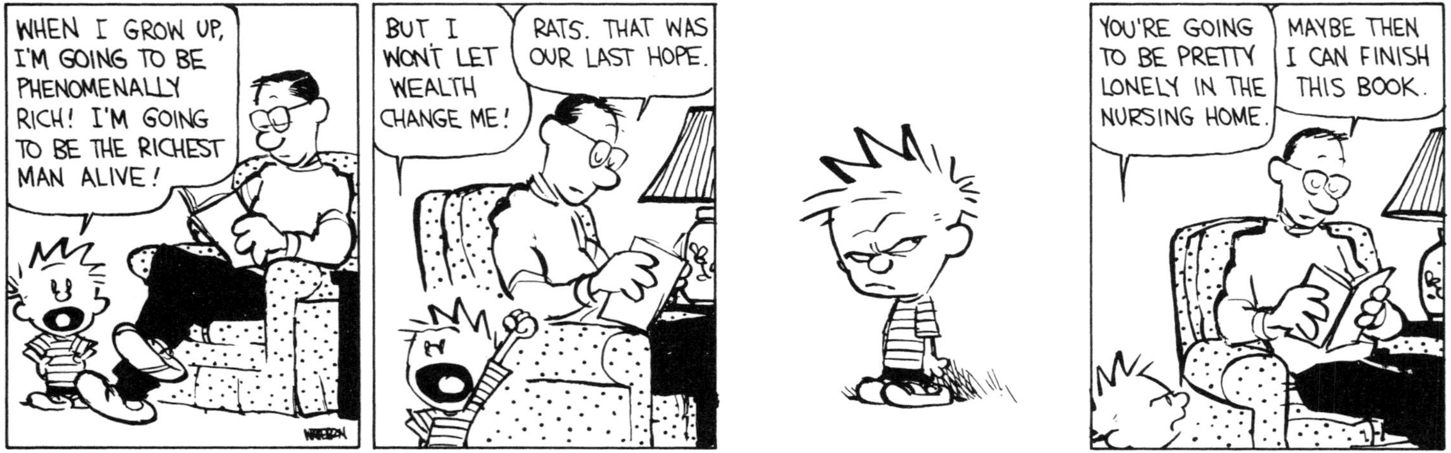
WHEN I GROW UP, I'M GOING TO BE PHENOMENALLY RICH! I'M GOING TO BE THE RICHEST MAN ALIVE!
BUT I WON'T LET WEALTH CHANGE ME!
RATS. THAT WAS OUR LAST HOPE.
YOU'RE GOING TO BE PRETTY LONELY IN THE NURSING HOME.
MAYBE THEN I CAN FINISH THIS BOOK.

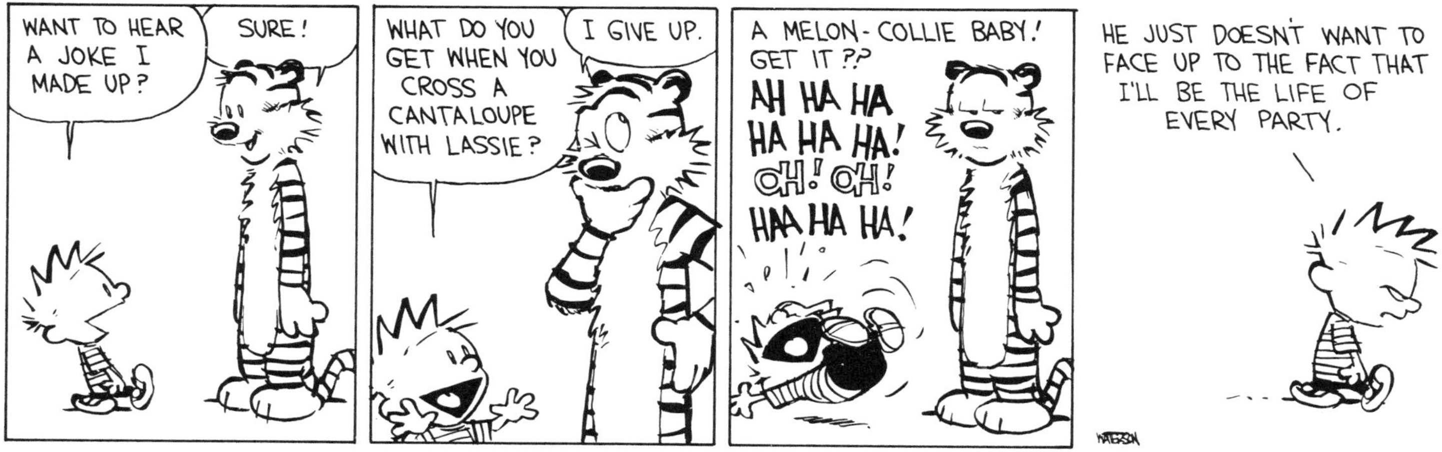
WANT TO HEAR A JOKE I MADE UP?
SURE!
WHAT DO YOU GET WHEN YOU CROSS A CANTALOUPE WITH LASSIE?
I GIVE UP.
A MELON-COLLIE BABY! GET IT?!?
AH HA HA HA HA HA! OH! OH! HAA HA HA!
HE JUST DOESN'T WANT TO FACE UP TO THE FACT THAT I'LL BE THE LIFE OF EVERY PARTY.

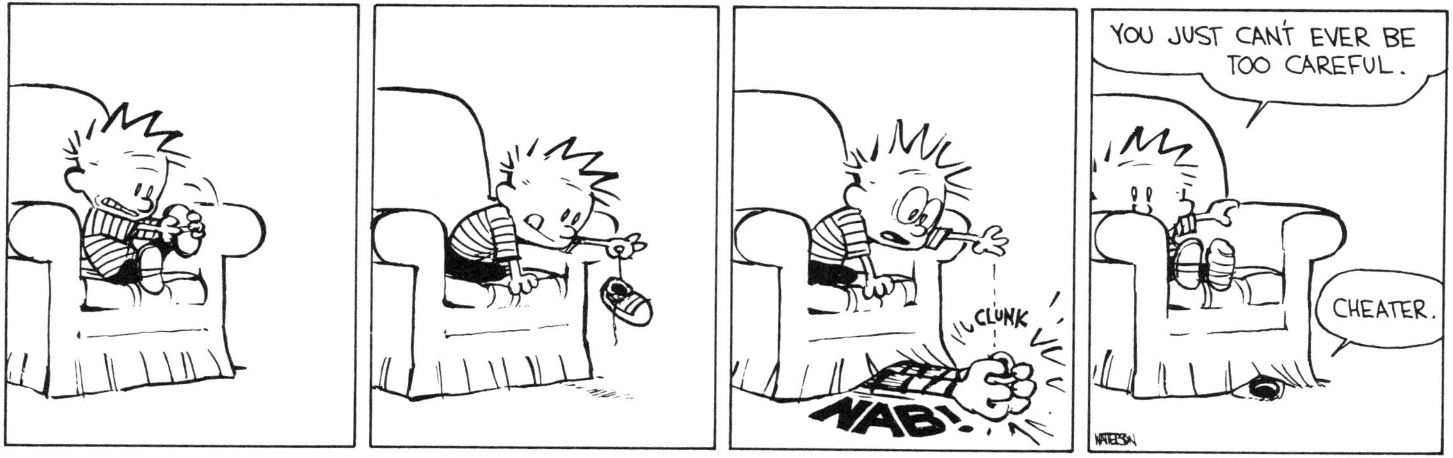
CLUNK
NAB!
YOU JUST CAN'T EVER BE TOO CAREFUL.
CHEATER.

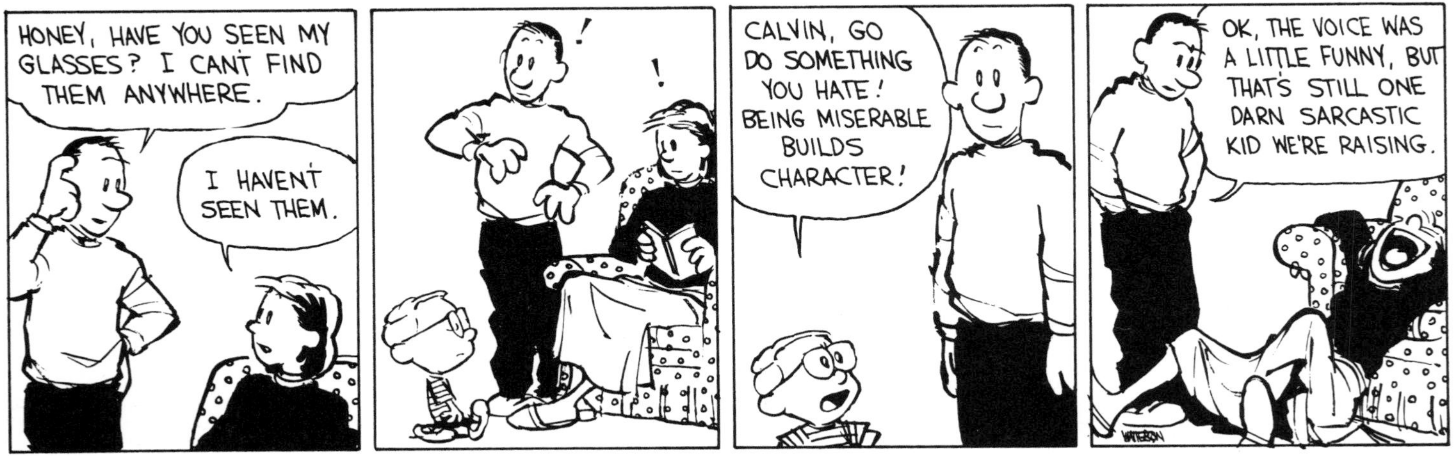

HONEY, HAVE YOU SEEN MY GLASSES? I CAN'T FIND THEM ANYWHERE.
I HAVEN'T SEEN THEM.
!
!
CALVIN, GO DO SOMETHING YOU HATE! BEING MISERABLE BUILDS CHARACTER!
OK, THE VOICE WAS A LITTLE FUNNY, BUT THAT'S STILL ONE DARN SARCASTIC KID WE'RE RAISING.

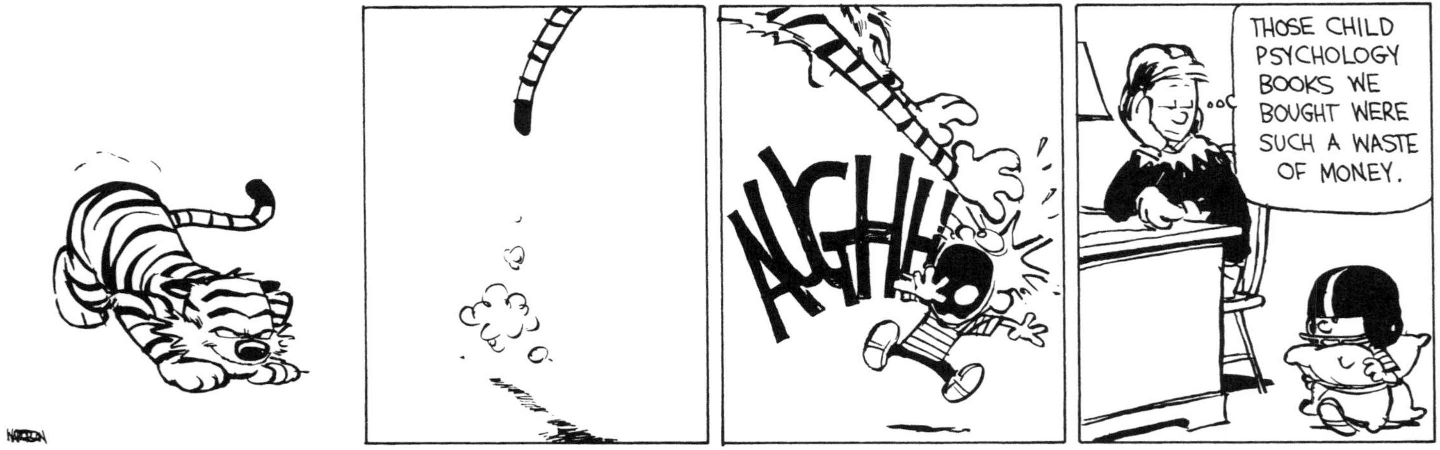

AUGHH!
THOSE CHILD PSYCHOLOGY BOOKS WE BOUGHT WERE SUCH A WASTE OF MONEY.

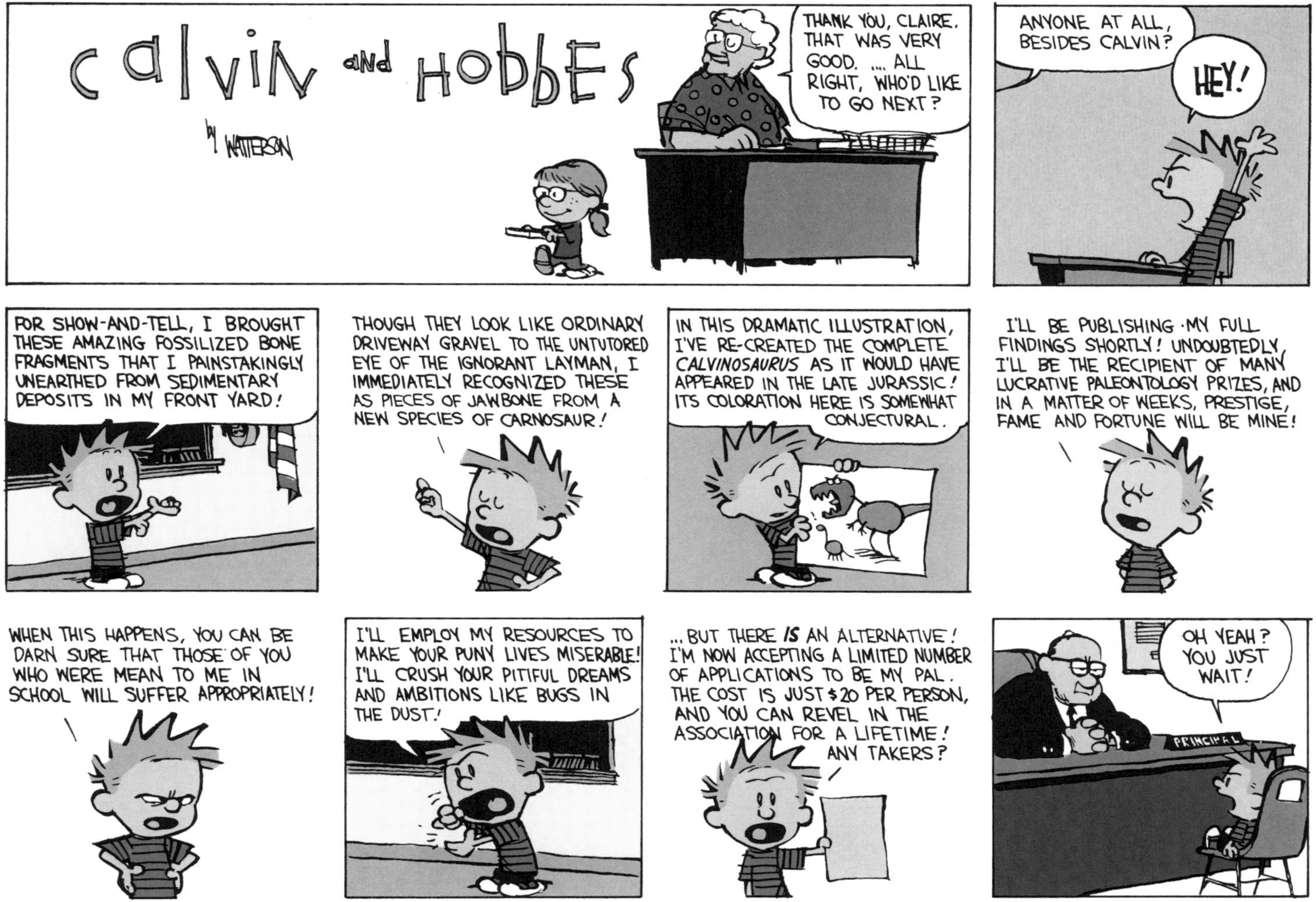

Calvin and Hobbes
by Watterson
THANK YOU, CLAIRE. THAT WAS VERY GOOD. .... ALL RIGHT, WHO'D LIKE TO GO NEXT?
ANYONE AT ALL, BESIDES CALVIN?
HEY!
FOR SHOW-AND-TELL, I BROUGHT THESE AMAZING FOSSILIZED BONE FRAGMENTS THAT I PAINSTAKINGLY UNEARTHED FROM SEDIMENTARY DEPOSITS IN MY FRONT YARD!
THOUGH THEY LOOK LIKE ORDINARY DRIVEWAY GRAVEL TO THE UNTUTORED EYE OF THE IGNORANT LAYMAN, I IMMEDIATELY RECOGNIZED THESE AS PIECES OF JAWBONE FROM A NEW SPECIES OF CARNOSAUR!
IN THIS DRAMATIC ILLUSTRATION, I'VE RE-CREATED THE COMPLETE *CALVINOSAURUS* AS IT WOULD HAVE APPEARED IN THE LATE JURASSIC! ITS COLORATION HERE IS SOMEWHAT CONJECTURAL.
I'LL BE PUBLISHING MY FULL FINDINGS SHORTLY! UNDOUBTEDLY, I'LL BE THE RECIPIENT OF MANY LUCRATIVE PALEONTOLOGY PRIZES, AND IN A MATTER OF WEEKS, PRESTIGE, FAME AND FORTUNE WILL BE MINE!
WHEN THIS HAPPENS, YOU CAN BE DARN SURE THAT THOSE OF YOU WHO WERE MEAN TO ME IN SCHOOL WILL SUFFER APPROPRIATELY!
I'LL EMPLOY MY RESOURCES TO MAKE YOUR PUNY LIVES MISERABLE! I'LL CRUSH YOUR PITIFUL DREAMS AND AMBITIONS LIKE BUGS IN THE DUST!
...BUT THERE ***IS*** AN ALTERNATIVE! I'M NOW ACCEPTING A LIMITED NUMBER OF APPLICATIONS TO BE MY PAL. THE COST IS JUST $20 PER PERSON, AND YOU CAN REVEL IN THE ASSOCIATION FOR A LIFETIME! ANY TAKERS?
PRINCIPAL
OH YEAH? YOU JUST WAIT!

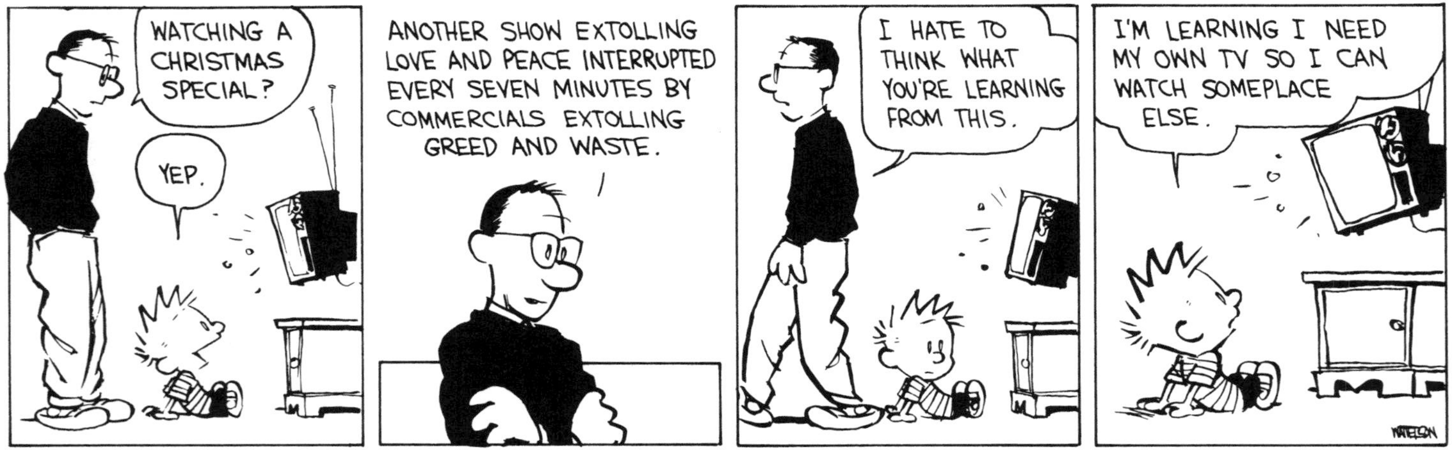
WATCHING A CHRISTMAS SPECIAL?
YEP.
ANOTHER SHOW EXTOLLING LOVE AND PEACE INTERRUPTED EVERY SEVEN MINUTES BY COMMERCIALS EXTOLLING GREED AND WASTE.
I HATE TO THINK WHAT YOU'RE LEARNING FROM THIS.
I'M LEARNING I NEED MY OWN TV SO I CAN WATCH SOMEPLACE ELSE.
WATTERSON

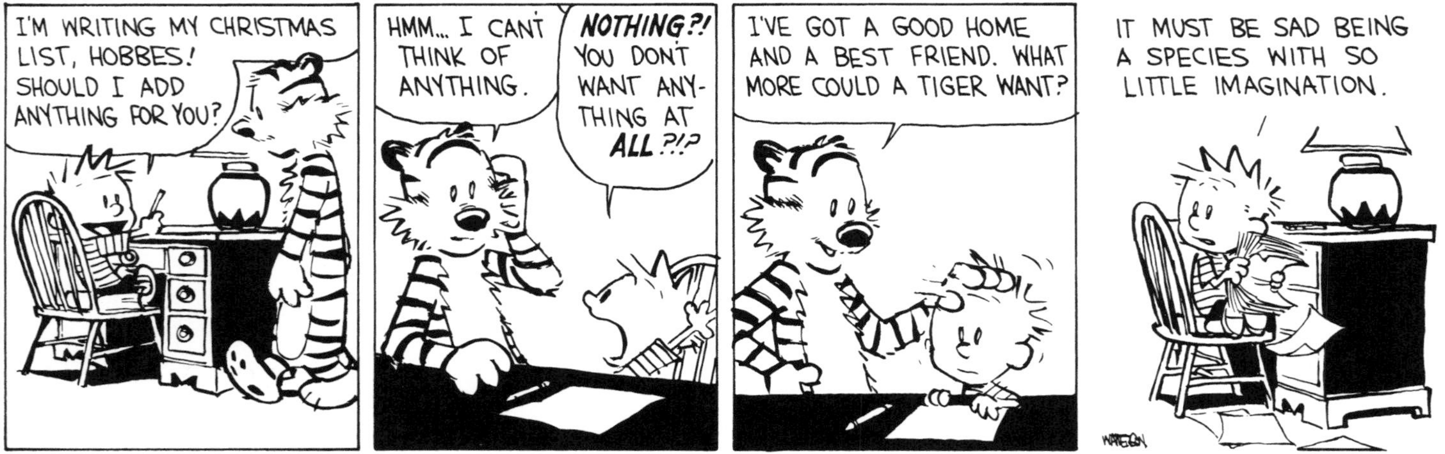
I'M WRITING MY CHRISTMAS LIST, HOBBES! SHOULD I ADD ANYTHING FOR YOU?
HMM... I CAN'T THINK OF ANYTHING.
NOTHING?! YOU DON'T WANT ANYTHING AT ALL?!?
I'VE GOT A GOOD HOME AND A BEST FRIEND. WHAT MORE COULD A TIGER WANT?
IT MUST BE SAD BEING A SPECIES WITH SO LITTLE IMAGINATION.
WATTERSON

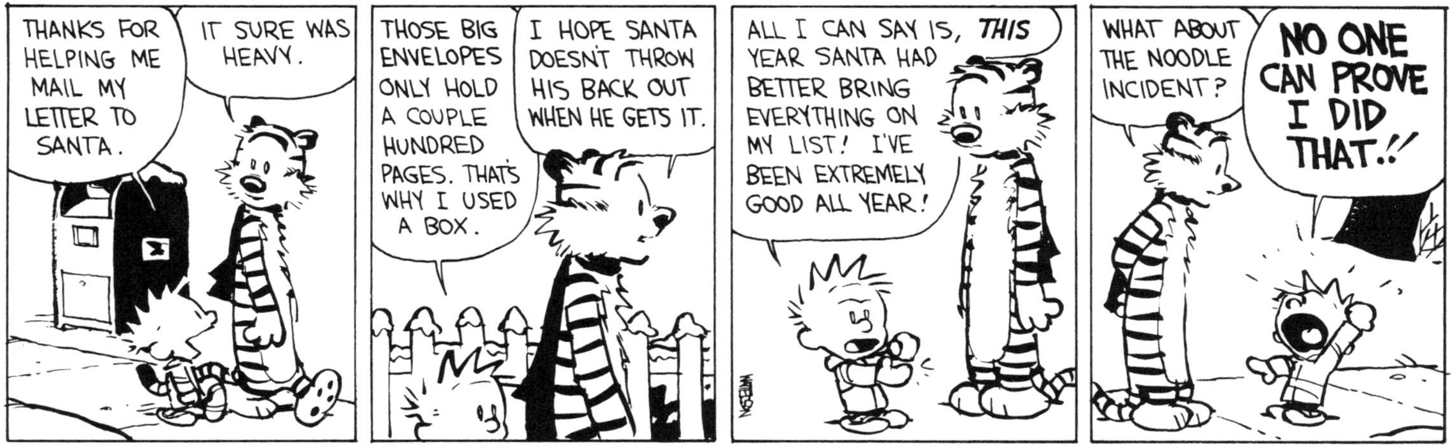
THANKS FOR HELPING ME MAIL MY LETTER TO SANTA.
IT SURE WAS HEAVY.
THOSE BIG ENVELOPES ONLY HOLD A COUPLE HUNDRED PAGES. THAT'S WHY I USED A BOX.
I HOPE SANTA DOESN'T THROW HIS BACK OUT WHEN HE GETS IT.
ALL I CAN SAY IS, THIS YEAR SANTA HAD BETTER BRING EVERYTHING ON MY LIST! I'VE BEEN EXTREMELY GOOD ALL YEAR!
WATERSON
WHAT ABOUT THE NOODLE INCIDENT?
NO ONE CAN PROVE I DID THAT!!

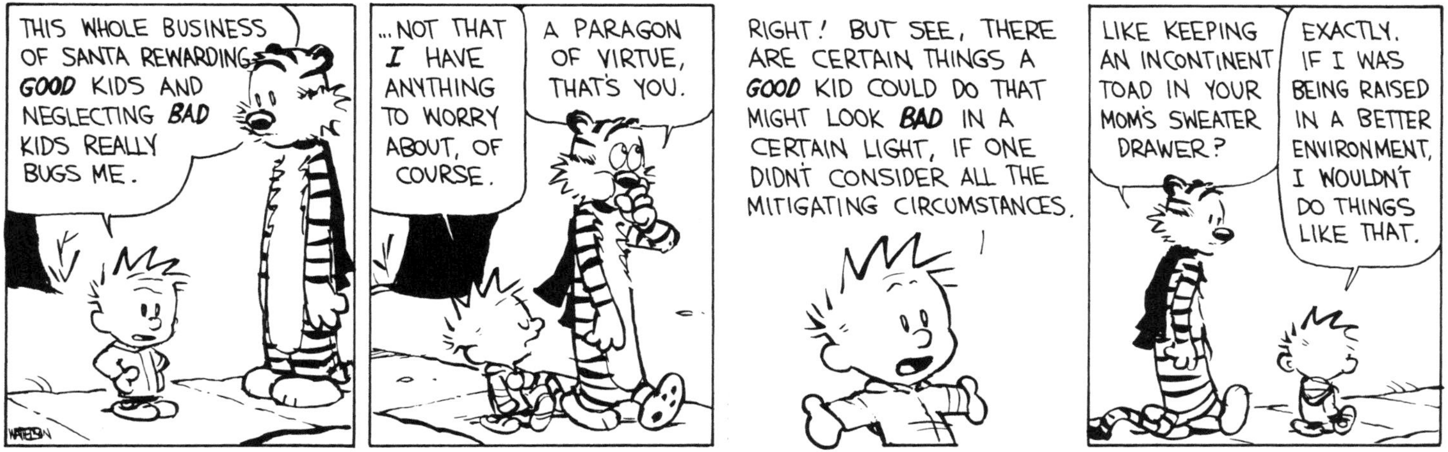
THIS WHOLE BUSINESS OF SANTA REWARDING GOOD KIDS AND NEGLECTING BAD KIDS REALLY BUGS ME.
WATERSON
...NOT THAT I HAVE ANYTHING TO WORRY ABOUT, OF COURSE.
A PARAGON OF VIRTUE, THAT'S YOU.
RIGHT! BUT SEE, THERE ARE CERTAIN THINGS A GOOD KID COULD DO THAT MIGHT LOOK BAD IN A CERTAIN LIGHT, IF ONE DIDN'T CONSIDER ALL THE MITIGATING CIRCUMSTANCES.
LIKE KEEPING AN INCONTINENT TOAD IN YOUR MOM'S SWEATER DRAWER?
EXACTLY. IF I WAS BEING RAISED IN A BETTER ENVIRONMENT, I WOULDN'T DO THINGS LIKE THAT.

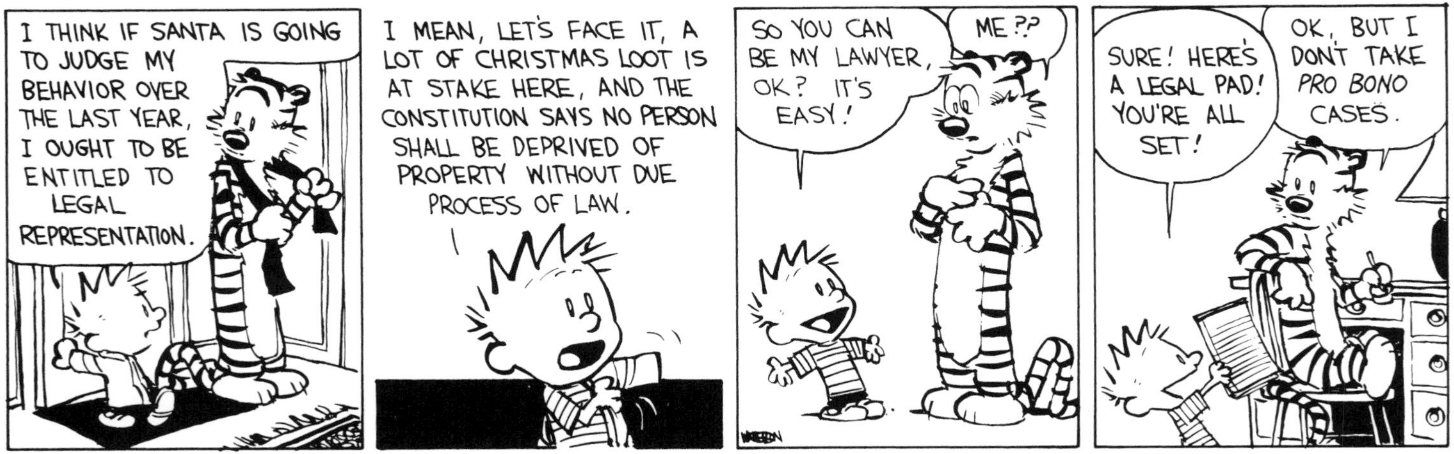
I THINK IF SANTA IS GOING TO JUDGE MY BEHAVIOR OVER THE LAST YEAR, I OUGHT TO BE ENTITLED TO LEGAL REPRESENTATION.
I MEAN, LET'S FACE IT, A LOT OF CHRISTMAS LOOT IS AT STAKE HERE, AND THE CONSTITUTION SAYS NO PERSON SHALL BE DEPRIVED OF PROPERTY WITHOUT DUE PROCESS OF LAW.
SO YOU CAN BE MY LAWYER, OK? IT'S EASY!
ME??
SURE! HERE'S A LEGAL PAD! YOU'RE ALL SET!
OK, BUT I DON'T TAKE *PRO BONO* CASES.

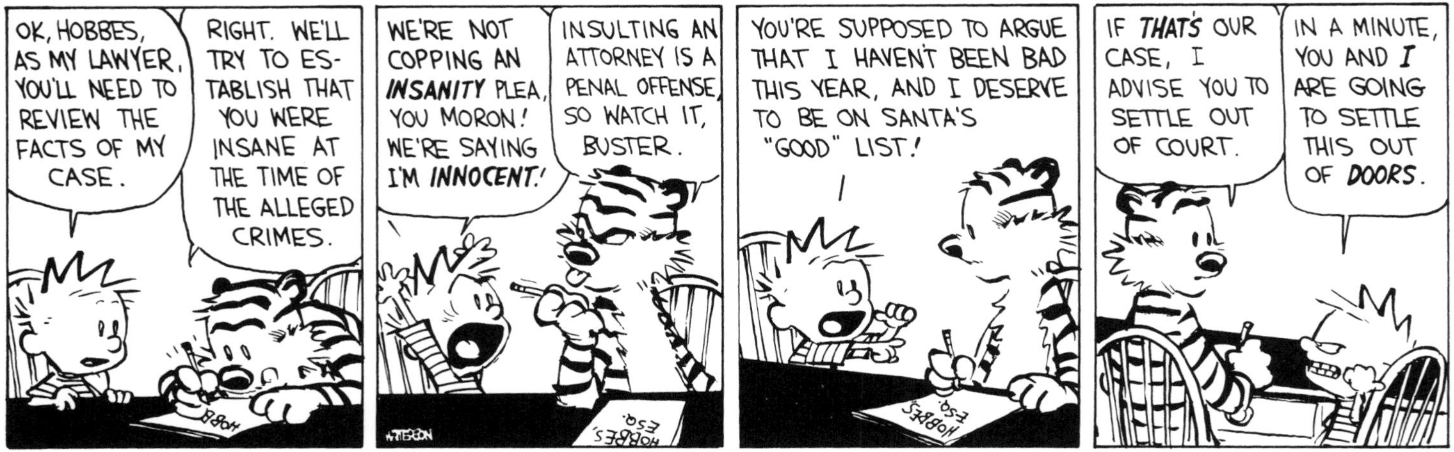
OK, HOBBES, AS MY LAWYER, YOU'LL NEED TO REVIEW THE FACTS OF MY CASE.
RIGHT. WE'LL TRY TO ESTABLISH THAT YOU WERE INSANE AT THE TIME OF THE ALLEGED CRIMES.
WE'RE NOT COPPING AN ***INSANITY*** PLEA, YOU MORON! WE'RE SAYING I'M ***INNOCENT***!
INSULTING AN ATTORNEY IS A PENAL OFFENSE, SO WATCH IT, BUSTER.
YOU'RE SUPPOSED TO ARGUE THAT I HAVEN'T BEEN BAD THIS YEAR, AND I DESERVE TO BE ON SANTA'S "GOOD" LIST!
IF ***THAT'S*** OUR CASE, I ADVISE YOU TO SETTLE OUT OF COURT.
IN A MINUTE, YOU AND ***I*** ARE GOING TO SETTLE THIS OUT OF ***DOORS***.

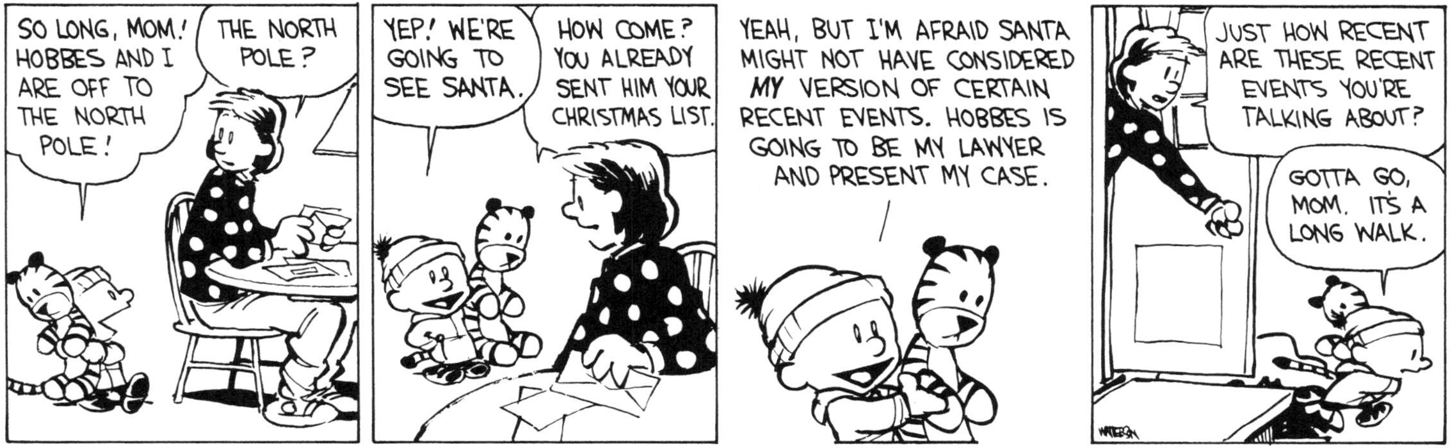
SO LONG, MOM! HOBBES AND I ARE OFF TO THE NORTH POLE!
THE NORTH POLE?
YEP! WE'RE GOING TO SEE SANTA.
HOW COME? YOU ALREADY SENT HIM YOUR CHRISTMAS LIST.
YEAH, BUT I'M AFRAID SANTA MIGHT NOT HAVE CONSIDERED *MY* VERSION OF CERTAIN RECENT EVENTS. HOBBES IS GOING TO BE MY LAWYER AND PRESENT MY CASE.
JUST HOW RECENT ARE THESE RECENT EVENTS YOU'RE TALKING ABOUT?
GOTTA GO, MOM. IT'S A LONG WALK.

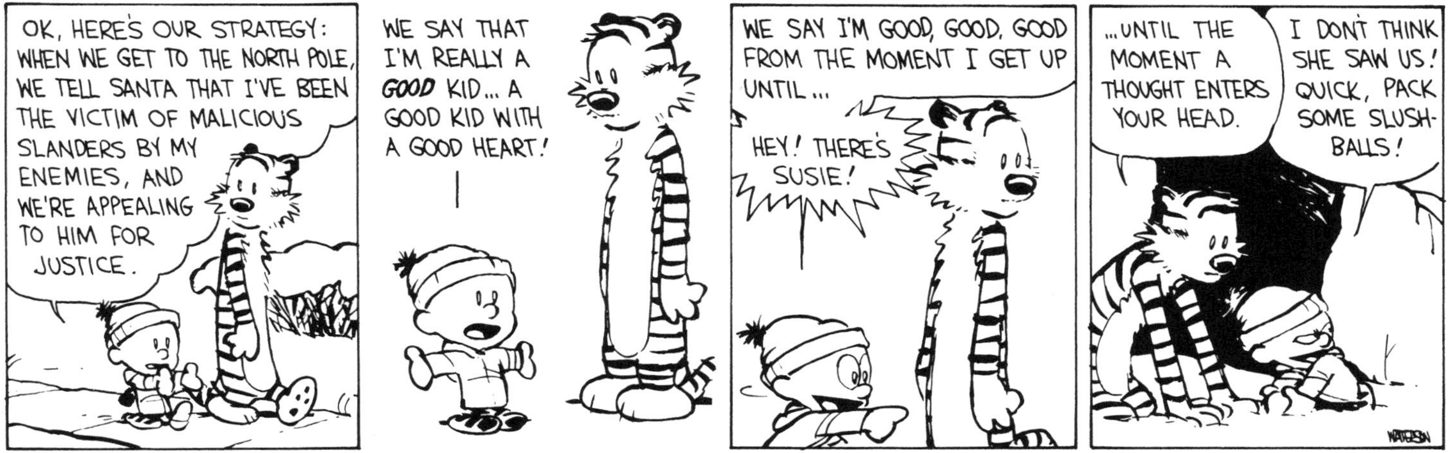
OK, HERE'S OUR STRATEGY: WHEN WE GET TO THE NORTH POLE, WE TELL SANTA THAT I'VE BEEN THE VICTIM OF MALICIOUS SLANDERS BY MY ENEMIES, AND WE'RE APPEALING TO HIM FOR JUSTICE.
WE SAY THAT I'M REALLY A *GOOD* KID... A GOOD KID WITH A GOOD HEART!
WE SAY I'M GOOD, GOOD, GOOD FROM THE MOMENT I GET UP UNTIL...
HEY! THERE'S SUSIE!
...UNTIL THE MOMENT A THOUGHT ENTERS YOUR HEAD.
I DON'T THINK SHE SAW US! QUICK, PACK SOME SLUSH-BALLS!

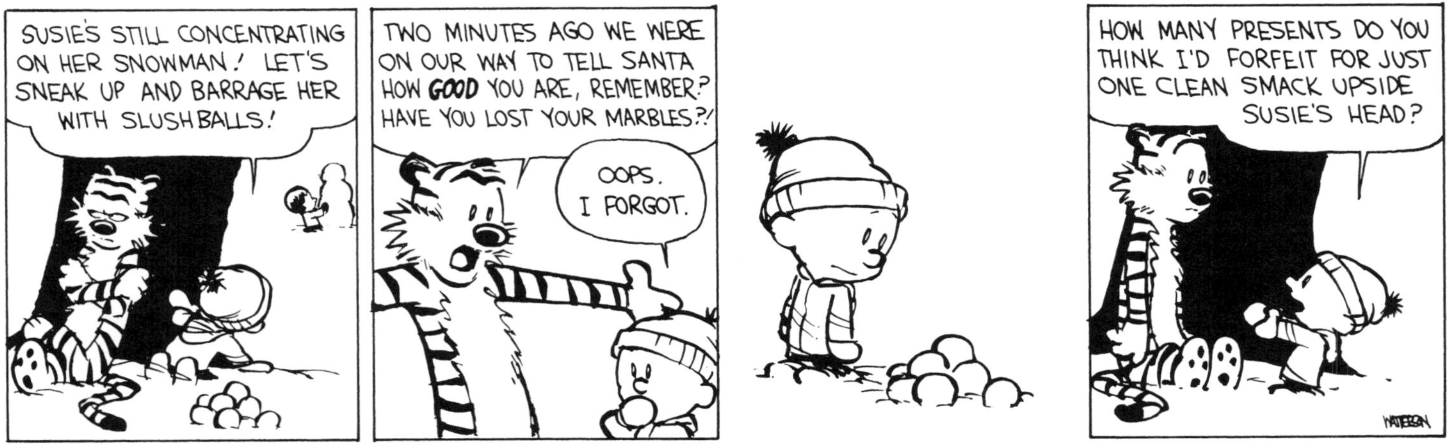
SUSIE'S STILL CONCENTRATING ON HER SNOWMAN! LET'S SNEAK UP AND BARRAGE HER WITH SLUSHBALLS!
TWO MINUTES AGO WE WERE ON OUR WAY TO TELL SANTA HOW GOOD YOU ARE, REMEMBER? HAVE YOU LOST YOUR MARBLES?!
OOPS. I FORGOT.
HOW MANY PRESENTS DO YOU THINK I'D FORFEIT FOR JUST ONE CLEAN SMACK UPSIDE SUSIE'S HEAD?
WATTERSON

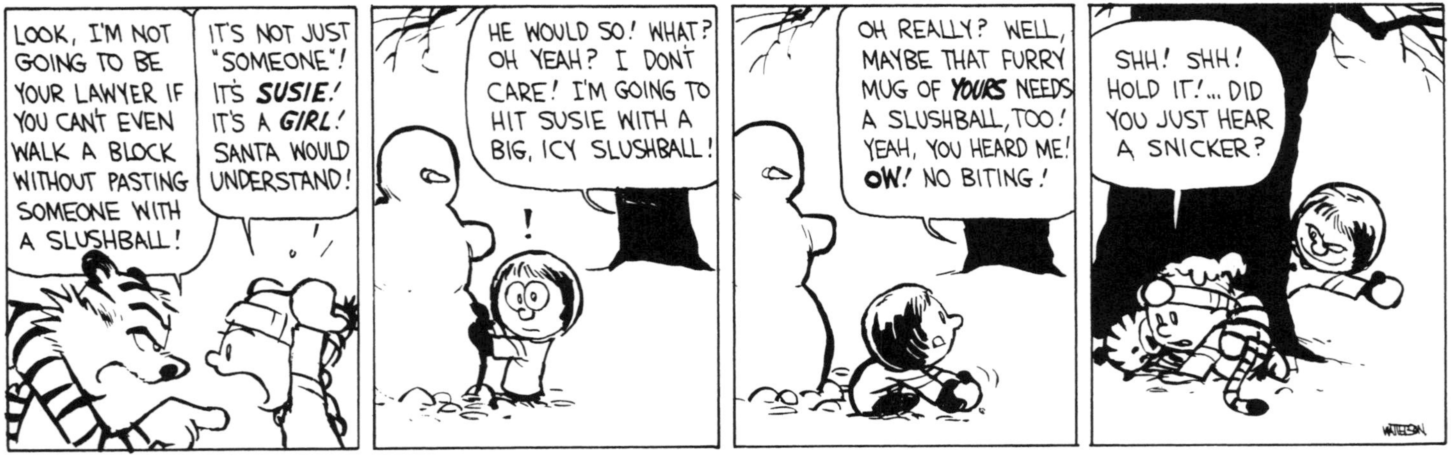
LOOK, I'M NOT GOING TO BE YOUR LAWYER IF YOU CAN'T EVEN WALK A BLOCK WITHOUT PASTING SOMEONE WITH A SLUSHBALL!
IT'S NOT JUST "SOMEONE"! IT'S SUSIE! IT'S A GIRL! SANTA WOULD UNDERSTAND!
HE WOULD SO! WHAT? OH YEAH? I DON'T CARE! I'M GOING TO HIT SUSIE WITH A BIG, ICY SLUSHBALL!
!
OH REALLY? WELL, MAYBE THAT FURRY MUG OF YOURS NEEDS A SLUSHBALL, TOO! YEAH, YOU HEARD ME! OW! NO BITING!
SHH! SHH! HOLD IT!... DID YOU JUST HEAR A SNICKER?
WATTERSON

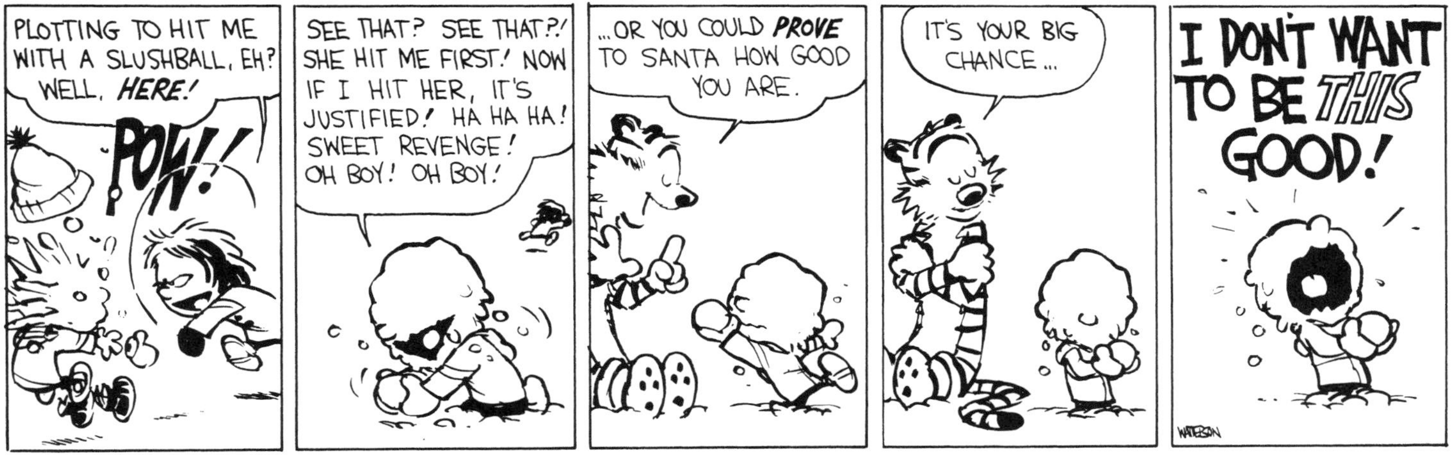
PLOTTING TO HIT ME WITH A SLUSHBALL, EH? WELL, HERE!
POW!
SEE THAT? SEE THAT?! SHE HIT ME FIRST! NOW IF I HIT HER, IT'S JUSTIFIED! HA HA HA! SWEET REVENGE! OH BOY! OH BOY!
...OR YOU COULD PROVE TO SANTA HOW GOOD YOU ARE.
IT'S YOUR BIG CHANCE...
I DON'T WANT TO BE THIS GOOD!
WATTERSON

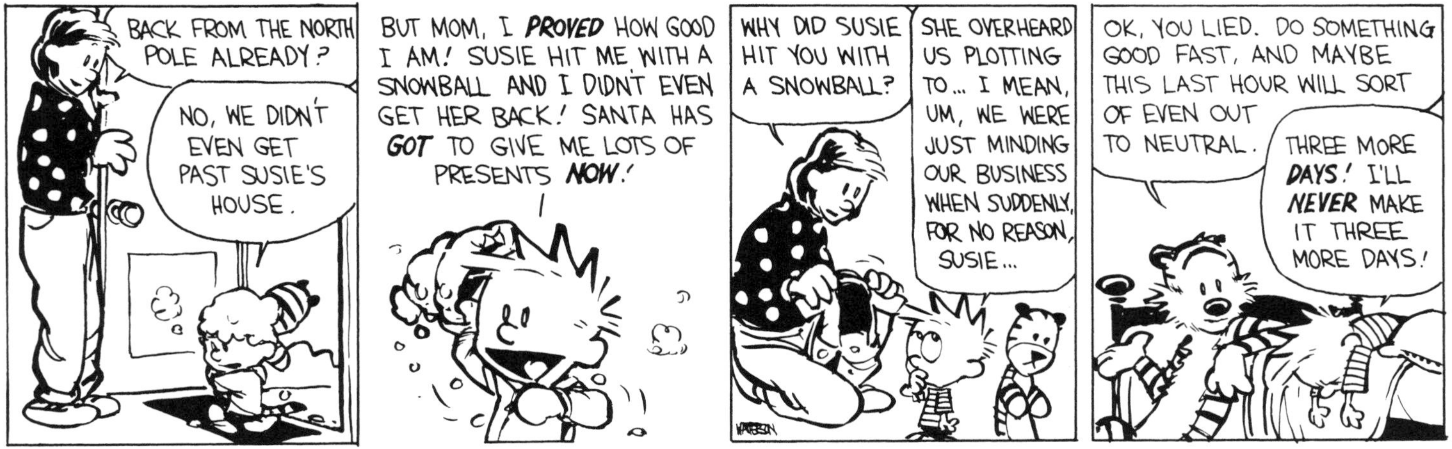
BACK FROM THE NORTH POLE ALREADY?
NO, WE DIDN'T EVEN GET PAST SUSIE'S HOUSE.
BUT MOM, I PROVED HOW GOOD I AM! SUSIE HIT ME WITH A SNOWBALL AND I DIDN'T EVEN GET HER BACK! SANTA HAS GOT TO GIVE ME LOTS OF PRESENTS NOW!
WHY DID SUSIE HIT YOU WITH A SNOWBALL?
SHE OVERHEARD US PLOTTING TO... I MEAN, UM, WE WERE JUST MINDING OUR BUSINESS WHEN SUDDENLY, FOR NO REASON, SUSIE...
OK, YOU LIED. DO SOMETHING GOOD FAST, AND MAYBE THIS LAST HOUR WILL SORT OF EVEN OUT TO NEUTRAL.
THREE MORE DAYS! I'LL NEVER MAKE IT THREE MORE DAYS!
WATTERSON

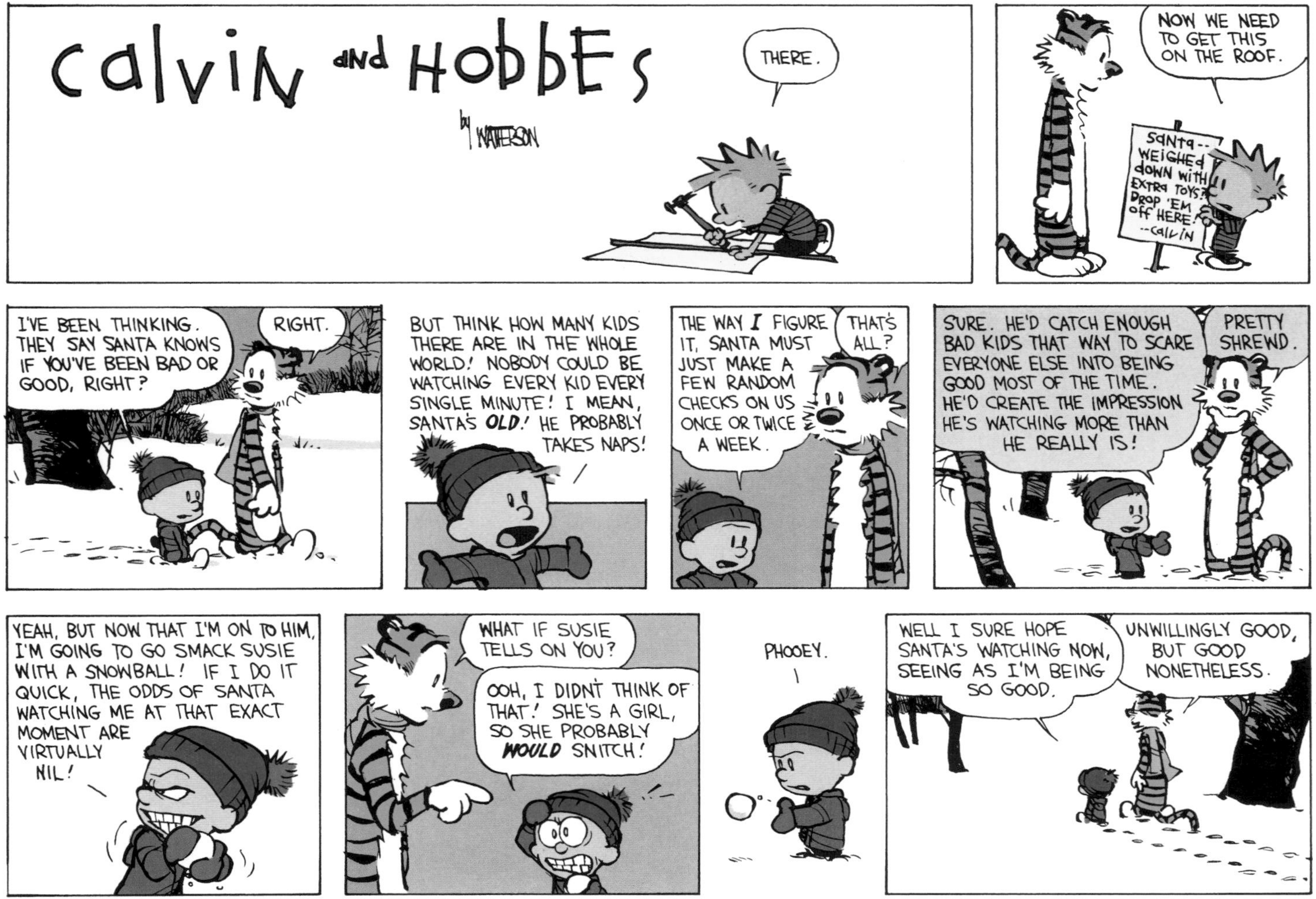
Calvin and HobbEs
by WATTERSON
THERE.
NOW WE NEED TO GET THIS ON THE ROOF.
SANTA-- WEIGHED DOWN WITH EXTRA TOYS? DROP 'EM OFF HERE! --CALVIN
I'VE BEEN THINKING. THEY SAY SANTA KNOWS IF YOU'VE BEEN BAD OR GOOD, RIGHT?
RIGHT.
BUT THINK HOW MANY KIDS THERE ARE IN THE WHOLE WORLD! NOBODY COULD BE WATCHING EVERY KID EVERY SINGLE MINUTE! I MEAN, SANTA'S OLD! HE PROBABLY TAKES NAPS!
THE WAY I FIGURE IT, SANTA MUST JUST MAKE A FEW RANDOM CHECKS ON US ONCE OR TWICE A WEEK.
THAT'S ALL?
SURE. HE'D CATCH ENOUGH BAD KIDS THAT WAY TO SCARE EVERYONE ELSE INTO BEING GOOD MOST OF THE TIME. HE'D CREATE THE IMPRESSION HE'S WATCHING MORE THAN HE REALLY IS!
PRETTY SHREWD.
YEAH, BUT NOW THAT I'M ON TO HIM, I'M GOING TO GO SMACK SUSIE WITH A SNOWBALL! IF I DO IT QUICK, THE ODDS OF SANTA WATCHING ME AT THAT EXACT MOMENT ARE VIRTUALLY NIL!
WHAT IF SUSIE TELLS ON YOU?
OOH, I DIDN'T THINK OF THAT! SHE'S A GIRL, SO SHE PROBABLY WOULD SNITCH!
PHOOEY.
WELL I SURE HOPE SANTA'S WATCHING NOW, SEEING AS I'M BEING SO GOOD.
UNWILLINGLY GOOD, BUT GOOD NONETHELESS.

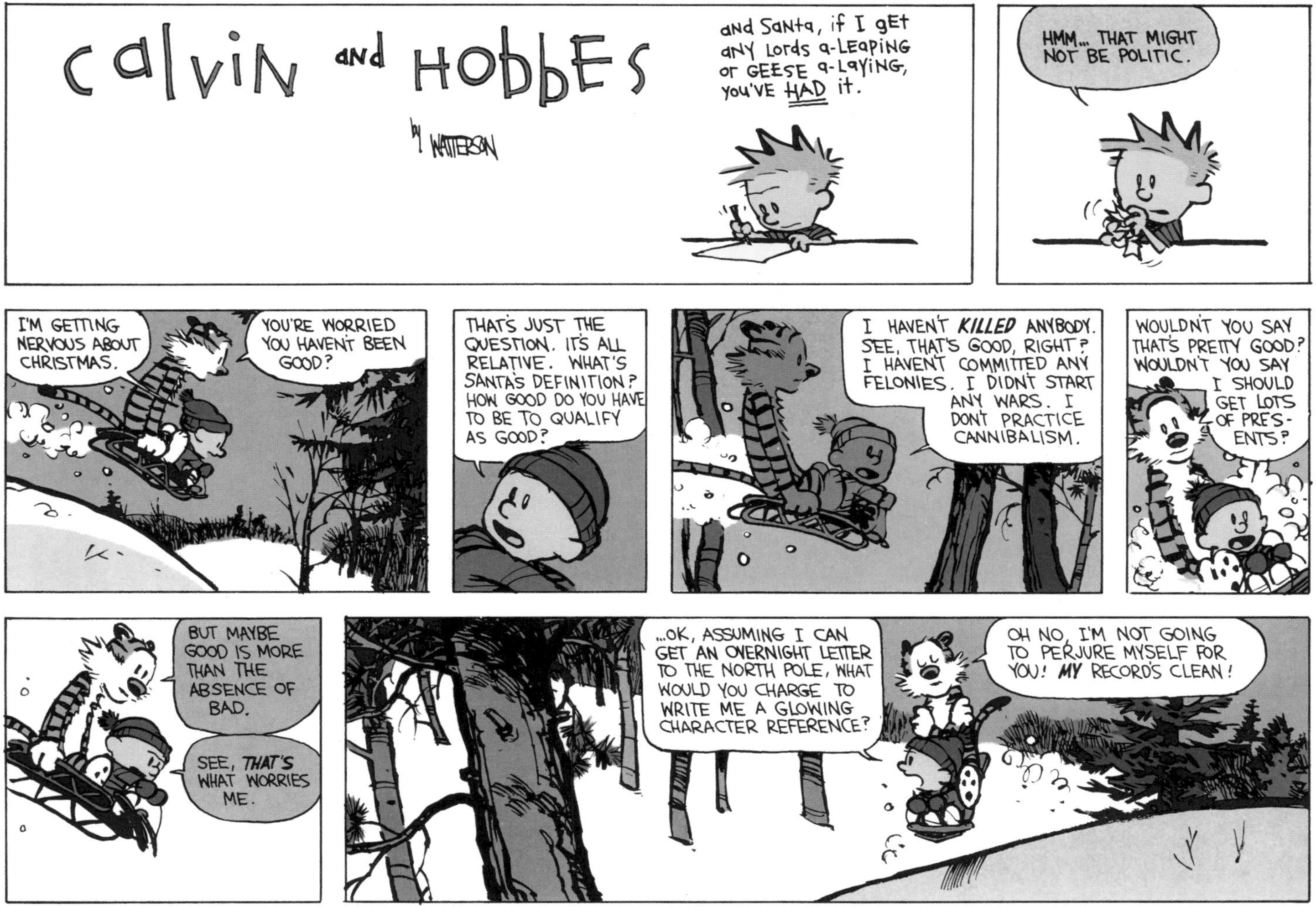
Calvin and Hobbes
by WATTERSON
and Santa, if I get any Lords a-Leaping or GEESE a-Laying, you've HAD it.
HMM... THAT MIGHT NOT BE POLITIC.
I'M GETTING NERVOUS ABOUT CHRISTMAS.
YOU'RE WORRIED YOU HAVEN'T BEEN GOOD?
THAT'S JUST THE QUESTION. IT'S ALL RELATIVE. WHAT'S SANTA'S DEFINITION? HOW GOOD DO YOU HAVE TO BE TO QUALIFY AS GOOD?
I HAVEN'T KILLED ANYBODY. SEE, THAT'S GOOD, RIGHT? I HAVEN'T COMMITTED ANY FELONIES. I DIDN'T START ANY WARS. I DON'T PRACTICE CANNIBALISM.
WOULDN'T YOU SAY THAT'S PRETTY GOOD? WOULDN'T YOU SAY I SHOULD GET LOTS OF PRES-ENTS?
BUT MAYBE GOOD IS MORE THAN THE ABSENCE OF BAD.
SEE, THAT'S WHAT WORRIES ME.
...OK, ASSUMING I CAN GET AN OVERNIGHT LETTER TO THE NORTH POLE, WHAT WOULD YOU CHARGE TO WRITE ME A GLOWING CHARACTER REFERENCE?
OH NO, I'M NOT GOING TO PERJURE MYSELF FOR YOU! MY RECORD'S CLEAN!

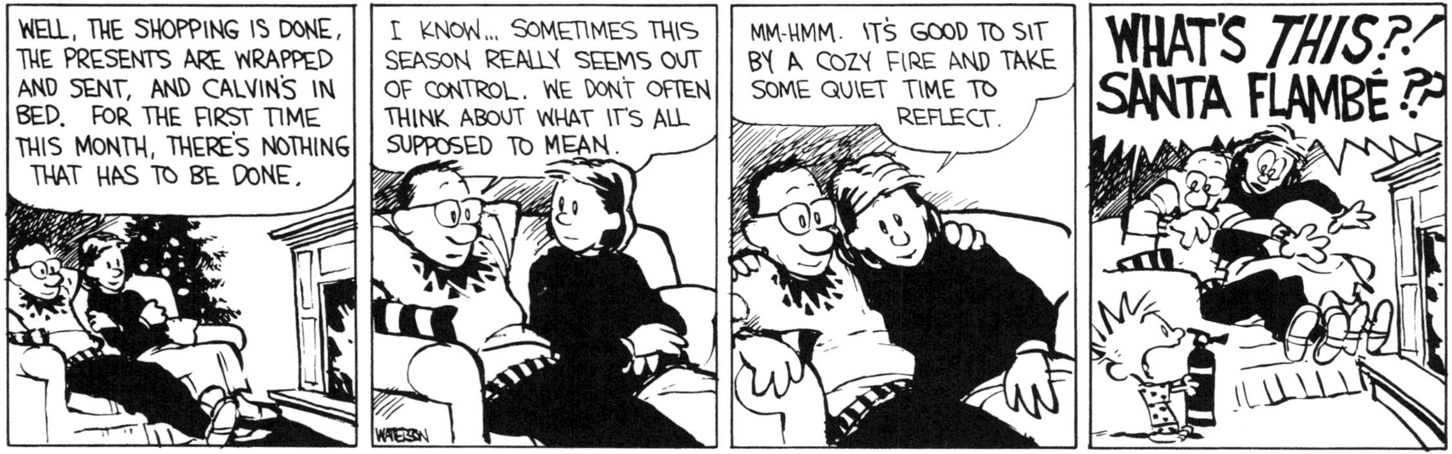
WELL, THE SHOPPING IS DONE, THE PRESENTS ARE WRAPPED AND SENT, AND CALVIN'S IN BED. FOR THE FIRST TIME THIS MONTH, THERE'S NOTHING THAT HAS TO BE DONE.
I KNOW... SOMETIMES THIS SEASON REALLY SEEMS OUT OF CONTROL. WE DON'T OFTEN THINK ABOUT WHAT IT'S ALL SUPPOSED TO MEAN.
WATTERSON
MM-HMM. IT'S GOOD TO SIT BY A COZY FIRE AND TAKE SOME QUIET TIME TO REFLECT.
WHAT'S *THIS* ?! SANTA FLAMBÉ ??

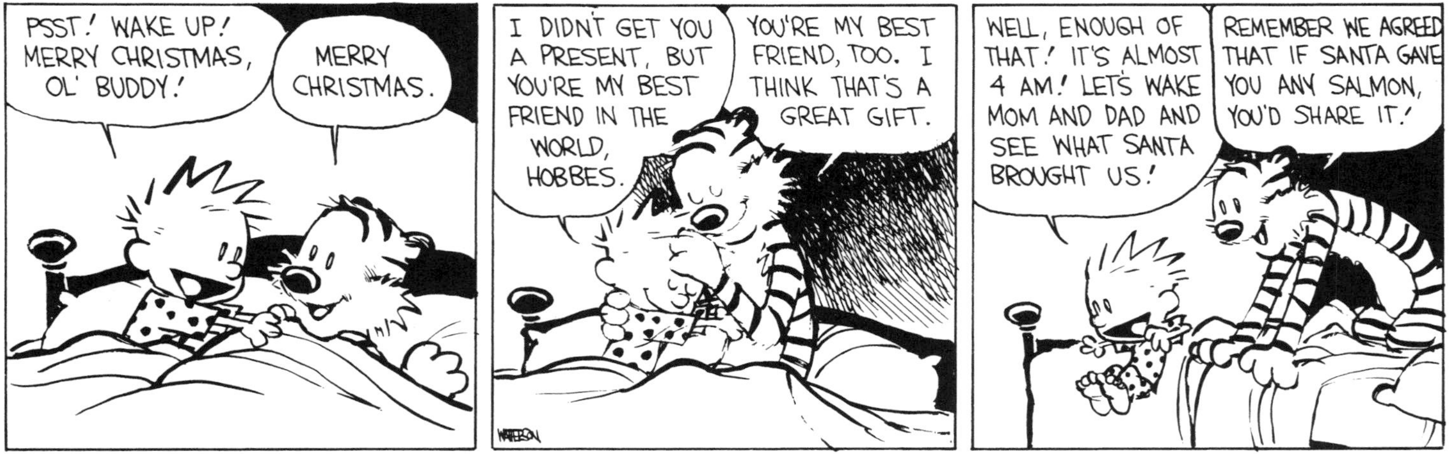
PSST! WAKE UP! MERRY CHRISTMAS, OL' BUDDY!
MERRY CHRISTMAS.
I DIDN'T GET YOU A PRESENT, BUT YOU'RE MY BEST FRIEND IN THE WORLD, HOBBES.
YOU'RE MY BEST FRIEND, TOO. I THINK THAT'S A GREAT GIFT.
WATTERSON
WELL, ENOUGH OF THAT! IT'S ALMOST 4 AM! LET'S WAKE MOM AND DAD AND SEE WHAT SANTA BROUGHT US!
REMEMBER WE AGREED THAT IF SANTA GAVE YOU ANY SALMON, YOU'D SHARE IT!

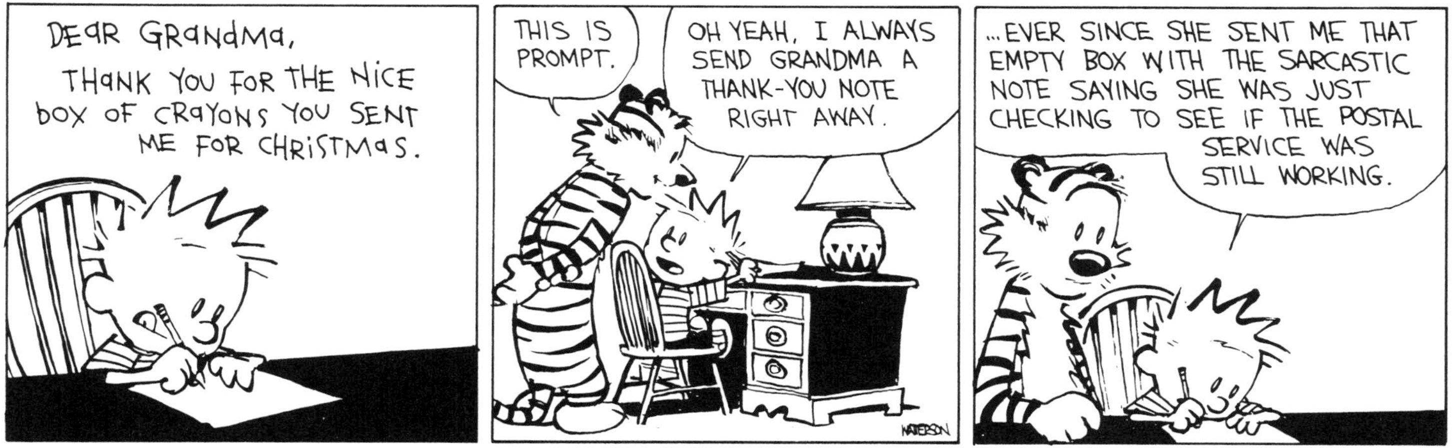
DEAR GRANDMA,
THANK YOU FOR THE NICE BOX OF CRAYONS YOU SENT ME FOR CHRISTMAS.
THIS IS PROMPT.
OH YEAH, I ALWAYS SEND GRANDMA A THANK-YOU NOTE RIGHT AWAY.
...EVER SINCE SHE SENT ME THAT EMPTY BOX WITH THE SARCASTIC NOTE SAYING SHE WAS JUST CHECKING TO SEE IF THE POSTAL SERVICE WAS STILL WORKING.
WATTERSON

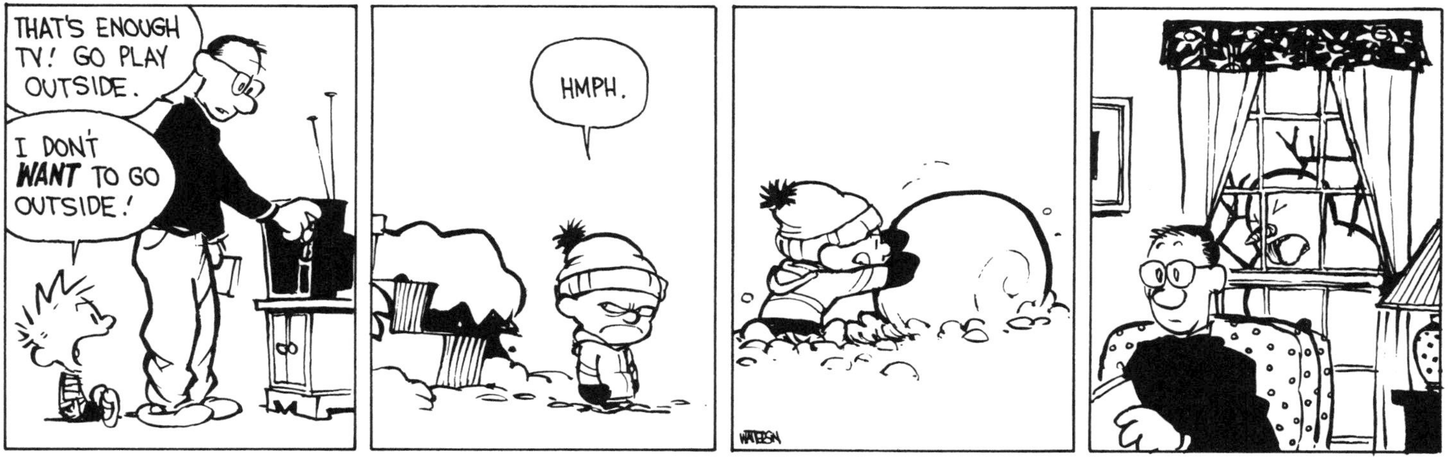
THAT'S ENOUGH TV! GO PLAY OUTSIDE.
I DON'T **WANT** TO GO OUTSIDE!
HMPH.
WATTERSON

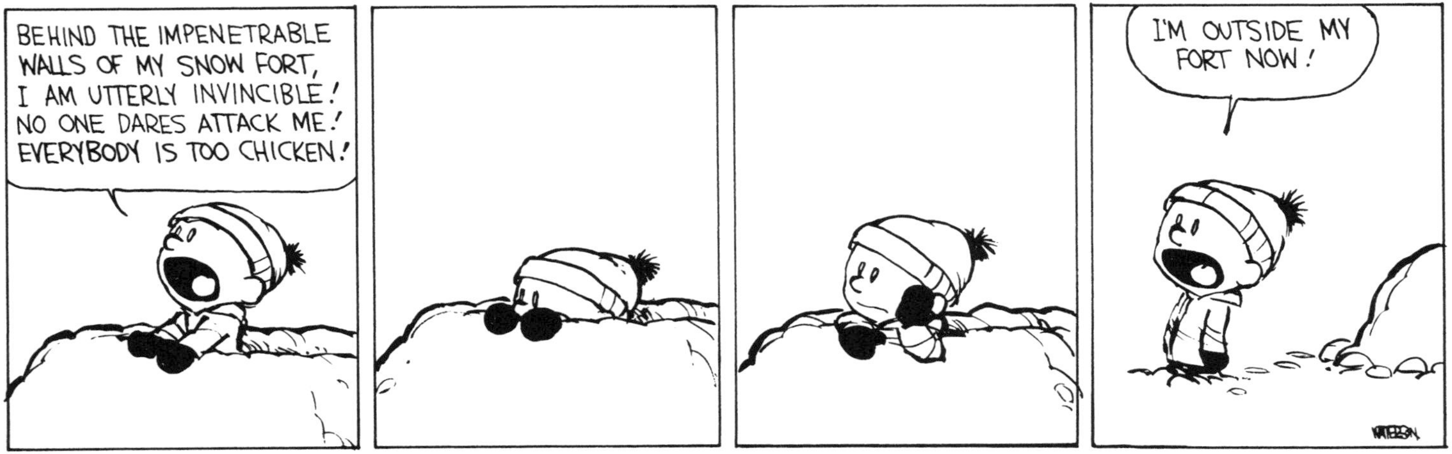
BEHIND THE IMPENETRABLE WALLS OF MY SNOW FORT, I AM UTTERLY INVINCIBLE! NO ONE DARES ATTACK ME! EVERYBODY IS TOO CHICKEN!
I'M OUTSIDE MY FORT NOW!

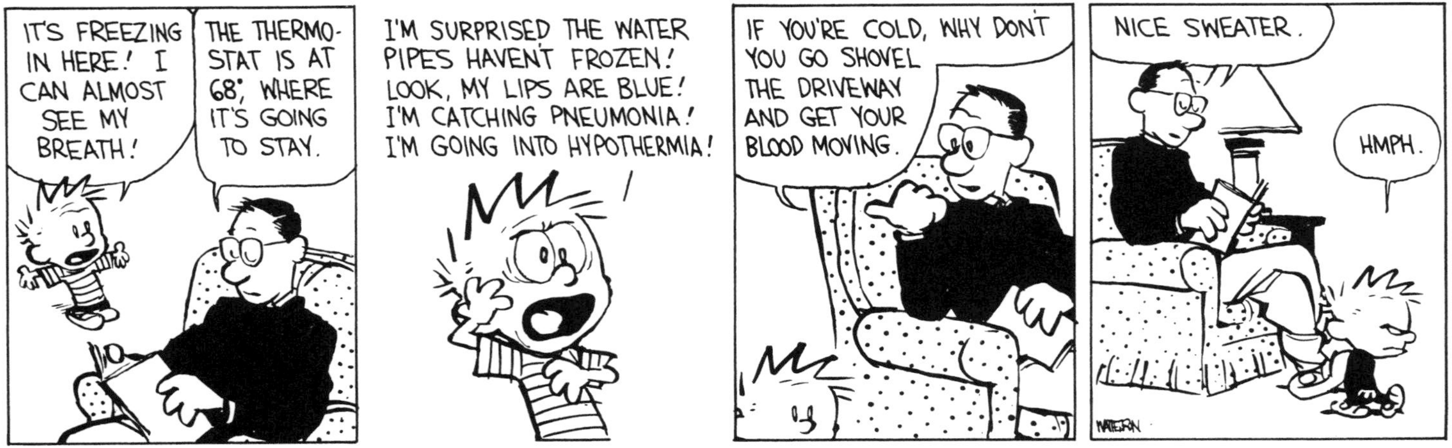
IT'S FREEZING IN HERE! I CAN ALMOST SEE MY BREATH!
THE THERMOSTAT IS AT 68°, WHERE IT'S GOING TO STAY.
I'M SURPRISED THE WATER PIPES HAVEN'T FROZEN! LOOK, MY LIPS ARE BLUE! I'M CATCHING PNEUMONIA! I'M GOING INTO HYPOTHERMIA!
IF YOU'RE COLD, WHY DON'T YOU GO SHOVEL THE DRIVEWAY AND GET YOUR BLOOD MOVING.
NICE SWEATER.
HMPH.

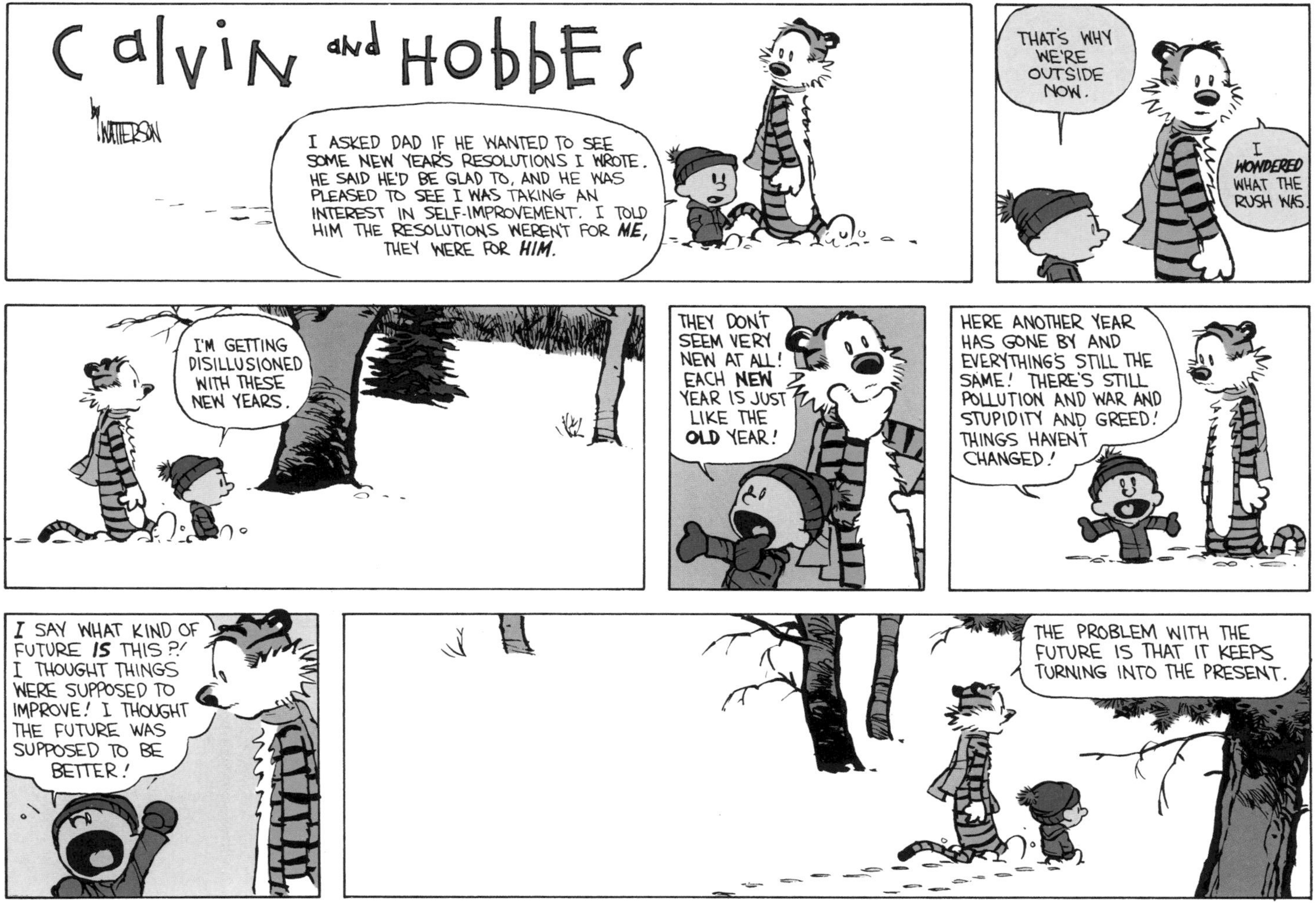
Calvin and HobbES
by WATTERSON
I ASKED DAD IF HE WANTED TO SEE SOME NEW YEAR'S RESOLUTIONS I WROTE. HE SAID HE'D BE GLAD TO, AND HE WAS PLEASED TO SEE I WAS TAKING AN INTEREST IN SELF-IMPROVEMENT. I TOLD HIM THE RESOLUTIONS WEREN'T FOR **ME**, THEY WERE FOR **HIM**.
THAT'S WHY WE'RE OUTSIDE NOW.
I **WONDERED** WHAT THE RUSH WAS.
I'M GETTING DISILLUSIONED WITH THESE NEW YEARS.
THEY DON'T SEEM VERY NEW AT ALL! EACH **NEW** YEAR IS JUST LIKE THE **OLD** YEAR!
HERE ANOTHER YEAR HAS GONE BY AND EVERYTHING'S STILL THE SAME! THERE'S STILL POLLUTION AND WAR AND STUPIDITY AND GREED! THINGS HAVEN'T CHANGED!
I SAY WHAT KIND OF FUTURE ***IS*** THIS?! I THOUGHT THINGS WERE SUPPOSED TO IMPROVE! I THOUGHT THE FUTURE WAS SUPPOSED TO BE BETTER!
THE PROBLEM WITH THE FUTURE IS THAT IT KEEPS TURNING INTO THE PRESENT.

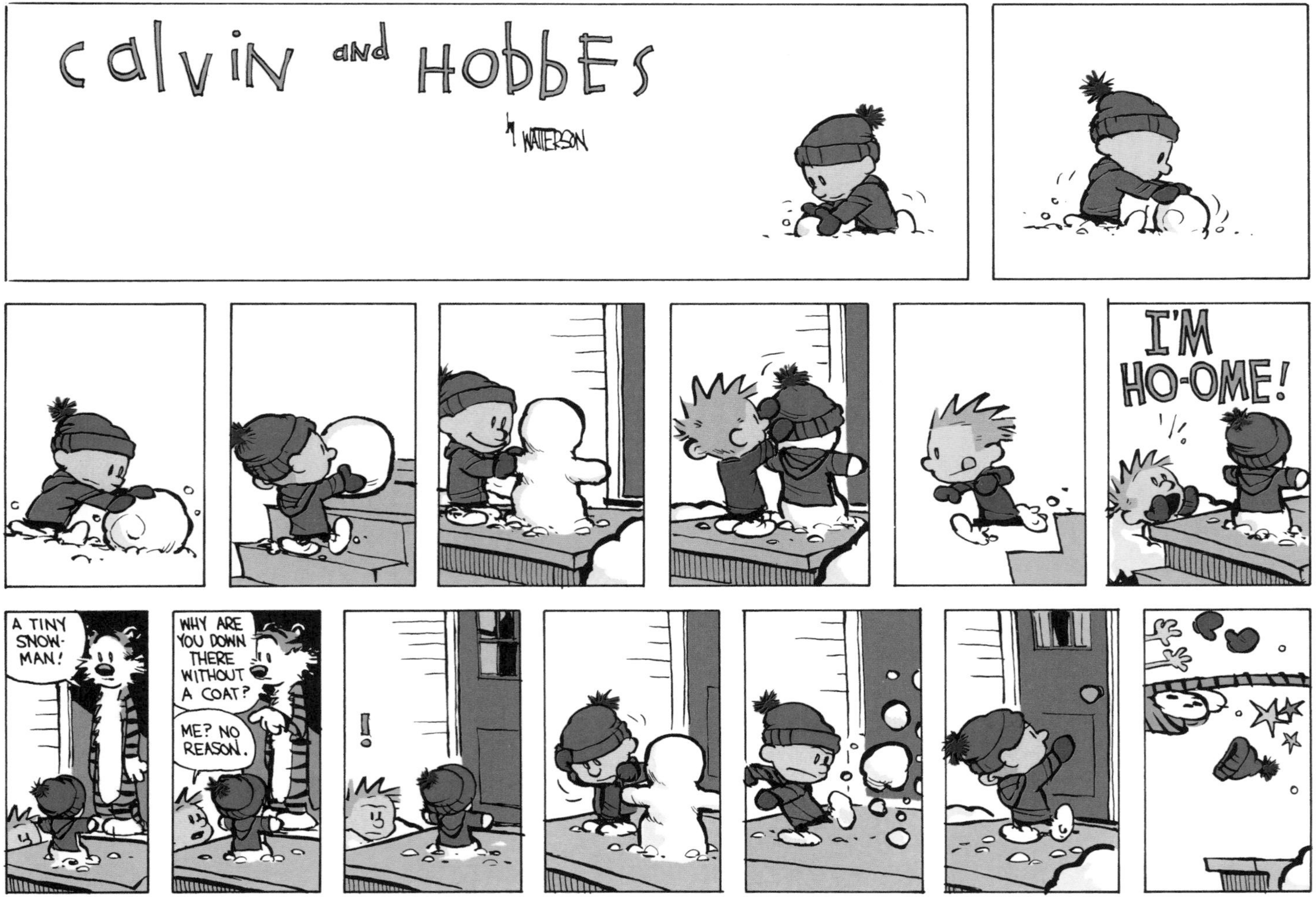
Calvin and HOBBES
by WATTERSON
I'M HO-OME!
A TINY SNOW-MAN!
WHY ARE YOU DOWN THERE WITHOUT A COAT?
ME? NO REASON.
!

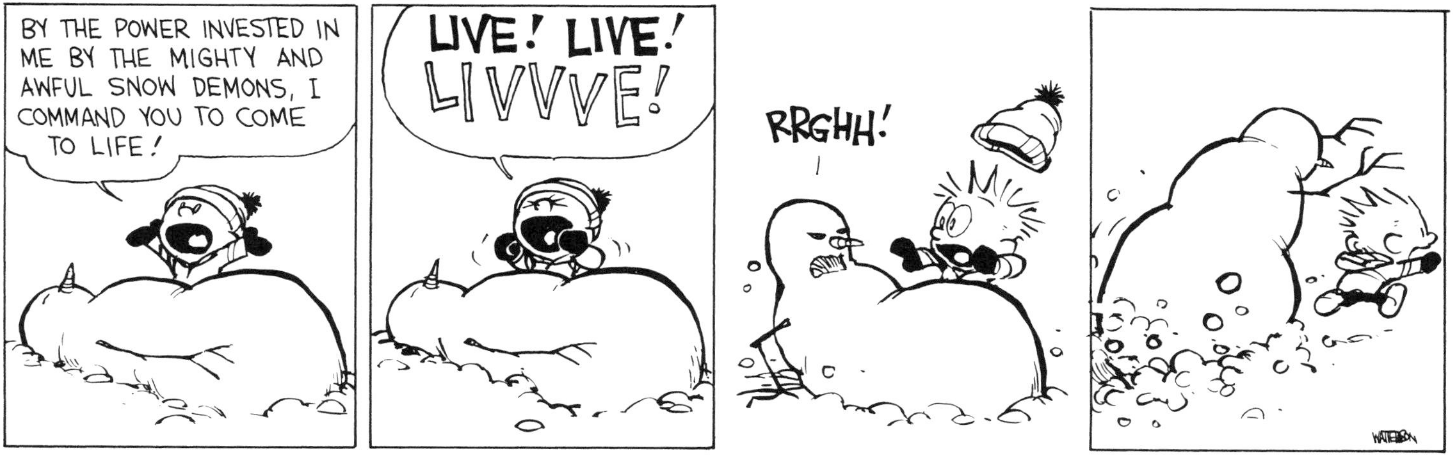
BY THE POWER INVESTED IN ME BY THE MIGHTY AND AWFUL SNOW DEMONS, I COMMAND YOU TO COME TO LIFE!
LIVE! LIVE! LIVVVE!
RRGHH!

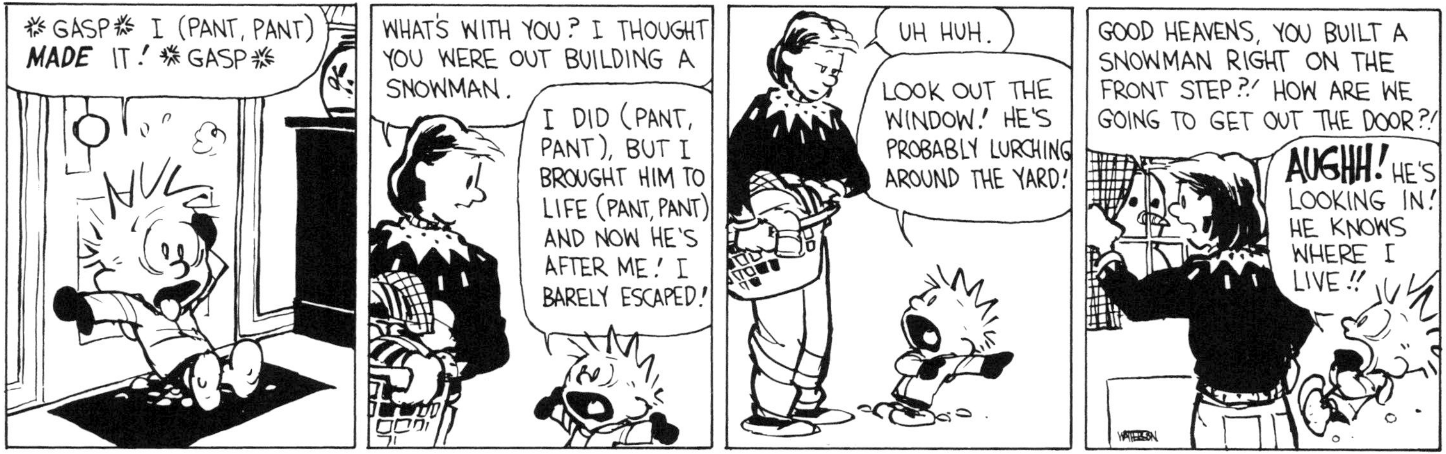
GASP I (PANT, PANT) MADE IT! *GASP*
WHAT'S WITH YOU? I THOUGHT YOU WERE OUT BUILDING A SNOWMAN.
I DID (PANT, PANT), BUT I BROUGHT HIM TO LIFE (PANT, PANT) AND NOW HE'S AFTER ME! I BARELY ESCAPED!
UH HUH.
LOOK OUT THE WINDOW! HE'S PROBABLY LURCHING AROUND THE YARD!
GOOD HEAVENS, YOU BUILT A SNOWMAN RIGHT ON THE FRONT STEP?! HOW ARE WE GOING TO GET OUT THE DOOR?!
AUGHH! HE'S LOOKING IN! HE KNOWS WHERE I LIVE!!

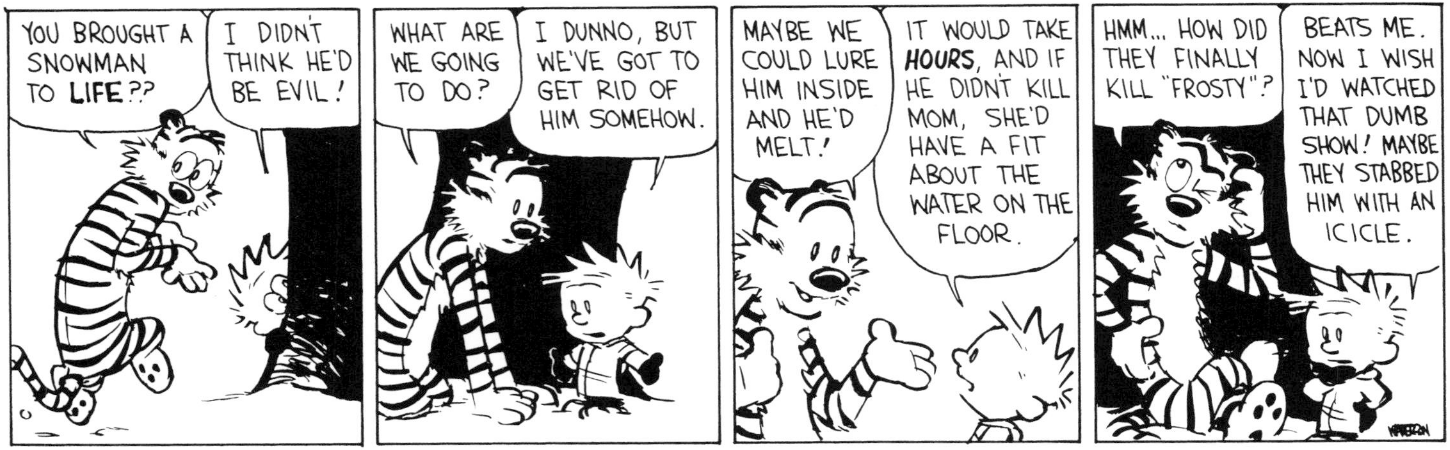
YOU BROUGHT A SNOWMAN TO **LIFE**??
I DIDN'T THINK HE'D BE EVIL!
WHAT ARE WE GOING TO DO?
I DUNNO, BUT WE'VE GOT TO GET RID OF HIM SOMEHOW.
MAYBE WE COULD LURE HIM INSIDE AND HE'D MELT!
IT WOULD TAKE **HOURS**, AND IF HE DIDN'T KILL MOM, SHE'D HAVE A FIT ABOUT THE WATER ON THE FLOOR.
HMM... HOW DID THEY FINALLY KILL "FROSTY"?
BEATS ME. NOW I WISH I'D WATCHED THAT DUMB SHOW! MAYBE THEY STABBED HIM WITH AN ICICLE.

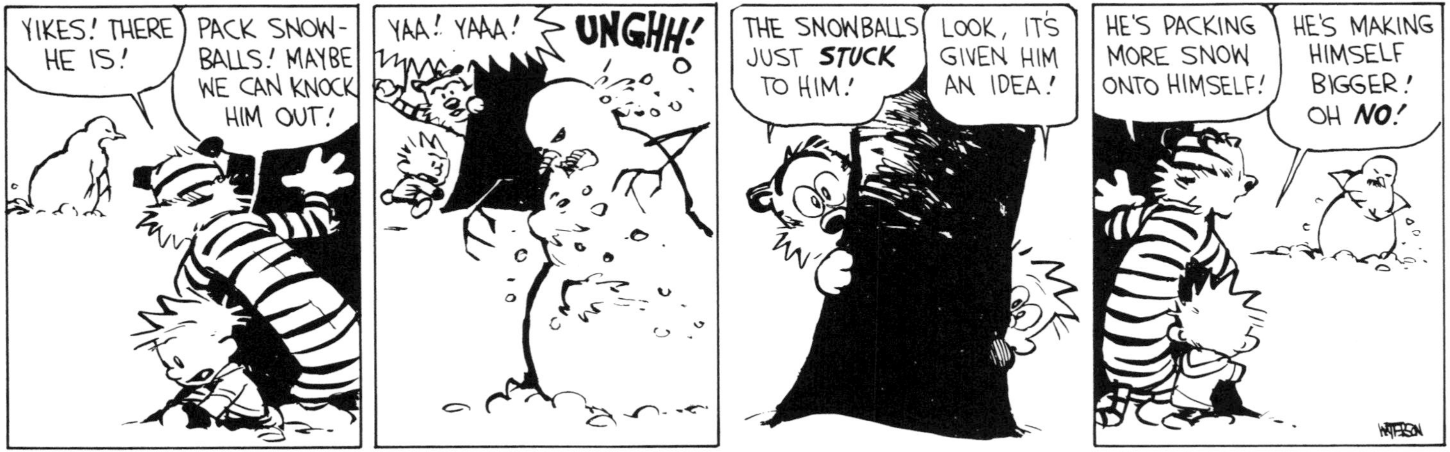
YIKES! THERE HE IS!
PACK SNOW-BALLS! MAYBE WE CAN KNOCK HIM OUT!
YAA! YAAA!
UNGHH!
THE SNOWBALLS JUST **STUCK** TO HIM!
LOOK, IT'S GIVEN HIM AN IDEA!
HE'S PACKING MORE SNOW ONTO HIMSELF!
HE'S MAKING HIMSELF BIGGER! OH **NO**!

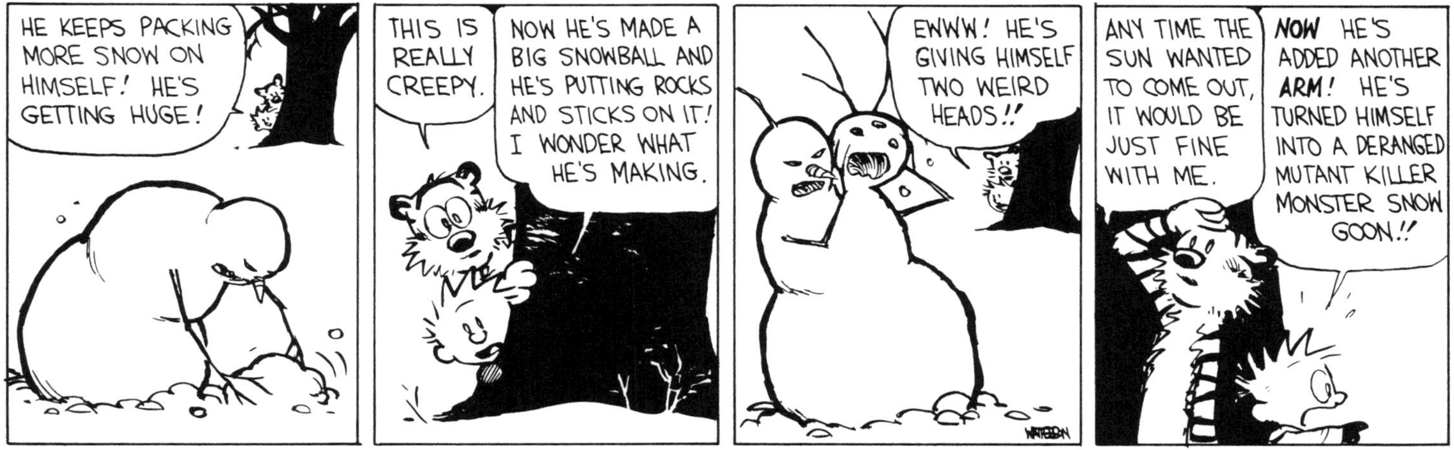
HE KEEPS PACKING MORE SNOW ON HIMSELF! HE'S GETTING HUGE!
THIS IS REALLY CREEPY.
NOW HE'S MADE A BIG SNOWBALL AND HE'S PUTTING ROCKS AND STICKS ON IT! I WONDER WHAT HE'S MAKING.
EWWW! HE'S GIVING HIMSELF TWO WEIRD HEADS!!
ANY TIME THE SUN WANTED TO COME OUT, IT WOULD BE JUST FINE WITH ME.
NOW HE'S ADDED ANOTHER **ARM**! HE'S TURNED HIMSELF INTO A DERANGED MUTANT KILLER MONSTER SNOW GOON!!

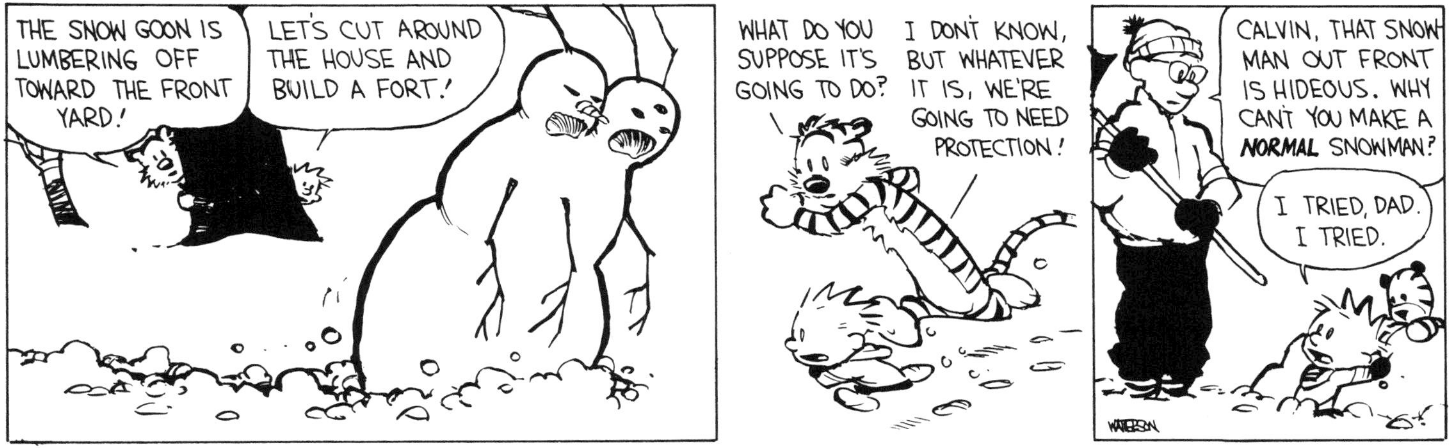
THE SNOW GOON IS LUMBERING OFF TOWARD THE FRONT YARD!
LET'S CUT AROUND THE HOUSE AND BUILD A FORT!
WHAT DO YOU SUPPOSE IT'S GOING TO DO?
I DON'T KNOW, BUT WHATEVER IT IS, WE'RE GOING TO NEED PROTECTION!
CALVIN, THAT SNOWMAN OUT FRONT IS HIDEOUS. WHY CAN'T YOU MAKE A **NORMAL** SNOWMAN?
I TRIED, DAD. I TRIED.

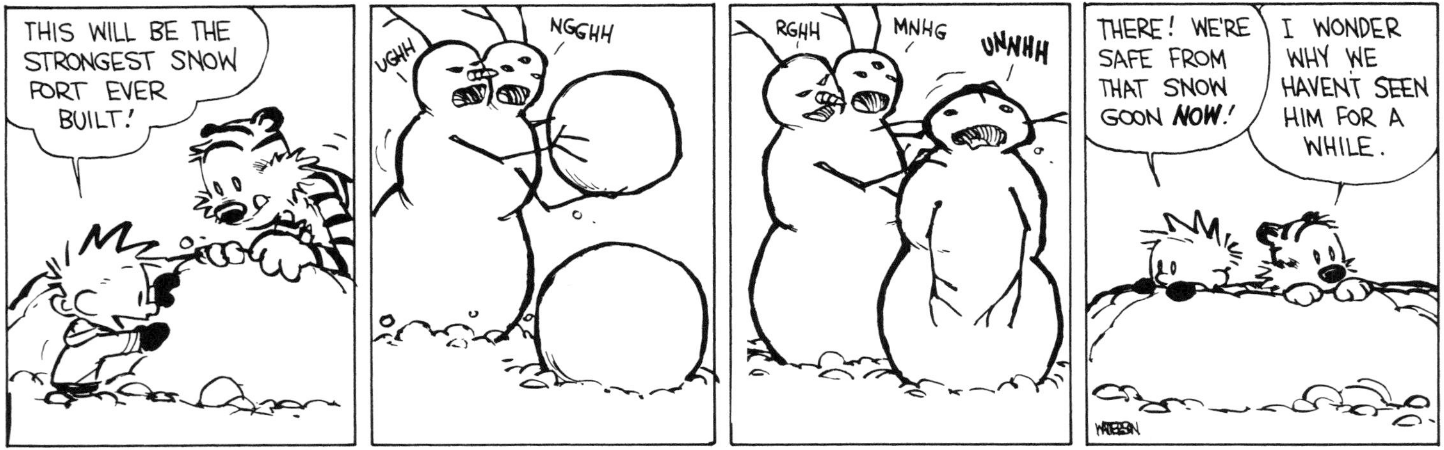
THIS WILL BE THE STRONGEST SNOW FORT EVER BUILT!
UGHH
NGGHH
RGHH
MNHG
UNNHH
THERE! WE'RE SAFE FROM THAT SNOW GOON NOW!
I WONDER WHY WE HAVEN'T SEEN HIM FOR A WHILE.
WATTERSON

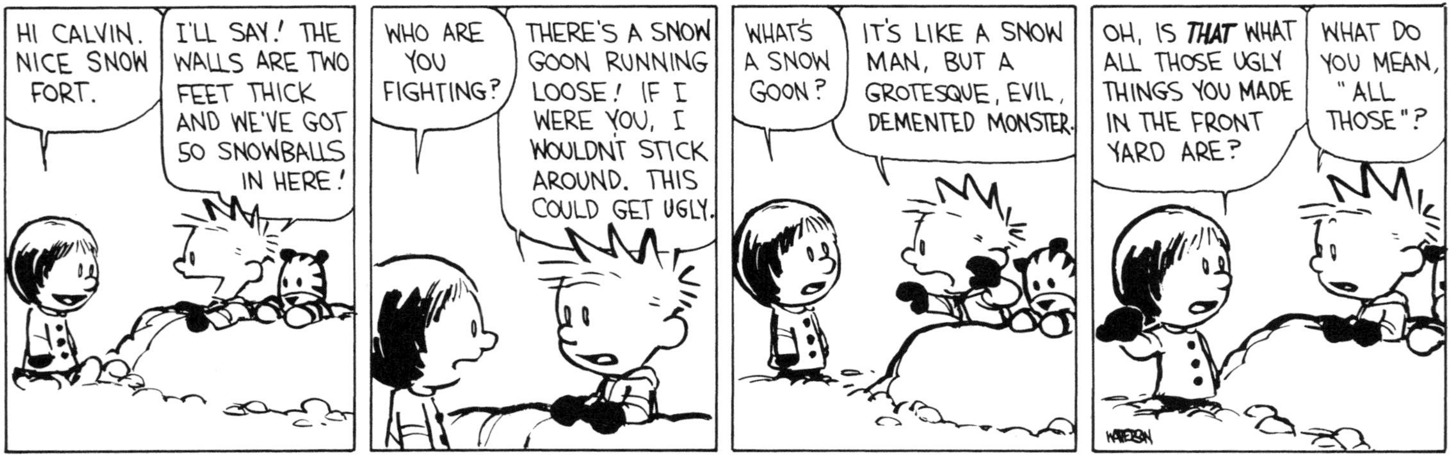
HI CALVIN. NICE SNOW FORT.
I'LL SAY! THE WALLS ARE TWO FEET THICK AND WE'VE GOT 50 SNOWBALLS IN HERE!
WHO ARE YOU FIGHTING?
THERE'S A SNOW GOON RUNNING LOOSE! IF I WERE YOU, I WOULDN'T STICK AROUND. THIS COULD GET UGLY.
WHAT'S A SNOW GOON?
IT'S LIKE A SNOW MAN, BUT A GROTESQUE, EVIL, DEMENTED MONSTER.
OH, IS THAT WHAT ALL THOSE UGLY THINGS YOU MADE IN THE FRONT YARD ARE?
WHAT DO YOU MEAN, "ALL THOSE"?
WATTERSON

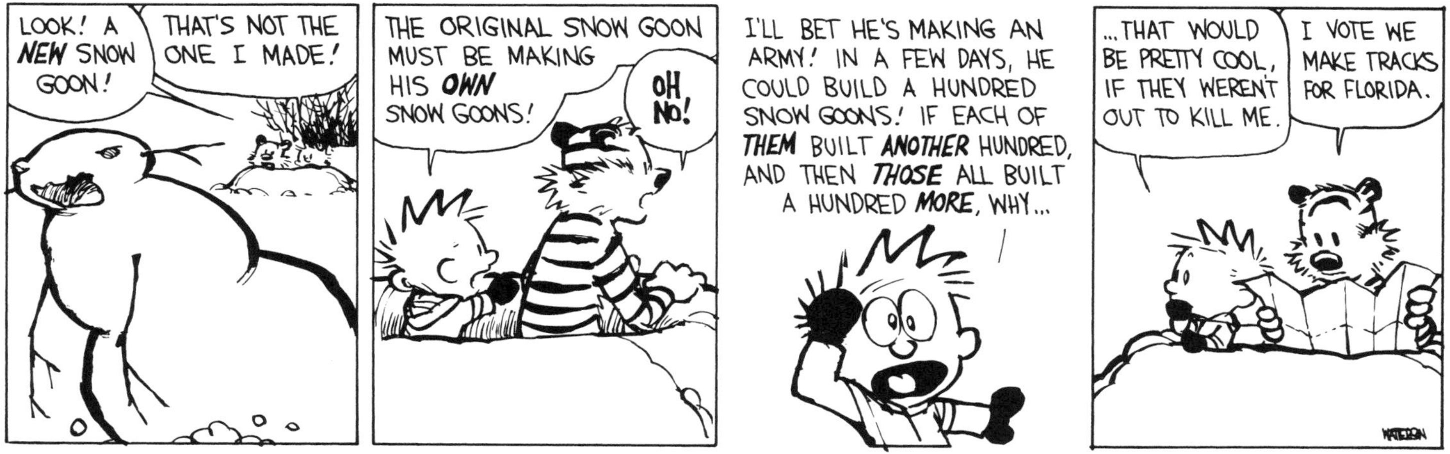
LOOK! A **NEW** SNOW GOON!
THAT'S NOT THE ONE I MADE!
THE ORIGINAL SNOW GOON MUST BE MAKING HIS **OWN** SNOW GOONS!
OH NO!
I'LL BET HE'S MAKING AN ARMY! IN A FEW DAYS, HE COULD BUILD A HUNDRED SNOW GOONS! IF EACH OF **THEM** BUILT **ANOTHER** HUNDRED, AND THEN **THOSE** ALL BUILT A HUNDRED **MORE**, WHY...
...THAT WOULD BE PRETTY COOL, IF THEY WEREN'T OUT TO KILL ME.
I VOTE WE MAKE TRACKS FOR FLORIDA.

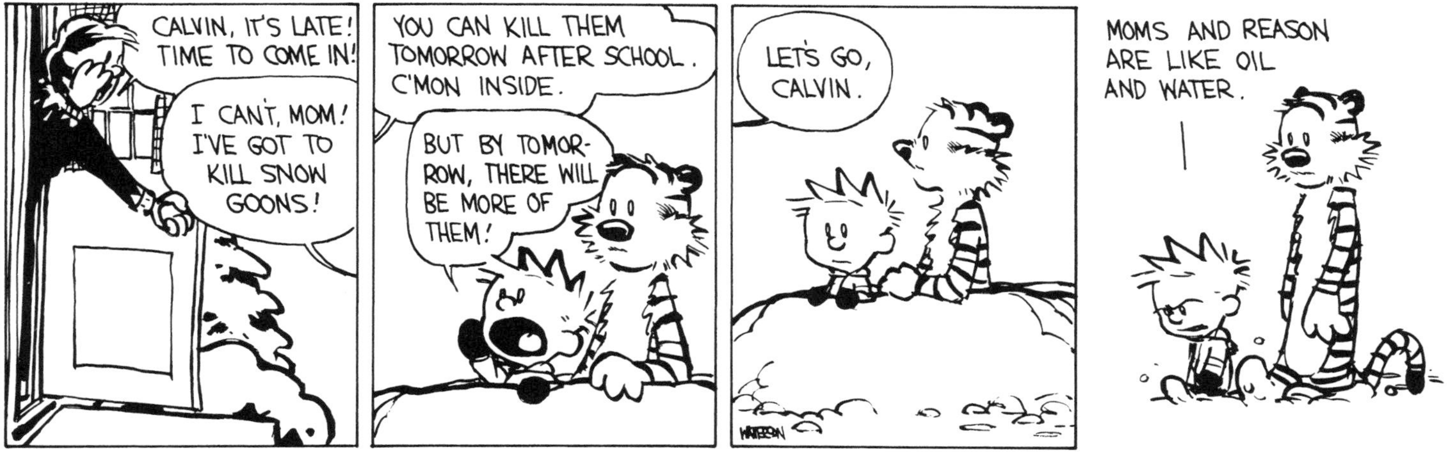
CALVIN, IT'S LATE! TIME TO COME IN!
I CAN'T, MOM! I'VE GOT TO KILL SNOW GOONS!
YOU CAN KILL THEM TOMORROW AFTER SCHOOL. C'MON INSIDE.
BUT BY TOMORROW, THERE WILL BE MORE OF THEM!
LET'S GO, CALVIN.
MOMS AND REASON ARE LIKE OIL AND WATER.

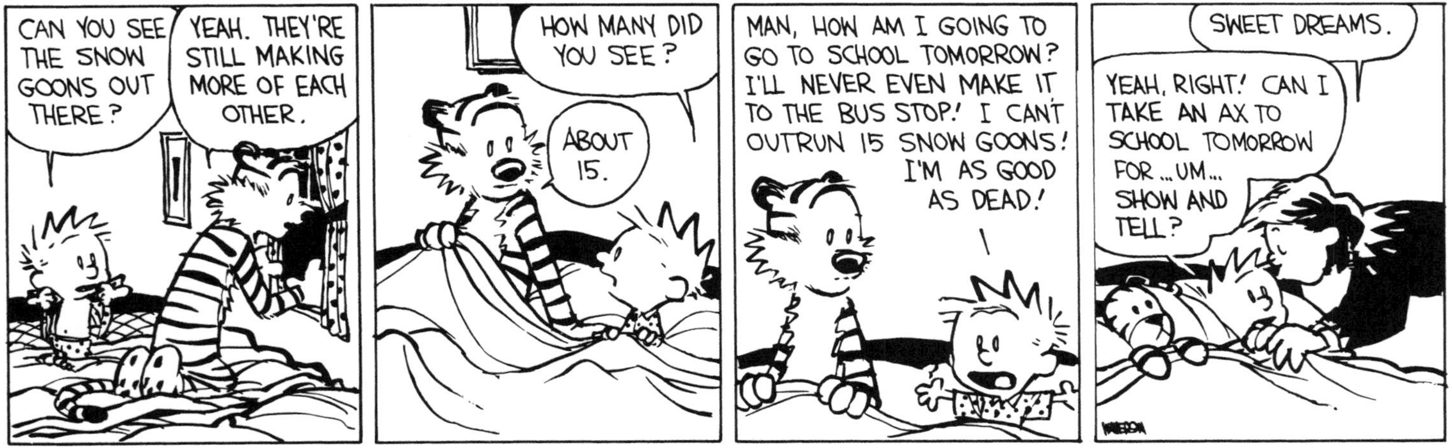
CAN YOU SEE THE SNOW GOONS OUT THERE?
YEAH. THEY'RE STILL MAKING MORE OF EACH OTHER.
HOW MANY DID YOU SEE?
ABOUT 15.
MAN, HOW AM I GOING TO GO TO SCHOOL TOMORROW? I'LL NEVER EVEN MAKE IT TO THE BUS STOP! I CAN'T OUTRUN 15 SNOW GOONS! I'M AS GOOD AS DEAD!
SWEET DREAMS.
YEAH, RIGHT! CAN I TAKE AN AX TO SCHOOL TOMORROW FOR ... UM ... SHOW AND TELL?

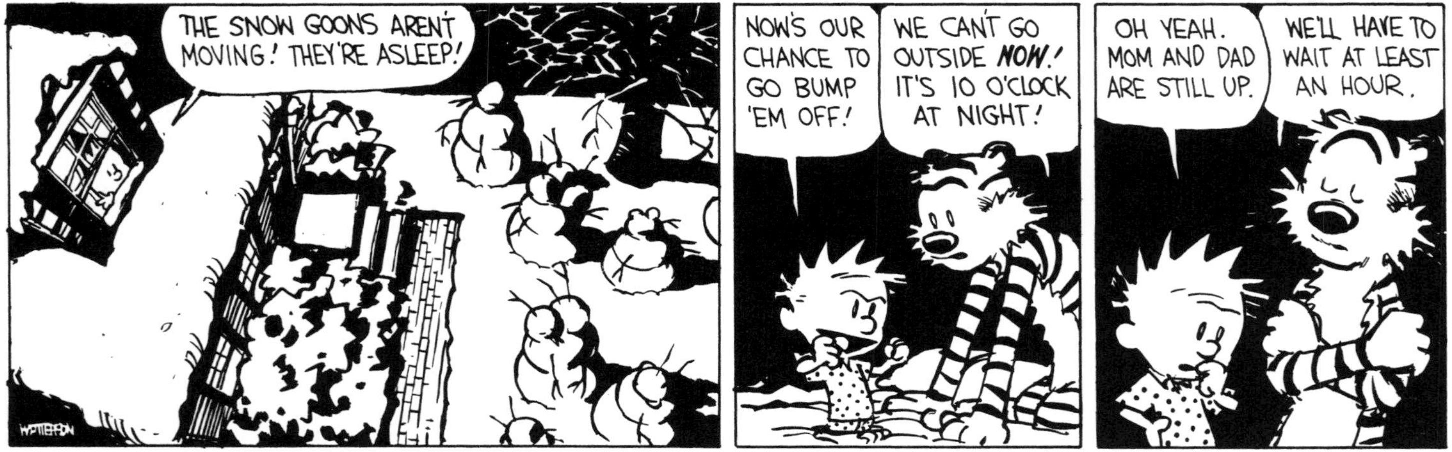
THE SNOW GOONS AREN'T MOVING! THEY'RE ASLEEP!
NOW'S OUR CHANCE TO GO BUMP 'EM OFF!
WE CAN'T GO OUTSIDE **NOW**! IT'S 10 O'CLOCK AT NIGHT!
OH YEAH. MOM AND DAD ARE STILL UP.
WE'LL HAVE TO WAIT AT LEAST AN HOUR.

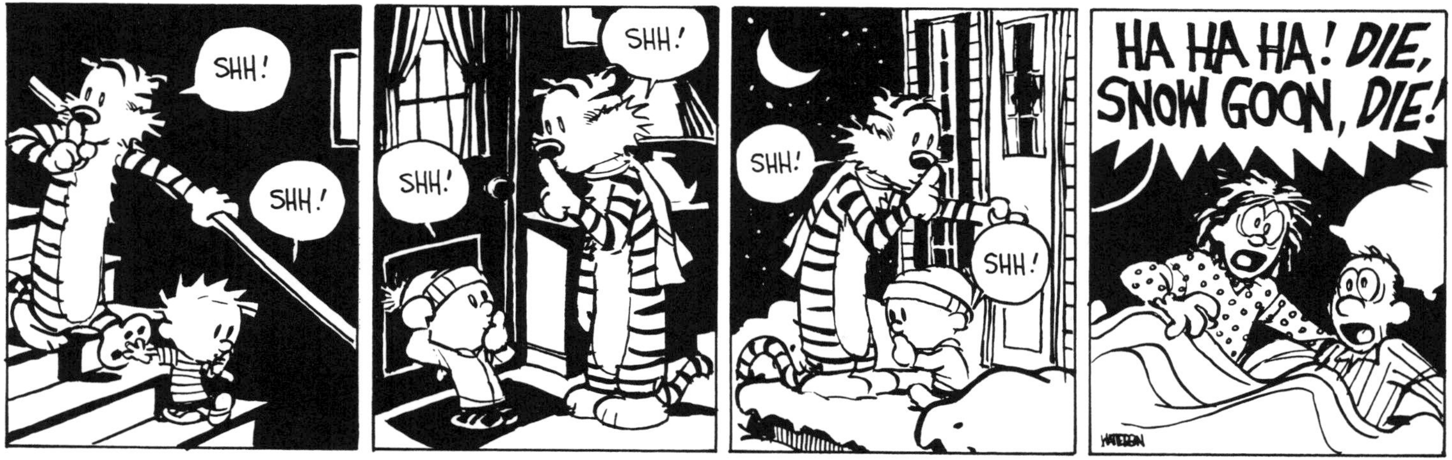
SHH!
SHH!
SHH!
SHH!
SHH!
SHH!
HA HA HA! DIE, SNOW GOON, DIE!
WATTERSON

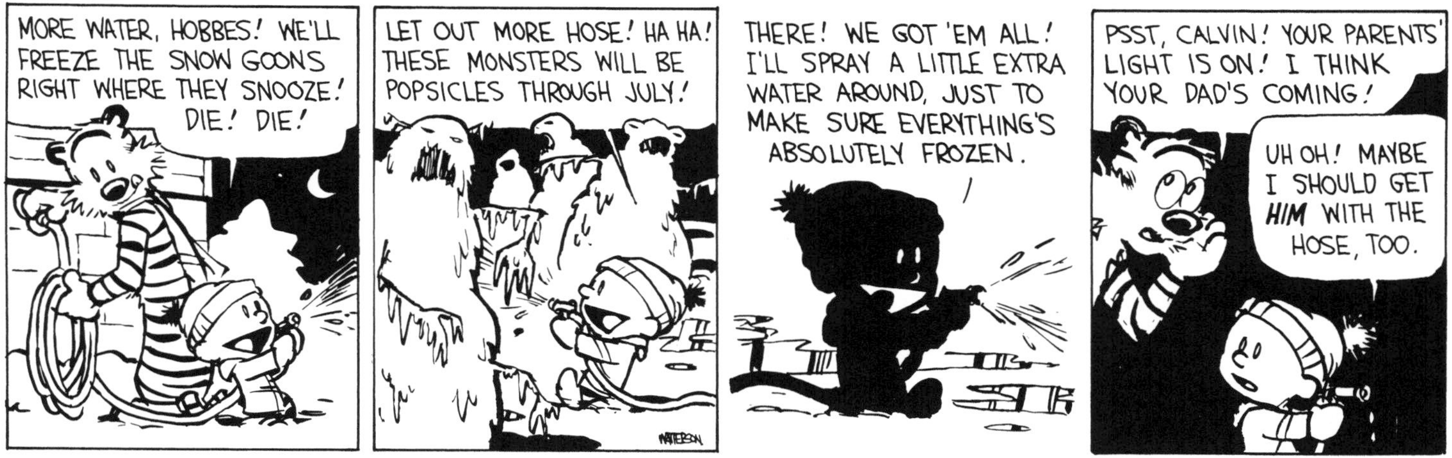
MORE WATER, HOBBES! WE'LL FREEZE THE SNOW GOONS RIGHT WHERE THEY SNOOZE! DIE! DIE!
LET OUT MORE HOSE! HA HA! THESE MONSTERS WILL BE POPSICLES THROUGH JULY!
WATTERSON
THERE! WE GOT 'EM ALL! I'LL SPRAY A LITTLE EXTRA WATER AROUND, JUST TO MAKE SURE EVERYTHING'S ABSOLUTELY FROZEN.
PSST, CALVIN! YOUR PARENTS' LIGHT IS ON! I THINK YOUR DAD'S COMING!
UH OH! MAYBE I SHOULD GET HIM WITH THE HOSE, TOO.

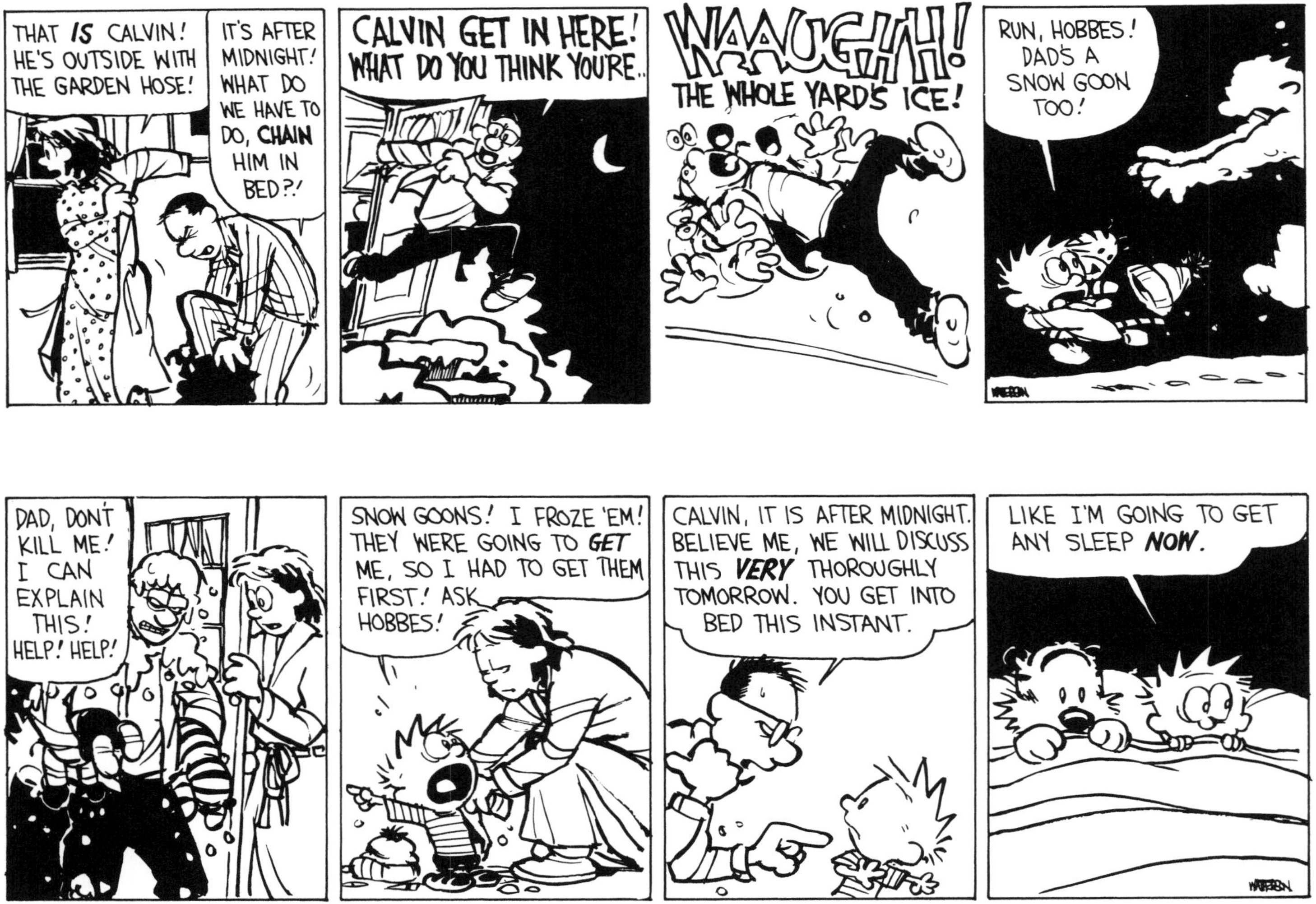
THAT IS CALVIN! HE'S OUTSIDE WITH THE GARDEN HOSE!
IT'S AFTER MIDNIGHT! WHAT DO WE HAVE TO DO, CHAIN HIM IN BED?!
CALVIN GET IN HERE! WHAT DO YOU THINK YOU'RE..
WAAUGHH!
THE WHOLE YARD'S ICE!
RUN, HOBBES! DAD'S A SNOW GOON TOO!
DAD, DON'T KILL ME! I CAN EXPLAIN THIS! HELP! HELP!
SNOW GOONS! I FROZE 'EM! THEY WERE GOING TO GET ME, SO I HAD TO GET THEM FIRST! ASK HOBBES!
CALVIN, IT IS AFTER MIDNIGHT. BELIEVE ME, WE WILL DISCUSS THIS VERY THOROUGHLY TOMORROW. YOU GET INTO BED THIS INSTANT.
LIKE I'M GOING TO GET ANY SLEEP NOW.

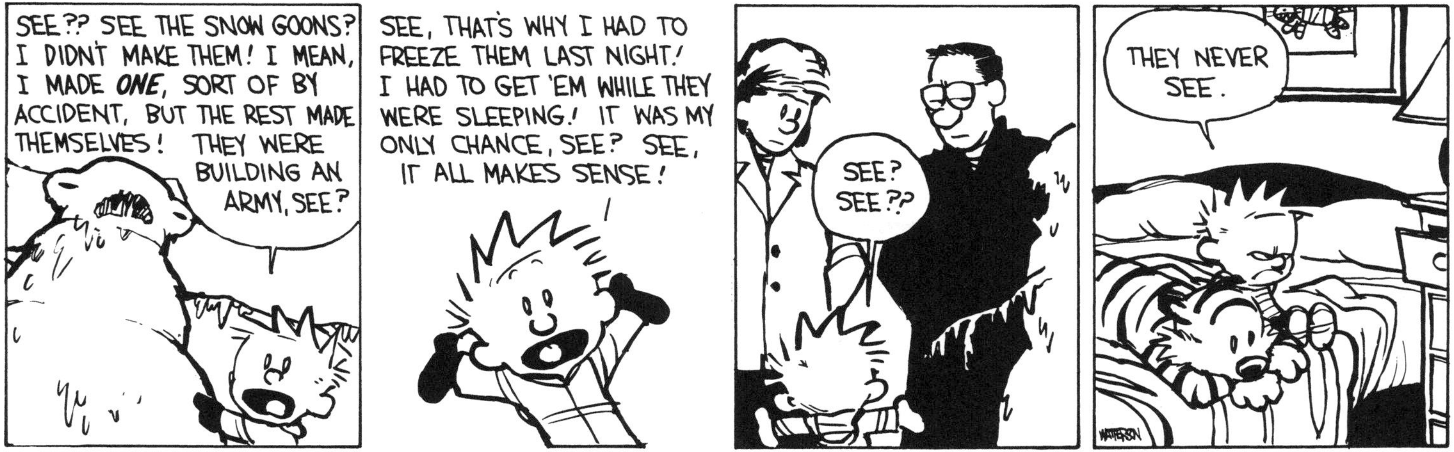
SEE?? SEE THE SNOW GOONS? I DIDN'T MAKE THEM! I MEAN, I MADE ONE, SORT OF BY ACCIDENT, BUT THE REST MADE THEMSELVES! THEY WERE BUILDING AN ARMY, SEE?
SEE, THAT'S WHY I HAD TO FREEZE THEM LAST NIGHT! I HAD TO GET 'EM WHILE THEY WERE SLEEPING! IT WAS MY ONLY CHANCE, SEE? SEE, IT ALL MAKES SENSE!
SEE? SEE??
THEY NEVER SEE.

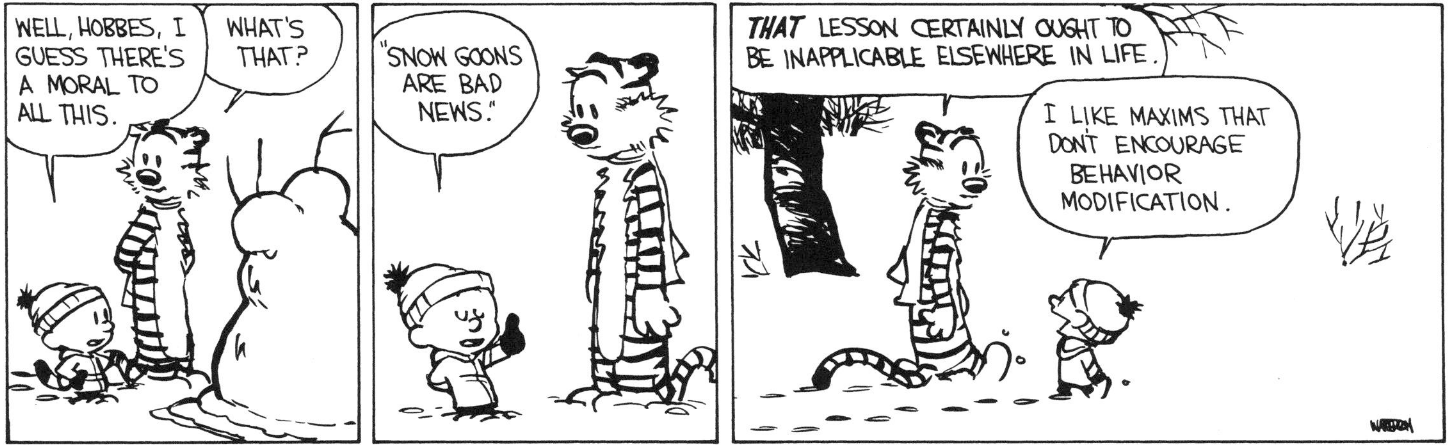
WELL, HOBBES, I GUESS THERE'S A MORAL TO ALL THIS.
WHAT'S THAT?
"SNOW GOONS ARE BAD NEWS."
THAT LESSON CERTAINLY OUGHT TO BE INAPPLICABLE ELSEWHERE IN LIFE.
I LIKE MAXIMS THAT DON'T ENCOURAGE BEHAVIOR MODIFICATION.

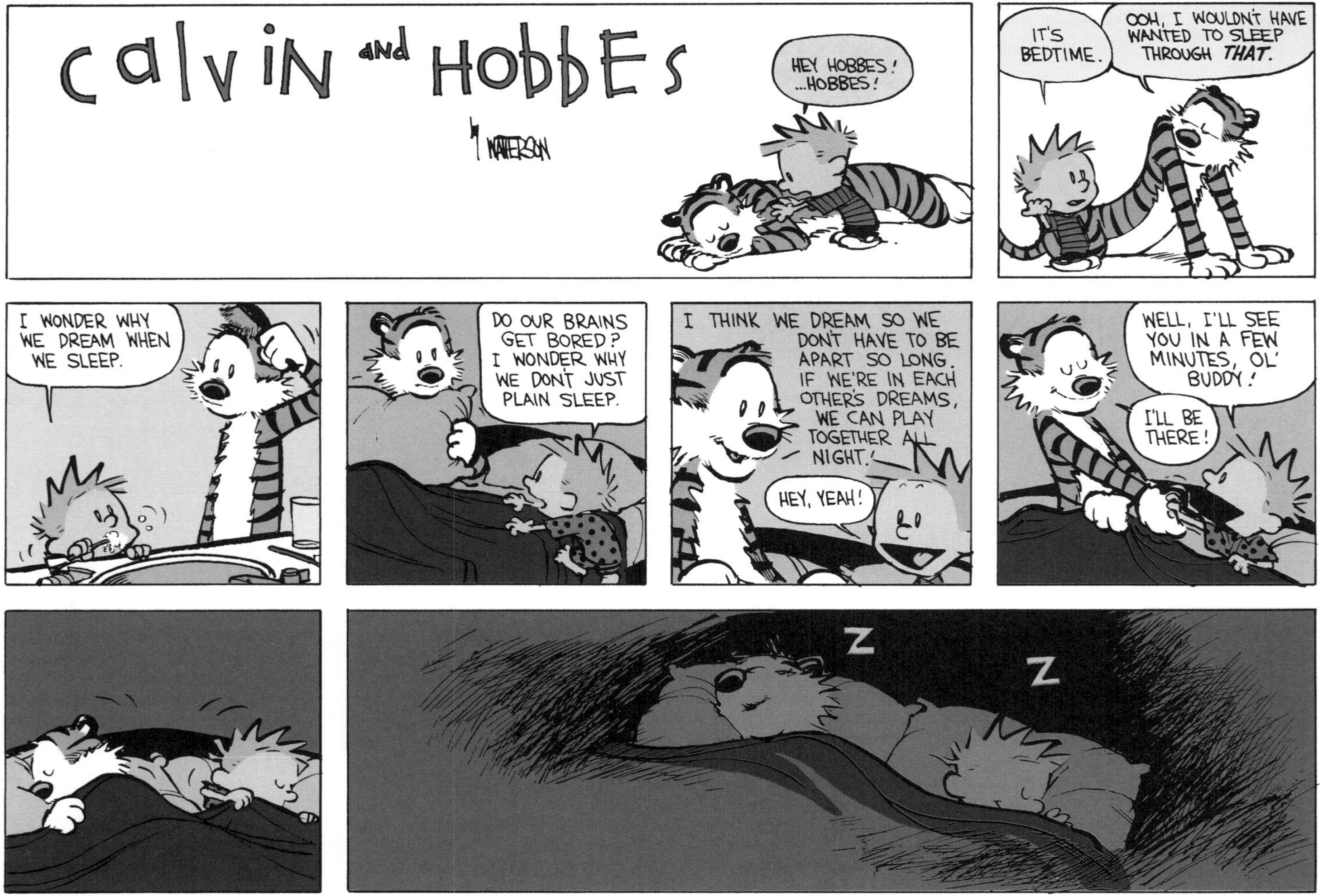
Calvin and Hobbes
by WATTERSON
HEY HOBBES! ...HOBBES!
IT'S BEDTIME.
OOH, I WOULDN'T HAVE WANTED TO SLEEP THROUGH THAT.
I WONDER WHY WE DREAM WHEN WE SLEEP.
DO OUR BRAINS GET BORED? I WONDER WHY WE DON'T JUST PLAIN SLEEP.
I THINK WE DREAM SO WE DON'T HAVE TO BE APART SO LONG. IF WE'RE IN EACH OTHER'S DREAMS, WE CAN PLAY TOGETHER ALL NIGHT.
HEY, YEAH!
WELL, I'LL SEE YOU IN A FEW MINUTES, OL' BUDDY!
I'LL BE THERE!
Z
Z

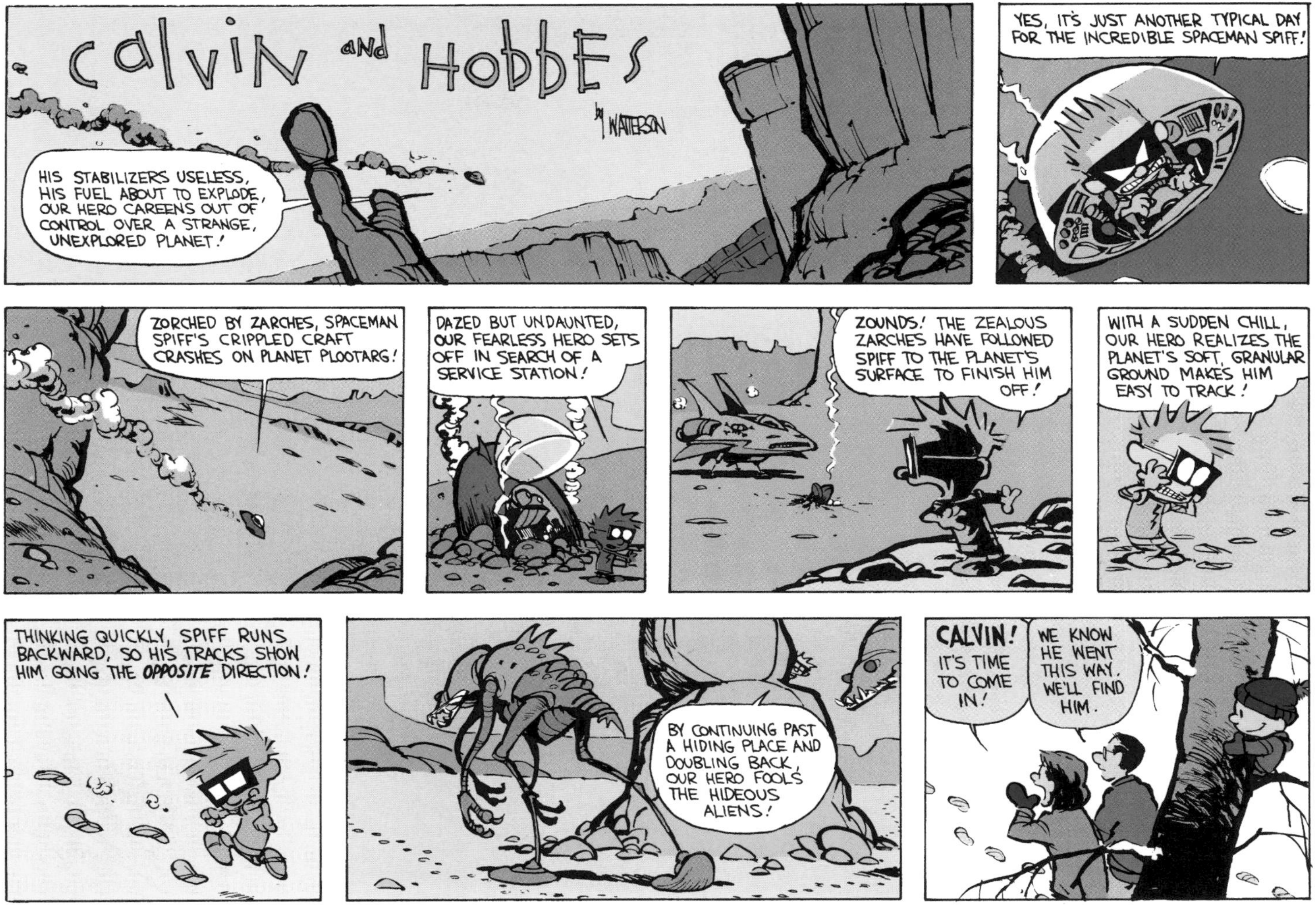
Calvin and Hobbes
by WATTERSON
HIS STABILIZERS USELESS, HIS FUEL ABOUT TO EXPLODE, OUR HERO CAREENS OUT OF CONTROL OVER A STRANGE, UNEXPLORED PLANET!
YES, IT'S JUST ANOTHER TYPICAL DAY FOR THE INCREDIBLE SPACEMAN SPIFF!
ZORCHED BY ZARCHES, SPACEMAN SPIFF'S CRIPPLED CRAFT CRASHES ON PLANET PLOOTARG!
DAZED BUT UNDAUNTED, OUR FEARLESS HERO SETS OFF IN SEARCH OF A SERVICE STATION!
ZOUNDS! THE ZEALOUS ZARCHES HAVE FOLLOWED SPIFF TO THE PLANET'S SURFACE TO FINISH HIM OFF!
WITH A SUDDEN CHILL, OUR HERO REALIZES THE PLANET'S SOFT, GRANULAR GROUND MAKES HIM EASY TO TRACK!
THINKING QUICKLY, SPIFF RUNS BACKWARD, SO HIS TRACKS SHOW HIM GOING THE OPPOSITE DIRECTION!
BY CONTINUING PAST A HIDING PLACE AND DOUBLING BACK, OUR HERO FOOLS THE HIDEOUS ALIENS!
CALVIN! IT'S TIME TO COME IN!
WE KNOW HE WENT THIS WAY. WE'LL FIND HIM.

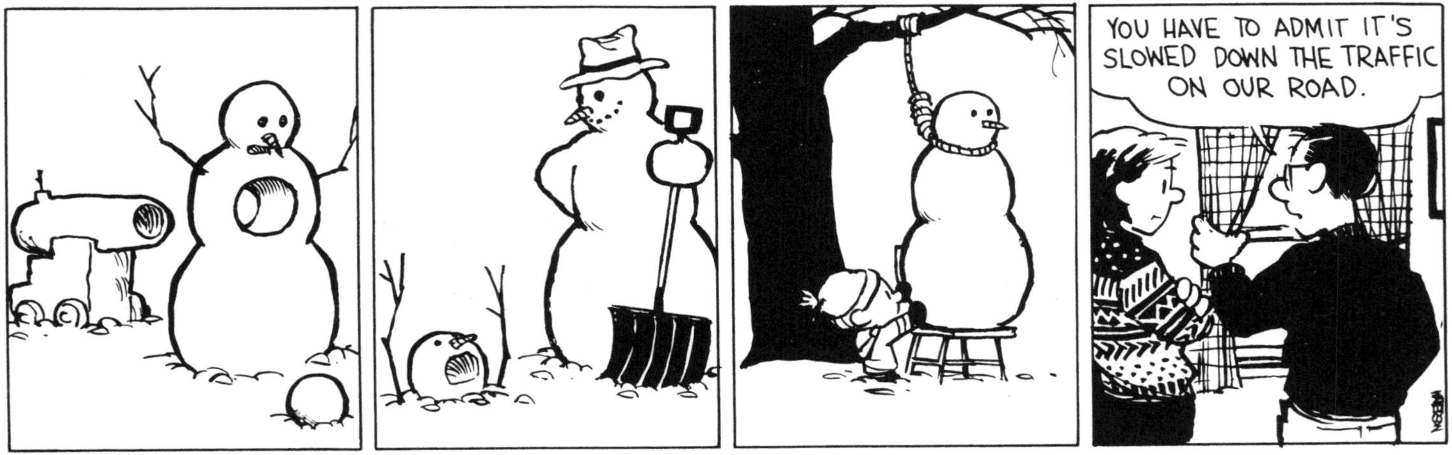
YOU HAVE TO ADMIT IT'S SLOWED DOWN THE TRAFFIC ON OUR ROAD.

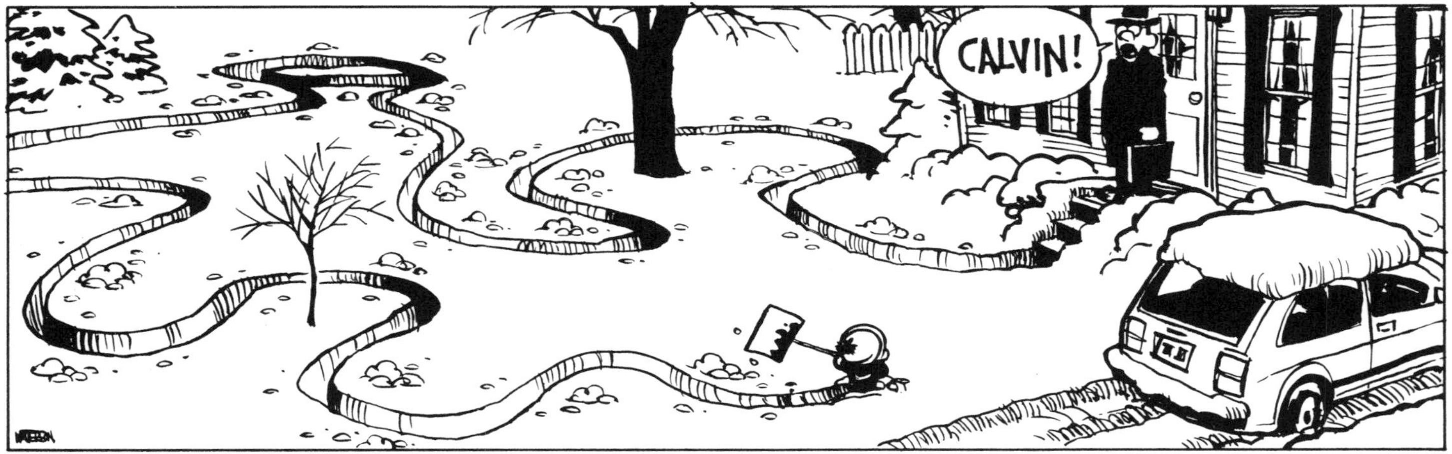
CALVIN!

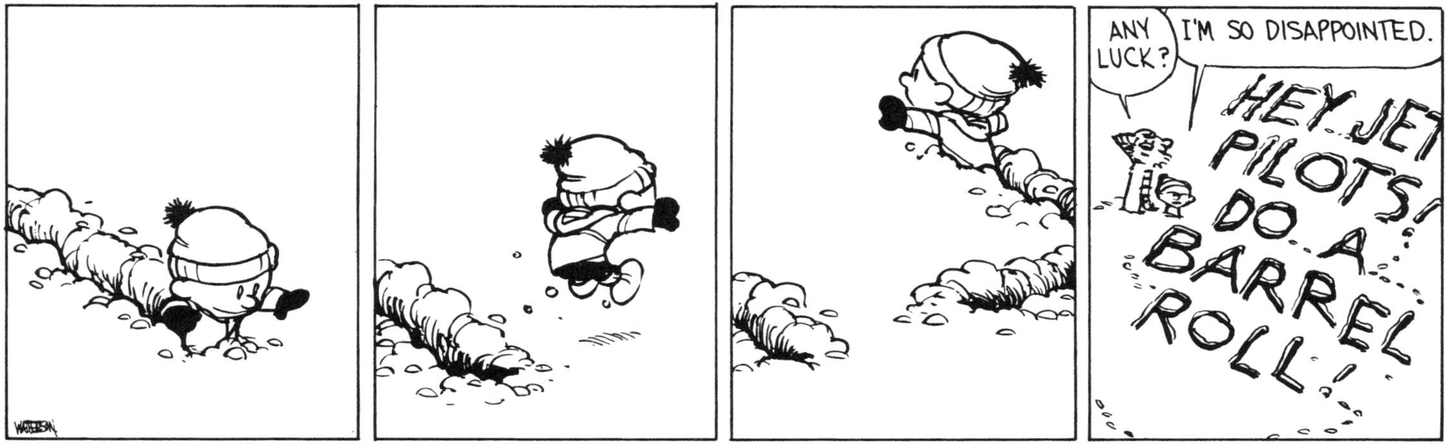
ANY LUCK?
I'M SO DISAPPOINTED.
HEY JET PILOTS! DO A BARREL ROLL!

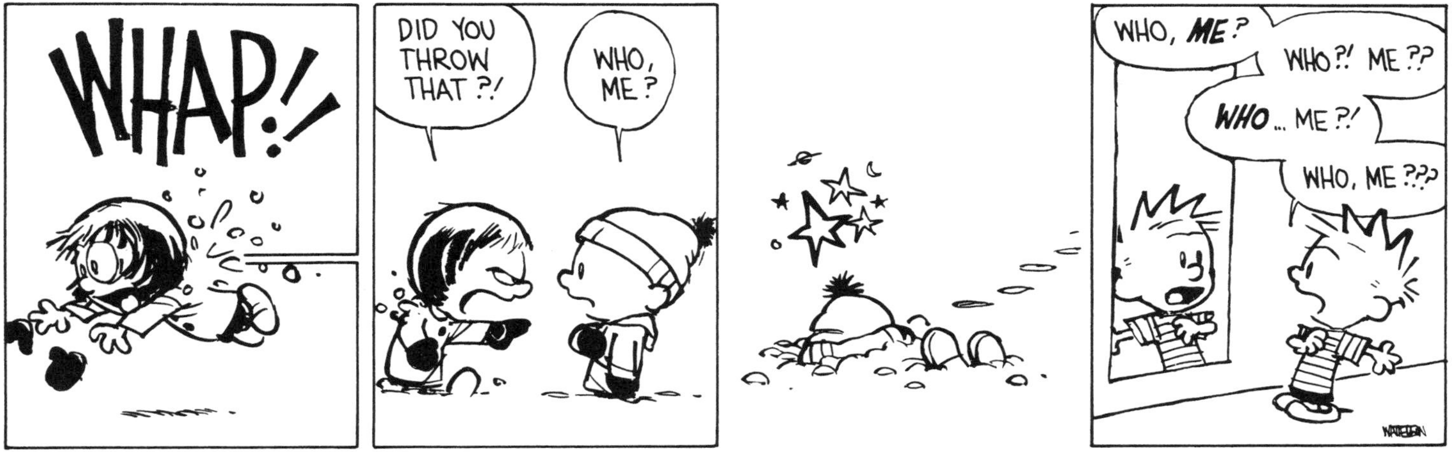
WHAP!!
DID YOU THROW THAT?!
WHO, ME?
WHO, ME?
WHO?! ME??
WHO... ME?!
WHO, ME???

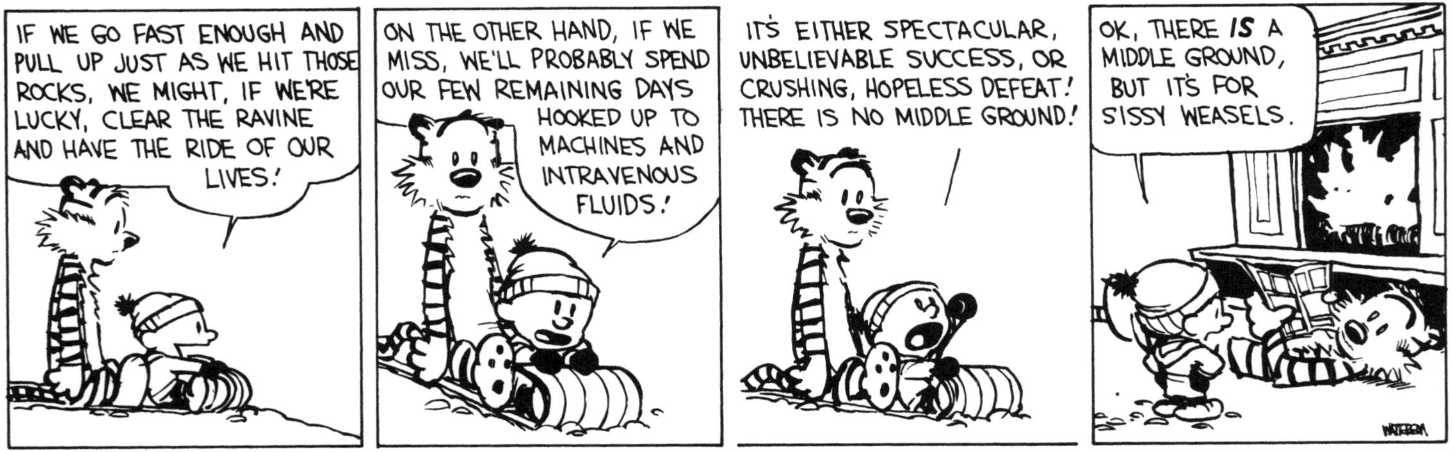
IF WE GO FAST ENOUGH AND PULL UP JUST AS WE HIT THOSE ROCKS, WE MIGHT, IF WE'RE LUCKY, CLEAR THE RAVINE AND HAVE THE RIDE OF OUR LIVES!
ON THE OTHER HAND, IF WE MISS, WE'LL PROBABLY SPEND OUR FEW REMAINING DAYS HOOKED UP TO MACHINES AND INTRAVENOUS FLUIDS!
IT'S EITHER SPECTACULAR, UNBELIEVABLE SUCCESS, OR CRUSHING, HOPELESS DEFEAT! THERE IS NO MIDDLE GROUND!
OK, THERE **IS** A MIDDLE GROUND, BUT IT'S FOR SISSY WEASELS.
WATTERSON

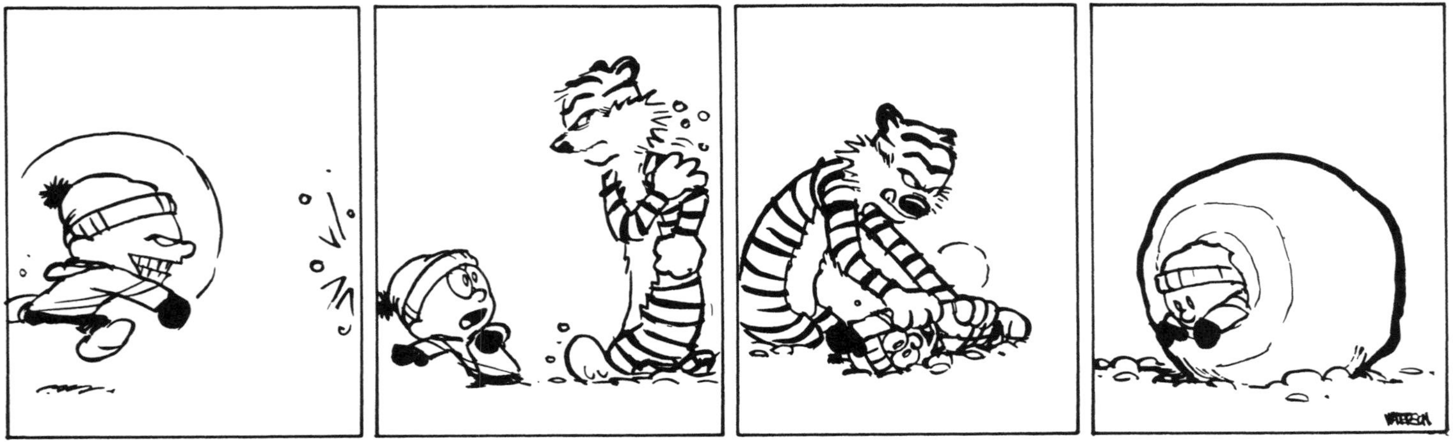
WATTERSON

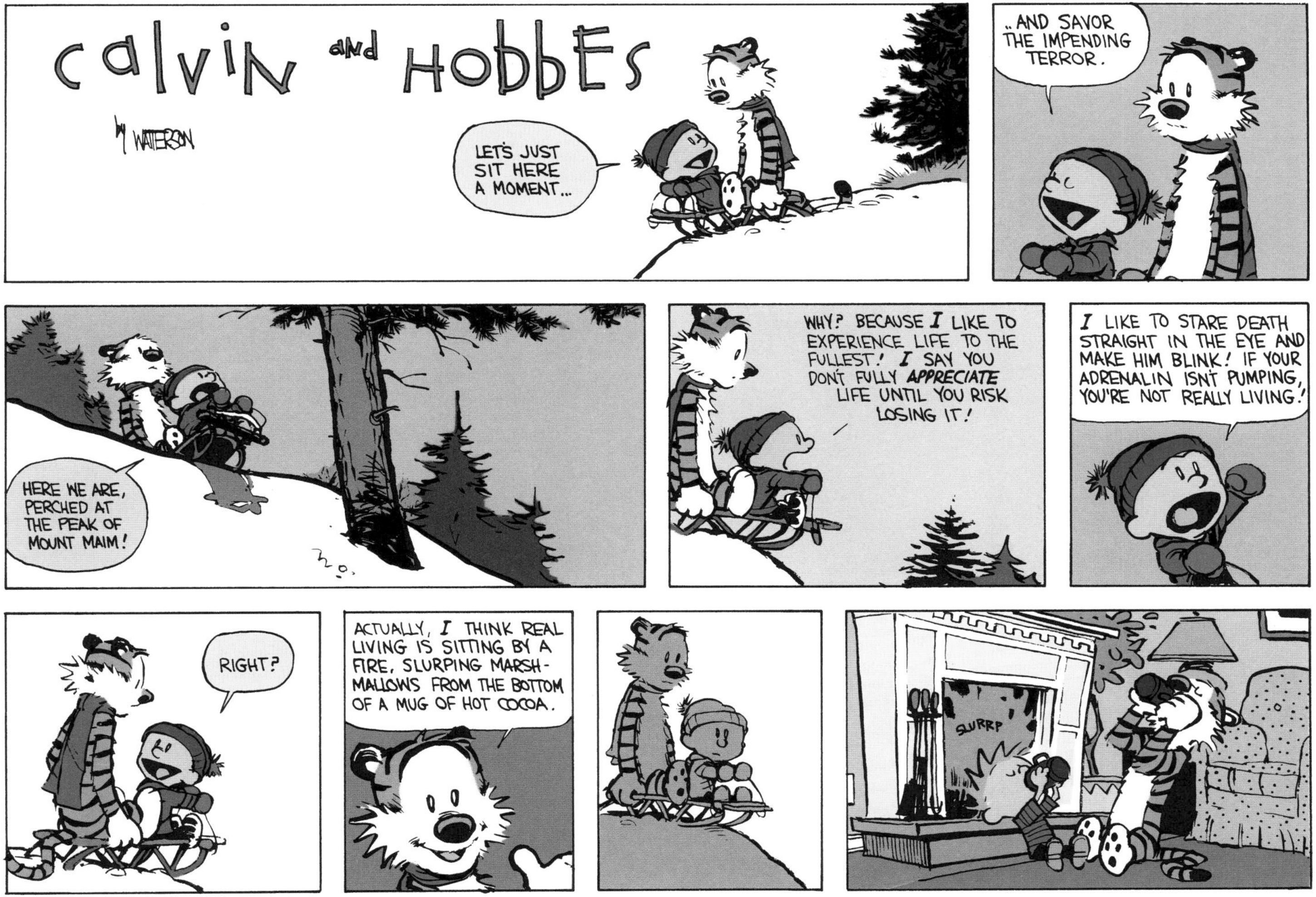
Calvin and Hobbes
by Watterson
LET'S JUST SIT HERE A MOMENT...
..AND SAVOR THE IMPENDING TERROR.
HERE WE ARE, PERCHED AT THE PEAK OF MOUNT MAIM!
WHY? BECAUSE I LIKE TO EXPERIENCE LIFE TO THE FULLEST! I SAY YOU DON'T FULLY APPRECIATE LIFE UNTIL YOU RISK LOSING IT!
I LIKE TO STARE DEATH STRAIGHT IN THE EYE AND MAKE HIM BLINK! IF YOUR ADRENALIN ISN'T PUMPING, YOU'RE NOT REALLY LIVING!
RIGHT?
ACTUALLY, I THINK REAL LIVING IS SITTING BY A FIRE, SLURPING MARSH-MALLOWS FROM THE BOTTOM OF A MUG OF HOT COCOA.
SLURRP

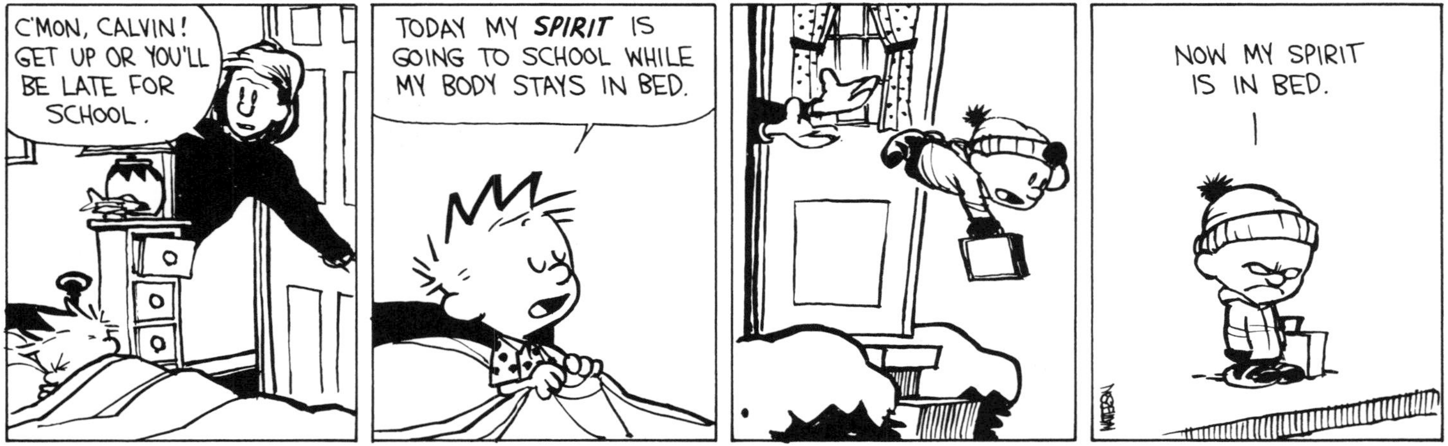
C'MON, CALVIN! GET UP OR YOU'LL BE LATE FOR SCHOOL.
TODAY MY SPIRIT IS GOING TO SCHOOL WHILE MY BODY STAYS IN BED.
NOW MY SPIRIT IS IN BED.

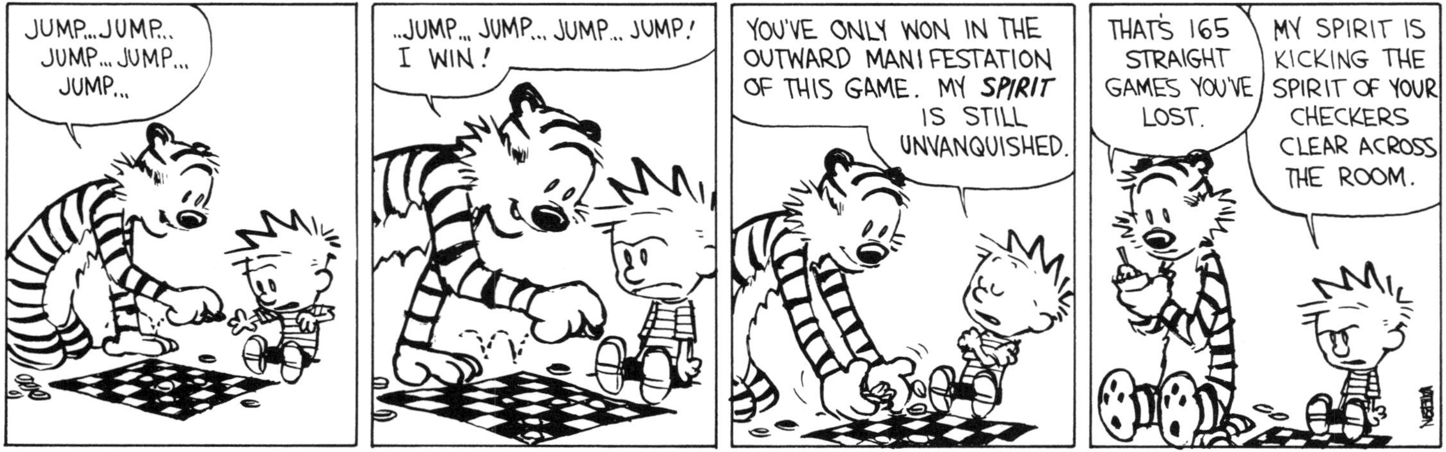
JUMP...JUMP... JUMP...JUMP... JUMP...
...JUMP... JUMP... JUMP... JUMP! I WIN!
YOU'VE ONLY WON IN THE OUTWARD MANIFESTATION OF THIS GAME. MY SPIRIT IS STILL UNVANQUISHED.
THAT'S 165 STRAIGHT GAMES YOU'VE LOST.
MY SPIRIT IS KICKING THE SPIRIT OF YOUR CHECKERS CLEAR ACROSS THE ROOM.

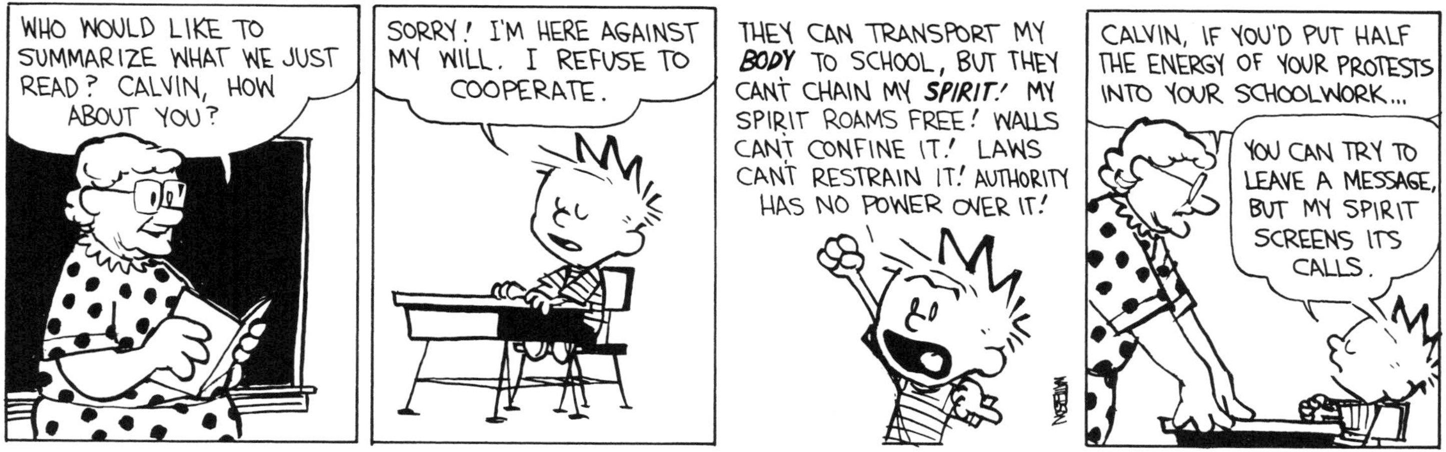
WHO WOULD LIKE TO SUMMARIZE WHAT WE JUST READ? CALVIN, HOW ABOUT YOU?
SORRY! I'M HERE AGAINST MY WILL. I REFUSE TO COOPERATE.
THEY CAN TRANSPORT MY **BODY** TO SCHOOL, BUT THEY CAN'T CHAIN MY **SPIRIT!** MY SPIRIT ROAMS FREE! WALLS CAN'T CONFINE IT! LAWS CAN'T RESTRAIN IT! AUTHORITY HAS NO POWER OVER IT!
CALVIN, IF YOU'D PUT HALF THE ENERGY OF YOUR PROTESTS INTO YOUR SCHOOLWORK...
YOU CAN TRY TO LEAVE A MESSAGE, BUT MY SPIRIT SCREENS ITS CALLS.

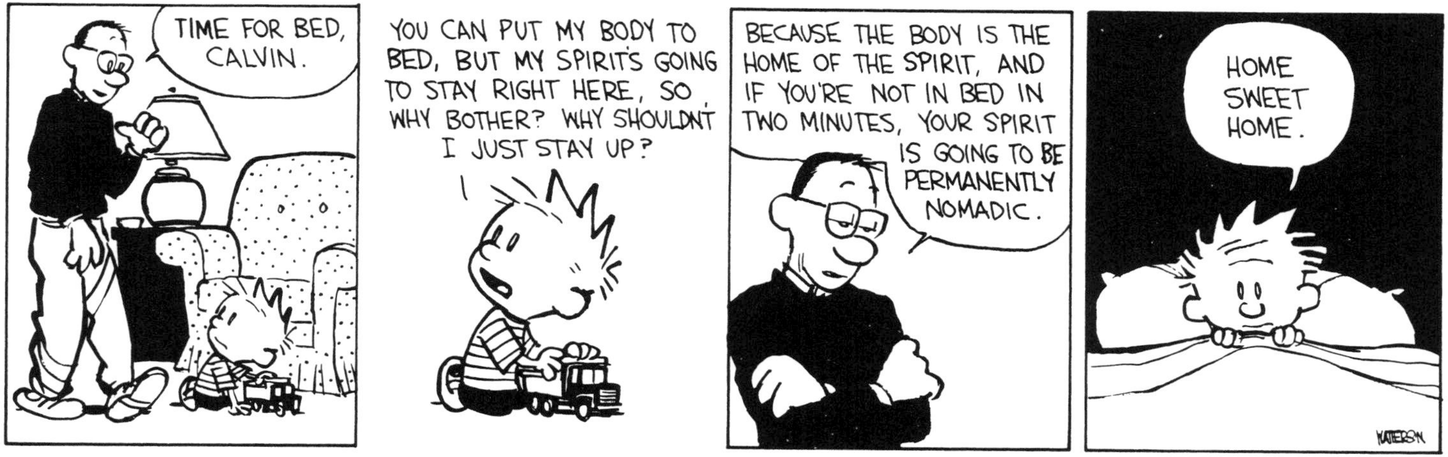
TIME FOR BED, CALVIN.
YOU CAN PUT MY BODY TO BED, BUT MY SPIRIT'S GOING TO STAY RIGHT HERE, SO WHY BOTHER? WHY SHOULDN'T I JUST STAY UP?
BECAUSE THE BODY IS THE HOME OF THE SPIRIT, AND IF YOU'RE NOT IN BED IN TWO MINUTES, YOUR SPIRIT IS GOING TO BE PERMANENTLY NOMADIC.
HOME SWEET HOME.

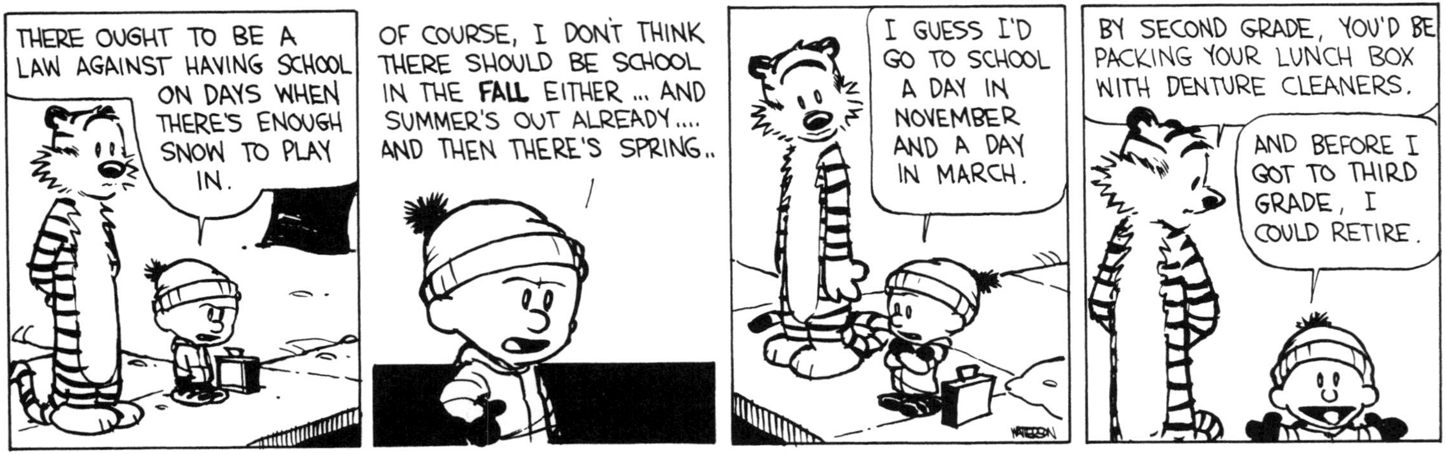
THERE OUGHT TO BE A LAW AGAINST HAVING SCHOOL ON DAYS WHEN THERE'S ENOUGH SNOW TO PLAY IN.
OF COURSE, I DON'T THINK THERE SHOULD BE SCHOOL IN THE **FALL** EITHER ... AND SUMMER'S OUT ALREADY.... AND THEN THERE'S SPRING..
I GUESS I'D GO TO SCHOOL A DAY IN NOVEMBER AND A DAY IN MARCH.
BY SECOND GRADE, YOU'D BE PACKING YOUR LUNCH BOX WITH DENTURE CLEANERS.
AND BEFORE I GOT TO THIRD GRADE, I COULD RETIRE.

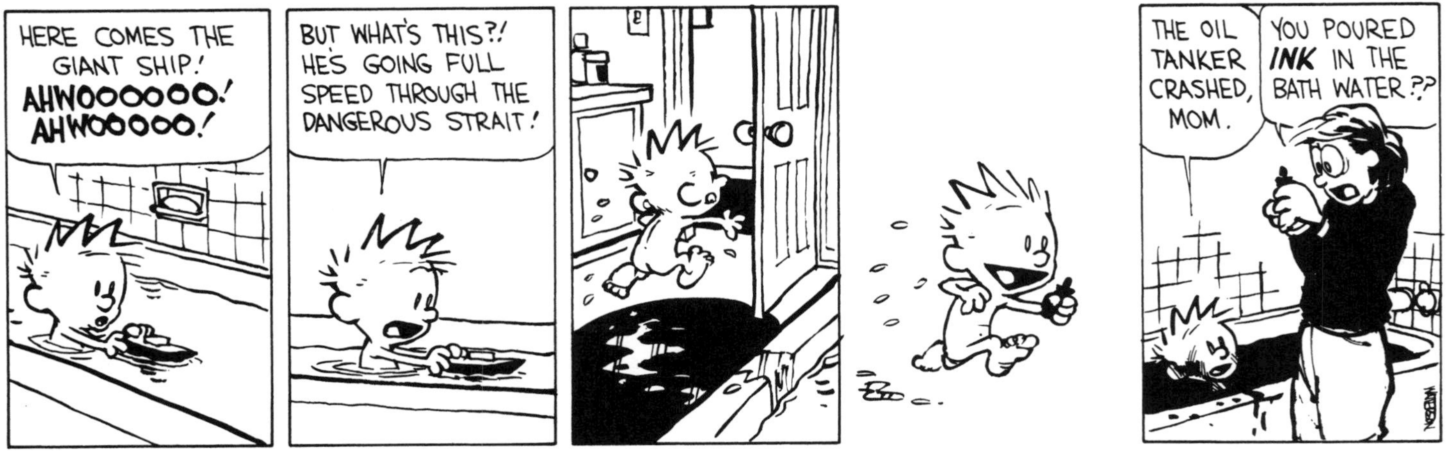
HERE COMES THE GIANT SHIP! **AHWOOOOOO! AHWOOOOO!**
BUT WHAT'S THIS?! HE'S GOING FULL SPEED THROUGH THE DANGEROUS STRAIT!
THE OIL TANKER CRASHED, MOM.
YOU POURED ***INK*** IN THE BATH WATER??

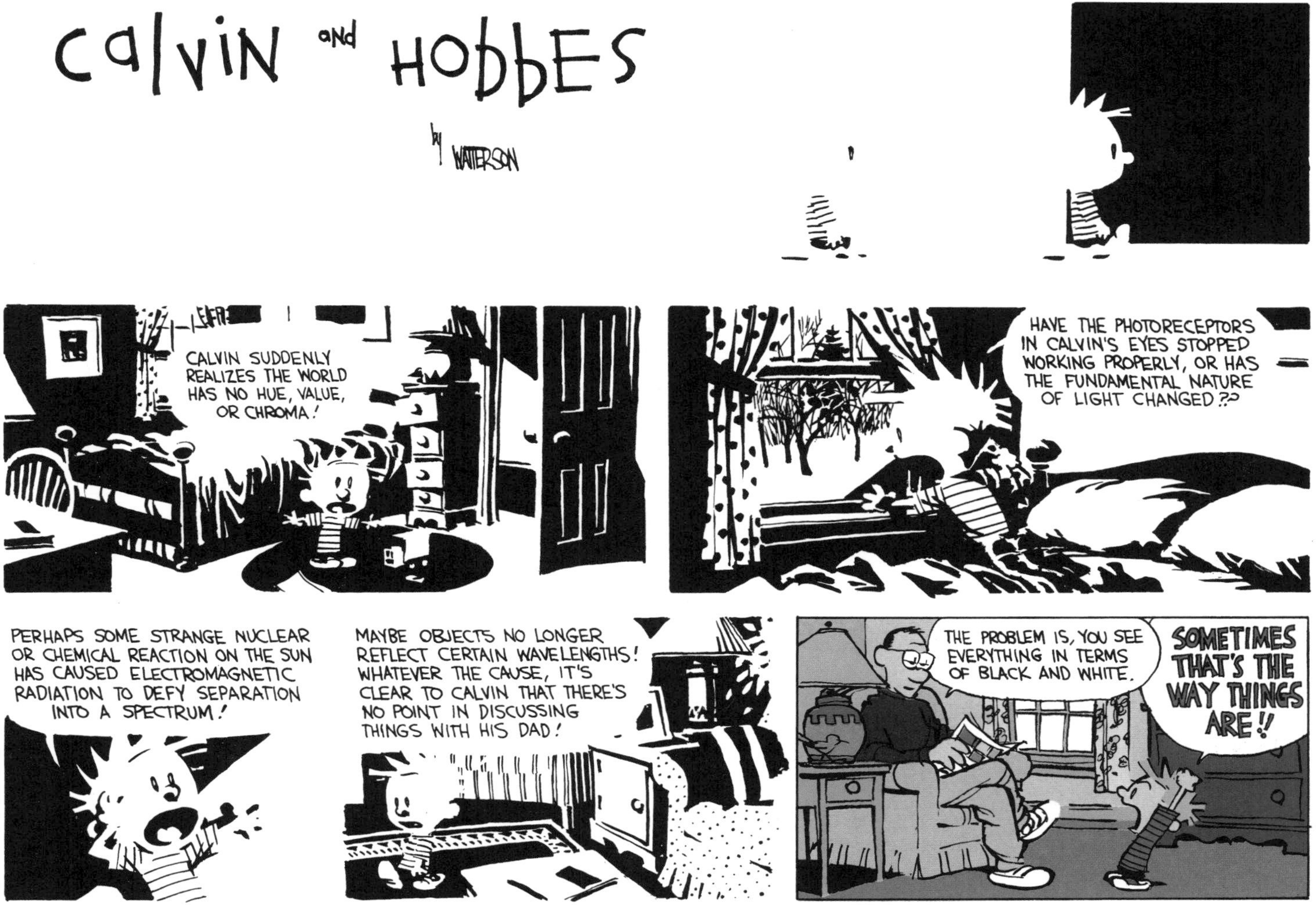

CALVIN AND HOBBES
by WATTERSON
CALVIN SUDDENLY REALIZES THE WORLD HAS NO HUE, VALUE, OR CHROMA!
HAVE THE PHOTORECEPTORS IN CALVIN'S EYES STOPPED WORKING PROPERLY, OR HAS THE FUNDAMENTAL NATURE OF LIGHT CHANGED?!
PERHAPS SOME STRANGE NUCLEAR OR CHEMICAL REACTION ON THE SUN HAS CAUSED ELECTROMAGNETIC RADIATION TO DEFY SEPARATION INTO A SPECTRUM!
MAYBE OBJECTS NO LONGER REFLECT CERTAIN WAVELENGTHS! WHATEVER THE CAUSE, IT'S CLEAR TO CALVIN THAT THERE'S NO POINT IN DISCUSSING THINGS WITH HIS DAD!
THE PROBLEM IS, YOU SEE EVERYTHING IN TERMS OF BLACK AND WHITE.
SOMETIMES THAT'S THE WAY THINGS ARE!!

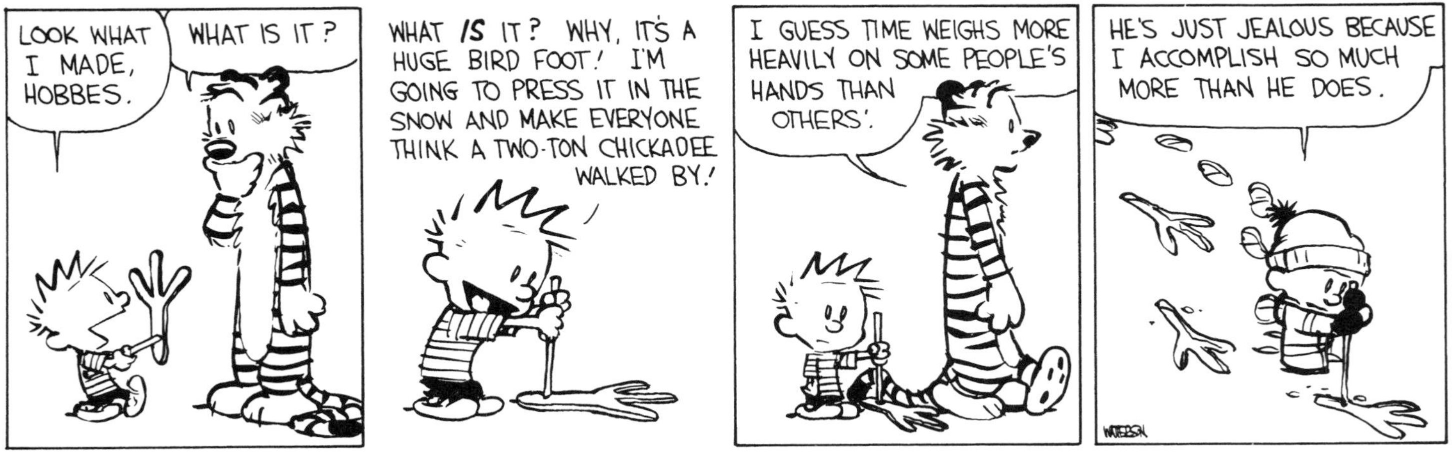

LOOK WHAT I MADE, HOBBES.
WHAT IS IT?
WHAT *IS* IT? WHY, IT'S A HUGE BIRD FOOT! I'M GOING TO PRESS IT IN THE SNOW AND MAKE EVERYONE THINK A TWO-TON CHICKADEE WALKED BY!
I GUESS TIME WEIGHS MORE HEAVILY ON SOME PEOPLE'S HANDS THAN OTHERS'.
HE'S JUST JEALOUS BECAUSE I ACCOMPLISH SO MUCH MORE THAN HE DOES.
WATTERSON

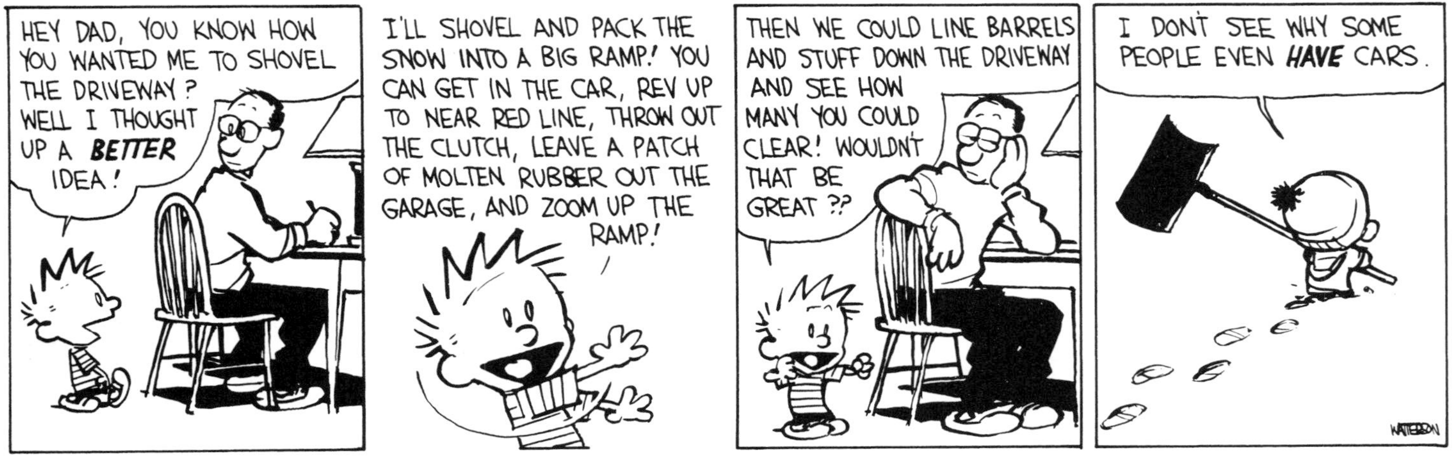

HEY DAD, YOU KNOW HOW YOU WANTED ME TO SHOVEL THE DRIVEWAY? WELL I THOUGHT UP A *BETTER* IDEA!
I'LL SHOVEL AND PACK THE SNOW INTO A BIG RAMP! YOU CAN GET IN THE CAR, REV UP TO NEAR RED LINE, THROW OUT THE CLUTCH, LEAVE A PATCH OF MOLTEN RUBBER OUT THE GARAGE, AND ZOOM UP THE RAMP!
THEN WE COULD LINE BARRELS AND STUFF DOWN THE DRIVEWAY AND SEE HOW MANY YOU COULD CLEAR! WOULDN'T THAT BE GREAT??
I DON'T SEE WHY SOME PEOPLE EVEN *HAVE* CARS.
WATTERSON

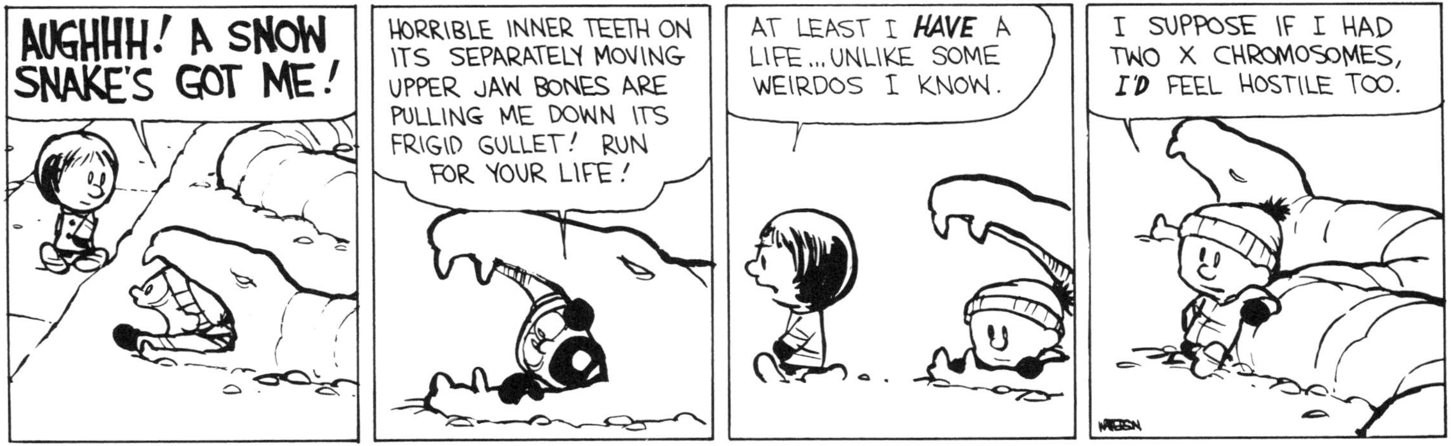
AUGHHH! A SNOW SNAKE'S GOT ME!
HORRIBLE INNER TEETH ON ITS SEPARATELY MOVING UPPER JAW BONES ARE PULLING ME DOWN ITS FRIGID GULLET! RUN FOR YOUR LIFE!
AT LEAST I *HAVE* A LIFE... UNLIKE SOME WEIRDOS I KNOW.
I SUPPOSE IF I HAD TWO X CHROMOSOMES, *I'D* FEEL HOSTILE TOO.

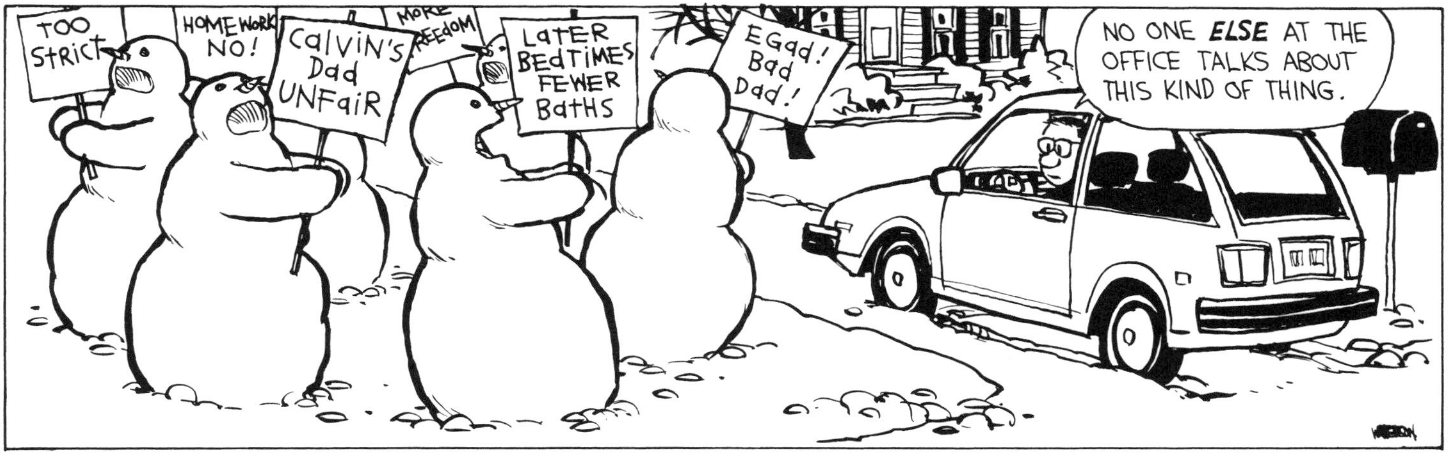
TOO StricT
HOMEWORK NO!
CalviN's Dad UNFaiR
MORE FREEDOM
LaTER BEdTIMES FEWER BaTHS
EGad! Bad Dad!
NO ONE *ELSE* AT THE OFFICE TALKS ABOUT THIS KIND OF THING.

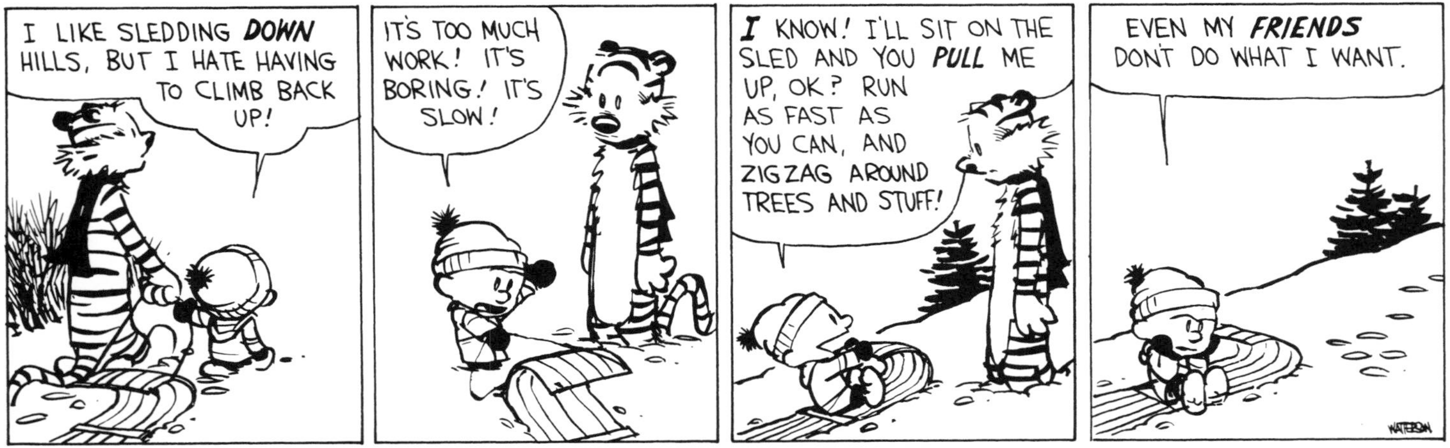
I LIKE SLEDDING **DOWN** HILLS, BUT I HATE HAVING TO CLIMB BACK UP!
IT'S TOO MUCH WORK! IT'S BORING! IT'S SLOW!
I KNOW! I'LL SIT ON THE SLED AND YOU **PULL** ME UP, OK? RUN AS FAST AS YOU CAN, AND ZIGZAG AROUND TREES AND STUFF!
EVEN MY **FRIENDS** DON'T DO WHAT I WANT.

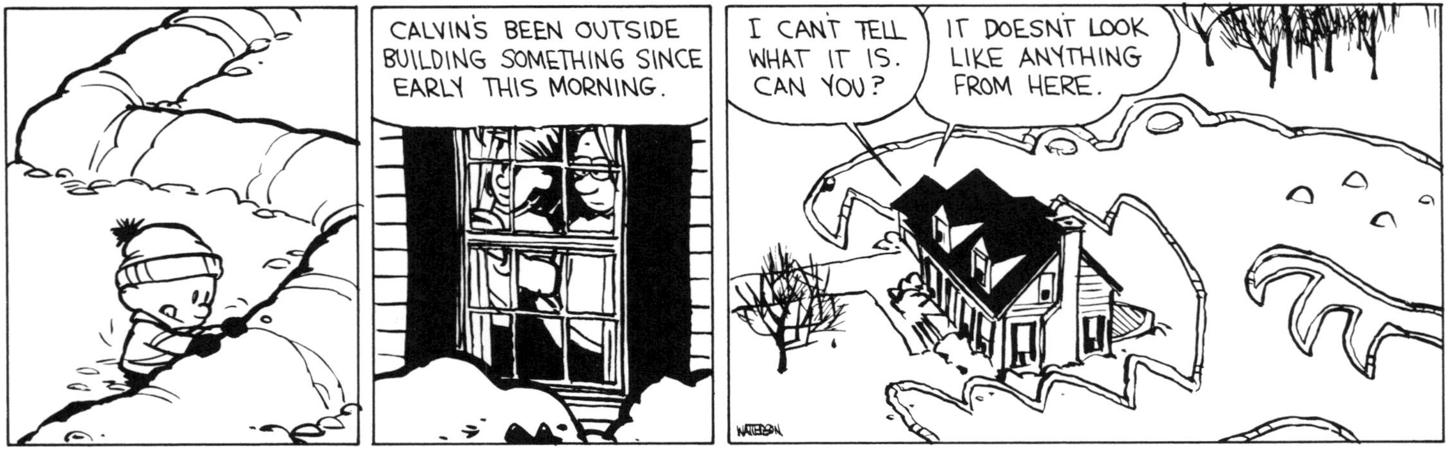
CALVIN'S BEEN OUTSIDE BUILDING SOMETHING SINCE EARLY THIS MORNING.
I CAN'T TELL WHAT IT IS. CAN YOU?
IT DOESN'T LOOK LIKE ANYTHING FROM HERE.

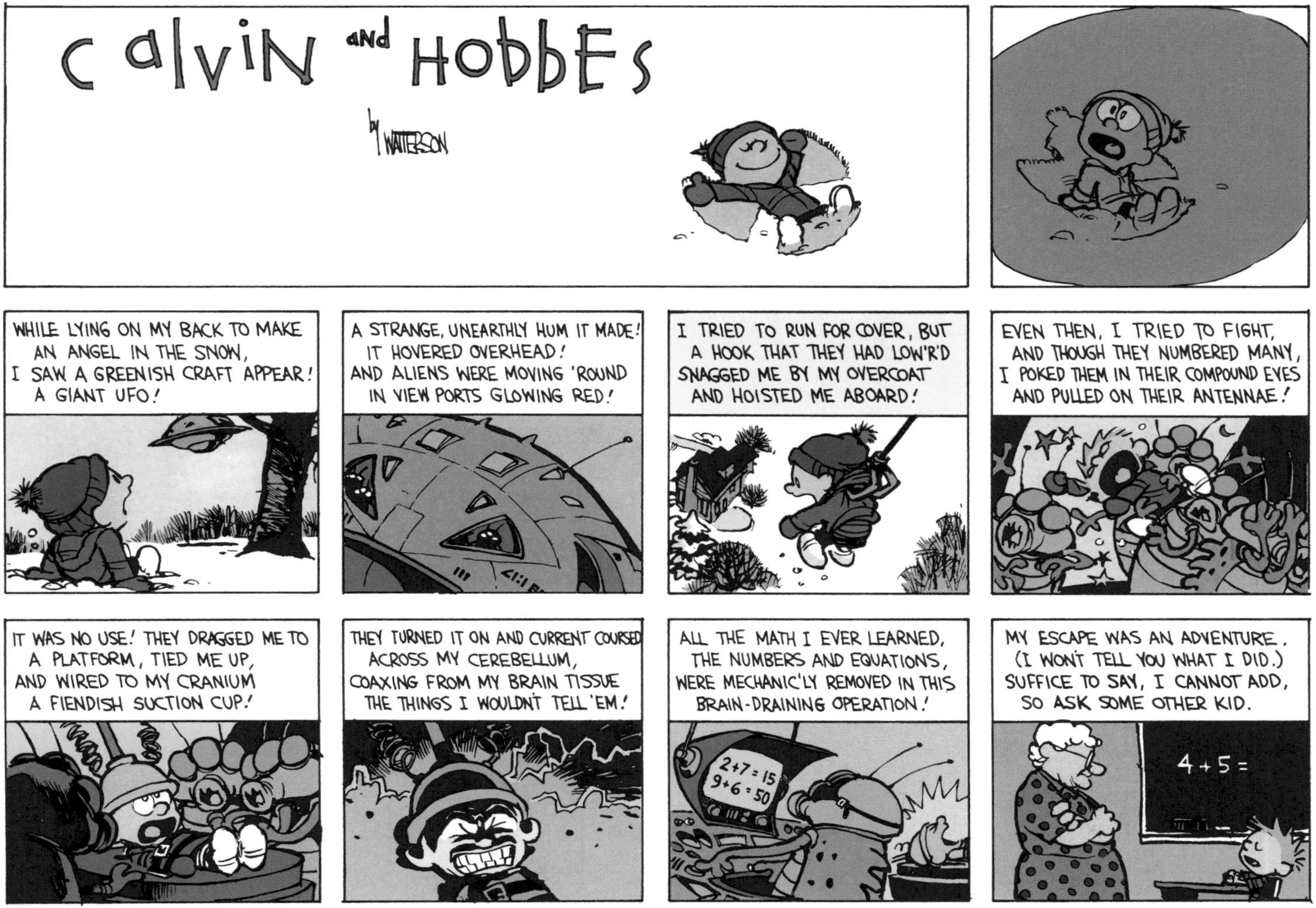
Calvin and Hobbes
by WATTERSON
WHILE LYING ON MY BACK TO MAKE AN ANGEL IN THE SNOW, I SAW A GREENISH CRAFT APPEAR! A GIANT UFO!
A STRANGE, UNEARTHLY HUM IT MADE! IT HOVERED OVERHEAD! AND ALIENS WERE MOVING 'ROUND IN VIEW PORTS GLOWING RED!
I TRIED TO RUN FOR COVER, BUT A HOOK THAT THEY HAD LOW'R'D SNAGGED ME BY MY OVERCOAT AND HOISTED ME ABOARD!
EVEN THEN, I TRIED TO FIGHT, AND THOUGH THEY NUMBERED MANY, I POKED THEM IN THEIR COMPOUND EYES AND PULLED ON THEIR ANTENNAE!
IT WAS NO USE! THEY DRAGGED ME TO A PLATFORM, TIED ME UP, AND WIRED TO MY CRANIUM A FIENDISH SUCTION CUP!
THEY TURNED IT ON AND CURRENT COURSED ACROSS MY CEREBELLUM, COAXING FROM MY BRAIN TISSUE THE THINGS I WOULDN'T TELL 'EM!
ALL THE MATH I EVER LEARNED, THE NUMBERS AND EQUATIONS, WERE MECHANIC'LY REMOVED IN THIS BRAIN-DRAINING OPERATION!
2+7=15
9+6=50
MY ESCAPE WAS AN ADVENTURE. (I WON'T TELL YOU WHAT I DID.) SUFFICE TO SAY, I CANNOT ADD, SO ASK SOME OTHER KID.
4+5=

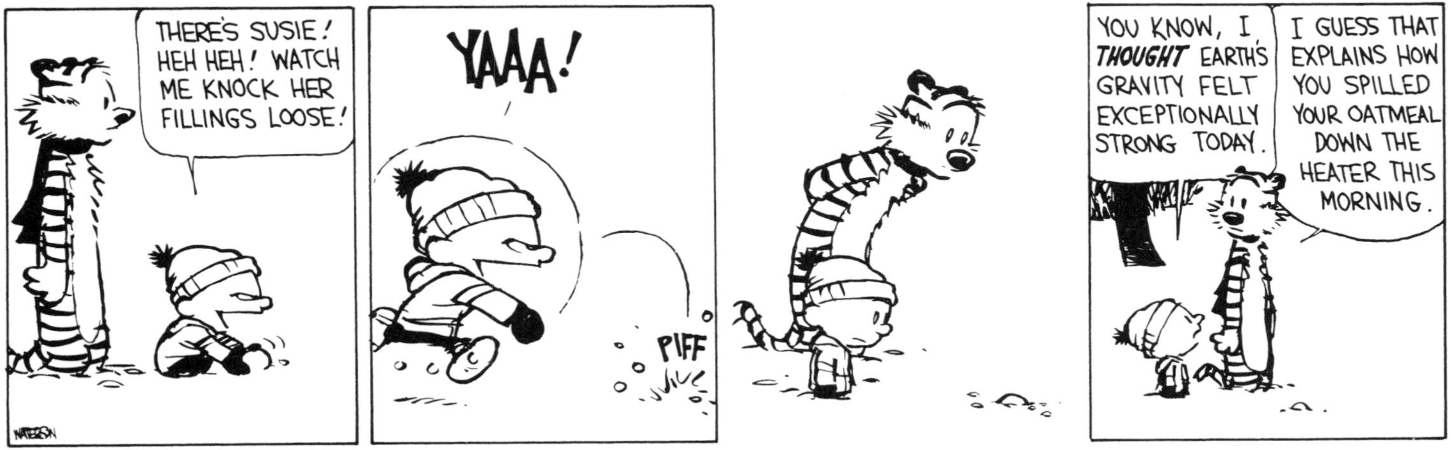
THERE'S SUSIE! HEH HEH! WATCH ME KNOCK HER FILLINGS LOOSE!
YAAA!
PIFF
YOU KNOW, I *THOUGHT* EARTH'S GRAVITY FELT EXCEPTIONALLY STRONG TODAY.
I GUESS THAT EXPLAINS HOW YOU SPILLED YOUR OATMEAL DOWN THE HEATER THIS MORNING.

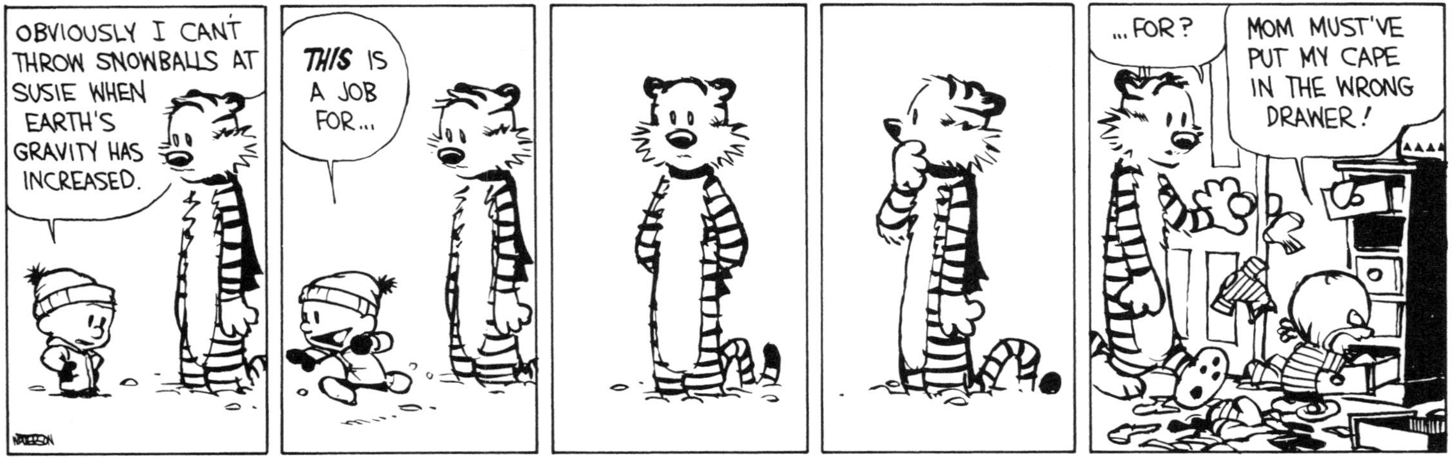
OBVIOUSLY I CAN'T THROW SNOWBALLS AT SUSIE WHEN EARTH'S GRAVITY HAS INCREASED.
THIS IS A JOB FOR...
...FOR?
MOM MUST'VE PUT MY CAPE IN THE WRONG DRAWER!

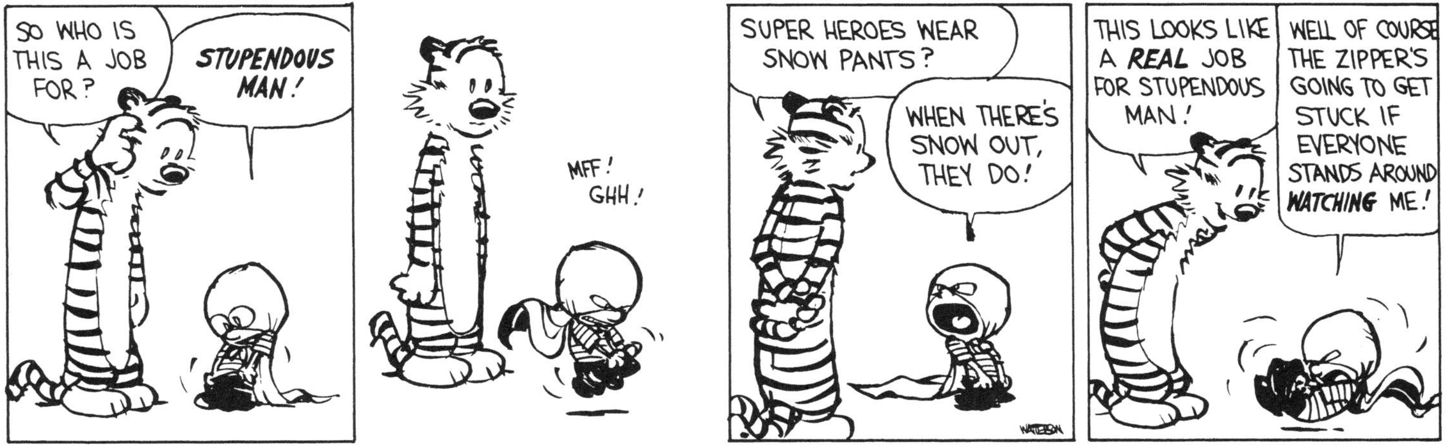
SO WHO IS THIS A JOB FOR?
STUPENDOUS MAN!
MFF! GHH!
SUPER HEROES WEAR SNOW PANTS?
WHEN THERE'S SNOW OUT, THEY DO!
THIS LOOKS LIKE A **REAL** JOB FOR STUPENDOUS MAN!
WELL OF COURSE THE ZIPPER'S GOING TO GET STUCK IF EVERYONE STANDS AROUND **WATCHING** ME!

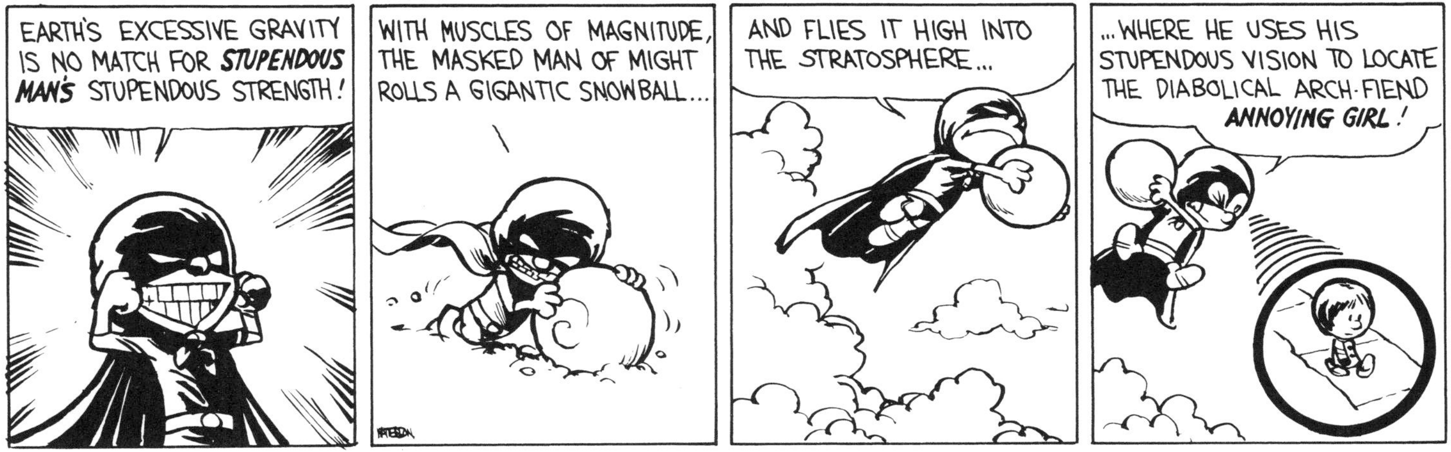
EARTH'S EXCESSIVE GRAVITY IS NO MATCH FOR **STUPENDOUS MAN'S** STUPENDOUS STRENGTH!
WITH MUSCLES OF MAGNITUDE, THE MASKED MAN OF MIGHT ROLLS A GIGANTIC SNOWBALL...
AND FLIES IT HIGH INTO THE STRATOSPHERE...
...WHERE HE USES HIS STUPENDOUS VISION TO LOCATE THE DIABOLICAL ARCH-FIEND **ANNOYING GIRL!**

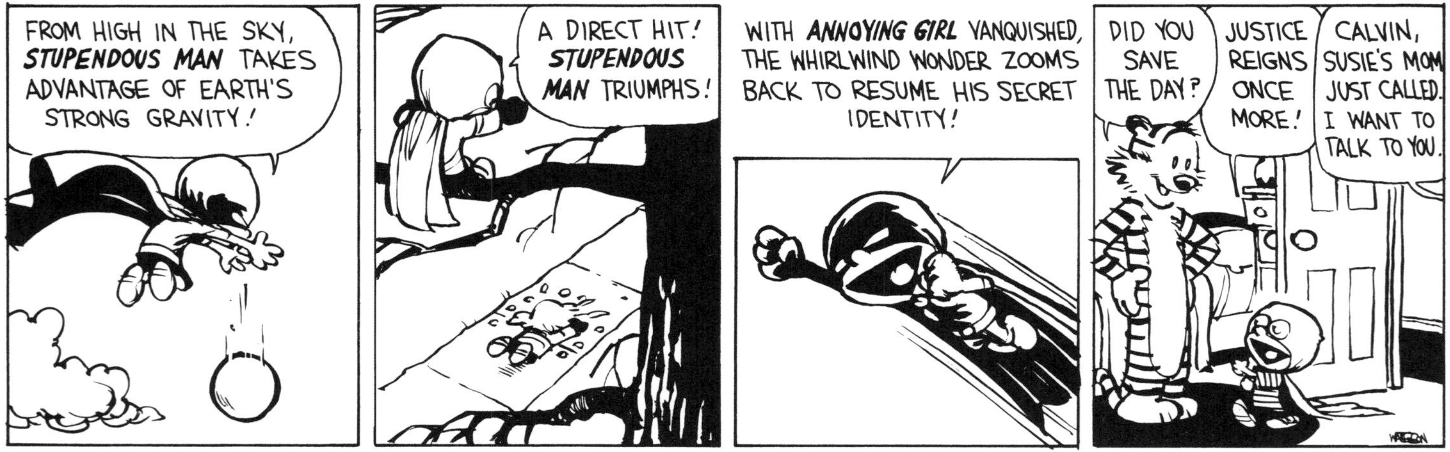
FROM HIGH IN THE SKY, STUPENDOUS MAN TAKES ADVANTAGE OF EARTH'S STRONG GRAVITY!
A DIRECT HIT! STUPENDOUS MAN TRIUMPHS!
WITH ANNOYING GIRL VANQUISHED, THE WHIRLWIND WONDER ZOOMS BACK TO RESUME HIS SECRET IDENTITY!
DID YOU SAVE THE DAY?
JUSTICE REIGNS ONCE MORE!
CALVIN, SUSIE'S MOM JUST CALLED. I WANT TO TALK TO YOU.

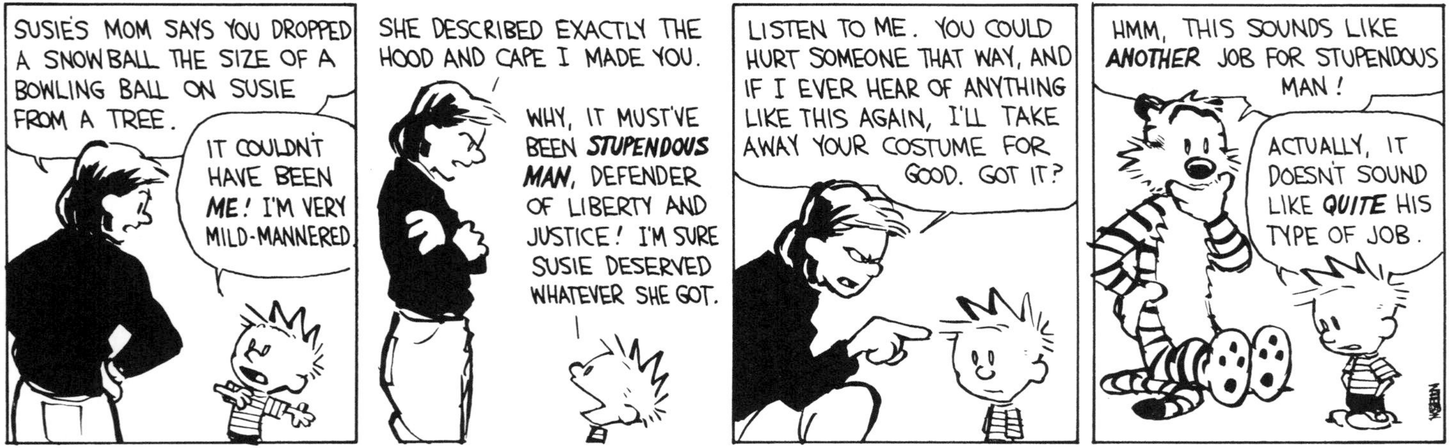
SUSIE'S MOM SAYS YOU DROPPED A SNOWBALL THE SIZE OF A BOWLING BALL ON SUSIE FROM A TREE.
IT COULDN'T HAVE BEEN ME! I'M VERY MILD-MANNERED.
SHE DESCRIBED EXACTLY THE HOOD AND CAPE I MADE YOU.
WHY, IT MUST'VE BEEN STUPENDOUS MAN, DEFENDER OF LIBERTY AND JUSTICE! I'M SURE SUSIE DESERVED WHATEVER SHE GOT.
LISTEN TO ME. YOU COULD HURT SOMEONE THAT WAY, AND IF I EVER HEAR OF ANYTHING LIKE THIS AGAIN, I'LL TAKE AWAY YOUR COSTUME FOR GOOD. GOT IT?
HMM, THIS SOUNDS LIKE ANOTHER JOB FOR STUPENDOUS MAN!
ACTUALLY, IT DOESN'T SOUND LIKE QUITE HIS TYPE OF JOB.

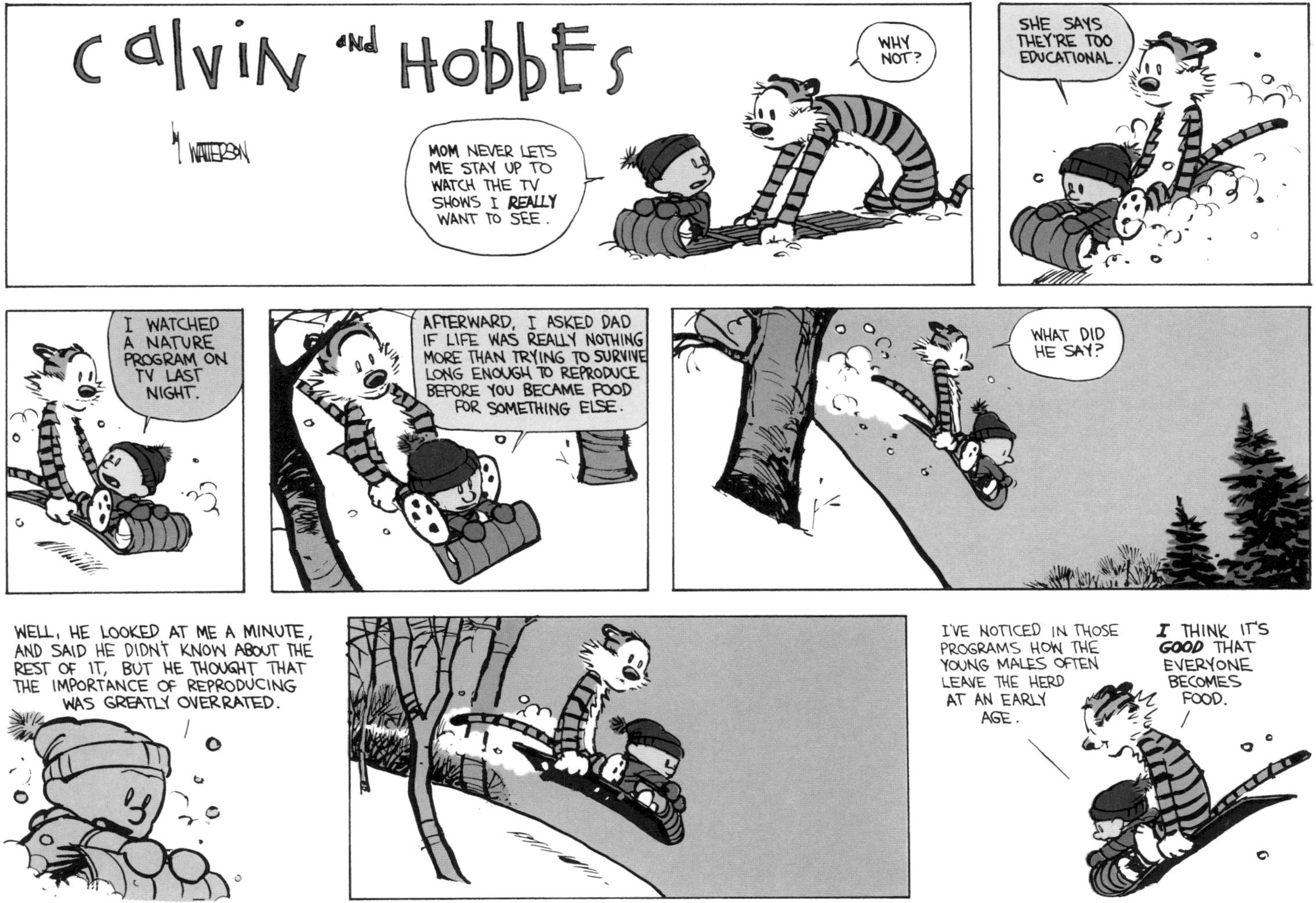
Calvin and Hobbes
by WATTERSON
MOM NEVER LETS ME STAY UP TO WATCH THE TV SHOWS I REALLY WANT TO SEE.
WHY NOT?
SHE SAYS THEY'RE TOO EDUCATIONAL.
I WATCHED A NATURE PROGRAM ON TV LAST NIGHT.
AFTERWARD, I ASKED DAD IF LIFE WAS REALLY NOTHING MORE THAN TRYING TO SURVIVE LONG ENOUGH TO REPRODUCE BEFORE YOU BECAME FOOD FOR SOMETHING ELSE.
WHAT DID HE SAY?
WELL, HE LOOKED AT ME A MINUTE, AND SAID HE DIDN'T KNOW ABOUT THE REST OF IT, BUT HE THOUGHT THAT THE IMPORTANCE OF REPRODUCING WAS GREATLY OVERRATED.
I'VE NOTICED IN THOSE PROGRAMS HOW THE YOUNG MALES OFTEN LEAVE THE HERD AT AN EARLY AGE.
I THINK IT'S GOOD THAT EVERYONE BECOMES FOOD.

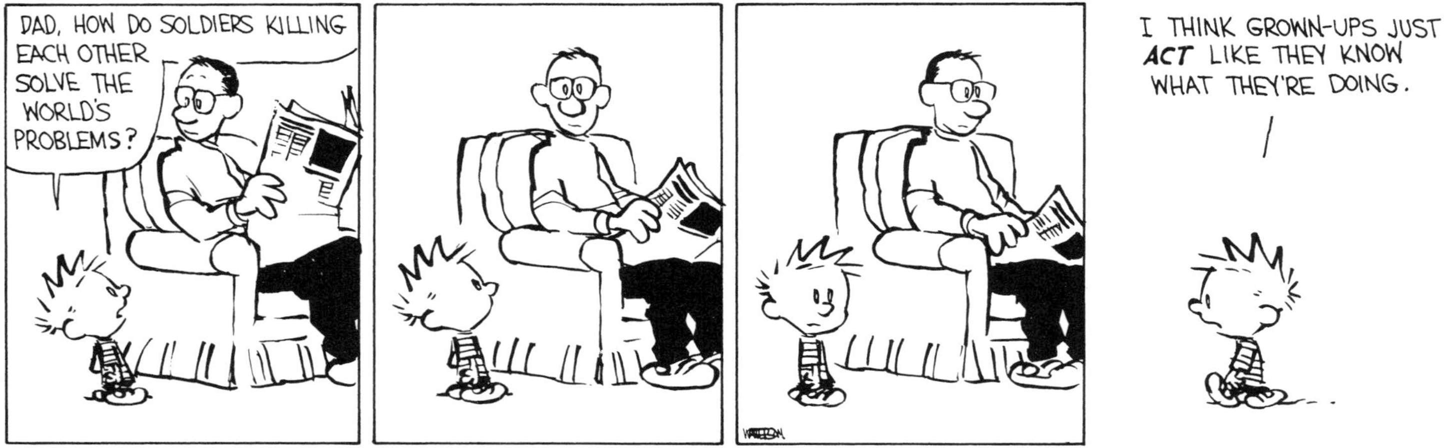
DAD, HOW DO SOLDIERS KILLING EACH OTHER SOLVE THE WORLD'S PROBLEMS?
I THINK GROWN-UPS JUST **ACT** LIKE THEY KNOW WHAT THEY'RE DOING.

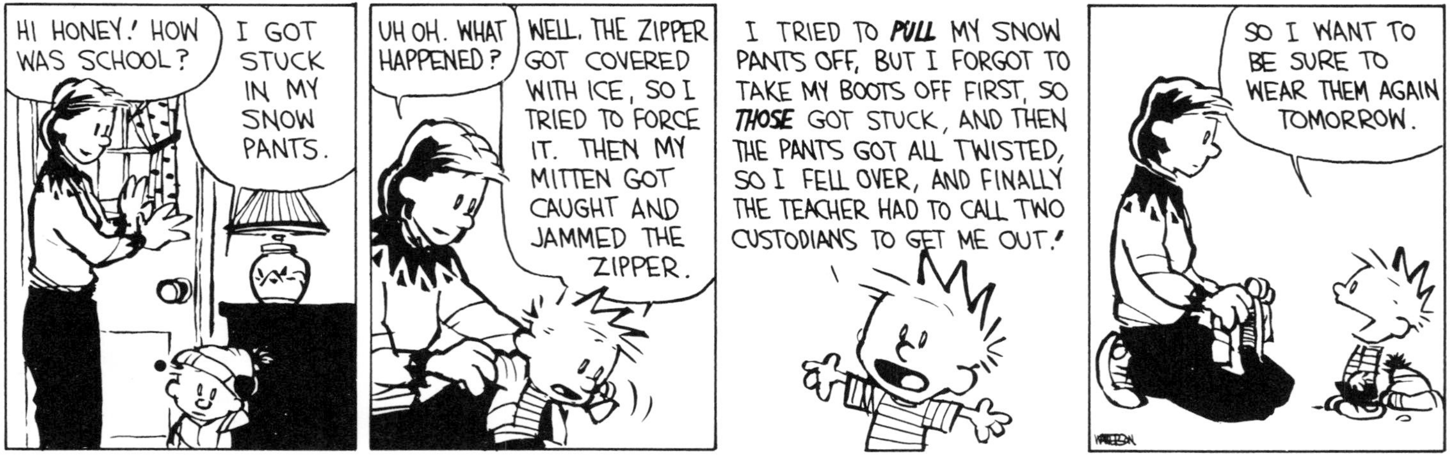
HI HONEY! HOW WAS SCHOOL?
I GOT STUCK IN MY SNOW PANTS.
UH OH. WHAT HAPPENED?
WELL, THE ZIPPER GOT COVERED WITH ICE, SO I TRIED TO FORCE IT. THEN MY MITTEN GOT CAUGHT AND JAMMED THE ZIPPER.
I TRIED TO **PULL** MY SNOW PANTS OFF, BUT I FORGOT TO TAKE MY BOOTS OFF FIRST, SO **THOSE** GOT STUCK, AND THEN THE PANTS GOT ALL TWISTED, SO I FELL OVER, AND FINALLY THE TEACHER HAD TO CALL TWO CUSTODIANS TO GET ME OUT!
SO I WANT TO BE SURE TO WEAR THEM AGAIN TOMORROW.

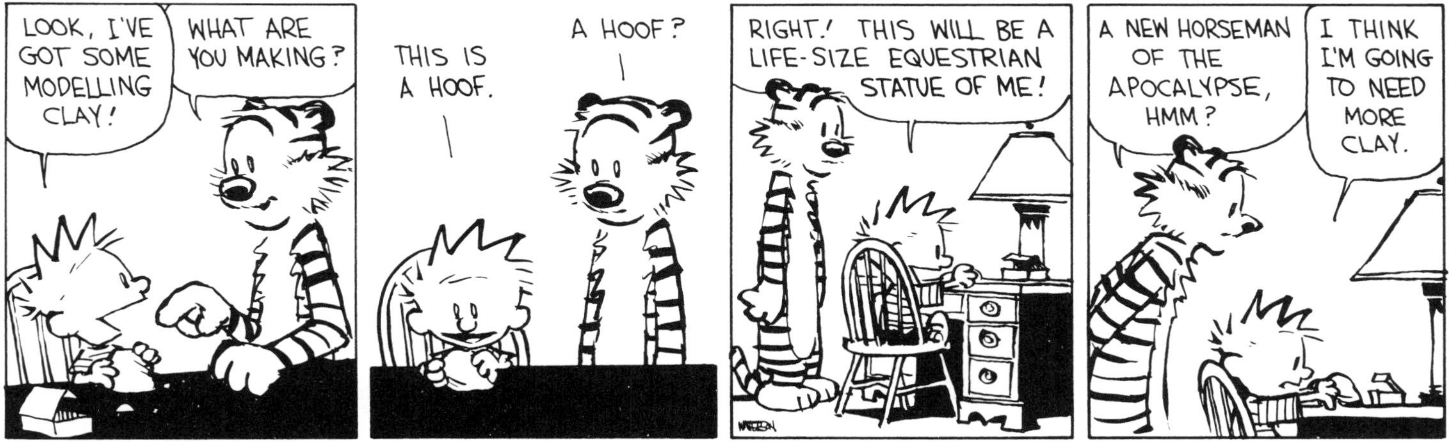
LOOK, I'VE GOT SOME MODELLING CLAY!
WHAT ARE YOU MAKING?
THIS IS A HOOF.
A HOOF?
RIGHT! THIS WILL BE A LIFE-SIZE EQUESTRIAN STATUE OF ME!
A NEW HORSEMAN OF THE APOCALYPSE, HMM?
I THINK I'M GOING TO NEED MORE CLAY.

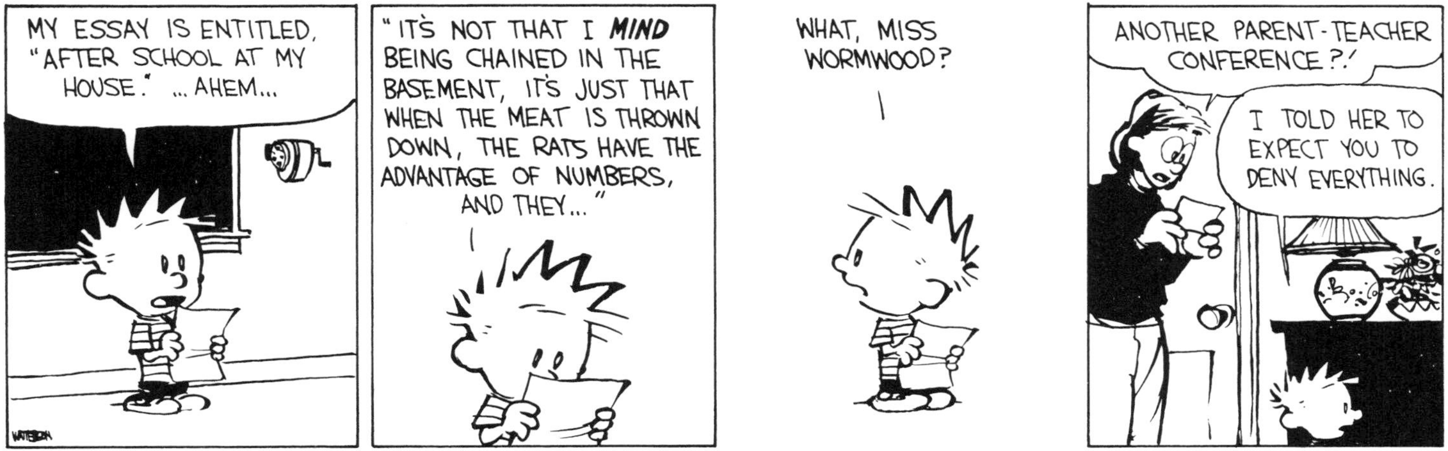
MY ESSAY IS ENTITLED, "AFTER SCHOOL AT MY HOUSE." ...AHEM...
"IT'S NOT THAT I **MIND** BEING CHAINED IN THE BASEMENT, IT'S JUST THAT WHEN THE MEAT IS THROWN DOWN, THE RATS HAVE THE ADVANTAGE OF NUMBERS, AND THEY..."
WHAT, MISS WORMWOOD?
ANOTHER PARENT-TEACHER CONFERENCE?!
I TOLD HER TO EXPECT YOU TO DENY EVERYTHING.

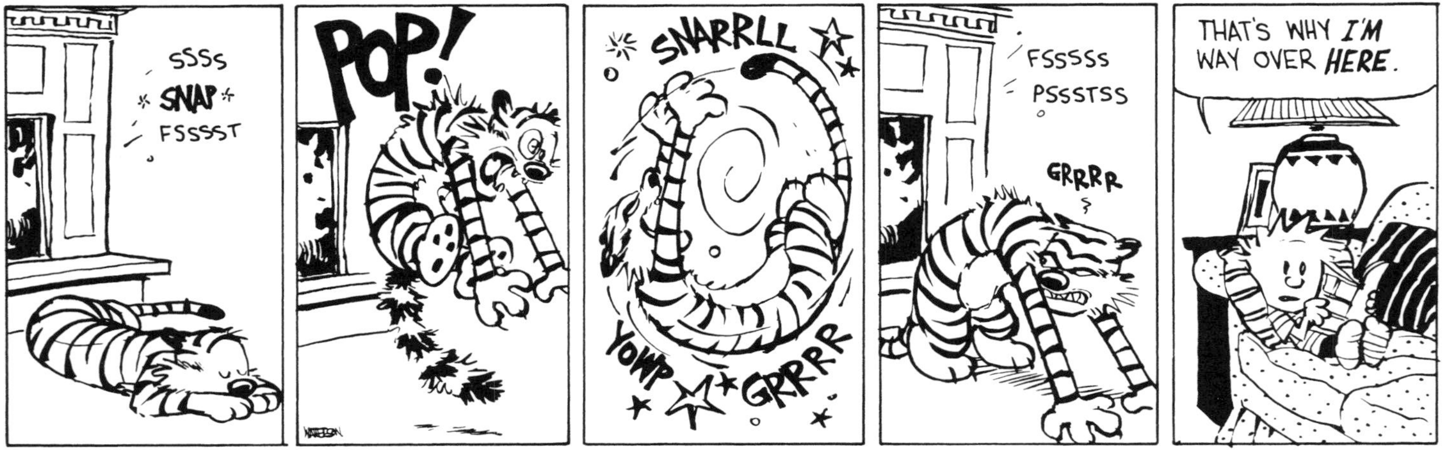
SSSS
SNAP
FSSSST
POP!
SNARRLL
YOWP
GRRRR
FSSSSS
PSSSTSS
GRRRR
THAT'S WHY I'M WAY OVER HERE.

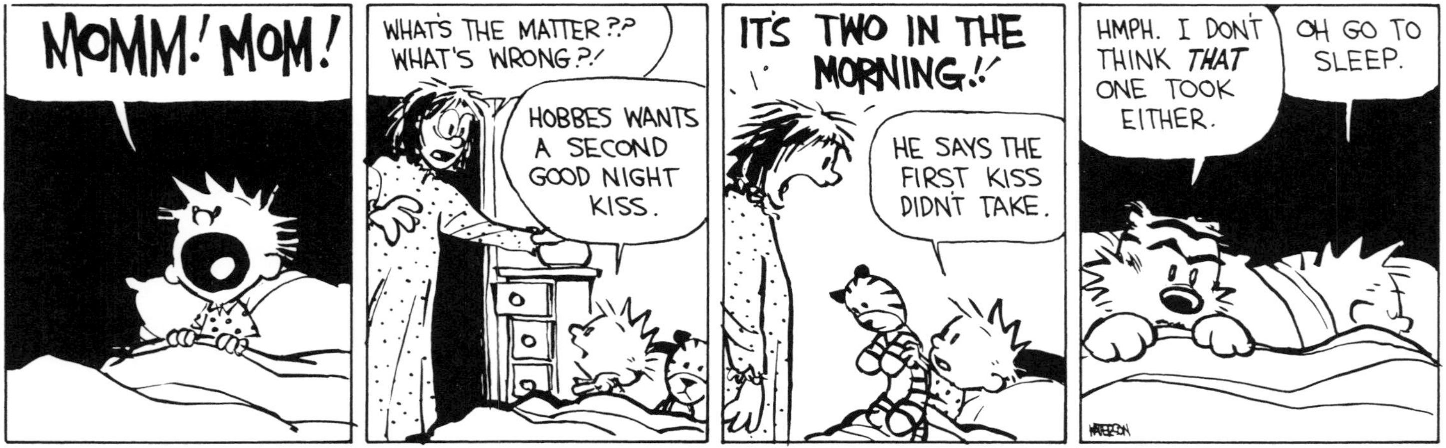
MOMM! MOM!
WHAT'S THE MATTER?? WHAT'S WRONG?!
HOBBES WANTS A SECOND GOOD NIGHT KISS.
IT'S TWO IN THE MORNING!!
HE SAYS THE FIRST KISS DIDN'T TAKE.
HMPH. I DON'T THINK THAT ONE TOOK EITHER.
OH GO TO SLEEP.

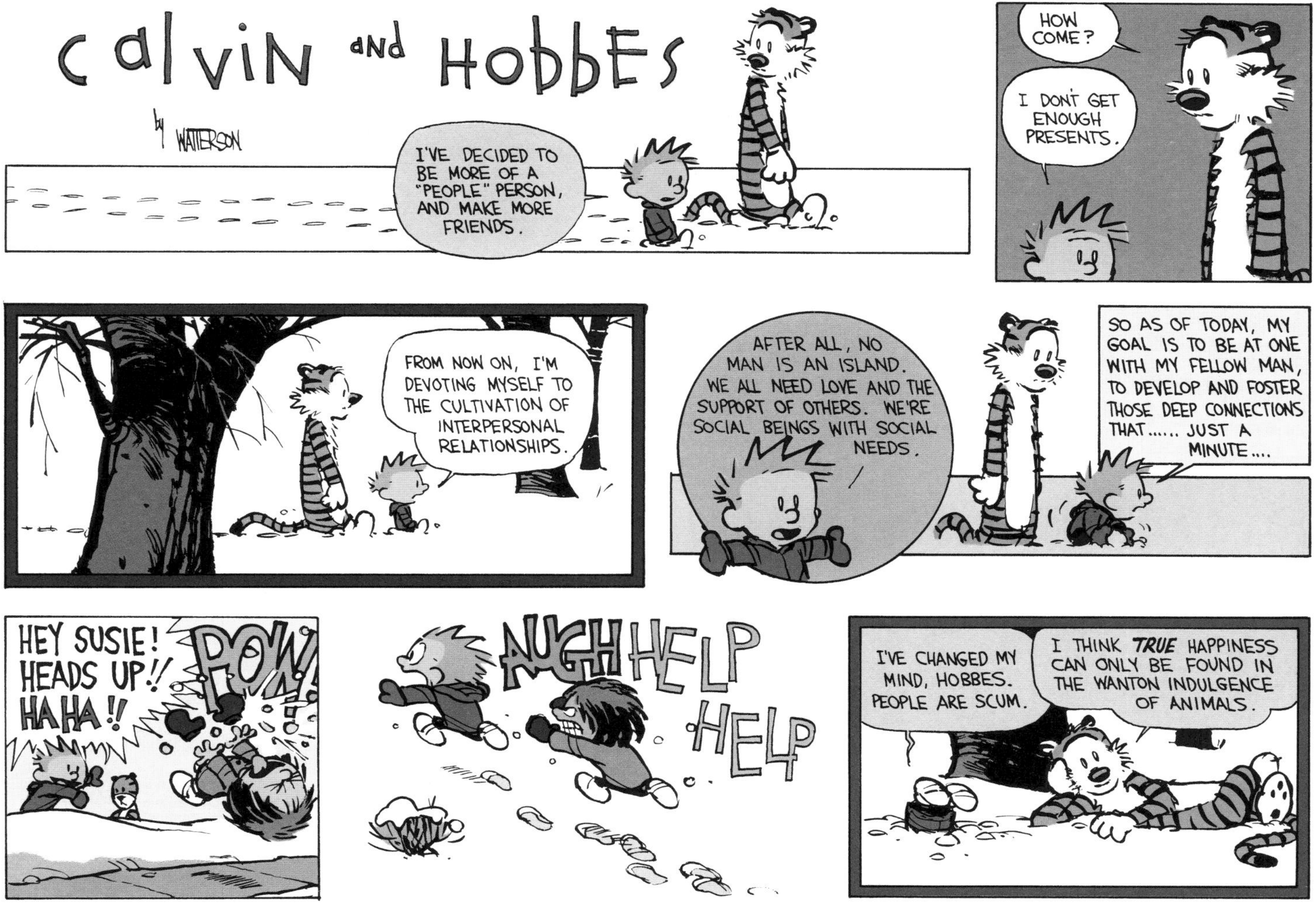
Calvin and HOBBES
by WATTERSON
I'VE DECIDED TO BE MORE OF A "PEOPLE" PERSON, AND MAKE MORE FRIENDS.
HOW COME?
I DON'T GET ENOUGH PRESENTS.
FROM NOW ON, I'M DEVOTING MYSELF TO THE CULTIVATION OF INTERPERSONAL RELATIONSHIPS.
AFTER ALL, NO MAN IS AN ISLAND. WE ALL NEED LOVE AND THE SUPPORT OF OTHERS. WE'RE SOCIAL BEINGS WITH SOCIAL NEEDS.
SO AS OF TODAY, MY GOAL IS TO BE AT ONE WITH MY FELLOW MAN, TO DEVELOP AND FOSTER THOSE DEEP CONNECTIONS THAT...... JUST A MINUTE....
HEY SUSIE! HEADS UP!! HAHA!!
POW!
AUGH
HELP
HELP
I'VE CHANGED MY MIND, HOBBES. PEOPLE ARE SCUM.
I THINK TRUE HAPPINESS CAN ONLY BE FOUND IN THE WANTON INDULGENCE OF ANIMALS.

Calvin and Hobbes is distributed internationally by Andrews McMeel Syndication.

The Calvin and Hobbes Portable Compendium Set 4 copyright © 2025 by Bill Watterson. All rights reserved.
Printed in China. No part of this book may be used or reproduced in any manner whatsoever without
written permission except in the case of reprints in the context of reviews.

Andrews McMeel Publishing
a division of Andrews McMeel Universal
1130 Walnut Street, Kansas City, Missouri 64106

www.andrewsmcmeel.com

25 26 27 28 29 SDB 10 9 8 7 6 5 4 3 2 1

ISBN: 978-1-5248-9061-2

Library of Congress Control Number: 2024943648

ATTENTION: SCHOOLS AND BUSINESSES
Andrews McMeel books are available at quantity discounts with bulk purchase for educational, business, or sales promotional use.
For information, please e-mail the Andrews McMeel Publishing Special Sales Department: sales@amuniversal.com.